ANCIENT GONZO WISDOM

Hunter S. Thompson (1937–2005) was an American journalist and author widely regarded as the father of gonzo journalism.

Also by Hunter S. Thompson

THE GONZO PAPERS ANTHOLOGY

THE GREAT SHARK HUNT

GENERATION OF SWINE

SONGS OF THE DOOMED

BETTER THAN SEX

SCREWJACK

HEY RUBE

Also by Anita Thompson

THE GONZO WAY

ANCIENT GONZO WISDOM

INTERVIEWS WITH HUNTER S. THOMPSON

EDITED BY ANITA THOMPSON

PICADOR

First published 2009 by Da Capo Press, Cambridge, MA and New York

First published in Great Britain 2009 by Picador

First published in paperback 2009 by Picador

This edition first published 2010 by Picador
an imprint of Pan Macmillan, a division of Macmillan Publishers Limited
Pan Macmillan, 20 New Wharf Road, London N1 9RR
Basingstoke and Oxford
Associated companies throughout the world
www.panmacmillan.com

ISBN 978-0-330-51072-1

3 5 7 9 8 6 4 2

A CIP catalogue record for this book is available from the British Library.

Printed and bound by CPI Group (UK) Ltd, Croydon, CR0 4YY

Ralph Steadman

George Stranahan

Doug Brinkley

Earth, receive an honoured guest;
William Yeats is laid to rest:
Let the Irish vessel lie
Emptied of its poetry.

Time, that is intolerant
of the brave and innocent,
And indifferent in a week,
To a beautiful physique,
Worships language and forgives
Everyone by whom it lives;
Pardons cowardice, conceit,
Lays its honours at their feet.

Time that with this strange excuse
Pardoned Kipling and his views,
And will pardon Paul Claudel,
Pardons him for writing well.

—W. H. AUDEN

Contents

Acknowledgments

This book is a compilation of Hunter's interviews made over the course of nearly forty years, and the manuscript took shape over the course of two years, so there are many people to thank.

Doug Brinkley, Hunter's literary executor, started the ball rolling when he urged me to provide this book to students and scholars of Hunter.

Brandon Wenerd, my godsend research and production assistant, began with multiple emails asking me how he could become an Owl Farm intern. After several months of persistence, he turned into the perfect match for this book and has stuck with me every step of the way and has proved to be professional in the true sense of Gonzo.

Jeff Posternack and Vaughn Shinall were helpful in getting the manuscript to an excellent publisher, and thanks to Gonzo Trustees George Tobia and Hal Haddon for their work in estate matters. I'd also like to thank Christopher Hitchens for his spicy introduction.

My editor, Ben Schafer at Da Capo Press, gently nudged me along and was very encouraging during the sometimes painful decision-making process: Which of Hunter's words to include and which to leave out? He was understanding of my personal attachment to Hunter's every syllable. So, thanks to his patience, I was able to edit hundreds of pages knowing I had Da Capo's support.

Jon Kenneth Williams, one of my teachers at Columbia University, helped me with the initial task of editing down the first 1,000+ pages, along with his humor and moral support. David Frank, Andrew Travers, and Jonathan Bastian were very helpful in giving me their valuable insight.

Alex Gibney, Don Fleming, Eric Shoaf, and Jigsaw Productions along with Sarah Funke of Horowitz Gallery were gracious to dust off, digitize and archive valuable files that had never been seen in print, until now.

Renee Caputo and Norman MacAfee, who helped edit the final manuscript, then the final of the final, then the final final manuscript, and did a lovely job. Thank you, guys.

Perhaps the biggest thanks goes to those brave and lucky individuals who interviewed Hunter over the forty years of his historic and spectacular life as a writer, and for asking those questions that had never been asked, or asking them again thirty years later, to find Hunter had the same wisdom to offer. You bought the ticket, and took the ride. Thanks for your contributions to this book.

Preface: A Whisper to the Reader

Given under my hand this twelfth day of February, 2009, in Butler Library at Columbia University, three miles back from Annabel Lee's kingdom by the sea—the same certainly affording the most charming view to be found on this planet, and with it the most dreamlike and enchanting sunsets to be found on any planet or even in any solar system—and given, too, with the busts of Cervantes and Sophocles and other grandees of this line looking approvingly down upon me as they used to look down upon Hunter and Barack Obama. . . .

Okay, I'll stop with the Mark Twain impersonation and get to the matter at hand, or, rather, in your hands. I am just the messenger or, as it were, the editor: Being the gal who spent his latter years with Hunter and who has read the letters and emails from so many of you who, especially after the volumes and films *about* him overwhelmed the bookshelves and movie screens since his death, wish you were given the chance to sit down with Hunter and simply talk and ask him some questions, without the external chatter.

Peter Olszewski, for instance, asked about the "lectures" that Hunter gave to young people, some of which I included in this volume, to which Hunter replied, "We could probably clear this up because this is a fairly major point. In truth I don't even give lectures. All I do is appear and take a lot of abuse, and sort of maintain a dialogue. . . . I like to get them up, get them moving, get them angry, but after that I just like to talk to people." Olszewski then asked, "Is there any particular thing you like talking about?"

"Whatever people want," Hunter replied. "I have nothing to say. I have no message. I'll talk with anyone who wants to talk."

This, dear reader, is the closest thing to that talk. His voice rings clear through the style of the interviews selected and from the transcribed tapes thereof, many of which have never seen print until now, though they comprise a goldmine of personal thoughts and laughs with the man we all love and love to study and who is and always will be missed by all who knew him. The beauty of the matter is that like those greats who look down upon me now in Butler Library, Hunter will live forever in his work, long after you and I are gone.

In these pages, you will see that just as Vladimir Nabokov's mind mirrored his homeland—Russia, with its vast memories of good and evil, its rich and profound literature, and its language tightly laced with double and triple meanings—Hunter S. Thompson's mind mirrored that of America: revolutionary, passionate, and intensely complex. Along with learning new aspects of his life and work in these interviews, some of which I had not even heard of before his death, I have been comforted to see in these interviews the same Hunter I know from our private life at Owl Farm. So I will now step back, and let you sit down and enjoy the conversation.

Your friend in Woody Creek,
Anita Thompson

(Writing from Hunter's alma mater,
Columbia University, New York City,
February 12, 2009)

Introduction

In the spring of 1990 I flew to Aspen, Colorado, to cover a summit meeting between Prime Minister Margaret Thatcher and President George Herbert Walker Bush. This fairly routine political event took on sudden significance when, on the evening before the talks were scheduled to begin, Saddam Hussein announced that the independent state of Kuwait had, by virtue of a massive deployment of military force, become a part of Iraq. We were not to know that this act—and the name Saddam Hussein—would dominate international politics for the next decade and more, but it was still possible to witness something extraordinary: the sight of Mrs. Thatcher publicly inserting quantities of lead into George Bush's pencil. The spattering quill of a Ralph Steadman would be necessary to do justice to such a macabre yet impressive scene.

The Aspen municipality had announced a cocktail party for the visiting media and I went with a group of friends to the top of the ski lift in order to attend it. There at the summit were white tablecloths and shining glasses, on trays borne by equally white and shining blondes with perfect sparkling smiles. I asked for a gin and tonic. "Sir, that wouldn't be appropriate at this altitude." "Say what?" The smile didn't contract even by a millimeter: "Sir, the effect of alcohol would be twice as great at this height. We can offer you a Chardonnay." "No, in that case I'll have a double gin." Did I imagine it or did the perfect smile fade just a fraction? "Sir, we can offer you a Chardonnay." This is the unironic Aspen of health and wealth and discreet background checks: a quiet authoritarianism behind the outdoorsy and sporty façade. "Come on," said one of my comrades. "Let's go." And within a short while we had sped down the ski lift, hailed a cab, and made it deposit us at the gates of Owl Farm, in the outlying district of Woody Creek, where the Woody Creek Inn, with its distinctive pig on the roof, offered a guiding landmark.

One could not easily, in such a short time and distance, have transported oneself to such an entirely different version of the American Dream. It was getting dark, and the host and denizen of Owl Farm, Dr. Hunter S. Thompson, was just getting up. Refreshments of all sorts were available without any reference to health-impact considerations, as were numerous stimulants and analgesics. A restless TV set changed channels as if by itself, sweeping the airwaves for fresh developments. Phone calls were placed, depending on time zones, to various sources and contacts around the known world.

The conversation zigzagged between the micro and macro: one minute it would be the circulation war that raged between Aspen's two papers (one of them pro-"development" and the other less so) and next would be the looming possibility of another war in the Middle East. At some point, towards the advent of the rosy-fingered dawn, it seemed important to go outside, set up some bottles and cans, and blast them into shards with high-velocity rifles. This may also have had something to do with reminding the Aspen sheriff's department to keep its distance.

I was only twice a visitor to Owl Farm and mustn't exaggerate the extent of my acquaintance with the good Doctor, but like everyone else of my age with even a tincture of interest in the depraved calling of journalism, I considered myself a considerable debtor long before I passed the piggy emblem at Woody Creek that alerted the pilgrim to journey's end. Hunter and I got on all right: We shared an electric loathing for Richard Nixon and Henry Kissinger that was so pure that it practically sang. But politics was about to become more banal as well as more ugly and more nuanced: The Cold War was only just over, and within a few months Jann Wenner and *Rolling Stone* would be discovering Sixties virtues in William Jefferson Clinton. Hunter seemed somewhat restless and discontented and—at least to me, who knew the symptoms of boredom so well because they terrified me, too—to be confronted with a certain quotient of anomie. Added to this, I decided on my second visit, was the strain imposed on him by visitors who wanted him to be outrageous, to do or to say something that was way over the top: tourists in effect who wanted their own "Hunter" anecdote to tell when they got home, or when his name could be dropped.

This of course happens to many veterans and celebrities, but I fear that it may have had an especially enervating effect on someone to whom the authenticity and spontaneity of the moment had always been so essential. If you, dear reader, should ever have the opportunity of viewing the documentary *Breakfast with Hunter,* you will perhaps be able to guess what I mean. Wherever he goes, and whoever he meets in this film, he is under pressure to perform, to be "Hunter," to do something "Gonzo." One can detect, in a certain dullness in his eye, a weariness with all this and a wish to be released from the demands of stereotype. There are also some episodes of rudeness and ill-temper which strike me as opportunities, gratefully if ineptly seized, to alleviate the general tedium of life. I write these sentences with the benefit—surely that is exactly the wrong word—of hindsight, but I was not the only one to become aware that Dr. Thompson was privately construing the old word "freedom" as "free doom" or in other words as the absolute and individual right to determine the time and place of one's own final exit.

A more recent movie—*Gonzo*—the product of a fruitful collaboration between Alex Gibney, Graydon Carter and Nicholas Fraser, succeeds in returning us to the themes that made Hunter Thompson so salient in the first place. When I first came to the United States in 1970, I went to call upon Carey McWilliams, then the editor of *The Nation.* He gave me a few useful addresses in California: the state that he had made particularly his own with his books and articles. But I was too young and green to know that this was the man who had commissioned Hunter to go and spend time with the Hell's Angels, thus inaugurating a span of counter-cultural reportage that stretched all the way through the turbulent Sixties to the hideous and upsetting dénouement of the Rolling Stones concert at Altamont, where the angels of hell became the pool-cue wielding forces of an improvised and fascistic mime of "law'n'order." Tom Wolfe once described Hunter as having been "embedded" with the Angels, and, anachronistic though the term is in (or out of) context, it can't be bettered as a summary of how committed he was to living the story, to being part of it and changing it by the way he wrote it. Which is ultimately what "Gonzo" means.

One of Hunter Thompson's most celebrated tropes—it occurs in his *Fear and Loathing in Las Vegas*—is the image of the great cresting wave of the nineteen-sixties, hitting a high-water mark and then receding, always receding, until a period of anticlimax and, well, recession set in. To be forced to live becalmed in those subsequent dreary shallows after having ridden the greatest wave of all was Hunter's fate, as it was to be asked continually by envious wannabes and emulators what it had really been "like." One senses that this line of questioning—very often to be found in these ensuing pages—came to bore and annoy him even as he strove to answer it seriously. Oscar Wilde once said that the secret lay in knowing how far you could go, and then going just that little bit further. My friend Mike Kinsley once updated this apercu for our time by observing that, if you ever worry if you have gone or are going too far, you very probably haven't gone quite far enough. This determination to live permanently on the edge while always knowing roughly where it was—an ambition that was reflected in his admiration for F. Scott Fitzgerald—could have been Hunter Thompson's initiating and sustaining spark. As he told his *Salon* interviewer in February 2003:

> By any widely accepted standard, I have had more than nine lives. I counted them up once and there were 13 times that I almost and maybe should have died—from emergencies with fires to violence, drowning, bombs. I guess I am an action junkie, yeah. There may be some genetic imperative that caused me to get into certain situations. It's curiosity, I guess. As long as I'm learning something I figure I'm OK—it's a decent day.

Allowance made for heroic exaggeration, this is the way in which many of us have imagined the craft of journalism: as a way of forcing the general public to continue paying for our free education indefinitely. But then let us not ignore the darker side of the impulsive optimism above. When asked by Marty Beckerman: "a lot of the figures from the '60s have passed on in the last 10 years—Ginsberg, Leary, Kesey—how does it feel to see that era fading away?" he responded: "You morbid little bastard . . . Yeah, how does it feel to be the last buffalo?"

A question necessarily arises as to how one could tell when Hunter was, and was not, joking. This conundrum has bedeviled the satirical since Juvenal, and may be one of the reasons that the good Doctor eventually succumbed to terminal weltschmerz: it can be exhausting when people assume you are merely being outrageous when in fact your intention is serious and sincere. (Mark Twain experienced the same exasperation during his protests against the imperialist war of 1898 in Cuba and the Philippines: Audiences assumed that he was always on duty being a humorist. He elsewhere drily observed that "if you give a man a reputation as an early riser, he can sleep till noon.")

When I was about fourteen I heard a whispered "inside" story about the late President John F. Kennedy, who hadn't been dead for very long. It appeared—so said those in the know at my boarding school—that on Air Force One on the flight back from Dallas, the newly sworn President Lyndon Johnson had been discovered in the back of the plane, gleefully fornicating in his deceased predecessor's head wound. I never met anyone who had not heard this story and at least half-believed it, and it certainly helped to color the impression one had of LBJ as the Vietnam madness intensified. Decades later I met Paul Krassner, who with the help of that other genius Terry Southern had put this fantastic, and fantastically successful, rumor into circulation with the help of a rogue magazine called *The Realist.* I couldn't decide whether to be depressed or impressed at the scale and speed of the hoax. I am recalling this because of Hunter Thompson's invention—or do I mean promulgation?—of "ibogaine."

After all, there had to be an explanation for the bizarre and awful conduct of one of Hunter's most despised enemies, Senator Ed Muskie, on the campaign trail in 1972. As the fount of Gonzo wisdom himself phrased it to P. J. O'Rourke, in a reminiscence published in *Rolling Stone* in November 1987:

> Muskie's weeping in New Hampshire, going crazy in elevators in Florida, bitching and whining. I happened to pick up a pharmaceutical newsletter. There was a report on ibogaine.
>
> **O'Rourke: Ibogaine? What is it?**
>
> Oh, it's a wonderful African drug. Natives in Africa use it when they want to sit by a watering hole and wait for beasts. It freezes you in a catatonic stupor. But it also makes you prone to sudden rages. This was what I'd been watching with Ed Muskie and I thought, "By God, that's what he must have been eating." So I wrote that a mysterious Brazilian doctor appeared, and the word was that he had brought in some ibogaine. Which explained all of Muskie's behavior. If I'm going to go into the fantastic, I have to have a firm grounding in the truth. Otherwise everything I write about politics might be taken as a hallucination.

It might indeed . . . O'Rourke sums up with a straight-ish face by asking: "The fantastic with its feet in the truth. Is that your definition of gonzo?" To which Thompson gave two surprisingly solemn replies. The first was:

> I give the ibogaine as an example of the Gonzo technique. It's essentially a "what if?" If Ed Muskie's acting like this here's an explanation. But I had to have his behavior down—talking with his innermost staff people. They were telling me things that they don't tell other reporters. Like, "Ye gods, man, how did I ever get involved with this campaign?"

And the second, more cautionary:

> I get all kinds of things in the mail, from journalism students, from kids trying to be gonzo journalists. If it doesn't work, man, it's horrible.

Indeed it is. Beware of imitations. But be aware, also, of those moments in public life that you could not hope to make up. As I write, Washington is in mourning for Tony Snow, who will be remembered by most of those reading this as a Fox News man (if he is remembered by them at all). I revered Tony, though, for his amazing if not alarming honesty. During the Gulf War in 1991 I heard from some usually reliable sources that President George Herbert Walker Bush had been taking the wrong prescription medication and that this had made him disoriented as well as delusional (and had caused him famously to launch his lunch all over Japanese Prime Minister Takeshita, thus sponsoring a slew of second-hand "next time, lunch is on me" jokes). Having the chance to interview Tony Snow on camera a short while later, he having been one of Bush's closest speech writers, I asked him for the record if there was any truth to the story. I had expected a routine denial and almost fell from my chair when he replied evenly that all those who worked for the president at the time had had the impression that he was taking the wrong drugs. As so often, the "straight" story was something a Gonzo operative could not have fabricated.

On the other hand (as Fay Wray actually did entitle her autobiography) when "it doesn't work, man, it's horrible." Here is Hunter, using the same crap methods that would make any basement-dwelling paranoid into a master strategist, and analyzing the real story behind September 11, 2001, for some rather indulgent interviewer from Australia:

> Well, I saw that the US government was going to benefit, and the White House, the Republican administration to take the mind of the public off the crashing economy. Now you want to keep in mind that every time a person named Bush gets into office, the nation goes into a drastic recession, as they call it.

This gives paranoia a bad name, and one feels the cringe as the interviewer wraps up with the condescending summary that this was "US journalist Hunter S. Thompson with a very personal and idiosyncratic view of September 11." Much better is the deadpan claim to want more time to spend on "my responsibilities as a clergyman." The 1974 *Playboy* interviewer seems momentarily uncertain as to how to take this:

> **You're not a real minister, are you?**
> HST: What? Of course I am. I'm an ordained doctor of divinity in the Church of the New Truth. I have a scroll with a big gold seal on it hanging on my wall at home. In recent months we've had more converts than we can handle. Even Ron Ziegler was on the brink of conversion during that last week in San Clemente, but the law of karma caught up with him before he could take the vows.

This is being said about, and during, the final days of the Nixon nightmare and the fact is: Nobody can say for absolutely sure how much of it is meant humorously. Much weirder things, involving much weirder religious figures like Rabbi Korff and the Reverend Moon, were happening every day. (As those final days receded, and as I read Thompson's discovery of a peanut farmer from Plains, Georgia, who wanted to be president, and read also that this peanut farmer could quote Bob Dylan, I did think that the Dylan bit at least must be a put-on. But no: In the obscure speech that caught Thompson's attention the governor actually did quote Dylan—even if it was only a couple of lines from "Maggie's Farm.")

To kindle a smidgeon of faith in a mere politician after the Nixon debacle was an almost touching display of something like innocence (though Hunter was never to fall as far in praise of Clinton as his boss Jann Wenner was later prepared to). In a sense, for the Doctor to credit anything or anybody under the Stars and Stripes with anything but the worst motives would be to have sold out and to risk disillusioning his terminally alienated constituency. Yet I have some private reason to think that he didn't always believe his own propaganda about 9/11 and its aftermath, and I certainly find much of the exaggeration on those subjects in these pages to be just that: a straining for effect that may well even have helped contribute to the final accidie. To return then, in closing, to that *Salon* interview from 2003:

> **You've also referred to your beat as the "Death of the American Dream." That was the ostensible subject of *Fear and Loathing in Las Vegas*. Has it just sort of been on its deathbed since 1968?**

HST: I think that's right.

A lot of people would argue with you about that anyway, and believe that the American Dream is alive and well.

HST: They need to take a better look around.

But in a way, haven't you lived the American Dream?

HST: Goddammit! [pause]. I haven't thought about it that way. I suppose you could say that in a certain way I have.

I suppose you could, too. On this occasion, I do not choose to think that Hunter Stockton Thompson was being sarcastic, and I like the idea of leaving open the question of whether that was an irony, and if so at whose expense.

—*Christopher Hitchens*

ABC News—February 20, 1967

Interview with reporter about Hell's Angels

Reporter: You spent over a year with the Hell's Angels. What kind of an impression did you come out with of certain individuals?

HST: It gives them recognition, a sense of companionship, group loyalty, and power. They get together and they can frighten people who might ordinarily frighten them. Especially now, since the California Attorney General* did an official report on them, they've gotten a massive amount of attention and national publicity. They made the cover of the *Saturday Evening Post,* movies, this book . . . There would be no other way for these people to do this without going out and doing something like "The Boston Strangler" or "The Mad Bomber." It's an easy way to get what they can't get in the square world. It's a whole subculture of dropouts and washouts and people who just can't make it in this automated technological society.

Reporter: How would you describe a typical Hell's Angels party?

HST: It varies from big ones—the runs—to the continuing round of beer parties here and there. On a run, they might get 150 to 200 bikes to anywhere up to 300 in a state park somewhere. They park them in a big ring around a massive bonfire, sometimes 215 feet tall. And they'd buy about, oh, 100 dollars worth of beer just as a starter for the afternoon. They'll drink hundreds of dollars worth of beer in a matter of two or three days. They've actually cleaned out a whole town's beer supplies. At the same time, they're taking amphetamine pills . . .

Reporter: LSD?

---

* In March 1965, California Attorney General Thomas C. Lynch published and distributed a fifteen-page report on the criminal activities of the Hell's Angels Motorcycle Club to police departments and municipalities across the state. The so-called "Lynch Report" was based on a ten-year study of the customs and exploits of the Hell's Angels, including details about felony arrests, convictions, and misdemeanors committed by motorcycle gang members.

HST: Well, that comes a little later. They start off with pills. Barbiturates and amphetamines, mixing them all together, then beer, then the wine starts, and later on there will be some LSD. Everything gets mixed in all together.

Reporter: Mr. Thompson, what does your book attempt?

HST: I just try to liken them to the other people—people like the Hell's Angels who don't wear the colors, like I say. There are thousands of losers and thugs, muggers and petty criminals, who would like to have this kind of attention but don't.

Reporter: To summarize, how would you explain a Hell's Angel?

HST: Well, he's between 20 and 40, though more likely around late 20s. He'd be a high school dropout. He'd have a minor police record with a lot of arrests and few convictions but not anything serious. Maybe a year or so in jail a few times for a small things. He'd be a motorcycle freak, a sort of lifetime bike rider. That would get him into the Hell's Angels. After that, he becomes sort of a creature of the club. And it gets more and more bizarre. His police record will start piling up because he's much more obvious.

Reporter: You spent at least a year knowing them and living with them. What was your most vivid impressions of them?

HST: Vivid impressions? Well, visually, there's no sight I can think of that compares to these Labor Day runs when they got several hundred of bikes out on the road.

Reporter: What is a "run" exactly?

HST: A run is just a sort of gigantic picnic or outing. They'd gather in one spot in the city then go to some sort of vacation in the mountains or the beach, or somewhere all together for a great big three-or four-day party. That's when they really frighten people because they're all together and they dress in the wildest way they can. They're all drunk out of their minds and eating pills. It's like an army of Huns has moved into your town.

They don't necessarily go to destroy the place, but they work themselves into such a frenzy, and there are so many of them. Of course, the townspeople are all worried and frightened and carrying weapons and locking up their doors and locking up their daughters in the basement. That sort of thing. It creates a very tense situation. The slightest thing can blow into a riot or an attack, and the police can't really handle two or three hundred of them running wild without a lot of reinforcements.

Reporter: Sometimes, in your book, I almost get the impression you're saying that their notoriety is overstated.

HST: Yeah. The Hell's Angels themselves aren't as dangerous or are not nearly as much of a mess as they seem to be. But if you just drop it at that and go on to say "They're not so dangerous, go on and ignore them," then you missed the whole point I was getting at about the Hell's Angels being thousands of other losers just by some other name. I'm much more aware of it now after all this sort of thing. I see Hell's Angels everywhere and they don't wear colors. Even as far as Chicago.

Reporter: Are these kind of people hopeless? I mean after observing them for a year and you say they can't make it in this automated society, is it a hopeless cause?

HST: Well they're hopeless as long as they decide to stay Hell's Angels and hopeless in the sense that you're talking about. They're not hopeless with themselves as long as they insist on being that obvious as a Hell's Angel. Why would you hire somebody with a gold earring and shoulder-length hair, stinking of old grease and slime with a police record two feet long? They're not really eligible for good jobs. Now, if they decided to quit this, you know, and shave . . .

Reporter: Do many decide to quit?

HST: Yeah. I'm not sure what the percentage would be. There are three ways to stop being a Hell's Angel: One is to die, and a lot of them do that; one is to go to prison, and a lot do that; the other is to quit. I guess it would be about more quit than go to prison and more go to prison than die. But those are the three exits they can make.

Reporter: Is it difficult to quit? Are there reprisals from the group if you do?

HST: Hmm . . . It depends on why you quit. Sometimes there are. And it depends on when you quit. It gets harder and harder as you get older because you've built up more of a police record and your friends become more of an in group, outlaw thing. I remember one of them saying he'd like to quit but he didn't have friends anywhere else. He didn't know how.

Reporter: What usually motivated a man to just quit?

HST: It depends on how intelligent he is. If he joins at 21 or something and if he has sense, and quite a few of them have enough sense to understand their situation. They don't understand how to handle it, but those who have a sense of options begin to realize that as they approach 30, they're losing all their options. It gets harder to get a job; it gets hard to find new friends, harder to do almost anything. So once past 30 it sort of confirms that it's either jail, a broad crash on a bike, or being shot by somebody. Younger ones quit.

Reporter: What's the relationship between the motorcycle and the personality of the Hell's Angels? Do you think there is one?

HST: Well obviously, it's like carrying a massive gun, a bazooka, around the street. It gives them a tremendous sense of power and freedom. It makes them very obvious. You can't ignore a Hell's Angel on one of his "chopped hogs" booming up and down the street cause the thing rattles windows and frightens pedestrians. So, without a motorcycle, he'd be just another punk. So, it's what I'd call an "equalizer."

Reporter: You pointed out in the book that sometimes they get an almost perverse pleasure in being exceedingly nice to crash their image.

HST: Yeah, when they run into a situation where people are obviously frightened of them. They already have the attention that they're looking for anyway, so it isn't necessary to tear up a place because it makes it sort of unpleasant if you get arrested or somebody gets cut. As long as they get the attention they're looking for, they enjoy it. They enjoy setting up this sort of tense situation and seeing people quiver like this: "Yes sir, you want some more coffee?" That sort of business. They'll take advantage of these things.

Reporter: You spoke about the intelligence of the Hell's Angels and you said some of them had real common sense. Would you say you found any geniuses among them?

HST: No, unless they were so disguised that I didn't realize it. You do find people who are much brighter than average. There are very few, but some. For instance, one of the brightest of the San Francisco Angels, Kent Reed, didn't go to school until the third grade. You find some with a very articulate instinct for what's happening, but they simply have a hard time saying it. Most of them are not really smart.

Reporter: Is there any conclusion at all to be reached?

HST: About the Hell's Angels? Only that it represents a sort of growing menace that might or might not be called "Hell's Angels." These people are breeding all over the country and the more complicated the job apparatus and the more qualified you have to be to get a job, the more people are going to be driven and forced out of the job market. There are motorcycle clubs starting everywhere and existing everywhere, for that matter. All these people don't ride motorcycles and they don't all wear jackets saying "Hell's Angels" but they're all around. And there are a lot more of them. You can draw your own conclusions on what's going to happen when we get to a certain level. I'm not sure what the level will ever be.

Sunday (Canadian Broadcasting Corporation)—1967(?)

Interview with host Alan Davis and Hell's Angel Cliff "Skip" Workman

Announcer: The bike rider is Cliff Workman, the treasurer of the Hell's Angels—the wildest bunch of outlaws to come out of the West since Billy the Kid. He's here to challenge his biographer, a tense young literary journalist named Hunter Thompson. It was Thompson who lived, drank, and rode with the Hell's Angels and wrote about them in a best seller. He was the first to compare them to the outlaws of the West. The critics have been unanimous in their praise of his book. But the Hell's Angels haven't been heard from yet. Tonight, *Sunday* makes author meet critic, bringing together the writer Hunter Thompson with the Hell's Angel, Cliff Workman.

Host (Alvin Davis): What'd you think of the book?

"Skip" Workman: Well, I'll tell you Al, and Hunter, and everybody in this room . . . that that book is 60 percent cheap trash.

Host: Cliff, what is a typical Hell's Angel?

"Skip" Workman: A typical Hell's Angel could be anybody in this room, somebody that likes to ride a motorcycle.

I got a home, I got a job, I got a boat and trailer. I do all things. I raise dogs. I do a little bit of everything.

HST: Well, let's face it—you're not a typical Angel. I know that and you know that . . . So let's not get ourselves in that story . . .

Host: Do you think the Angels sent Cliff here as an emissary, as a minister of planted pedantry with a high college degree and a yearning for bourgeois respectability? Is he different?

HST: Those are all your words.

Host: But is he different? You said he's not typical.

HST: No. I mean . . .

"Skip" Workman: You see, actually, there are none of us that care what anybody thinks. 'Cause we are us. I am me. What I do in my home is

nobody's business. I don't give a damn. If they don't like me on my motorcycle, it's too bad.

HST: You say you've read the book and you think that I wasn't saying that?! No, I know exactly what I said. I spent two years on the damn . . .

"Skip" Workman: I'd like to, then, get to the end of it, then, on why, after you spend a year with us, why you got your head thumped on.

HST: All right, get to it.

"Skip" Workman: I want to know why we didn't get the two kegs of beer you promised us. This guy here, he's sitting here making a million dollars . . .

HST: Ohhh . . . Help! Help! Help!

"Skip" Workman: Ah, well maybe not quite that much.

HST: If you knew what I was making on this, you wouldn't sell me that bike on credit.

"Skip" Workman: Well you're making something on it anyway. We helped you make it, right?

HST: Yeah.

"Skip" Workman: There was nothing about money, nothing about a share in the book, nothing about anything. All we wanted was a couple kegs of beer so we could all get drunk—and a copy of the book to each of the Oakland members.

HST: Yeah . . . and I said that . . . wait a minute . . .

"Skip" Workman: When you got your head thumped on, you wrote a letter to Ralph,* and you said, "See and I got my head thumped on . . . I don't owe you guys nothing."

HST: Well I didn't figure I did.

"Skip" Workman: Yeah, but you didn't tell the people why you got your head thumped on . . .

HST: Wait a minute, but which two kegs of beer? Which two kegs of beer are you talking about?

"Skip" Workman: The two kegs you were going to give us. We've had you in our home, we've fed you, we've given you beer. You didn't pay for nothing when you went on those runs . . . donated out of our pocket and all.

---

*Hell's Angels leader Ralph "Sonny" Barger.

HST: Oh wait a minute. I don't think you've been in my house, but a lot of Angels have been in my house and drank a hell of a lot of my beer . . . so I think it's fairly even.

"Skip" Workman: Well sure and they still like you.

HST: They do?

"Skip" Workman: They just don't like what you're doing.

Host: Why did they thump him?

"Skip" Workman: This man here got into a man's personal argument.

HST: That's an outright lie.

"Skip" Workman: No, no. It isn't. This is my side of what happened.

HST: OK. You weren't there, so why don't you preface it with that?

"Skip" Workman: This is what happened, and you see if this isn't right. "Junkie George" was beating his old lady.

HST: If you say so . . .

"Skip" Workman: I'm serious, this is what happened. Junkie George was beating his old lady . . . now, listen to this, Junkie George's dog bit him . . .

HST: I didn't say that . . .

"Skip" Workman: To me, this is a personal feud. If a guy wants to beat his wife and his dog bites him, that's between the three of them, right?

But here came the peacemaker, right? He doesn't have a patch on and he isn't in the club, ya know. Junkie George is stiff. You walked right up to him and said, "Only a punk beats his wife and dog."

These were your words. Now you said it. You said it to this man and you backed up . . .

And he said, "Hunter, you want some of this?" and you said "No." But you got it anyways. And when he hit you, three or four others of 'em hit you too . . .

HST: More than that . . .

"Skip" Workman: You got in your car and you left. That's when in your book you found Magoo asleep in the back of your car. So you stopped and he got out. But the next day, if you would have had any guts after living with all these people, you'd have come back up there, had a beer, and sat down with everyone and said, "All right, I made a mistake . . . " or "Somebody made a mistake, so what? Let's have a drink." But we've never seen you since . . . We've never seen our two kegs of beer and we've never seen our book!

HST: Are you finished?! Here's the thing . . . I was talking to "Crip." It was about three in the morning and we were talking about whether my BSA 650 would run with his chopper. And we were comparing ratios, top speeds, and roads . . . And I was watching what's his name—"Junkie" George? I don't know, I didn't know the guy. But there was somebody about 30 feet to the left beating his wife to a pulp on the rocks.

I thought, "Well, that's . . . you know, kind of ugly, but that's the way the game is played in this city."

"Skip" Workman: If he were beating her that bad, somebody would have stopped her . . .

HST: Oh no! You're kidding me and you're going to kid everybody else! Nobody stopped him and you know he was beating his wife up. You just said it, right?!

"Skip" Workman: He was beating his wife up, but he didn't have her head on the ground with a big rock up or something . . .

HST: Oh no, but she was lying on the rocks and he was giving her this . . . motion with hands . . .

"Skip" Workman: No. To keep a woman in line, you got to beat them like a rug once in a while.

HST: Well I wasn't paying that much attention 'cause I'd been around . . .

"Skip" Workman: So Junkie George kicked his dog, ya know!

HST: Well wait a minute, let me just get to it.

"Skip" Workman: If it would have been me and I was going to say something about it, I'd say, "Go ahead and beat your old lady but don't kick your dog anymore."

HST: You said that . . .

Host: I'm sorry Hunter . . . We're finished.

HST: In other words, I don't get my own version of it?!

Host: I'm afraid you'll have to do it privately.

HST: All right, all right!

Host: Thank you both very much for coming.

WBZ 1030 AM Radio (Boston, Massachusetts)—August 8, 1972

Interview with Jerry Williams

Jerry Williams: With me now is Hunter Thompson. He's a freelance writer and, the book says, a failed politician from Woody Creek, Colorado. Anybody who comes from Woody Creek is something you can't put words on. By the way, he is currently burning himself out as the Washington Correspondent for *Rolling Stone.* I met him about five or six years ago when the book *Hell's Angels* came out. Were you a Hell's Angel?

Hunter S. Thompson: No. They thought I was, which led to some trouble. I was presumed to be a member.

Jerry Williams: And?

HST: Well, I was a writer. I've always thought of myself as a writer.

Jerry Williams: You call yourself sort of a counter-culture, underground, freak George Plimpton?

HST: Oh no. No. I don't say that.

Jerry Williams: Assuming the role of going into the Hell's Angels. People would liken that sort of thing to Plimpton.

HST: Yeah, but you'll recall when we talked in Chicago, I kept trying to say that I did that book because I was a writer and I was broke. At the time, the rent was due and I had a Chinese landlord who was beating on the door yelling, "I want 100 bucks a month!" I didn't have it. My phone had been taken out. I had written a book about hammerhead sharks and gotten down in the water with them in the San Francisco Bay. People don't really grasp that about writers . . . you get a job and you do it.

Jerry Williams: Have you done anything with the Hell's Angels since then?

HST: Well, I've avoided them, more or less. (laughs) That sounds melodramatic. The people I knew and liked there are either dead or locked up. The book has had a prophetic kind of doom quality.

Jerry Williams: Is there a change? There's been a change in everything. Has there been a change in the Hell's Angels since you've written a book about them?

HST: Yes, definitely. Back then it was very much an up sort of thing. It was adventuresome.

Jerry Williams: And now?

HST: Now it's back into the same thing as the dope culture . . . the drug culture. It's sort of a downer, aggressive, resentful, vengeful sort of trip.

Jerry Williams: Would you consider these guys in the Hell's Angels lower-middle-class or on the lower echelon of society? Not being able to identify with blacks or Chicanos?

HST: No . . . they're very anti-black.

Jerry Williams: They don't have a rallying point or cause? It seems like because they have no great cause within them, they drift into this business of being hostile against the whole society.

HST: It's like the Wallace* vote in the last election. It's the kind of people who I saw in a place like Serb Hall in Milwaukee, this really rabid, relatively same kind of crowd. It was a Wallace crowd that had come out there for no other reason than to see Wallace. They told me that they were there because he was the one person in American politics who really made sense when you cut through the bullshit and get things done. They wanted to get the truth back. As much as I was appalled by it, the whole mood, I was struck by the intensity they were feeling. There are people in this country who really feel that they are not only left out, but the world is deaf to them.

Jerry Williams: Yeah. I get that feeling sometimes. I sit here nightly hearing a lot of those people. Nobody really believes it. Others who listen to the voices of estranged people try to categorize them as nuts.

HST: There are a lot of nuts. There's a hard, red line of truth in that. It's hard to pick out and you have to listen very closely to hear the truth.

Jerry Williams: I want to indicate to you that I think your writings about the campaign are the most interesting I've read in the press.

---

*Former Alabama governor and Democratic presidential candidate, George Wallace.

HST: Thank you. I'm not sure it's for the best . . .

Jerry Williams: It's another angle. It's not James Reston* . . . it's not Mary McGrory† . . .

HST: Yes, there's a big area on the left, or somewhere on the right, that nobody ever touches. It's very easy to do that, to sort of wander in and just write what you hear. People call it a new kind of journalism. But it's not new at all, really. It's the simplest kind of journalism.

Jerry Williams: Hunter also ran for political office. There was a locally based political movement called the Aspen Freak Power Uprising, and it had to do with Hunter Thompson running for sheriff. Am I right now? Could you give us a little background on that?

HST: Yeah . . . well, it's a pretty twisted sort of story.

Jerry Williams: Just a short synopsis, because I really want to talk politics with you.

HST: The idea of me becoming sheriff was just as big of a joke then as it is now. What I wanted was the power to name the sheriff. So I ran on a very drastic platform. Let's say that I would hire a professional cop of my choosing to run the sheriff's office. The sheriff we had there was a real monster, a redneck. The kind of person who really enjoyed getting out of bed at 2:30 in the morning and raiding a house or a cabin of kids up in the boondocks just to find four joints or people not married sleeping in the same bag. That kind of thing.

So the idea was to run, and not become sheriff, but to turn the political process around to the point, to the idea of the Freak Power. We didn't want power so much, but control over the power. My idea was to become sheriff and then name a sub-sheriff and become a sort of ombudsman and give my salary over to the sheriff, whom I would hire. There are a lot of good cops in the country, which is sort of interesting to me . . . a lot of frustrated cops that like to do the right thing.

Jerry Williams: I think it was an indication of what you found down in Miami. The police work in Miami was very effective. The local Miami Beach police chief did a fantastic job, rather than adhere to what some of**

---

*James Reston was a Pulitzer prize-winning journalist, editor, and columnist for the *New York Times* from 1964 to 1989.

†Mary McGory was a Pulitzer-prize winning journalist and columnist for the *Washington Star* and the *Washington Post.*

**The 1972 Democratic National Convention was held in Miami Beach from July 10 to 13. Hunter wrote extensively about this in *Fear and Loathing on the Campaign Trail, 1972.*

the people in Miami Beach were thundering about—how they had to arrest people because they were smoking some pot down in Flamingo Park—and the mayor of Miami himself. I think they did a fantastic job, talking about good policemen.

HST: Oh yeah, they were very good . . . particularly on that Wednesday afternoon with that disoriented crowd. They came in there for different reasons. One girl had a bullhorn. There were many different factions. It was mainly a harassment kind of thing. I'm glad that people were very concerned about not having a scene, so they had the police back off. It was sort of embarrassing in a way. I remember when I talked to you last was right before the Chicago things.*

Jerry Williams: Yes. It was right before Chicago. What a difference in approach, huh?

HST: Yeah, the validity of it, too. The Chicago protests and demonstrations were very valid. And this was, I think, Ed Sanders† put it best, who was sort of half-running it, saying that the people who should have been demonstrating were inside on the floor with McGovern.** In four years, the people that had been outside in Chicago were inside with McGovern.

Jerry Williams: I'm just saying, as kind of an aside on the fact, there are policemen that really know what they're doing . . . who handle their job well.

HST: But the police recognize that, I think. They saw that. The McGovern people said, "Stay out and let them say what they want" and the police had been sort of warned and half-trained. There's no need to just immediately rush out and use a Billy club and tear gas.

Jerry Williams: Yeah. Nevertheless, you weren't elected sheriff of Aspen? Was it close?

HST: I lost what you call the rural wards. I think I won three out of six wards and lost one really badly, like ten to one. Which is probably one of the luckiest things to ever happen.

Jerry Williams: Is that an indication of the McGovern campaign this year? You lost in Aspen, obviously you split the community into two camps.

---

*The riots at the 1968 Democratic National Convention in Chicago.

†Ed Sanders is an American counterculture poet, musician, and social activist.

**George McGovern served as the Democratic senator for South Dakota from 1963 to 1981. McGovern was the Democratic presidential nominee in the 1972 election against Richard Nixon.

Those who were with you, who were against you? Is this any indication of the McGovern race?

HST: Well, that's a weird story. You say they are split in two camps. We ran a campaign the year before. We figured out, since there were two parties, if we ran a third party, we'd win. So we ran a twenty-nine-year-old kind of freak bike racer lawyer for sheriff. We lost by six votes. But the sheriff's campaign was based on the premise there would be a three-party, three-way race for the next year round.

So I ran for sheriff and another guy ran for county commissioner, which were the really important posts. I'd seen earlier the mayor candidate the year before had taken a lot of blind hate votes, the "he's too young, he's too crazy, he's too weird" votes. So I thought that I would run for sheriff. I figured I would really freak them out, and take the hate vote, be the lightning-rod vote.

But what happened was the national press swarmed over us in a beastly scene where we couldn't move without camera crews and tripods and lights. I think the BBC sent an eight-man team for three weeks.

Jerry Williams: Gee that's really exciting. It gives me an idea, just gives an idea for Massachusetts.

HST: No it was a nightmare. It frightened the people in the town to death. It just scared the hell out of them.

Jerry Williams: I wasn't aware it was so big. Were there any articles about that? Was there a New York Times Magazine* section piece on that?

HST: There was not a paper in the country that didn't write a piece about it of some kind. But the only person who knew the story was me. And I was so much into it.

Jerry Williams: Well, how did you get to be Washington Correspondent for *Rolling Stone?* I mean, if I were thinking of a Washington Correspondent for *Rolling Stone,* you simply wouldn't come to mind.

HST: It came out of the campaign. I was arguing with the *Rolling Stone* editors out in San Francisco that rock music was not the sole expression of the culture for the next two or three years, and we should look to politics rather than backing off. And they all agreed, and there was a silence in the room, and somebody said, "Well who's going to write about it?" And I didn't

---

*Anthony Ripley, "'Freak Power' Candidate May Be the Next Sheriff in Placid Aspen, Colo.," the *New York Times,* October 19, 1970.

want to . . . I was happy out in Woody Creek. But it ended up, since it was my idea, I had to do it.

Jerry Williams: I have a collection of all the columns you've written in *Rolling Stone* about the campaign. As I went along, I read them from beginning to end; I found that you were fooled like a great many other people in terms of George McGovern early in the campaign. You didn't think he had much for chance early, did you?

HST: No. I knew him from November on. It's still a little baffling to me just what he's put together in terms of what it means with the politics we're talking about in Aspen. He's certainly no Freak Power candidate. He's really a conservative candidate. He's just barely conservative enough for me. I think that explains why, although you pretend to be objective, you really view a candidate in terms of whatever point on the spectrum you find yourself. McGovern struck me first as being a very limited candidate in terms of the whole one-issue thing, and second, not a very forceful one. In the beginning, I had no idea, and nobody else did either—and the staff is very defensive about this now—the idea that he'd been putting his staff together for two or three years. Even before he began in New Hampshire, he had the whole entire state of Wisconsin wired from corner to corner.

Jerry Williams: Well, this is the way I look at it. He couldn't have possibly put this together without the one issue—the war—as the center and core . . .

HST: No . . . I think one of his main problems, which is also one of his main strengths, is the fact McGovern is a vehicle for a lot of people who have different notions, like me. And he's barely acceptable to me. I like him, personally. I think he's a good, very straight politician. For a politician, he's one of the most honest people I've ever seen.

But I don't really agree with him. I think his thing with Eagleton and Shriver is a disastrous return to the old politics, which betrays a lot of his talk about the "new politics." But I don't think McGovern really ever claimed to be this. He didn't come up like McCarthy,* saying, "Rise up, I'm the man on the white horse, follow me . . ." It wasn't the politics of Armageddon, which is really like what we were doing in Aspen—the fires on the hillside, the drums, the shouts, the instant takeover.

---

*Eugene McCarthy was a United States senator and representative from Minnesota. McCarthy ran for the Democratic presidential nomination in 1968, 1972, and 1992. He also attempted presidential bids as an Independent candidate in 1976 and for the Progressive Party in 1988.

He's a very reasonable kind of guy. I think he has a very good chance of winning . . . which is kind of crazy to say right now. He's a transitional figure. If he wins, he's a person between the old politics and what I'd like to get to.

Jerry Williams: All right, let's return now. We're here with Hunter Thompson, the Washington Correspondent for *Rolling Stone*. If you read *Rolling Stone*, fine. If you don't, you ought to, at least just to read Hunter Thompson's correspondences on the campaign because it's really been the most colorful stuff written about the campaign. I don't want to get into doing quotations. I just want to talk to Hunter about his observations on the campaign. It seems to me, and correct me if I'm wrong, that Humphrey* destroyed McGovern up to California. Humphrey was a viable candidate and McGovern was destroyed by the intensity of the campaign in California. McGovern, up to California, was doing fairly well. He could occupy some sort of center in the American political spectrum—didn't lose the Jews, didn't lose the Catholic blue-collar workers, didn't get pushed into the so-called radical left—until California. Humphrey went after him on the defense budget, welfare proposals, all of those things and really tore up the pieces in terms of his own campaign. That was a telltale blow against McGovern in terms of his flexibility. Up to this point . . .

HST: No. That is a totally wrong analysis, I think. I was with McGovern at the first debate and something that doesn't come across too often in public—I've never seen him angry before; I've never seen him almost trembling. When he came out, after they took the makeup off for the CBS videos he was almost in a trembling rage. I was talking to John Holman, his speechwriter, and I said, "What the hell, George looks shaken." George couldn't believe Humphrey would have come on him like that, with these obvious debate tactics and absolutely false charges, which Humphrey knew were wrong and so did McGovern.

Jerry Williams: But what I'm saying is that it worked. It didn't work for Humphrey, but it worked in terms of George McGovern's credibility with a large group of people who were pro-Humphrey, who now are going into the Nixon camp.

HST: Well, if it worked, it's too bad, because one of the secrets of understanding, I saw Humphrey change his whole tack in the next debate, completely back off. I called the station after that and oddly enough no

*Hubert Humphrey was vice president under Lyndon B. Johnson and a Democratic presidential nominee in 1968.

one else did. They had 160 calls in 55 minutes, and that window was pro-Humphrey, which surprised me. The press interpretation was that Humphrey had won the first debate, because of that first attack. I think one of the things nobody had really grasped about McGovern, I didn't either for a while, is that he's almost dangerously naïve in a way. He's straight in a way most politicians aren't. It's very difficult for him to cope with things like the California challenge,* which really stunned him, that somebody would actually use a parliamentary ploy to take delegates he's spent weeks and millions to win.

Jerry Williams: Did anyone see George Meany?†

HST: Only I think on Friday. The convention ended on Thursday, and he was photographed on Friday leaving the Americana, where he had been totally incognito in what appeared to be a sort of heinous funk.

Jerry Williams: Well you had indicated in one of the columns that he was very sick and had a stroke?

HST: Oh. That was part of my style.

Jerry Williams: Was it really? I read it several times and wasn't sure if you were just kidding about it or putting him on or whether it actually had happened.

HST: Did I say a stroke? I said brain bubbles. I guess that's an aneurysm . . . yeah, that's a stroke. Well, in effect, politically, yeah, he had a stroke. That's one of the troubles with my column.

Jerry Williams: Oh, OK. I'll accept that.

HST: Humphrey was . . . the ABM movement. The Anybody But McGovern movement was directed by Meany and Al Barken, who was the director of the Committee for Political Education, called COPE, which is the political arm for the AFL-CIO. They were the ones that put together that last-ditch stand. When Humphrey went down on the South Carolina challenge . . . that was it for labor . . . that was it for Meany's veto power over

---

* In 1972 McGovern narrowly won California's winner-takes-all-delegates primary. One month later, during the Democratic National Convention in Miami, delegates from California attempted to challenge McGovern's nomination by threatening to cast their votes in favor of Hubert Humphrey. Delegates supporting McGovern voted down the California Challenge at the Convention by abandoning their support for the South Carolina Challenge, which promoted gender equity amongst the South Carolina delegation.

† George Meany was an influential organized labor leader and president of the AFL-CIO from 1955 to 1979.

Democratic politics. I'm afraid that "small-minded" is probably the right word for it. I'm afraid Meany would prefer to have control over a losing party than to be a secondary power in a winning party. I'm afraid that kind of thinking might cost McGovern the election, even though Meany has really had a gut-issue battle with Nixon for four years now.

Jerry Williams: There was a story the other day Meany was playing golf with the president . . .

HST: Yeah. From what I've seen of that kind of thinking—the Daley-Meany mentality—Daley* seems to come around faster. Meany's not coming around. But, Daley appears to be thinking in realistic terms. If you're looking at control of a party, maybe it might be better to have control of a losing party than to be a small frog in a big pond.

Jerry Williams: Do you think McGovern has lost the mental health vote? I think in today's New York Times, Reston indicates, and I had that feeling a week ago, he's gone.† He lost the mental health vote. A lot of people in this country who resent or have at one time themselves had some problems.

HST: Oh Christ . . . the whole Congress.

Jerry Williams: So I wonder whether or not the mental health vote or the union vote is bigger here.

HST: Well, that goes back to a problem that really is at the root of the campaign. I think you mentioned somewhere in California, you noticed McGovern began to lose some kind of credibility. It was somewhere about the point where the Field Poll in California, which is this sort of the Gallup Poll of California . . . it's a respected, authoritative kind of poll, came out about a week before the election, showing him with an eighteen-point lead. All of a sudden, you'll notice all the old boys in politics coming aboard the McGovern camp. That's when they saw the candidate right there. They knew Humphrey was doomed. They also knew control of the party had passed to McGovern and his people. From that point on, the campaign, to me, kind of peaked. In Miami they were really just holding on. They knew they had a . . . it was a procedural fight, which I described in that last *Rolling Stone* column . . . well, I didn't, but

---

* Richard Daley was the mayor of Chicago from 1955 to 1976 and an influential old-time Democratic Party boss—who was, of course, loathed by Hunter.

† James Reston, "Psychology and Politics," the *New York Times*, August 8, 1972.

Rick Stearns* did, which was brilliant work. The fact that they could do that and baffle these old pros, who had known every trick in the book. They had Humphrey's campaign manager, Jack Chestnut, climbing the walls. He had no idea what was happening. Humphrey himself knew. They baffled all the journalists . . . it was just straight, technical politics.

Jerry Williams: With me now is Hunter Thompson, a freelance writer and a failed politician from Woody Creek, Colorado. His first book was *Fear and Loathing in Las Vegas,* and his other book was called *Hell's Angels* because he was involved, secretly as a writer as one of the Hell's Angels, until they found him out.

HST: Oh no. No, no. That was no secret. I was up front about that. They knew I was writing. Oh yeah. They knew I was a writer. They wanted me to join because they thought writers should be part of the team.

Jerry Williams: He also ran for sheriff with the whole Aspen "Freak Power" uprising. And he's now the Washington Correspondent for *Rolling Stone.* In case you're tuning in late, *Rolling Stone* is generally a music magazine. It could be called underground, semi-underground, whatever. Many young people read it. It's a national publication, a weekly magazine and Hunter Thompson is the Washington Correspondent. By the way, he was written for many magazines, including *Esquire, The Nation,* the *New York Times Magazine, Scanlan's.* He is currently living in Washington and following the campaign of George McGovern.

We were discussing the business of California. It is my contention that McGovern began to lose credibility as a result of the attacks upon him by Hubert Humphrey. Nobody much cared about McGovern's views on the defense establishment, welfare, guaranteed annual income until Humphrey dramatized it and everybody started to get uptight about it. And that's where it began, the whole business of examining McGovern rather than examining the president. The issue was supposed to be based around the administration's four years, but what the campaign has been so far has been an examination of George McGovern.

HST: Yes, I keep insisting that Humphrey dramatized it falsely. But I agree that McGovern responded. What Humphrey did was drag McGovern down to his level of debate.

---

*Rick Stearns served as special assistant to Senator George McGovern during the 1972 presidential campaign.

Jerry Williams: Yeah, I'm not contending truth was involved. I'm merely trying to analyze the events as they occur.

HST: I think you're right then. At some point, about a week or ten days before the end of the California primary, the McGovern campaign turned somehow back toward the old politics. Which, to me, is the politics of ploy, counterploy; move, countermove. Tactical politics instead of thinking politics.

Jerry Williams: Well, is it possible that George McGovern and Mankiewicz* and the other wheels within the campaign figured they could not win without moving back into the center of the old politics?

HST: No, no. That's not it. What I think happened was when the power people in the party saw McGovern would win, and California was the final test, instead of fighting him any longer, they decided to come on board: the Kennedy camp, the labor people, like the avant-garde laborer, Woodcock,† the UAW—people like that. Instead, it became clear in California a week before the election that McGovern would be the nominee, period. And that, like him or not, they'd have to deal with him. So, all the sudden, the ship of state, as it would be, was weighted very much in the center, the front, the prow, whatever, by people that hadn't been there before.

Jerry Williams: But didn't you discover also that the McGovern people knew they had made some very serious mistakes as result of the thrust upon them by Humphrey in California. That the mistakes were things George McGovern had been talking about, the thousand-dollar annual stipend for each member of the family? They had made some serious errors and had to move back to so-called old politics to right the errors that they made?

HST: I'm afraid that's right. I hate to say it because, having covered McGovern for so long, I've come to know him and like him, and I'm for him. But I do see a turn back to that. Maybe it's a retreat, like you say. Maybe it's not a conscious move . . . McGovern is inclined toward, not a radical politics,

---

* Frank Mankiewicz, who had been Robert Kennedy's press secretary for his 1968 presidential campaign, was directing McGovern's presidential campaign. They became good friends and it was Mr. Mankiewicz who said that Hunter's book on the campaign was "by far the least factual and most accurate book written about any campaign."

† Leonard Woodcock was an influential labor union leader, president of the United Automobile Workers from 1970 from 1976, and the first United States ambassador to China under the Carter administration.

but the kind of radicalism of the old IWW,* the radicalism of the Plains . . . Minnesota liberal labor.

Jerry Williams: The Wobblies.†

HST: Yeah, the Wobblies. That's really his roots. Compared to me, he's way, way to the right of any sort of politics I stand for. But I recognize in McGovern a reluctant kind of grasping for a kind of politics he personally is not really ready for. And I'm not sure anybody is. You can't really say that we want to turn over the world and get started in a different way. But McGovern has an open mind, and he understands that things are not going right. Whether that means that he's going to, under pressure . . . there's a terrible pressure that comes when you get close to a power you thought you'd never approach. I saw it in Miami when all of a sudden they realized they were about to get the nomination. The staff got all tense and wild. The loose atmosphere around the McGovern campaign disappeared. They had been saying all along "we'll win, we'll win . . . we have the right program, we have the right kind of organization" and all of a sudden, it appeared to them, out of nowhere, that they were going to win.

Jerry Williams: Yeah . . . When you get close to the seat of that awesome power . . .

HST: And there is a tremendous amount of power there. And I think that's what accounted for the Eagleton affair.

Jerry Williams: Up to that point, it seemed to me it's just kind of a game. You know, "Well, we may win and we'll have a lot of fun and laughs and we'll see if we can beat and out-maneuver the other guy." But when you get to the point when you're right near the seat and you've won . . . Wow. I think a whole new area of thinking begins to invade. At least in my brain.

HST: Oh yeah. That happened to me in Aspen. I put out two platforms. When I first began to run for sheriff, when I first announced it, I said I was doing it as a lightning rod, a sort of bogus candidate. I put out a platform deliberately to scare the hell out of the populace. One of the platforms was to tear up the streets immediately, rip them right up, put grass down. All dishonest swindlers would be put in stocks in front of the courthouse. Then

---

* Industrial Workers of the World is an international labor union and advocacy group based in Cincinnati, Ohio.

† The "Wobblies" is a nickname for the Industrial Workers of the World.

when I realized I was going to win the city, is when I realized it was going to be a serious campaign. We had to go back over it and come up with what still amounts to a very progressive sheriff campaign.

Jerry Williams: *Fear and Loathing in Las Vegas:* Were you in your right mind when you wrote most of that book?

HST: (laughs). Really, it's a very disciplined book. It had about four rewrites. It's a writer's book. It's probably one of the most disciplined things I've ever written, much more so than the political writing.

Jerry Williams: Well, I get the feeling that the political things, they ramble around with odd thoughts here and there, which is what I like about it. I guess you aren't encumbered by space with the political writing, were you?

HST: Usually the reverse. I have too much space. I have eight pages to fill on Wednesday or Monday night, and they're due on Tuesday.

Jerry Williams: Do you think McGovern can win, and was the Eagleton nomination a mistake to begin with? What was your reaction?

HST: Unfortunately, which is bizarre now in retrospect, McGovern assumed until the very end Kennedy* would do it. So there was never really any serious contingency plan for any second or third or fourth choice. They got into a real panic state on Thursday because Kennedy, after refusing it on Wednesday night, asked for one last review of it on Thursday morning. So about noon on Thursday, before McGovern realized he had to go to the field (because the rules of the national Democratic committee said that the choice of the candidate had to be in by four o'clock). In other words, if he had missed the four o'clock deadline, it would have been an open convention for the vice president. So they called a press conference for one first then for two. They got us all out of bed. The lobby of the Doral Hotel was a madhouse with every known correspondent and TV person, all of them waiting and yelling and demanding. It became increasingly apparent they were in trouble. And McGovern sent staff people down to calm the press and take them down to the coffee shop. It was 4:05 before Mankiewicz came down to announce this with a fishy look on his face, a very unhappy look. And the staff people were not happy at all. As I recall I was standing with Dave Sugarman, who ran the press thing up here in Massachusetts and we were yelling about the old politics. There was a pall that settled on the campaign at that point. They knew that somehow the

---

* Edward "Ted" Kennedy is a Democratic senator from Massachusetts.

momentum of the purist element of the McGovern campaign had been seriously tainted by Eagleton. So in a way, they got what they deserved.

Jerry Williams: Did you have a chance to look at Eagleton close up?

HST: No. I met him once in a steam bath. There wasn't a piece of copy anywhere about him at all. They put out a list on Friday before the convention of candidates under consideration . . . Jimmy Carter, the governor of Georgia; Dale Bumpers, the governor of Arkansas. But to me to me, Eagleton was just a young, ambitious Catholic candidate with ties to labor.

Jerry Williams: My observation was there were a great many people who could have made much better decisions than they could at that stage of the game. It was a poor decision, poorly timed, and poorly examined. The whole thing was a bad scene.

HST: Well, Kennedy deserves some of the blame for that. He could have let them know very firmly early on that he wasn't going to do it. That would have given them more time. If you want to look at it cynically, which I do, I think Kennedy sort of sandbagged them in a way. I don't think Kennedy really feels it's in his interest to have McGovern win this time. That's a harsh thing to say, but looking at it as a politician with the kind of adrenalin that comes up when you think that way, I thought about it, and I defend that. Kennedy could have made it easier and made it very clear ahead of time that he wasn't going to be there. Mrs. McGovern, on Wednesday afternoon, almost at the last second, was giving interviews saying they were sure Kennedy would take it, once George got over the hump.

Jerry Williams: Can McGovern win? What are they talking about now, since you're fairly close?

HST: I think so, yeah. They think they can win. Oh Christ yeah they think they can win.

Jerry Williams: What is the coalition they think they can put together? They have their hard-core support of the antiwar people. They have a lot of young people. Undoubtedly, they have most of the blacks, minorities, Chicanos, people like that pretty well solid in there. Labor vote: questionable. Jewish vote: questionable. Blue-collar, Catholic workers: questionable.

HST: Well, it'd be a terrible irony though if the Jewish vote and the labor vote went for Nixon against McGovern. That would baffle me and turn all sorts of political assumptions around. Why would that be?

Jerry Williams: Well, there's a fear of change. The change McGovern represents. McGovern represents change.

HST: But the Jewish vote has always been more progressive. Labor has always been progressive, toward change.

Jerry Williams: Well, there's a piece tonight on ABC television examining the Jewish vote. There were some of the big fundraisers in the Jewish community in Los Angeles indicating they are going Nixon. They were for Humphrey, but now they're for Nixon. And they are raising money. One of the big fundraisers indicated he was raising money and not having a hard time doing it.

HST: For Nixon?

Jerry Williams: Yes. And the interview said he was raising as much money as the law will allow.

HST: Sigh. That's really depressing to me to think two of the most progressive forces in the country in the last twenty years, the Jewish vote and the labor vote, would be so afraid of change now. Not so much afraid of specified change, but by the threat of change.

Jerry Williams: Well what are they saying. What are the McGovern people saying about that?

HST: I had dinner the other night in Chicago with Eugene McCarthy and Carl Wagner* . . . Eugene McCarthy is in charge of Chicago and Illinois, which demonstrates his importance to the organization, and Wagner is in charge of Michigan. These are two key states. They believe they can win, not by changing peoples' minds so much, or by arguing the issues, but by getting out the vote. They believe that the vote in this country is essentially weighted against Nixon. Their idea is "if the vote comes out, we'll win."

Jerry Williams: I think Mr. Nixon and his people are very hip to that. They understand that. I think they'll devote a lot of money getting out the vote pro-Nixon as well. They understand how serious that matter is. You don't hear anyone downgrading the fact there will be a runaway fight. Nixon is running scared and always has been running scared. He isn't going to take this business of being a pushover too seriously.

HST: Yeah. I recall months ago talking to Mankiewicz over the phone. I asked if there were enough of us to beat them. That was when we were still talking on shadow terms. And he said, "Yeah." That's really the assumption of the McGovern campaign—if you say the right things to the right number

*Carl Wagner is a progressive political strategist who worked heavily on McGovern's 1972 presidential campaign.

people, they will come out and vote. And the hook of that is backsliding into things like the Eagleton botch and resorting to the old politics.

That was our assumption in Aspen—that there was a contingency for a new politics. You couldn't come out, for instance, and say: "Hey I'll eat mescaline when I'm off duty, but not while on." Which is one of the more absurd aspects of it. But I believe it. If you give the people in this country a viable alternative, a real one, they'll vote for it.

Jerry Williams: You've watched the candidates and you've watched the people's reaction to them. There's a lot of hostility for McGovern, particularly in the South. I don't think he's going to take one Southern state. Have they given up on that?

HST: No, no. McGovern believes, and he seriously believes it and there is some basis for it, if he talks to enough people personally, they'll vote for him. And I guarantee you there is some truth in that. He's kind of anti-convincing in a way. And he's convincing in a way that comes around behind you. It's like reading a book you don't really enjoy too much and then you finish it and you're like, "Wow—what was that?" He really is as straight as he seems. The problem is he's naïve. His father was a minister. He has a lot of that in him. It worries me sometimes how he misunderstands the power surges and vacuums in American politics. But, of course, we could talk about that after misjudging his chances in New Hampshire six months ago as madness.*

Jerry Williams: I'm wondering what they are hoping for in the campaign. They must have some hopes there will be some bumbling by the other side.

HST: Well, I'm reading Fred Dutton's book *Changing Sources of Power: American Politics in the 1970s.* Dutton has a very good point that Nixon won in '68 with fewer votes than he lost by in '60. While the population went up, the vote itself went down. There are four different splits in the McGovern camp; Dutton represents one of those newer, looser thinkers. The population is rising, but the number of voters is falling. There is a huge dropout vote that is not necessarily in the 18-to-24 demographic, which alone is 25 million on paper. There are another 20 million that have backed off politics. The assumption is to get that vote, the huge dropout vote.

Jerry Williams: We're going to take a few callers now.

Phone Caller #1: I'd like to speak to Hunter Thompson. I'm a great admirer of yours; I've read all your pieces in *Rolling Stone*, and I think you're

---

*George McGovern lost the 1972 New Hampshire Primary to Maine senator Ed Muskie.

one of the few political commentators these days that tells the unvarnished truth. I've got a couple questions for you. I voted for McGovern, and I did some work for him. I voted in the primary for him. But I've been growing more and more disenchanted with this campaign. You mentioned this backsliding into this old politics, and that's been concerning me, too. I think pretty clearly this Eagleton affair was a cave-in to the moneybags in the party. There was an item with your interview with Rick Stearns from your latest piece in the *Stone* that struck me quite a bit. You were talking about the crucial California confrontation about the South Carolina vote.* Apparently this is a direct quote from Stearns: "What it really came down to is they had less guts then we had. We were willing to sell out the women but we weren't willing to sell out a Southern governor."

HST: Yeah. That's true. It wasn't edited out of the transcript. That sums up what it was all about.

Phone Caller #1: What I was wondering is how many more people are they going to sell out between now and the election? Have they really gotten power-mad? He's been backtracking on everything from amnesty to residual troops in Vietnam. How many more of their ideals are they going to ditch in their lust for power?

HST: Well, it worries me quite frankly. The closer you get to power, the more tempting it is to shave points here and there. And I think one of the main levers we have on them is to remind McGovern and his people if they do that, it will turn into another Nixon-Humphrey race. I think the real thrust in this country is for a new politics. Not just the same old . . . I don't give a damn whether McGovern wins or not, frankly, if he's just a down-the-road politician. I think it's important people speak up and say that to him. The proximity of power creates a kind of tunnel vision. Whereas, four months ago I could sit with Mankiewicz and argue with him, it's impossible now for me to do it. There's too much press around. But I think it's important for

---

*Immediately preceding the opening of the 1972 Democratic National Convention in Miami, a women's interest group challenged the gender composition of the all-male South Carolina delegation by threatening a parliamentary action during the convention. Democratic nominee George McGovern supported the group's position for a half-male, half-female South Carolina delegation. On the opening roll call on July 10, however, delegates dumped votes on the position to avoid a parliamentary challenge regarding the results of the California primary, which McGovern narrowly won by 5 percent.

this type of attitude to penetrate. And so far it hasn't. They're very close, and they can smell it. The drool is there. It worries me.

Jerry Williams: The question is, Where do you draw the line?

HST: Yeah. That's my problem right now. I wonder just how far I'm willing to go with McGovern just to beat Nixon.

Phone Caller #1: Well it's hard to say.

HST: Well, we have to say! We have two months.

Phone Caller #1: There's time, but I get pressure from people I know that have nothing to do with politics at all. I did vote for him in the primary, I did a little work for him. I'm sort of in the middle. I'm prepared to involve myself in this type of politics. But sometimes they make it very difficult to do it.

Jerry Williams: I think we have the gist of that. There's a guy in the McGovern camp and doesn't know where to draw the line yet. Twenty minutes to midnight. We've got Hunter Thompson here. Hello.

Phone Caller #2: I would like to ask Mr. Thompson if Eunice Shriver's* tremendous work with the mentally retarded will at all offset the Eagleton blunder?

HST: You can't equate the idea of retarded children with the mental health vote.

Jerry Williams: Well I hate to talk in those terms, those so-called political terms.

Phone Caller #2: Isn't it disgraceful?

Jerry Williams: The lady is saying Eunice Shriver has done some fantastic work among the mentally retarded. Is that enough to offset, because obviously some people feel very alienated about Tom Eagleton?

HST: No, put in those terms, I wouldn't think so. They're two different issues altogether. Eunice Shriver is also on a stump making speeches against abortion, which I am totally for. That is one of the issues McGovern has been the most backed off on and the cheapest. It started in Nebraska, where Humphrey accused him of being an abortionist, a dope dealer, God knows what else. Instead of being straight about it, because he does favor free abortion, he backed off.

---

*Eunice Kennedy Shriver is a member of the influential Kennedy family from Massachusetts. She is a founder of the Special Olympics and an international advocate for improving and enhancing the lives of the mentally disabled.

Phone Caller #2: Don't you think though that the Democratic Party cannot stand with liberals alone? You cannot just chop off the ones that have been Democrats for years and years . . . you can't just exclude them completely. I mean, after all, if you don't want to vote Republican and you still want to be classified as a Democrat and you're not entirely liberal and you're not entirely conservative, you're more or less a middle-of-the-roader, why can't everybody be in the same party?

HST: I think a growing number of people think the two-party system is a detriment to this country. I think one of McGovern's main mistakes is nailing his fortune to the Democratic Party, which I think should be destroyed by fire, ice, whatever means it takes. I think when you get into that, you identify yourself with old, worn-out policies. Which I think he's done.

Phone Caller #3: Hi. I heard you talking about the Jewish vote in Los Angeles. While George McGovern and his aides were vacationing, Nixon was picking up the Jewish vote in New York. There was a big meeting with the leaders of the Jewish communities, and Henry Kissinger was there. After that, Mr. Nixon was able to pick up quite a bit of money from there. The other thing I wanted to say was about the Catholic vote. Senator McGovern says it's not necessary to have the parochial schools. And Mr. Nixon has told the Catholic people he's going to arrange to have credits up to 100 dollars for each student in a private school. This is always going to get some of the Jewish vote because they want to keep the Hebrew schools open. And the other thing I wanted to comment on was about Senator Kennedy sandbagging McGovern by not telling them until Thursday. Do you think also he's the one who sandbagged Mayor [Kevin] White* so he would not be the leader of the Democratic liberals in Massachusetts?

Jerry Williams: My observation was from Father Drinan,† who led the opposition against Kevin White.

HST: The Kennedy thing is a speculation on my part. It's a fairly cynical and probably cruel speculation. But having seen politicians for a while, I think it's correct.

---

* Kevin White is a former Democratic mayor of Boston. He served as mayor between 1968 and 1984.

† Father Robert Drinan was an influential Jesuit priest, lawyer, and Democratic representative from Massachusetts.

Phone Caller #3: Do you think Senator Kennedy is willing to let Senator McGovern take over the liberal Democrats in the country? If he does, he's finished.

HST: But if he loses, he won't?

Phone Caller #3: If Senator McGovern loses, Senator Kennedy will still be the head of the liberals in this county. If Senator McGovern wins, Kennedy is lost.

HST: That's exactly what I'm saying. This is why I'm cynical enough to think that Kennedy was not going out of his way to help McGovern win.

Phone Caller #3: I saw that thing the other night, and I never saw anybody look so bored as Senator Kennedy did. And Sargent Shriver* turned to him right during the middle of his speech and said, "Why are you looking so pensive?"

HST: That's right.

Jerry Williams: During the Democratic National Convention?

Phone Caller #3: Right during the middle of his speech! And then he said that finally the family was allowing him to run.

HST: Well, the family was against Shriver running. There was a lot of pressure on him not to run, not to take it.

Phone Caller #3: I know. They never let him do anything. Anytime he wanted to do anything he was shipped somewhere. And I'm just wondering because the Kennedys must be very upset in a way because, as you know, Teddy Kennedy is supposed to be the one who's next. But I don't think they'd appreciate Shriver, or let him in before Teddy.

HST: You seem to have the whole thing wired. You have to draw your own conclusions about what he did in Miami.

Jerry Williams: It seems to me Sargent Shriver is his own man. He wanted to run for political office and elected office, but he's pretty much his own guy.

HST: He might not have been before yesterday, but sure. In '68 Humphrey wanted him to run.

Phone Caller #3: They said it was Bobby Kennedy's turn, but he wasn't allowed to do anything.

HST: No, Teddy Kennedy's turn.

---

*Robert "Sargent" Shriver is married to Eunice Kennedy Shriver. He was the first director of the Peace Corps and served as the United States ambassador to France under presidents Lyndon B. Johnson and Richard Nixon. George McGovern chose Shriver as a Democratic vice-presidential running mate after Thomas Eagleton's history of mental health problems was made public.

Phone Caller #3: In '68?

HST: Yeah. Bobby was dead. After Humphrey got the nomination, Shriver came up, but the Kennedy brain trust vetoed it because it was Teddy's turn.

Phone Caller #3: That's why I can't understand it now. Kennedy must be sure McGovern is going to lose because otherwise, his entire career is absolutely ruined.

HST: I think you're right smack on target.

Phone Caller #4: Yes, I'd like to comment on what I think is an unfair force which Mr. Thompson and the rest are putting on McGovern. I think too many people are asking McGovern to play the role of a radical instead of a politician. I think it's impossible to be a rigid ideologue in two-party politics, and they're simply asking him to play a role . . .

HST: No, I said that earlier! I said that was one of McGovern's problems. There were too many people, like me, who had made him a vehicle. I think there is a tremendous energy in this country for some kind of new politics. And nobody knew what it was until all of a sudden McGovern emerged. I don't think even McGovern understands how many weird people and twisted ideas are behind him.

Phone Caller #4: I just think these demands . . . It's so unfortunate, because I think they're destroying what could be a successful campaign.

HST: It's not fair. It's a fact. Let's just live with it. If you want to get out on the road there and say, "I'm the candidate of the new politics," which he's done, you have to take some peculiar baggage with you.

Phone Caller #4: See, I don't think the new politics has to have a rigid ideologue.

HST: Who said that? What do you have in mind?

Phone Caller #4: I just think too many people that call themselves practitioners of the new politics feel that way.

HST: McGovern doesn't. He's one of the most flexible people I've ever seen in politics. He is, let's face it, the alternative to Nixon. There's never been a more classic example of the old politics. He can't sift and sort his supporters like he could in New Hampshire back in February.

Phone Caller #4: I think part of it is McGovern's fault also. In the primaries he had to take this role to distinguish himself from the vital center of Muskie* and Humphrey and others. In a sense, he has two campaign

*Edmund Muskie was a senator and governor from Maine. He was a candidate for the Democratic presidential nomination in 1972. Muskie served as secretary of state under the Carter administration.

strategies so wholly different that he's asked for this problem himself. In a sense, it wasn't his fault, though, because he had to pursue it with an ideological position in the primaries.

HST: He knew this. That's no accident. If you emerge from a twelve-man primary as the one alternative to an incumbent Republican president, you're damn well going to take some weird people with you.

Phone Caller #4: It's just the role of a radical to prod. And McGovern played the role of a radical in the primaries.

HST: I don't think he ever . . .

Phone Caller #4: One of his Senate speeches in which he said every man in this chamber is responsible for dying boys in Vietnam and this chamber reeks of blood.

HST: That's not radical. I think that's a flat-out conservative truth.

Phone Caller #4: Well certainly it's more outspoken.

HST: Why is it radical?

Phone Caller #4: From the standpoint of viewing it against the vital center on a position against Vietnam. They don't speak on those terms.

HST: That's not McGovern's fault. If their feet aren't clean, it doesn't make you a radical to point it out.

Phone Caller #4: Well you know everything is relative of course.

HST: Well, I think McGovern is basically a centrist politician. That's been his whole stance from the start.

Playboy—November 1974

Playboy Interview: Hunter Thompson

BY CRAIG VETTER

Early in the year, *Playboy* sent Craig Vetter to interview Thompson.

Vetter's report:

"This interview was hammered and stitched together over seven months, on the road, mostly, in Mexico and Washington, San Clemente and Colorado, and as I write this, we are in Chicago, where tornado warnings are out, and we are up against a hell-fire deadline that has me seeing ghosts and has Dr. Thompson locked in a penthouse full of mirrors on the 20th floor of an Astor Street high-rise. He has the heavy steel window louvers cranked shut, there is a lamp behind him that has had its neck snapped off and he is bent over a coffee table cursing. We are trying to salvage this interview, making changes, corrections, additions—all of them unnecessary until nine days ago, when Richard Nixon quit. Thompson is mumbling that the motor control in his pen hand is failing and he is not kidding. You can't read his Rs anymore and all five vowels may become illegible soon. We might have finished this thing like gentlemen, except for Richard Nixon, who might as well have sent the plumbers' unit to torch the entire second half, the political half, of the manuscript we have worked on so long. All of it has had to be redone in the past few sleepless days and it has broken the spirit of nearly everyone even vaguely involved.

"We're well into the 30th hour now and there won't be many more, no matter what. Thompson is working over his last few answers, still talking to himself, and I think I just heard him say, 'The rest will have to be done by God,' which may mean that he is finished.

"And though this long and killing project is ending here in desperate, guilty, short-tempered ugliness, it began all those months ago, far from this garden of agony, on a sunshine island in the Caribbean where Thompson and Sandy and I had gone to begin taping.

"The first time I turned on the tape recorder, we were sitting on a sea wall, in damp, salty bathing suits, under palm trees. It was warm, Nixon was still our President and Thompson was sucking up bloody marys, vegetables and all, and he had just paid a young newsboy bandit almost one dollar American for a paper that would have cost a straighter, more sober person 24 cents."*

Playboy: You just paid as much for your morning paper as you might for a good hit of mescaline. Are you a news junkie, too?

HST: Yeah, I must have the news. One of these mornings, I'm gonna buy a paper with a big black headline that says, "Richard Nixon Committed Suicide Last Night." Jesus . . . can you imagine that rush?

Playboy: Do you get off on politics the same way you get off on drugs?

HST: Sometimes. It depends on the politics, depends on the drugs . . . there are different kinds of highs. I had this same discussion in Mexico City one night with a guy who wanted me to do Zihuatanejo with him and get stoned for about 10 days on the finest flower tops to be had in all of Mexico. But I told him I couldn't do that; I had to be back in Washington.

Playboy: That doesn't exactly fit your image as the drug-crazed outlaw journalist. Are you saying you'd rather have been in the capital, covering the Senate Watergate hearings or the House Judiciary Committee debate on Nixon's impeachment, than stoned on the beach in Mexico with a bunch of freaks?

HST: Well—it depends on the timing. On Wednesday, I might want to go to Washington; on Thursday, I might want to go to Zihuatanejo.

Playboy: Today must be Thursday, because already this morning you've had two bloody marys, three beers and about four spoons of some white substance and you've been up for only an hour. You don't deny that you're heavily into drugs, do you?

HST: No, why should I deny it? I like drugs. Somebody gave me this white powder last night. I suspect it's cocaine, but there's only one way to find out—look at this shit! It's already crystallized in this goddamn humidity. I can't even cut it up with the scissors in my Swiss-army knife. Actually, coke is a worthless drug, anyway. It has no edge. Dollar for dollar, it's probably the most inefficient drug on the market. It's not worth the effort or the risk or

*Feeling that Craig Vetter's initial words were important to set up this interview, I included them, but for reasons of space, I did edit his words a bit—Anita Thompson.

the money—at least not to me. It's a social drug; it's more important to offer it than it is to use it. But the world is full of cocamaniacs these days and they have a tendency to pass the stuff around, and this morning I'm a little tired and I have this stuff, so . . .

Playboy: What do you like best?

HST: Probably mescaline and mushrooms: That's a genuine high. It's not just an up—you know, like speed, which is really just a motor high. When you get into psychedelics like mescaline and mushrooms, it's a very clear kind of high, an interior high. But really, when you're dealing with psychedelics, there's only one king drug, when you get down to it, and that's acid. About twice a year you should blow your fucking tubes out with a tremendous hit of really good acid. Take 72 hours and just go completely amuck, break it all down.

Playboy: When did you take your first acid trip?

HST: It was while I was working on the Hell's Angels book. Ken Kesey wanted to meet some of the Angels, so I introduced him and he invited them all down to his place in La Honda. It was a horrible, momentous meeting and I thought I'd better be there to see what happened when all this incredible chemistry came together. And, sure as shit, the Angels rolled in—about 40 or 50 bikes—and Kesey and the other people were offering them acid. And I thought, "Great creeping Jesus, what's going to happen now?"

Playboy: Had the Angels ever been into acid before that?

HST: No. That was the most frightening thing about it. Here were all these vicious bikers full of wine and bennies, and Kesey's people immediately started giving them LSD. They didn't know what kind of violent crowd they were dealing with. I was sure it was going to be a terrible blood, rape and pillage scene, that the Angels would tear the place apart. And I stood there, thinking, "Jesus, I'm responsible for this, I'm the one who did it." I watched those lunatics gobbling the acid and I thought, "Shit, if it's gonna get this heavy I want to be as fucked up as possible." So I went to one of Kesey's friends and I said, "Let me have some of that shit; we're heading into a very serious night. Perhaps even ugly." So I took what he said was about 800 micrograms, which almost blew my head off at the time . . . but in a very fine way. It was nice. Surprised me, really. I'd heard all these stories when I lived in Big Sur a couple of years before from this psychiatrist who'd taken the stuff and wound up running naked through the streets of Palo Alto, screaming that he wanted to be punished for his crimes. He didn't know what his crimes were and nobody else did, either, so they took him away and he spent a long time in a loony bin somewhere, and I thought, "That's not what I need." Because if a guy who seems levelheaded like that is going to flip out and tear off his clothes and beg the citizens to punish him, what the hell might I do?

Playboy: You didn't beg to be scourged and whipped?

HST: No . . . and I didn't scourge anybody else, either, and when I was finished, I thought, "Jesus, you're not so crazy, after all; you're not a basically violent or vicious person like they said." Before that, I had this dark fear that if I lost control, all these horrible psychic worms and rats would come out. But I went to the bottom of the well and found out there's nothing down there I have to worry about, no secret ugly things waiting for a chance to erupt.

Playboy: You drink a little, too, don't you?

HST: Yeah . . . obviously, but I drink this stuff like I smoke cigarettes; I don't even notice it. You know—a bird flies, a fish swims, I drink. But you notice I very rarely sit down and say, "Now I'm going to get wasted." I never eat a tremendous amount of any one thing. I rarely get drunk and I use drugs pretty much the same way.

Playboy: Do you like marijuana?

HST: Not much. It doesn't mix well with alcohol. I don't like to get stoned and stupid.

Playboy: What would you estimate you spend on drugs in a year?

HST: Oh, Jesus . . .

Playboy: What the average American family spends on an automobile, say?

HST: Yeah, at least that much. I don't know what the total is; I don't even want to know. It's frightening, but I'll tell you that on a story I just did, one of the sections took me 17 days of research and $1,400 worth of cocaine. And that's just what I spent. On one section of one story.

Playboy: What do you think the drugs are doing to your body?

HST: Well, I just had a physical, the first one in my life. People got worried about my health, so I went to a very serious doctor and told him I wanted every fucking test known to man: EEG, heart, everything. And he asked me questions for three hours to start with, and I thought, "What the hell, tell the truth, that's why you're here." So I told him exactly what I'd been doing for the past 10 years. He couldn't believe it. He said, "Jesus, Hunter, you're a goddamn mess"—that's an exact quote. Then he ran all the tests and found I was in perfect health. He called it a "genetic miracle."

Playboy: What about your mind?

HST: I think it's pretty healthy. I think I'm looser than I was before I started to take drugs. I'm more comfortable with myself. Does it look like it's fucked me up? I'm sitting here on a beautiful beach in Mexico; I've written three books; I've got a fine 100-acre fortress in Colorado. On that evidence, I'd have to advise the use of drugs. . . . But of course I wouldn't, never in hell—or at least not all drugs for all people. There are some people who should never be allowed to take acid, for instance. You can spot them after about 10 minutes: people with all kinds of bad psychic baggage, stuff they haven't cleaned out yet, weird hostilities, repressed shit—the same kind of people who turn into mean drunks.

Playboy: Do you believe religious things about drugs?

HST: No, I never have. That's my main argument with the drug culture. I've never believed in that guru trip; you know, God, nirvana, that kind of oppressive, hipper-than-thou bullshit. I like to just gobble the stuff right out in the street and see what happens, take my chances, just stomp on my own accelerator. It's like getting on a racing bike and all of a sudden you're doing 120 miles per hour into a curve that has sand all over it and you think, "Holy Jesus, here we go," and you lay it over till the pegs hit the street and metal starts to spark. If you're good enough, you can pull it out, but sometimes you end up in the emergency room with some bastard in a white suit sewing your scalp back on.

Playboy: Is that what you call "edge work"?

HST: Well, that's one aspect of it, I guess—in that you have to be good when you take nasty risks, or you'll lose it, and then you're in serious trouble.

Playboy: Why are you smiling?

HST: Am I smiling? Yeah, I guess I am . . . well, it's fun to lose it sometimes.

Playboy: What kind of flack do you get for being so honest about the drugs you use?

HST: I'm not too careful about what I say. But I'm careful in other ways. I never sell any drugs, for instance; I never get involved in the traffic or the marketing end of the drug business. I make a point of not even knowing about it. I'm very sensitive about maintaining my deniability, you know—like Nixon. I never deal. Simple use is one thing—like booze in the Twenties—

but selling is something else: They come after you for that. I wouldn't sell drugs to my mother, for any reason . . . no, the only person I'd sell drugs to would be Richard Nixon. I'd sell him whatever the fucker wanted . . . but he'd pay heavy for it and damn well remember the day he tried it.

Playboy: Are you the only journalist in America who's ridden with both Richard Nixon and the Hell's Angels?

HST: I must be. Who else would claim a thing like that? Hell, who else would admit it?

Playboy: Which was more frightening?

HST: The Angels. Nobody can throw a gut-level, king-hell scare into you like a Hell's Angel with a pair of pliers hanging from his belt that he uses to pull out people's teeth in midnight diners. Some of them wear the teeth on their belts, too.

Playboy: Why did you decide to do a book on the Hell's Angels?

HST: Money. I'd just quit and been fired almost at the same time by *The National Observer.* They wouldn't let me cover the Free Speech thing at Berkeley and I sensed it was one of the biggest stories I'd ever stumbled onto. So I decided, "Fuck journalism," and I went back to writing novels. I tried driving a cab in San Francisco, I tried every kind of thing. I used to go down at five o'clock every morning and line up with the winos on Mission Street, looking for work handing out grocery-store circulars and shit like that. I was the youngest and healthiest person down there, but nobody would ever select me. I tried to get weird and rotten-looking; you know—an old Army field jacket, scraggly beard, tried to look like a bad wino. But even then, I never got picked out of the line-up.

Playboy: You couldn't even get wino's work?

HST: No, and at that point I was stone-broke, writing fiction, living in a really fine little apartment in San Francisco—looking down on Golden Gate Park, just above Haight Street. The rent was only $100 a month—this was 1965, about a year before the Haight-Ashbury madness started—and I got a letter from Carey McWilliams, the editor of *The Nation,* and it said, "Can you do an article on the Hell's Angels for us for $100?" That was the rent, and I was about ready to get back into journalism, so I said, "Of course. I'll do anything for $100."

Playboy: How long did the article take?

HST: I worked about a month on it, put about $3,000 worth of effort into it, got no expenses—and about six weeks after the fucker came out, my mailbox piled up with book offers. My phone had been cut off by then. I couldn't believe it: editors, publishers, people I'd never heard of. One of them offered me $1,500 just to sign a thing saying that if I decided to write the book, I'd do it for them. Shit, at that point I would have written the definitive text on hammer-head sharks for the money—and spent a year in the water with them.

Playboy: How did you first meet the Angels?

HST: I just went out there and said, "Look, you guys don't know me, I don't know you, I heard some bad things about you, are they true?" I was wearing a fucking madras coat and wing tips, that kind of thing, but I think they sensed I was a little strange—if only because I was the first writer who'd ever come out to see them and talk to them on their own turf. Until then, all the Hell's Angels stories had come from the cops. They seemed a little stunned at the idea that some straight-looking writer for a New York literary magazine would actually track them down to some obscure transmission shop in the industrial slums of south San Francisco. They were a bit off balance at first, but after about 50 or 60 beers, we found a common ground, as it were . . . Crazies always recognize each other. I think Melville said it, in a slightly different context: "Genius all over the world stands hand in hand, and one shock of recognition runs the whole circle round."* Of course, we're not talking about genius here, we're talking about crazies—but it's essentially the same thing. They knew me, they saw right through all my clothes and there was that instant karmic flash. They seemed to sense what they had on their hands.

Playboy: Had you been into motorcycles before that?

HST: A little bit, not much. But when I got the advance on the book, I went out and bought the fastest bike ever tested by *Hot Rod* magazine: a BSA 650 Lightning. I thought, "If I'm gonna ride with these fuckers, I want the fastest bike known to man."

Playboy: They all rode Harley-Davidsons, right?

HST: Yeah, and they didn't like it that I was riding a BSA. They kept offering to get me hot bikes. You know—a brand-new Harley Sportster for $400, stuff like that. No papers, of course, no engine numbers—so I said no. I had enough trouble as it was. I was always getting pulled over. Jesus, they

---

*In August, 1850, Herman Melville originally used these words to praise fellow writer Nathanial Hawthorne in an essay titled "Hawthorne and His Mosses."

canceled my car insurance because of that goddamn bike. They almost took my driver's license away. I never had any trouble with my car. I drove it full bore all over San Francisco all the time, just wide open. It was a good car, too, a little English Ford. When it finally developed a crack in one of the four cylinders, I took it down to a cliff in Big Sur and soaked the whole interior with ten gallons of gasoline, then executed the fucker with six shots from a .44 magnum in the engine block at point-blank range. After that, we rolled it off the cliff—the radio going, lights on, everything going—and at the last minute, we threw a burning towel in. The explosion was ungodly; it almost blew us into the ocean. I had no idea what ten gallons of gas in an English Ford could do. The car was a mass of twisted, flaming metal. It bounced about six times on the way down—pure movie-stunt shit, you know. A sight like that was worth the car: it was beautiful.

Playboy: It seems pretty clear you had something in common with the Angels. How long did you ride with them?

HST: About a year.

Playboy: Did they ever ask you to join?

HST: Some of them did, but there was a very fine line I had to maintain there. Like when I went on runs with them, I didn't go dressed as an Angel. I'd wear Levis and boots but always a little different from theirs; a tan leather jacket instead of a black one, little things like that. I told them right away I was a writer, I was doing a book and that was it. If I'd joined, I wouldn't have been able to write about them honestly, because they have this "brothers" thing . . .

Playboy: Were there moments in that year when you wondered how you ever came to be riding with the meanest motorcycle outlaws in the world?

HST: Well, I figured it was a hard dollar—maybe the hardest—but actually, when I got into it, I started to like it. My wife, Sandy, was horrified at first. There were five or six from the Oakland and Frisco chapters that I got to know pretty well, and it got to the point that they'd just come over to my apartment any time of the day or night—bring their friends, three cases of stolen beer, a bunch of downers, some bennies. But I got to like it; it was my life, it wasn't just working.

Playboy: Was that a problem when you actually started to write?

HST: Not really. When you write for a living and you can't do anything else, you know that sooner or later that the deadline is going to come screaming down on you like a goddamn banshee. There's no avoiding it—not even when you have a fine full-bore story like the Angels that's still running . . . so one day you just don't appear at the El Adobe bar anymore; you shut the door, paint the windows black, rent an electric typewriter and become the monster you always were—the writer. I'd warned them about that. I'd said, "It's going to come, I'm not here for the fun of it, it's gonna happen." And when the time came, I just did it. Every now and then, somebody like Frenchy or Terry would drop by at night with some girls or some of the others, but even when I'd let them read a few pages of what I'd written they didn't really believe I was actually writing a book.

Playboy: How long did it take?

HST: About six months. Actually it took six months to write the first half of the book and then four days to write the second half. I got terrified about the deadline; I actually thought they were going to cancel the contract if I didn't finish the book exactly on time. I was in despair over the thing, so I took the electric typewriter and about four quarts of Wild Turkey and just drove north on 101 until I found a motel that looked peaceful, checked in and stayed there for four days. Didn't sleep, ate a lot of speed, went out every morning and got a hamburger at McDonald's and just wrote straight through for four days—and that turned out to be the best part of the book.

Playboy: In one of the last chapters, you described the scene where the Angels finally stomped you, but you described it rather quickly. How did it happen?

HST: Pretty quickly . . . I'd been away from their action for about six months, I'd finished most of the writing and the publisher sent me a copy of the proposed book cover and I said, "This sucks. It's the worst fucking cover I've seen on any book"—so I told them I'd shoot another cover if they'd just pay the expenses. So I called Sonny Barger, who was the head Angel, and said, "I want to go on the Labor Day run with you guys; I've finished the book, but now I want to shoot a book cover." I got some bad vibes over the phone from him. I knew something was not right, but by this time I was getting careless.

Playboy: Was the Labor Day run a big one?

HST: Shit, yes. This was one of these horrible things that scare the piss out of everybody—200 bikes. A mass Hell's Angels run is one of the most terrifying things you'll ever hope to see. When those bastards come by you on the road, that's heavy. And being a part of it, you get this tremendous feeling of humor and madness. You see the terror and shock and fear all around you and you're laughing all the time. It's like being in some kind of horror movie where you know that sooner or later the actors are going to leap out of the screen and burn the theater down.

Playboy: Did the Angels have a sense of humor about it?

HST: Some of them did. They were running a trip on everybody. I mean, you don't carry pliers and pull people's teeth out and then wear them on your belt without knowing you're running a trip on somebody. But on that Labor Day, we went up to some beach near Mendocino and I violated all my rules: First, never get stoned with them. Second, never get really drunk with them. Third, never argue with them when you're stoned and drunk. And fourth, when they start beating on each other, leave. I'd followed those rules for a year. But they started to pound on each other and I was just standing there talking to somebody and I said my bike was faster than his, which it was—another bad mistake—and all of a sudden, I got it right in the face, a terrific whack; I didn't even see where it came from, had no idea. When I grabbed the guy, he was small enough so that I could turn him around, pin his arms and just hold him. And I turned to the guy I'd been talking to and said something like, "Jesus Christ, look at this nut, he just hit me in the fucking face, get him away from here," and the guy I was holding began to scream in this high wild voice because I had him helpless, and instead of telling him to calm down, the other guy cracked me in the side of the head—and then I knew I was in trouble. That's the Angels' motto: One on all, all on one.

Playboy: Were there police around or other help?

HST: No, I was the only nonbiker there. The cops had said, "All right, at midnight we seal this place off and anybody who's not a part of this crowd get the hell out or God's mercy on him." So here I was, suddenly rolling around on the rocks of that Godforsaken beach in a swarm of stoned, crazy-drunk bikers. I had this guy who'd hit me in a death grip by now, and there were people kicking me in the chest and one of the bastards was trying to bash my head in with a tremendous rock . . . but I had this screaming Angel's head right next to mine, and so he had to be a little careful. I don't know how long it went on, but just about the time I knew I was going to die, Tiny suddenly showed up and said. "That's it, stop it," and they stopped as fast as they started, for no reason.

Playboy: Who was Tiny?

HST: He was the sergeant at arms and he was also one of the guys who I knew pretty well. I didn't know the bastards I was fighting with. All the Angels I might have counted on for help—the ones I'd come to think of as friends by that time—had long since retired to the bushes with their old ladies.

Playboy: How badly were you hurt?

HST: They did a pretty good job on my face. I went to the police station and they said, "Get the fuck out of here—you're bleeding in the bathroom." I was wasted, pouring blood, and I had to drive 60 miles like that to Santa Rosa, where I knew a doctor. I called him, but he was in Arizona and his partner answered the phone and said something like, "Spit on it and run a lap"; you know, that old football-coach thing. I'll never forgive him for that. So then I went to the emergency room at the Santa Rosa hospital and it was one of the worst fucking scenes I'd ever seen in my life. A bike gang called the Gypsy Jokers had been going north on Labor Day and had intersected with this horrible train of Angels somewhere around Santa Rosa and these fuckers were all over the emergency room. People screaming and moaning, picking up pieces of jawbones, trying to fit them back in, blood everywhere, girls yelling, "He's dying, please help us! Doctor, doctor! I can't stop the bleeding!" It was like a bomb had just hit.

Playboy: Did you get treatment?

HST: No. I felt guilty even being there. I had only been stomped. These other bastards had been cranked out with pipes, run over, pinned against walls with bikes—mangled, just mangled. So I left, tried to drive in that condition, but finally I just pulled over to the side of the road and thought, "I'd better set this fucking nose, because tomorrow it's going to be hard." It felt like a beanbag. I could hear the bone chips grinding. So I sat there and drank a beer and did my own surgery, using the dome light and the rearview mirror, trying to remember what my nose had looked like. I couldn't breathe for about a year, and people thought I was a coke freak before I actually was, but I think I did a pretty good job.

Playboy: Who are the Hell's Angels, what kind of people?

HST: They're rejects, losers—but losers who turned mean and vengeful instead of just giving up, and there are more Hell's Angels than anybody can count. But most of them don't wear any colors. They're people who got moved out—you know, musical chairs—and they lost. Some people just lie down when they lose; these fuckers come back and tear up the whole game. I was a Hell's Angel in my head for a long time. I was a failed writer for 10 years and I was always in fights. I'd do things like go into a bar with a 50-pound sack of lime, turn the whole place white and then just take on anyone who came at me. I always got stomped, never won a fight. But I'm not into that anymore. I lost a lot of my physical aggressiveness when I started to sell what I wrote. I didn't need that trip anymore.

Playboy: Some people would say you didn't lose all your aggressiveness, that you come on like journalism's own Hell's Angel.

HST: Well, I don't see myself as particularly aggressive or dangerous. I tend to act weird now and then, which makes people nervous if they don't know me—but I think that's sort of a stylistic hangover from the old days . . . and I suppose I get a private smile or two out of making people's eyes bulge once in a while. You might call that a Hell's Angels trait—but otherwise, the comparison is ugly and ominous. I reject it—although I definitely feel myself somewhat apart. Not an outlaw, but more like a natural freak . . . which doesn't bother me at all. When I ran for sheriff of Aspen on the Freak Power ticket, that was the point. In the rotten fascist context of what was happening to America in 1969, being a freak was an honorable way to go.

Playboy: Why did you run for sheriff?

HST: I'd just come back from the Democratic Convention in Chicago and been beaten by vicious cops for no reason at all. I'd had a billy club rammed into my stomach and I'd seen innocent people beaten senseless and it really jerked me around. There was a mayoral race a few months later in Aspen and there was a lawyer in town who'd done some good things in local civil rights cases. His name is Joe Edwards and I called him up one midnight and said, "You don't know me and I don't know you, but you've got to run for mayor. The whole goddamn system is getting out of control. If it keeps going this way, they'll have us all in pens. We have to get into politics—if only in self-defense." Now, this guy was a bike rider, a head and a freak in the same sense I am. He said, "We'll meet tomorrow and talk about it." The next day, we went to see *The Battle of Algiers* and when we came out, he said, "I'll do it; we're going to bust these bastards."

Playboy: How close did you come?

HST: Edwards lost by six votes. And remember, we're talking about an apolitical town and the hardest thing was to get our people to register. So one of the gigs I used to get people into it was to say, "Look, if you register and vote for Edwards, I'll run for sheriff next year, if he wins." Well, he didn't win, but when the next county elections came up, I found myself running for sheriff anyway. I didn't take it seriously at first, but when it began to look like I might win, everybody took it seriously.

Playboy: As a matter of fact, you announced you were going to eat drugs in the sheriff's office if you won, didn't you?

HST: Yeah and that scared a lot of people. But I'd seen the ignorant hate vote that the Edwards campaign brought out the year before. You know, when the freaks get organized, the other side gets scared and they bring out people on stretchers who are half dead, haven't voted for 25 years. And I thought. "Well, if they want somebody to hate, I'll give them one they can really hate." And meanwhile, on the same ticket, I figured we could run a serious candidate for a county commissioner, which is the office we really wanted. Hell, I didn't want to be sheriff, I wanted to scare the piss out of the yahoos and the greed-heads and make our county-commissioner candidate look like a conservative by contrast. That's what we did, but then this horrible press coverage from all over the goddamn world poured in and we finally couldn't separate the two races.

Playboy: There was a whole Freak Power slate, wasn't there?

HST: Yeah, a friend of mine, who lived next door at the time, ran for coroner, because we found out the coroner was the only official who could fire the sheriff. And we decided we needed a county clerk, so we had somebody running for that. But finally, my lightning-rod, hate-candidate strategy back lashed on them, too. It got a little heavy. I announced that the new sheriff's posse would start tearing up the streets the day after the election—every street in Aspen, rip 'em up with jackhammers and replace the asphalt with sod. I said we were going to use the sheriff's office mainly to harass real-estate developers.

Playboy: Sounds like that could heat up a political contest.

HST: Indeed. The greedheads were terrified. We had a series of public debates that got pretty brutal. The first one was in a movie theater, because that was the only place in town that could hold the crowd. Even then, I arrived a half hour early and I couldn't get in. The aisles were jammed, I had to walk over people to get to the stage. I was wearing shorts, with my head shaved completely bald. The yahoos couldn't handle it. They were convinced the Anti-Christ had finally appeared—right there in Aspen. There's something ominous about a totally shaved head. We took questions from the crowd and sort of laid out our platforms. I was not entirely comfortable, sitting up there with the incumbent sheriff and saying, "When I drive this corrupt thug out of office, I'm going to go in there and maybe eat a bit of mescaline on slow nights. . . ." I figured from then on I had to win, because if I lost, it was going to be the hammer for me. You just don't admit that kind of thing on camera, in front of a huge crowd. There was a reporter from the *New York Times* in the front row, NBC, an eight-man team from the BBC filming the whole thing, the *Los Angeles Times,* the *Washington Post*—incredible.

Playboy: You changed the pitch toward the end, toned it down, didn't you?

HST: Yeah, I became a creature of my own campaign. I was really surprised at the energy we could whip up for that kind of thing, latent political energy just sitting around.

Playboy: What did your platform finally evolve into?

HST: I said I was going to function as an Ombudsman, create a new office—unsalaried—then turn my sheriff's salary over to a good experienced lawman and let him do the job. I figured once you got control of the sheriff's office, you could let somebody else carry the badge and gun—under your control, of course. It almost worked.

Playboy: What was the final vote?

HST: Well, there were six precincts that mattered and I won the three in town, broke even in number four and then got stomped brutally in the two precincts where most of the real-estate developers and subdividers live.

Playboy: Are you sorry you lost?

HST: Well, I felt sorry for the people who worked so hard on the campaign. But I don't miss the job. For a while, I thought I was going to win, and it scared me.

Playboy: There's been talk of your running for the Senate from Colorado. Is that a joke?

HST: No. I considered it for a while, but this past year has killed my appetite for politics. I might reconsider after I get away from it for a while. Somebody has to change politics in this country.

Playboy: Would you run for the Senate the same way you ran for sheriff?

HST: Well, I might have to drop the mescaline issue, I don't think there'd be any need for that—promising to eat mescaline on the Senate floor. I found out last time you can push people too far. The backlash is brutal.

Playboy: What if the unthinkable happened and Hunter Thompson went to Washington as a Senator from Colorado? Do you think you could do any good?

HST: Not much, but you always do some good by setting an example—you know, just by proving it can be done.

Playboy: Don't you think there would be a strong reaction in Washington to some of the things you've written about the politicians there?

HST: Of course. They'd come after me like wolverines. I'd have no choice but to haul out my secret files—all that raw swill Ed Hoover* gave me just before he died. We were good friends. I used to go to the track with him a lot.

Playboy: You're laughing again, but that raises a legitimate question: Are you trying to say you know things about Washington people that you haven't written?

HST: Yeah, to some extent. When I went to Washington to write *Fear and Loathing: On the Campaign Trail '72,* I went with the same attitude I take anywhere as a journalist: hammer and tongs—and God's mercy on anybody who gets in the way. Nothing is off the record, that kind of thing. But I finally realized that some things have to be off the record. I don't know where the line is, even now. But if you're an indiscreet blabber-mouth and a fool, nobody is going to talk to you—not even your friends.

Playboy: What was it like when you first rode into Washington in 1971?

HST: Well, nobody had ever heard of *Rolling Stone,* for one thing. "Rolling what? . . . Stones? I heard them once: noisy bastards, aren't they?" It was a nightmare at first, nobody would return my calls. Washington is a horrible town, a cross between Rome, Georgia, and Toledo, Ohio—that kind of mentality. It's basically a town full of vicious, powerful rubes.

Playboy: Did they start returning your calls when you began writing things like "Hubert Humphrey should be castrated" so his genes won't be passed on?

HST: Well, that was a bit heavy, I think—for reasons, I don't want to get into now. Anyway, it didn't take me long to learn that the only time to call politicians is very late at night. Very late. In Washington, the truth is never told in daylight hours or across a desk. If you catch people when they're very tired or drunk or weak, you can usually get some answers. So I'd sleep days, wait till these people got their lies and treachery out of the way, let them relax, then come on full speed on the phone at two or three in the morning. You have to wear the bastards down before they'll tell you anything.

---

*First director of the United States Federal Bureau of Investigation (FBI), J. Edgar Hoover.

Playboy: Your journalistic style has been attacked by some critics—most notably, the *Columbia Journalism Review*—as partly commentary, partly fantasy and partly the ravings of someone too long into drugs.

HST: Well, fuck the *Columbia Journalism Review.* They don't pay my rent. That kind of senile gibberish reminds me of all those people back in the early Sixties who were saying, "This guy Dylan is giving Tin-Pan Alley a bad name—hell, he's no musician. He can't even carry a tune." Actually, it's kind of a compliment when people like that devote so much energy to attacking you.

Playboy: Well, you certainly say some outrageous things in your book on the 1972 Presidential campaign; for instance, that Edmund Muskie was taking Ibogaine, an exotic form of South American speed or psychedelic, or both. That wasn't true, was it?

HST: Not that I know of, but if you read what I wrote carefully, I didn't say he was taking it. I said there was a rumor around his headquarters in Milwaukee that a famous Brazilian doctor had flown in with an emergency packet of Ibogaine for him. Who would believe that shit?

Playboy: A lot of people did believe it.

HST: Obviously, but I didn't realize that until about halfway through the campaign—and it horrified me. Even some of the reporters who'd been covering Muskie for three or four months took it seriously. That's because they don't know anything about drugs. Jesus, nobody running for President would dare touch a thing like Ibogaine. Maybe I would, but no normal politician. It would turn his brains to jelly. He'd have to be locked up.

Playboy: You also said that John Chancellor* took heavy hits of black acid.

HST: Hell, that was such an obvious heavy-handed joke that I still can't understand how anybody in his right mind could have taken it seriously. I'd infiltrated a Nixon youth rally at the Republican Convention and I thought I'd have a little fun with them by telling all the grisly details of the time that John Chancellor tried to kill me by putting acid in my drink. I also wrote that if I'd had more time, I would have told these poor yo-yos the story about Walter Cronkite† and his white-slavery racket with Vietnamese orphan girls—

---

* John Chancellor was an American television journalist and the anchor of *NBC Nightly News* from 1970 to 1982.

† Walter Cronkite was an American television journalist and the anchor of *CBS Evening News* from 1962 to 1981.

importing them through a ranch in Quebec and then selling them into brothels up and down the East Coast . . . which is true, of course; *Collier's* magazine has a big story on it this month, with plenty of photos to prove it . . . What? You don't believe that? Why not? All those other waterheads did. Christ, writing about politics would paralyze my brain if I couldn't have a slash of weird humor now and then. And, actually, I'm pretty careful about that sort of thing. If I weren't, I would have been sued long ago. It's one of the hazards of Gonzo Journalism.

Playboy: What is Gonzo Journalism?

HST: It's something that grew out of a story on the Kentucky Derby for *Scanlan's* magazine. It was one of those horrible deadline scrambles and I ran out of time. I was desperate. Ralph Steadman had done the illustrations, the cover was printed and there was this horrible hole in the interviews. I was convinced I was finished, I'd blown my mind, couldn't work. So finally I just started jerking pages out of my notebook and numbering them and sending them to the printer. I was sure it was the last article I was ever going to do for anybody. Then when it came out, there were massive numbers of letters, phone calls, congratulations, people calling it a "great breakthrough in journalism." And I thought, "Holy shit, if I can write like this and get away with it, why should I keep trying to write like the *New York Times?*" It was like falling down an elevator shaft and landing in a pool full of mermaids.

Playboy: Is there a difference between Gonzo and the new journalism?

HST: Yeah, I think so. Unlike Tom Wolfe or Gay Talese, for instance, I almost never try to reconstruct a story. They're both much better reporters than I am, but then I don't really think of myself as a reporter. Gonzo is just a word I picked up because I liked the sound of it—which is not to say there isn't a basic difference between the kind of writing I do and the Wolfe/Talese style. They tend to go back and re-create stories that have already happened, while I like to get right in the middle of whatever I'm writing about—as personally involved as possible. There's a lot more to it than that, but if we have to make a distinction, I suppose that's a pretty safe way to start.

Playboy: Are the fantasies and wild tangents a necessary part of your writing?

HST: Absolutely. Just let your mind wander, let it go where it wants to. Like with that Muskie thing; I'd just been reading a drug report from some lab in California on the symptoms of Ibogaine poisoning and I thought, "I've seen that style before, and not in West Africa or the Amazon; I've seen those symptoms very recently." And then I thought, "Of course: rages, stupors, being able to sit for days without moving—that's Ed Muskie."

Playboy: Doesn't that stuff get in the way of your serious political reporting?

HST: Probably—but it also keeps me sane. I guess the main problem is that people will believe almost any twisted kind of story about politicians or Washington. But I can't help that. Some of the truth that doesn't get written is a lot more twisted than any of my fantasies.

Playboy: You were the first journalist on the campaign to see that McGovern was going to win the nomination. What tipped you off?

HST: It was the energy; I could feel it. Muskie, Humphrey, Jackson,* Lindsay†—all the others were dying on the vine, falling apart. But if you were close enough to the machinery in McGovern's campaign, you could almost see the energy level rising from one week to the next. It was like watching pro-football teams toward the end of a season. Some of them are coming apart and others are picking up steam; their timing is getting sharper, their third-down plays are working. They're just starting to peak.

Playboy: The football analogy was pretty popular in Washington, wasn't it?

HST: Yes, because Nixon was into football very seriously. He used the language constantly; he talked about politics and diplomacy in terms of power slants, end sweeps, mousetrap blocks. Thinking in football terms may be the best way to understand what finally happened with the whole Watergate thing: Coach Nixon's team is fourth and 32 on their own ten, and he finds out that his punter is a junkie. A sick junkie. He looks down the bench: "OK, big fella—we need you now!" And this guy is stark white and vomiting, can't even stand up, much less kick. When the game ends in disaster for the home team, then the fans rush onto the field and beat the players to death with rocks, beer bottles, pieces of wooden seats. The coach makes a desperate dash for the safety of the locker room, but three hit men hired by heavy gamblers nail him before he gets there.

Playboy: You talked football with Nixon once, didn't you, in the back seat of his limousine?

---

* Democratic Senator Henry M. Jackson of Washington.

† Former Republican mayor of New York City from 1966 to 1973 and 1972 Democratic presidential candidate, John Lindsay.

HST: Yeah, that was in 1968 in New Hampshire; he was just starting his comeback then and I didn't take him seriously. He seemed like a Republican echo of Hubert Humphrey: just another sad old geek limping back into politics for another beating. It never occurred to me that he would ever be President. Johnson hadn't quit at that point, but I sort of sensed he was going to and I figured Bobby Kennedy would run—so that even if Nixon got the Republican nomination, he'd just take another stomping by another Kennedy. So I thought it would be nice to go to New Hampshire, spend a couple of weeks following Nixon around and then write his political obituary.

Playboy: You couldn't have been too popular with the Nixon party.

HST: I didn't care what they thought of me. I put weird things in the pressroom at night, strange cryptic threatening notes that they would find in the morning. I had wastebaskets full of cold beer in my room in the Manchester Holiday Inn. Oddly enough, I got along pretty well with some of the Nixon people—Ray Price,* Pat Buchanan,† Nick Ruwe**—but I felt a lot more comfortable at Gene McCarthy's headquarters in the Wayfarer, on the other side of town. So I spent most of my spare time over there.

Playboy: Then why did Nixon let you ride alone with him?

HST: Well, it was the night before the vote and Romney had dropped out. Rockefeller wasn't coming in, so all of a sudden the pressure was off and Nixon was going to win easily. We were at this American Legion hall somewhere pretty close to Boston. Nixon had just finished a speech there and we were about an hour and a half from Manchester, where he had his Learjet waiting, and Price suddenly came up to me and said, "You've been wanting to talk to the boss? OK, come on." And I said, "What? What?" By this time I'd given up; I knew he was leaving for Key Biscayne that night and I was wild-eyed drunk. On the way to the car, Price said, "The boss wants to relax and talk football; you're the only person here who claims to be an expert on that subject, so you're it. But if you mention anything else—out. You'll be

---

* Ray Price is a former American journalist and chief speechwriter for President Richard Nixon.

† Patrick Buchanan is an American political strategist, author, and journalist, and served as senior advisor to presidents Richard Nixon and Ronald Reagan. Buchanan sought the Republican presidential nomination in 1992 and 1996.

** Nick Ruwe was a high-ranking Republican supporter and senior staff member for the campaign of Richard Nixon and Ronald Reagan. He served as United States ambassador to Iceland from 1984 to 1989.

hitchhiking back to Manchester. No talk about Vietnam, campus riots—nothing political; the boss wants to talk football, period."

Playboy: Were there awkward moments?

HST: No, he seemed very relaxed. I've never seen him like that before or since. We had a good, loose talk. That was the only time in 20 years of listening to the treacherous bastard that I knew he wasn't lying.

Playboy: Did you feel any sympathy as you watched Nixon go down, finally?

HST: Sympathy? No. You have to remember that for my entire adult life, Richard Nixon has been the national boogeyman. I can't remember a time when he wasn't around—always evil, always ugly, 15 or 20 years of fucking people around. The whole Watergate chancre was a monument to everything he stood for: This was a cheap thug, a congenital liar. . . . What the Angels used to call a gunsel, a punk who can't even pull off a liquor-store robbery without shooting somebody or getting shot, or busted.

Playboy: Do you think a smarter politician could have found a man to cover it up after the original break-in? Could Lyndon Johnson have handled it, say?

HST: Lyndon Johnson would have burned the tapes. He would have burned everything. There would have been this huge wreck out on his ranch somewhere—killing, oddly enough, all his tape technicians, the only two Secret Servicemen who knew about it, his executive flunky and the Presidential tapemeisters. He would have had a van go over a cliff at high speed, burst into flames and they'd find all these bodies, this weird collection of people who'd never had any real reason to be together, lying in a heap of melted celluloid at the bottom of the cliff. Then Johnson would have wept—all of his trusted assistants—"Goddamn it, how could they have been in the same van at the same time? I warned them about that."

Playboy: Do you think it's finally, once and for all, true that we won't have Richard Nixon to kick around anymore?

HST: Well, it looks like it, but he said an incredible thing when he arrived in California after that last ride on Air Force One. He got off the plane and said to his crowd that was obviously rounded up for the cameras—you know: winos, children, Marine sergeants . . . they must have had a hell of a time lashing that crowd together. No doubt Ziegler* promised to pay well, and

* Ron Ziegler was Richard Nixon's press secretary and assistant.

then welshed, but they had a crowd of 2,000 or 3,000 and Nixon said: "It is perhaps appropriate for me to say very simply this, having completed one task does not mean that we will just sit and enjoy this marvelous California climate and do nothing." Jesus Christ! Here's a man who just got run out of the White House, fleeing Washington in the wake of the most complete and hideous disgrace in the history of American politics, who goes out to California and refers to "having completed one task." It makes me think there must have been another main factor in the story of his downfall, in addition to greed and stupidity; I think in the past few months he was teetering on the brink on insanity. There were hints of this in some of the "inside reports" about the last days; Nixon didn't want to resign and he didn't understand why he had to; the family never understood. He probably still thinks he did nothing wrong, that he was somehow victimized, ambushed in the night by his old and relentless enemies. I'm sure he sees it as just another lost campaign, another cruel setback on the road to greatness; so now it's back to the bunker for a while—lick the wounds and then come out fighting again. He may need one more whack. I think we should chisel his tombstone now and send it to him with an epitaph, in big letters, that says, Here Lies Richard Nixon: He Was a Quitter.

Playboy: Do you think that his resignation proves that the system works?

HST: Well, that depends on what you mean by "works." We can take some comfort, I guess, in knowing the system was so finely conceived originally—almost 200 years ago—that it can still work when it's absolutely forced to. In Nixon's case, it wasn't the system that tripped him up and finally destroyed his Presidency; it was Nixon himself, along with a handful of people who actually took it upon themselves to act on their own—a bit outside the system, in fact; maybe even a bit above and beyond it. There were a lot of "highly respected" lawyers, for instance—some of them alleged experts in their fields—who argued almost all the way to the end that Judge Sirica* exceeded his judicial authority when he acted on his own instinct and put the most extreme kind of pressure on the original Watergate burglars to keep the case from going into the books as the cheap-Jack "third-rate burglary" that Nixon,

* John Sirica was the Washington D.C. district court judge presiding over the Watergate break-in and resulting scandal. He demanded Richard Nixon disclose tapes of White House conversations.

Haldeman* and Ehrlichman† told Ziegler to call it when the news first broke. If Sirica had gone along with the system, like the original Justice Department prosecutors did, McCord** would never have cracked and written that letter that opened the gates to the White House. Sirica was the flywheel in that thing, from start to finish, when he put the final nail in the coffin by forcing James St. Clair, Nixon's lawyer of last resort, to listen to those doomsday tapes that he had done everything possible to keep from hearing. But when he heard the voices, that pulled the rip cord on Nixon, once St. Clair went on record as having listened to the tapes—which proved his client guilty beyond any doubt—he had only two choices: to abandon Nixon at the eleventh hour or stay on and possibly get dragged down in the quicksand himself. Sirica wasn't the only key figure in Nixon's demise who could have played it safe by letting the system take its traditional course. The *Washington Post* editors who kept Woodward and Bernstein on the story could have stayed comfortably within the system without putting their backs to the wall in a showdown with the whole White House power structure and a vengeful bastard of a President like Nixon. Leon Jaworski, the special prosecutor, couldn't even find a precedent in the system for challenging the President's claim of "Executive privilege" in the U.S. Supreme Court.

Hell, the list goes on and on . . . but in the end, the Nixon Watergate saga was written by mavericks who worked the loneliest outside edges of the system, not by the kind of people who played it safe and followed the letter of the law. If the system worked in this case, it was almost in spite of itself. Jesus, what else could the Congress have done—faced with the spectacle of a President going on national TV to admit a felony? Nixon dug his own grave, then made a public confession. If his resignation somehow proves the system works, you have to wonder how well that same system might have worked if we'd had a really blue-chip, sophisticated criminal in the White House—instead of a half-mad used-car salesman. In the space of ten months, the two top executives of this country resigned rather than risk impeachment and trial; and they

* H. R. Haldeman was a chief of staff to President Richard Nixon. Haldeman was convicted of conspiracy and obstruction of justice for his role in the Watergate scandal.

† John Ehrlichman was a White House aide to President Richard Nixon. Ehrlichman was convicted of conspiracy, perjury, and obstruction of justice for his role in the Watergate scandal.

** James McCord was the security director of Richard Nixon's "The Committee for Reelection of the President" and was one of the Watergate burglars.

wouldn't even have had to do that if their crimes hadn't been too gross to ignore and if public opinion hadn't turned so massively against them. Finally, even the chickenshit politicians in Congress will act if the people are outraged enough. But you can bet that if the public-opinion polls hadn't gone over 50 percent in favor of his impeachment, he'd still be in the White House.

Playboy: Is politics going to get any better?

HST: Well, it can't get much worse. Nixon was so bad, so obviously guilty and corrupt, that we're already beginning to write him off as a political mutant, some kind of bad and unexplainable accident. The danger in that is that it's like saying, "Thank God! We've cut the cancer out . . . you see it? . . . It's lying there . . . just sew up the wound . . . cauterize it . . . No, no, don't bother to look for anything else . . . just throw the tumor away, burn it," and then a few months later the poor bastard dies, his whole body rotten with cancer. I don't think purging Nixon is going to do much to the system except make people more careful. Even if we accept the idea that Nixon himself was a malignant mutant, his Presidency was no accident. Hell, Ford is our accident. He's never been elected to anything but Congress . . . But Richard Nixon has been elected to every national office a shrewd mutant could aspire to: Congressman, Senator, Vice President, President. He should have been impeached, convicted and jailed, if only as a voter-education project.

Playboy: Do you think that over the course of the Watergate investigation, Congress spent as much energy covering up its own sins as it did in exposing Richard Nixon's?

HST: Well, that's a pretty harsh statement; but I'm sure there've been a lot of tapes and papers burned and a lot of midnight phone calls, saying things like, "Hello, John, remember that letter I wrote you on August fifth? I just ran into a copy in my files here and, well, I'm burning mine, why don't you burn yours, too, and we'll just forget all about that matter? Meanwhile, I'm sending you a case of Chivas Regal and I have a job for your son here in my office this summer—just as soon as he brings me the ashes of that fucking letter."

Playboy: Does Gerald Ford epitomize the successful politician?

HST: That's pretty obvious, isn't it? Somehow he got to be President of the U.S. without ever running for the office. Not only that but he appointed his own Vice President. This is a bizarre syndrome we're into: For six years we were ruled by lunatics and criminals, and for the next two years we're going to have to live with their appointees. Nixon was run out of town, but not before he named his own successor.

Playboy: It's beginning to look as if Ford might be our most popular President since Eisenhower. Do you think he'll be tough to beat in 1976?

HST: That will probably depend on his staff. If it's good, he should be able to maintain this Mr. Clean, Mr. Good Guy, Mr. Reason image for two years; and if he can do that, he'll be very hard to beat.

Playboy: Will you cover the 1976 campaign?

HST: Well, I'm not looking forward to it, but I suspect I will. Right now, though, I need a long rest from politics—at least until the '76 campaign starts. Christ, now there's a junkie talking—"I guess I'll try one more hit . . . this will be the last, mind you. I'll just finish off what's here and that's it." No, I don't want to turn into a campaign junkie. I did that once, but the minute I kicked it, I turned into a Watergate junkie. That's going to be a hard one to come down from. You know, I was actually in the Watergate the night the bastards broke in. Of course, I missed the whole thing, but I was there. It still haunts me.

Playboy: What part of the Watergate were you in?

HST: I was in the bar.

Playboy: What kind of a reporter are you, anyway, in the bar?

HST: I'm not a reporter, I'm a writer. Nobody gives Norman Mailer this kind of shit. I've never tried to pose as a goddamn reporter. I don't defend what I do in the context of straight journalism, and if some people regard me as a reporter who's gone bad rather than a writer who's just doing his job—well, they're probably the same dingbats who think John Chancellor's an acid freak and Cronkite is a white slaver.

Playboy: You traveled to San Clemente with the White House press corps on the last trip Nixon made as President, and rumor had it that you showed up for one of the press conferences in pretty rocky shape.

HST: Rocky? Well, I suppose that's the best interpretation you could put on it. I'd been up all night and I was wearing a wet Mexican shirt, swimming trunks, these basketball shoes, dark glasses. I had a bottle of beer in my hand, my head was painfully constricted by something somebody had put in my wine the night before up in L.A. and when Rabbi Korff* began his demented rap about Nixon's being the most persecuted and maligned President in American history, I heard myself shouting, "Why is that, Rabbi? . . . Why? . . . Tell us why . . . " And he said something like, "I'm only a smalltime rabbi," and

---

* Baurch Korff was a Jewish community activist and outspoken Nixon supporter who became known as "Nixon's Rabbi."

I said, "That's all right, nobody's bigoted here. You can talk." It got pretty ugly—but then, ugliness was a sort of common denominator in the last days of the Nixon regime. It was like a sinking ship with no ratlines.

Playboy: How did the press corps take your behavior?

HST: Not too well. But it doesn't matter now. I won't be making any trips with the President for a while.

Playboy: What will you do? Do you have any projects on the fire other than the political stuff?

HST: Well, I think I may devote more time to my ministry, for one thing. All the hellish running around after politicians has taken great amounts of time from my responsibilities as a clergyman.

Playboy: You're not a real minister, are you?

HST: What? Of course I am. I'm an ordained doctor of divinity in the Church of the New Truth. I have a scroll with a big gold seal on it hanging on my wall at home. In recent months we've had more converts than we can handle. Even Ron Ziegler was on the brink of conversion during that last week in San Clemente, but the law of karma caught up with him before he could take the vows.

Playboy: How much did it cost you to get ordained?

HST: I prefer not to talk about that. I studied for years and put a lot of money into it. I have the power to marry people and bury them. I've stopped doing marriages, though, because none of them worked out. Burials were always out of the question; I've never believed in burials except as an adjunct to the Black Mass, which I still perform occasionally.

Playboy: But you bought your scroll, didn't you?

HST: Of course I did. But so did everybody else who ever went to school. As long as you understand that. . . .

Playboy: What's coming up as far as your writing goes?

HST: My only project now is a novel called "Guts Ball," which is almost finished on tape but not written yet. I was lying in bed one night, the room was completely black, I had a head full of some exotic weed and all of a sudden it was almost as if a bright silver screen had been dropped in front of me and this strange movie began to run. I had this vision of Haldeman and Ehrlichman and a few other Watergate-related casualties returning to California in disgrace. They're on a DC-10, in the first-class cabin; there's also a Secret Serviceman on board whose boss has just been gunned down by junkies in Singapore for no good reason and he's got the body in the baggage bowels of the plane, taking it home to be buried. He's in a vicious frame of mind, weeping and cursing junkies, and these others have their political disaster grinding on them, they're all half crazy for vengeance—and so to unwind, they start to throw a football around the cabin. For a while, the other passengers go along with it, but then the game gets serious. These crewcut, flinty-eyed buggers begin to force the passengers to play, using seats as blockers; people are getting smacked around for dropping passes, jerked out of the line-up and forced to do push-ups if they fumble. The passengers are in a state of terror, weeping, their clothes are torn . . . And these thugs still have all their official White House identification, and they put two men under arrest for refusing to play and lock them in the bathroom together. A man who can't speak English gets held down in a seat and shot full of animal tranquilizer with a huge hypodermic needle. The stewardesses are gobbling tranquilizers . . . You have to imagine this movie unrolling: I was hysterical with laughter. I got a little tape recorder and laid it on my chest and kept describing the scene as I saw it. Just the opening scenes took about 45 minutes. I don't know how it's going to end, but I like it that way. If I knew how it ended, I'd lose interest in the story.

Playboy: When you actually sit down to start writing, can you use drugs like mushrooms or other psychedelics?

HST: No. It's impossible to write with anything like that in my head. Wild Turkey and tobacco are the only drugs I use regularly when I write. But I tend to work at night, so when the wheels slow down, I occasionally indulge in a little speed—which I deplore and do not advocate—but you know, when the car runs out of gas, you have to use something. The only drug I really count on is adrenaline. I'm basically an adrenaline junkie. I'm addicted to the rush of the stuff in my own blood and of all the drugs I've ever used, I think it's the most powerful. [Coughing] Mother of God, here I go. [More coughing] Creeping Jesus, this is it . . . choked to death by a fucking . . . poisoned Marlboro. . . .

Playboy: Do you ever wonder how you have survived this long?

HST: Yes. Nobody expected me to get much past 20. Least of all me. I just assume, "Well, I got through today, but tomorrow might be different." This is a very weird and twisted world; you can't afford to get careless; don't fuck around. You want to keep your affairs in order at all times.

Loose Licks (Australia)—Spring 1976

Interview by Peter Olszewski

Olszewski: Many of your readers here are surprised that you're leaving the States so soon before the election. Why aren't you getting on the Campaign Trail in '76?

HST: OK. I can answer that one. You want me to do it now?

Olszewski: Yeah.

HST: I assume that the general election will be even duller than the primary election and I could bet right now, a lot of money on Carter, and I don't see any point in going out there and suffering to cover it.

Olszewski: So there won't be a "Fear and Loathing on the Campaign Trail" book for '76?

HST: No, it's too much work. And the work is too rotten. I told a *New York Times* reporter friend of mine that I went out and did it for about two months, and I couldn't handle it. It was just too depressing. And when he asked me why I was quitting I said, "Well Christ, you should know." He thought for a minute, and he said, "Yeah, it's not fit work for a grown man is it?" A perfect epitaph for covering campaigns.

Olszewski: So you've still got your money on Carter?

HST: Oh yeah, that's why I don't see any point in having it covered. As a gambler right now I would bet on him about 3 to 2 over Ford or Reagan.

Olszewski: I read a report the other day (*The Australian* July 5) that Carter is thinking of running for office with your old friend Ed Muskie. What do you think about that?

HST: I don't think he's going to do that. He's summoning one vice presidential candidate a day down to Plains, and he doesn't really tell you much about it except who is not going to be there. I hope he picks Church, Frank Church.*

---

* Frank Church was a Democratic senator from Idaho.

[Editor's note: Since this interview, Carter has named his running partner—Thompson was right, Muskie didn't get it, but neither did Thompson's hopeful, Frank Church. The job went to Walter "Fritz" Mondale.]

Olszewski: Who do you think is the greatest president the U.S. has ever had?

HST: I would think Thomas Jefferson. Very easily.

Olszewski: Why?

HST: I suppose in the context of his time, I think he was, in terms of human quality, intelligence, and talent, here's an example: I just remembered this. When John Kennedy had a bunch of White House dinners for poets and composers and writers, it was a vast assemblage of American establishment-like talent, and when he sat down for dinner at the White House he kindly observed that he thought that never before had so much talent been assembled for a dinner at the White House. Then he added, "Except for when Thomas Jefferson dined alone."*

So when I say Jefferson, it's no bizarre judgment. He was a very special person.

Olszewski: You said in your Campaign '72 book that after you watched a TV rerun of JFK's head exploding, you went to your room and felt rather ill. Do you have any theory on Kennedy's death? Do you subscribe to any particular conspiracy theory?

HST: The only theory I subscribe to in total is that we don't know yet the full story of it. I don't have any favorite conspiracy theory, no. I'm convinced that sooner or later we'll hear the real story and it's going to be quite a surprise.

Olszewski: So you don't think any of the conspiracies aired yet have been the real conspiracy?

HST: No. I wouldn't know where to look right now. If I did, I'd be there.

Olszewski: What was your immediate reaction when you heard that Nixon had finally resigned?

HST: Well, I've been on that case for about fifteen years. I went down to the White House lawn on the day he left, and I was sitting right next to his helicopter. I was the last person Nixon saw in Washington. I stayed up all night. I just wanted to make sure the bastard looked at me.

---

* John F. Kennedy's speech at a White House dinner honored forty-nine Nobel Laureates on April 29, 1962.

Olszewski: Did he acknowledge your presence when he saw you? Maybe he remembered you from your car ride with him?

HST: He was so full of clorazine and downers that they had to lead him to the plane.

Olszewski: He was pretty drugged out, was he?

HST: Oh yeah, he was. They had him on tranquilizers. He was just about to crack.

Olszewski: A broken man?

HST: Absolutely. And no man ever deserved it more.

Olszewski: Given the opportunity to mete out punishment to Nixon, what would you prescribe?

HST: As punishment for him now? Let's see. For Nixon I think he should be forced to hitchhike back and forth constantly across the country. Sort of like Philip Nolan.* They put the man without a country on a ship, they should put Nixon on the road. Naked. Make him hitchhike back and forth from San Clemente to Washington. Constantly. Never resting for more than one night. He'd have to be on the road hitchhiking and people could pick him up and abuse him if they wanted to, beat him if they wanted to, they could do anything they wanted to, but I think he should be forced to come out in public.

Olszewski: Have you ever thought of running for the presidency?

HST: I've thought about it, but when you think about running for president you also have to think about what's going to happen to you if you win. And I think life is too short to do that sort of thing unless you're crazy.

Olszewski: You think a president is a sure target for assassination?

HST: I wouldn't care about being assassinated. I think it's just the bullshit and living-in-a-fish-bowl atmosphere. I wouldn't like that sort of lack of privacy. I think you'd just have to be a little bit nuts to want to do that.

Olszewski: Just say, by some strange quirk of fate, you did attain the presidency. What's the first thing you'd do?

---

* Phillip Nolan was a merchant in late-1700s in the Spanish controlled territory of Texas. He eventually lost his passport privileges in the territory and was forced to travel across the territory illegally. In 1863, Phillip Nolan's legacy was popularized by American writer Edward Everett Hale in the story "A Man Without a Country," published in *The Atlantic Monthly.* In Hale's fictitious story, Nolan is a Union solider in the Civil War that damns his allegiance to the United States. He is sentenced to living his life on navy warships, never again to set foot or receive news from the U.S. Ultimately, Nolan painfully learns the value of patriotism through the desperation of losing his homeland.

HST: If I attained the presidency?

Olszewski: Yeah.

HST: Oh. The first thing I'd do? Well, If I behaved in such a way that I could attain the presidency the first thing I'd do would be something I wouldn't be able to tell you now. Probably in all honesty, I would take some immediate and terrifying vengeance on somebody. I would have to make some very serious enemies and I would punish them.

Olszewski: If you were president is there any instance in which you'd press the button and unleash the Big One?

HST: I don't think so. I don't see any reason to. Why blow up the whole world? If they're going to blow us up, what the hell, we can't save ourselves. So I'd rather not press the button.

Olszewski: You don't seem over-enchanted with the present model of American politics, and you certainly don't seem to be the kind of person who could live comfortably within a socialist state such as exists in the Soviet bloc. Is there any particular political philosophy to which you adhere?

HST: No. That's one of my problems. I'm essentially an anarchist. I think an anarchist party would kind of have a hard time qualifying for election. But maybe not. If I ran, I would probably run on some ticket that would be anarchism in disguise. But that's a problem nobody yet has quite worked out: How to be an anarchist and keep the system running. That's one of the reasons I'm not running for president.

Olszewski: What did you do on bicentennial day?

HST: Bicentennial day? Let's see. Oh, I ate a lot of acid and set off a tremendous amount of fireworks and just wandered around and acted like an American. Like cowboys. Just played cowboys. Threw bombs into crowds, things like that.

Olszewski: Do you think America can survive another 200 years?

HST: Probably so, but in a very altered condition. Something a bit like England. Like the coccyx bone of the spine of the world. You know the bone at the end of the spine? It's the remnant of the tail. This bone has no function except to give you a tremendous amount of pain if you break it. And in about 200 years I think America would be serving that kind of function in the world. A useless appendage until you break it. Then it causes a lot of trouble.

Olszewski: Let's leave the world of politics now and get on to your writing. You seem to have this strange obsession with what the murkier recesses of the human mind can unleash. Leaping out of the pages of your books

are all sorts of monsters and animals one associates with darkness—Gila monsters, colored bats, hammerhead sharks, ravens whose droppings smell like dead flesh, and . . .

HST: Hey, you talk faster than I do—you must be a speed freak?

Olszewski: Pardon?

HST: You talk faster than I do.

Olszewski: Do I?

HST: I hurry along myself but you're really getting it on.

Olszewski: OK. I'll slow down.

HST: Yeah.

Olszewski: Anyway, you have all these sorts of monsters, and the subject of your first book was about one of the more monstrous forms of human life, the Hell's Angels. The point I'm getting to is that in one sense you follow the tradition set by Mailer,* for example, in embracing the psychopath, and yet you're warier of what the unleashed human psyche is capable of. For example you often refer to [Charles] Manson. Do you, as Mailer suggests, consider that the psychopath is the stepping stone to a newer and higher level of human consciousness, or do you think civilization will be stomped into extinction by the greatest psychopath of all?

HST: Yeah, the psychopath. The psychopath is really a sort of a synonym for politician in a way. So I don't agree with Mailer that the psychopath could be an advance. I think it's a sort of an inevitable state.

Olszewski: But all the same you seem to be fascinated by genuine crazies, people who push the limit, you know?

HST: Oh yes, I like those people. Sometimes they can be dangerous, but I enjoy people who are crazy. I like to stay with my own kind, as it were.

Olszewski: Are you a psychopath?

HST: A psychopath? No. No. I look a little further ahead. A psychopath can only see to the end of his nose. Psychopaths are similar to a fly traveling towards a light. He becomes a different person every day. A very adjustable person.

Olszewski: You don't seem to dwell on women in your books.

HST: Women in my books?

Olszewski: Yeah.

---

* American novelist and journalist Norman Mailer, author of *The Naked and the Dead* and *The Executioner's Song*.

HST: Now let's see . . . there is an answer to that but I'm not going to tell you. Well, given the subject, you don't seem to run across women much.

You don't seem to run across them as much as mommas.* In politics you run across bimbos a lot. In Las Vegas you got hookers. I just haven't got to that subject really. I've just signed a contract, however, for a novel which will have a woman as one of the main characters. Yeah, I don't understand women. That's one of the reasons I don't write about them. I've given up the idea that I'll ever understand them. They're a different race. They fascinate me, but I'd be worried about writing about them until I learn to speak their language.

Olszewski: Are you surprised by your success as a writer?

HST: I'm not surprised at being successful. I'm surprised that the success has come as it has. It's sort of a peculiar. I didn't expect to be one of the most famous crazy persons of my time.

Olszewski: Well, you've done that pretty well.

HST: That wasn't my plan, but it happened somehow.

Olszewski: You're credited as the Dean of Gonzo Journalism.

HST: Oh yeah.

Olszewski: Exactly what does it mean?

HST: I've never been really sure. I just thought if I'm going to be a journalist I may as well be my own kind.

Olszewski: Where does the word "Gonzo" come from?

HST: It's some old Boston word meaning a little bit crazy and off the wall. Sort of a high crazy. Demented craziness.

Olszewski: I notice another of your favorite words is "cazart." What does that mean?

HST: That means run like a bastard, trouble is coming. You don't know where it's coming from but the shit rain is about to start.

Olszewski: What's the origin of that word?

HST: I made it up. But it is now in the dictionary.

Olszewski: Is it?

HST: I lie to people and tell them that I did make it up. You'd be surprised what people believe.

Olszewski: I've noticed that mass media journalists here, or straight journos if you want to use that term, are strangely fascinated by your writ-

---

* The Hell's Angels referred to certain women as mommas, as Hunter noted in *Hell's Angels.*

ing, yet repulsed as though you are perpetrating some travesty of journalism or political writing.

HST: Repulsed?

Olszewski: Yeah.

HST: Are these people that are going to be covering my "speeches"?

Olszewski: Some of them will be.

HST: Well tell them to get ready. If they're repulsed by what they've read, wait until they have to deal with me in person.

Olszewski: I notice occasionally references to you in things like *Time* or *Newsweek.* These people are aware of what you are doing to them, but they don't credit you as being a valid journalist, a writer with the capital W.

HST: That's true. I have people like that all around. I have people who would like to kill me and have me locked up. I don't know what I do, but I make a lot of enemies somehow. I don't really care what they think. If they come into my yard I'll shoot them. If they don't come into my yard, they don't bother me.

Olszewski: Exactly what sort of doctor are you?

HST: I'm a doctor of divinity, and a doctor of chemotherapy, and a doctor of Gonzo journalism. That's three doctorates.

Olszewski: How did you earn these?

HST: You have no doctorates?

Olszewski: Pardon?

HST: You fuckers have no doctorates. Are you one of these journalists who don't like 'em?

Olszewski: Oh, I don't care one way or another. I'm just interested in where you got them?

HST: Where I got my doctorates from?

Olszewski: Yeah.

HST: Well I got my doctor of, let's see, of chemotherapy from Berkeley, my doctorate of divinity from the Church of the New Truth, and my doctorate of journalism from Columbia.

Olszewski: From Columbia?

HST: I'd like to bring my sheepskins down for you to have a look at, but they may be too heavy for the baggage.

Olszewski: Well let's move from doctors to an area associated with them. Drugs. What's the most volatile drug you've experienced?

HST: The most volatile? By far the most terrifying single experience I've had ever, was with an animal tranquilizer called PCPA. But in general the most powerful, well among head drugs anyway, is LSD. You can get just about wherever you want to go on that one.

Olszewski: Let's just imagine you've indulged in some ultra-powerful acid and you start to get into a reincarnation thing. You know you can come back as any person, except yourself. Who would you come back as?

HST: How can I come back as a person?

Olszewski: I don't know. Let's just assume that it's the particular property of this batch of acid.

HST: As a person. Shit. Ah, I'd probably have to come back as myself right now because I could manage that.

Olszewski: Yeah, but remember, with this acid you can't come back as yourself.

HST: Oh. Well, let's see. I can't think of anyone. I'm afraid to think. I'm working hard at it. There's some state I could come back in, but there's nobody there now so I couldn't identify it by using somebody's name. I can't think of anyone I'd like to come back as. Can you?

Olszewski: Well, I would have thought, what with the way you whoop around on motorcycles, and with your attachment for your .44 Magnum, and the way you shoot your cars with it, etc., that you'd be more at home riding the range. I would have thought you might like to ride with the Jesse James gang.

HST: I don't want to start any arguments but till I'm convinced I'm going to stick with what I have now.

Olszewski: Let's move to future projects. I read in *Playboy* that you were working on a novel called "Guts Balls."

HST: That's in limbo right now. I haven't finished it and I might incorporate it into something else.

Olszewski: Earlier you said you were working on another book with a woman as . . .

HST: That's a different novel. I'm just starting it.

Olszewski: What sort of novel will that be?

HST: It's going to have something to do with Texas, that's all I know right now.

Olszewski: Texas?

HST: Violence, Texas, and drugs.

Olszewski: I heard there are movie rights for *Fear and Loathing in Las Vegas* in the offing. Is this so?

HST: Apparently so. Nobody's really certain, but it seems to be on its way to being a film, yeah.

Olszewski: How can such a book be translated onto the screen?

HST: Oh, I don't know. That's been one of the problems. I'm interested in seeing how they're going to solve it.

Olszewski: Yes it will be interesting. About your forthcoming tour of Australia. Do you have any impressions of this place?

HST: I have no impression of Australia. That's why I thought I might come down and take a look at it. I'm not totally ignorant about it. I know just enough about the place to make me curious. I know there's an outback, and there are several cities there. And most of the people I've met from Australia I like. So that's always a good advertisement, unlike South Africans. Maybe Australia's a monstrous place. I have no idea.

Olszewski: Do you lecture very often?

HST: No. I don't like it. We could probably clear this up because this is a fairly major point. In truth I don't even give lectures. All I do is appear and take a lot of abuse, and sort of maintain a dialogue.

Olszewski: Well, what sort of formats do your shows run to?

HST: I like to get them up, get them moving, get them angry, but after that I just like to talk to people.

Olszewski: Is there any particular thing you like talking about?

HST: Whatever people want. I have nothing to say. I have no message. I'll talk with anyone who wants to talk. I want to make sure that people don't expect me to come and make a speech.

New Times—December 10, 1976

The Hunter Thompson Interview

BY ROBERT SAM ANSON

Snow was beginning to fall on Aspen, when the Great Gonzo made his appearance. He timed it beautifully. As he swept through the door of the Jerome Bar, togged out in parka, sunglasses, and safari shorts, the clock was just striking midnight. The very witching hour. What better moment to meet the Mad-Dog Prince himself.

He collected a bet (the Cowboys had just defeated the Bills by 7 points, and Hunter was holding a 14-point spread), ordered a double margarita, adjusted his cigarette holder to a rakish angle, corrected a bartender who had called him "Mr. Thompson" ("That's Doctor, and don't forget it"), turned to me and uttered what I took to be a sound of greeting: "aaarrrggghhh."

Thus commenced a talk that, in different times, places and states of sobriety, stretched out some sixteen hours, a conversation sprinkled with literary allusions, observations on the state of the nation, pro football, *Rolling Stone,* and the good doctor himself (who is feeling just fine, thank you). Some excerpts:

ON COMING TO *ROLLING STONE*:

HST: It was mutuality of interests. I was running for sheriff, and I wanted to write a piece where people would see it, kind of an ad for myself. *Rolling Stone* seemed like the best place. That's why it worked so well for so many of us, that mutuality of interests. We all got something out of it. *Rolling Stone* was the first place I had been where I could write exactly what I felt. It was terrific.

ON HIS WRITING:

HST: I'd do the end first, and then the beginning, and then try to figure out everything that was supposed to go in between. I used to drive some of the

Rolling Stone people nuts. There would be all these excerpts: X, XX, XXX. They had to learn a whole new language. They didn't know that it was driving me nuts. I'd be just about finished, and Jann would call and say, "We just lost a couple of ad pages—can you give me two more pages?" So then things would get very long. I would write about what I had for breakfast, and how it tasted, and what I had for lunch, and how it tasted, and on and on. But it was like that. Basically, he paid by the word. The more you wrote, the more money you made.

ON HIS EXPENSE ACCOUNT:

HST: Not nearly as much as everyone believes, I'll tell you that. Sometimes there would be these editors' notes about things I was buying—the $6,000 fluegelhorns, for instance—they weren't true. They just added to the legend. Of course, if I thought I needed a $6,000 fluegelhorn to communicate with Frank Mankiewicz, I wouldn't hesitate a moment. Expenses, for me, was sort of a way of evening the score with Jann. You had two choices. You could either be a cheat or be honest. I opted for excess. Jann saw money as entirely something else. In a way, it was the great equalizer for him. That was the way he could assert authority over people he otherwise had no control over. My god, Crouse* had to get stubs for taxicabs he was taking in New York. This has an eroding effect on your sense of who you are, and what your relationship is to the magazine. Everyone has the wrong impression about *Rolling Stone*—that it's this luxurious, decadent place, where people are living it up. It's not like that at all. I remember the first time I went to a party at *Playboy*, and thinking to myself, "Hell, this is what I thought *Rolling Stone* was supposed to be."

ON WORKING FOR WENNER:

HST: When you deal with Jann, you think of the worst possible result of what you are doing, and the best possible result, and a lot of the time you end up with both. He has this capriciousness, a kind of dazed arrogance, like

* Timothy Crouse is an American journalist and author of *The Boys on the Bus* about the 1972 presidential campaign.

a cocoon case of John Mitchellism.* He could be your friend at night, and then do something horrible to you the next day, and then ask you out to dinner again that night. He could never quite grasp why people were pissed at him. He'd say hideous things you thought were a joke and then he'd turn around the next day and do them. A lot of writers can't stand up to it. It's like he leads them down this long tunnel, and they discover too late that there is no way to go back up. He breaks people's confidence in themselves, by doing chicken-shit things, like arbitrary salary cuts. It's like he's giving a guy a gig in the military for having something wrong at inspection. Jann's trouble is that he never paid his dues. Everything has been right for him from the beginning, so he can't understand the troubles he always causes for people who have paid their dues.

ON WHY HE QUIT:

HST: It just drifted away. I suppose you always think that people will learn—the Bobby Kennedy syndrome. And I was doing everything to make him learn except knocking his head against a wall. I was always the middleman; explain to people why they had been fucked. That's not the kind of thing I want to do for the next ten years. No amount of money is worth the constant haggling. I sensed that it would be a nice time to stop. I just kind of turned off the tap one day. It went as easily as it came.

ON *ROLLING STONE*'S FUTURE:

HST: I don't know. I haven't read it in months. But there are a lot of bad signs. Jann's much more interested now in what goes on the cover, what will sell magazines, than whether what is inside is worth reading. The product has gotten very watery. I don't think it stands on its own weight. There is no second level there. I don't know who would run the place if one day Jann gets run over by a black truck. Which is a real problem. Since there are a lot of people I know who would like to run him over with a black truck.

---

* John Mitchell was a former attorney general for the Nixon administration. He played a key role in the Watergate scandal as the head of the Committee for the Reelection of the President and was convicted on charges of perjury, conspiracy, and obstruction of justice.

ON WHAT MIGHT HAVE BEEN:

HST: Hell, it could have been great. After Elko,* I thought we were going to run wide open. I had worked on a lot of bad trains, running on a lot of awful tracks. Being on *Rolling Stone* was like riding the Metroliner. I wanted to put my foot down to the floor. There was Heineken running in the taps. We could have done anything. I wanted to use *Rolling Stone* for political leverage, to bring on real change. I wanted to bring in every good writer in the country. And then Wenner sold the railroad. He was carrying the ball for all of us and he dropped it. And it was all over such small stuff. That's the real tragedy. Jann really could have had the world—he was that close—if he could have just reached out and been decent for a minute or two. Instead, he reached out for nickels and dimes.

ON HIS NEW BOOK:

HST: It'll have to wait a while; I don't work during the football season. But it's about Texas and gunrunning and the American Dream. That's what I've always been interested in: whatever happened to the American Dream.

---

* In the winter of 1974, *Rolling Stone* publisher, Jann Wenner, and Hunter S. Thompson organized a secret political symposium at the Stockmen Hotel in Elko, Nevada. The goal was to set the groundwork of a progressive national political agenda and the future of *Rolling Stone*'s political coverage. Guests included McGovern strategists Rick Stearns and Frank Mankiewicz, pollster Pat Caddell, Ted Kennedy's chief of staff David Burke, and Robert Kennedy speechwriter Adam Walinsky.

90 Minutes Live (Canadian Broadcasting Corporation)—April 12, 1977

Interview with Peter Gzowski

Peter Gzowski: Welcome back. Even though a lot of journalists are acquiring a kind of stardom of their own these days, it's pretty rare when one of them becomes, even in the eyes of his most devoted readers or followers, almost more interesting himself than the people and the events that he writes about. One such person is my next guest. He's the author that went to live with the Hell's Angels of California. In the pages of *Rolling Stone* magazine he turned the same kind of eye on American and world politics. Would you welcome him, please—Dr. Hunter S. Thompson.

Gzowski: Doctor . . .

HST: Doctor, thank you, yes.

Gzowski: You call yourself a doctor when you write . . .

HST: Well I'm a doctor.

Gzowski: A doctor of?

HST: Divinity.

Gzowski: Who gave you a doctor of divinity?

HST: I worked for it in night school.

Gzowski: Did you really?

HST: Yeah. The Catholic Church in Aspen challenged my authority to perform marriages but they lost . . . and the priests lucked out.

Gzowski: So you have a license?

HST: Oh yes. I can perform marriages.

Gzowski: In the beginning of the program I said you were the king of the Gonzo journalists of North America . . .

HST: Well, there's only one.

(Audience laughs and cheers)

Gzowski: Where did the word "Gonzo" come from?

HST: It's an old Boston street word. It's one of those Charles River things that started when you're twelve years old on the banks of the Charles River. "Gonzo" is a word that Bill Cardoso, who's an editor at the *Boston Globe,* came up with to describe some of my writing. I just liked it. And I thought, "Well, am I a new journalist? Am I a political journalist?" I'm a Gonzo journalist . . . And why not?

Gzowski: Coming back to your background as a sports writer, if Gonzo journalism, if the kind of gut feeling . . . it's so hard to put any labels and descriptive adjectives to the way you write or your style or your approach . . .

HST: I've never been able to explain it myself at all.

Gzowski: Is it possible to say, in a general way, that you come at politics as a sports writer. That you look at the taste and the feel of the event and look for people lying all the time, because everyone lies to sports writers and no one lies to political writers.

HST: Well that's true, actually. There's a lot more freedom in sports writing, I would think, than any other kind of writing. You have a tremendous latitude with the use of verbs and adjectives and action. When you get forced into political writing, you miss that. In sports writing people are "pounced on" and "stomped" and "whipped" and "torn." And then you get into politics and somebody loses by 400 votes and he is "edged out. " It just doesn't seem right. You want somebody "pounced" . . . "stomped." And so if you bring that kind of vocabulary to politics—and the same kind of mind, as you say—they're all lying anyway.

The stock market is very much so the same. There's a whole article—I guess you have to say "South of the border" here in Canada—about taking a company public. You kind of nurture it, get the profit picture up, cheat all the employees, fire half the staff, get the profit picture huge, then you go public and sell the stock just like you said. So then it's "Oh yes . . . of course! I must have that!"—like me—and then "Bang! Zip!"

Gzowski: When you first turned your eye to politics during the '72 campaign, you were looked on by the establishment press corps as, just a guy from *Rolling Stone,* this weird hippie magazine. Second, there were questions about what little background you had other than the Hell's Angels and some sports writing. They did not accept you.

HST: I miss that. I'd really like to get that anonymity back. It's a tremendous advantage.

Gzowski: Really?

HST: Oh yeah. To be anonymous. Everyone thought I was a dingbat and just sort of a piece of furniture on the campaign. It's a huge advantage.

Gzowski: Because people would tell you things they would not tell someone from the *New York Times*?

HST: Yeah. They thought I was just a bag carrier.

Gzowski: What kind of thing would they tell you?

HST: Whatever I asked them. And if I'd ask them at 10 o'clock at night or 10 in the morning and they didn't answer, I'd call at 8 o'clock at night . . . then 10 at night . . . then 12 . . . then 2 . . . then 4 . . . and then, eventually, they'd finally answer.

Gzowski: And the fact that you weren't one of the regulars from the *Washington Post* made it all right for you?

HST: That's what they thought.

Gzowski: What did you do to Ed Muskie?

HST: Nothing. Ed Muskie did it to himself.

Gzowski: What was the drug that you said he was on?

HST: Ibogaine.

Gzowski: Ibogaine?

HST: It's a very powerful hallucinogenic root of *Trepentha ibogaine [Tabernanthe iboga]* or something. If you eat it—just a chunk of it—you can sit for three days in a very quiet stupor, without sleeping, and watching a water hole. Pygmies in Africa and South America have done this and it helps them to outlast the beast. You can sit there with your blowgun at the waterhole for three days. You're just frozen and all you can think about is killing the animal. There are other manifestations, such as sudden blind rages, unexplainable frenzies . . . but mainly you're after the animal, like Muskie.

Gzowski: Well two things happened. The first was the rumor began to spread everywhere among all the people that were covering the campaign that Muskie was in fact on this bizarre drug, right? And the other one was you finally said you made it all up.

HST: Well I had to! I couldn't believe people took this sort of thing seriously. But halfway through the campaign, I suddenly realized all these poor bastards reading *Rolling Stone* believed this madness.

It didn't occur to me until the very end of the book, at the end of the campaign, that people really believed that Muskie was eating Ibogaine. I never said he was. I said there was a rumor in Milwaukee that he was. Which was true and I started the rumor in Milwaukee.

Yeah. If you look carefully, I'm a very accurate journalist.

Gzowski: Does being a little bit crazy yourself help reflect a world that is very largely crazy?

HST: Well this is either slanderous or libelous, one of the two, but . . .

Gzowski: I just made it up, so I felt free to say it.

HST: I'll see you in court. Yeah . . . It does help. It will help me probably sue you for a million and a half dollars.

Gzowski: Then you are crazy. You've come to the right place. Better you should buy some penny stock in Vancouver. It will go for a million and a half for me.

HST: I'll go right to my stockbroker friends in New York. I remember getting my first money I ever got from a book . . . I think it was an $11,000 royalty check and I thought "Man. Jesus Christ . . . I haven't paid taxes in five years." I didn't know what to do with it . . . I walked around Aspen for about five days with that thing in the pocket of my Levis and it got all moldy and weird. I was afraid to deposit it in the bank and I didn't want to tell anyone I had it. I was embarrassed I had this money.

Finally some friend talked me into talking with a stockbroker who guaranteed he could double it within a year. And I charted it from then on down. The stock market peaked and dropped. At the end of the year, I just told him to get rid of it. And I said, "If I ever see you again, I'll pull all your teeth with a pair of pliers." If I do see him again, I will still pull out all his teeth.

Gzowski: In Colorado you ran as sheriff and very nearly came quite close to getting elected.

HST: Far too close, yeah. It was four percentage points. I'm now on the sheriff's advisory committee. I hire and fire deputies . . . think about that.

Gzowski: Is it a good idea for a person who is an observer such as yourself to get inside the political arena and act from within?

HST: I used to think so, but I don't think so now. It makes working much more difficult. All the stuff you were saying earlier about a journalist being more interesting than the people you're writing about. It's really true, but it makes it very hard to work. When I went out on the campaign trail in New Hampshire and Massachusetts with Carter, I'd go to press conferences and the Secret Service was baffled . . . I'd come in there and have to sign more autographs than Carter. It's very embarrassing. The press resents it. Nobody knows what to make of it. Carter resented it. So, I quit. You do something once and it's better not to go back.

Gzowski: You are known about doing drugs and all that stuff. Your book *Fear and Loathing in Las Vegas* is a deep, some people would say bitter, exposition and look into the American psyche. Here's a quotation I've come across that fascinates me. It's Kurt Vonnegut Jr. talking about you:

"Hunter Thompson's disease is that he feels America can be as easily led to beauty as to ugliness, to truth as to public relations, and to joy as to bitterness."*

Can you respond to that?

HST: I appreciate that. It was a very elegant sort of tribute in a way. I'm not sure I believe that anymore. I went into politics thinking that, but I really doubt I think it now. I think the system is much more essentially rotten than I believed four years ago.

Gzowski: What about, then, Jimmy Carter? I'm not going to use the word "endorsement," although *Rolling Stone* used it on the cover.†

HST: That was a real horror. Imagine writing the story, and then the cover comes back and says "endorsement." Plus it left out the speech that I was talking about and the Carter tapes . . . what can you do?

Gzowski: But it was written by someone who came away from a six-hour conversation with Jimmy Carter and was sure impressed by him.

HST: Well I was . . . I still am. I think he's one of the three meanest men I've ever met. The other two were Muhammad Ali and Sonny Barger, the president of the Hell's Angels. Those three men are a whole cut above everybody else I've ever run into in terms of sheer functional meanness . . .

Gzowski: Functional meanness?

HST: Yeah, meaning the ability to get to A or B . . . C . . . Z . . . whatever you want. Carter would cut my head off to carry North Dakota. He'd cut both your legs off to carry a ward in the Bronx. He'd never apologize for it. He understands the system. That's why he won. That's really all I said.

I admire that a person played the game as well as he did and the sort of "magnolia shade" that he played in for a while. He was perceived as sort of a

---

* Kurt Vonnegut Jr., "A Political Disease," *Harper's Magazine*, July, 1973.

† Hunter S. Thompson, "Jimmy Carter and the Great Leap of Faith," *Rolling Stone*, June 3, 1976.

Southern dingbat. But I saw him push Teddy Kennedy around down in Athens and I'd never seen Kennedy pushed around in anywhere.

I was stunned . . . And I thought "uh oh." This was 1974. I thought, "Oops . . . this is a bad one. I have to watch him." Sure enough he announced he was running for president some four or five months later. When he did, I took a ride down to see him and wished him good luck.

Gzowski: Were you as impressed by his references to Bob Dylan and things as you appeared to be? Or were you doing another little bit of Ibogaine writing?

HST: No, what he did in that speech that I consistently referred to in the article . . .

Gzowski: The Law Day Speech.*

HST: Yeah—which *Rolling Stone* did not run and left me hanging on some hideous limb—was just lay the whips, the serious whips, on all these lawyers at the Law Day Alumni Speech. This wasn't just all the alumni of the University of Georgia Law School, it was the distinguished alumni of the Law School. All the state senators and judges. He just beat the hell out of them. He'd been governor for three and a half years and they'd given him a hard time—the whole house had been against him—and he stomped on them, in public. I'd never seen a politician do that before. He just pushed Teddy aside and thought, "Out of the way, I got work to do. Move aside."

Kennedy was stunned. I was stunned.

I don't tape politicians' speeches normally, but about ten minutes into it I went to the car and got my tape recorder and thought I've never heard anything like this in my life . . . and I still haven't, from Carter either.

Gzowski: But what you're impressed by is the toughness and the naked . . .

HST: Oh yeah. He will eat your shoulder right off if he thinks it's right.

Gzowski: Have you changed your original impression of him since he's come to power?

HST: No. That's what I thought he was going to do and that's what he's done. He's just eating Russian shoulders instead of Humphrey's. He's a very hard person. He believes in exactly what he's doing. The question is whether he's right or wrong. He's going to walk as close to the edge as he can. Take it for what you want.

---

* Jimmy Carter's address at the University of Georgia on May 4, 1974.

Gzowski: That's a different impression than I got from reading the piece. I thought there was something else that you perceived about him or saw . . .

HST: What did you perceive?

Gzowski: What I read you perceiving was a kind of openness and a kind of willingness to be with . . .

HST: He was totally open! They were looking for men that are devious Humphrey and Muskie–type subterfuges and players. And I kept telling them, "Just look at the man! Listen to him. What he's saying is what he is." And that's exactly what he played. In terms of politics he's one of the most open and dangerously honest and aggressive . . . Well, honest is a dangerous word in politics.

Gzowski: Isn't it less dangerous to have an open man than a devious one?

HST: Yeah, but not if you perceive him as being devious. If you understand him as being open, that's fine. But, the reporters on the campaign were so used to these hack ball politicians that when Carter said, "I'll tell you my foreign policy when I'm president" . . . they would throw him weird reasons for this and strange strategies. That's what he meant. So when he became president, it was, "I'll tell you my foreign policy." It was a thundering sort of statement to lay on a state like Massachusetts, the home to all these serious third-, fourth-, and fifth-generation politicians. They couldn't understand it. It was just too direct. If he says he's going to put a cruise missile into Leningrad, he's willing to do it . . . and if you don't believe it . . . well, that doesn't matter, does it?

High Times—September 1977

Hunter S. Thompson: The Good Doctor Tells All . . . About Carter, Cocaine, Adrenaline, and the Birth of Gonzo Journalism

BY RON ROSENBAUM

The first time I met Hunter S. Thompson was back in 1970, at the America's Cup yacht race where Hunter had chartered a huge power yacht and was preparing to sail it full steam right into the middle of the race course. (This was shortly after his spectacular but unsuccessful run for the office of the sheriff of Aspen, Colorado, on a mescaline-eating "Capitalist Freak Power" ticket.) When I arrived on board the huge yacht, I found Thompson ensconced on the command deck, munching on a handful of psilocybin pills and regarding the consternation of the snooty Newport sailing establishment with amusement.

We never did manage to cross the path of the cup contenders and *Scanlan's* magazine went bankrupt before Hunter wrote up the whole fiasco, but I did learn one thing: this is a guy who understands the importance of perspective. He rode the Hell's Angels—and got himself a nasty beating in the process of getting a unique perspective on them. He leaded his car, his bloodstream and his brain cells full of dangerous drugs to cover a conference of drug-busting D.A.s and turned that experience into *Fear and Loathing in Las Vegas,* a brilliant exploration of the dark side of the drug scene at the peak of Nixon's power.

When he covered the 1972 presidential campaign as national affairs editor for *Rolling Stone,* Thompson's special dead-line-and-drug-crazed "Gonzo" journalism—his own patented mix of paranoia, nightmare, recklessness and black humor—would fill the nervous secret service agents with fear and loathing on the campaign trail. Ever since then, Thompson's become a kind of national character with millions of people following the exploits of "Uncle Duke," in the *Doonesbury* comic strip.

This year too, Thompson had another very special but very different perspective: he's widely reported to have become close to Jimmy Carter and to Carter's inner circle from the time back in 1974 when he heard Carter's now-famous Law Day speech. But curiously, there have been more articles speculating about Thompson—his relations with Jimmy Carter and Jann Wenner—this year than by him. He's never put his own role into perspective until now.

Ron Rosenbaum: How have your attitudes toward politics changed since you wrote about the '72 presidential election in *Fear and Loathing on the Campaign Trail*?

HST: Well, I think the feeling that I've developed since '72 is that an ideological attachment to the presidency or the president is very dangerous. I think the president should be a businessman; probably he should be hired. It started with Kennedy, where you got sort of a personal attachment to the president, and it was very important that he agree with you and you agree with him and you knew he was on your side. I no longer give a fuck if the president's on my side, as long as he leaves me alone or doesn't send me off to any wars or have me busted. The president should take care of business, mind the fucking store and leave people alone.

Ron Rosenbaum: So you developed a tired-of-fighting-the-White-House theory?

HST: I think I've lost my sense that it's a life-or-death matter whether someone is elected to this, that or whatever. Maybe it's losing faith in ideology or politicians—or maybe both. Carter, I think, is an egomaniac, which is good because he has a hideous example of what could happen if he fucks up. I wouldn't want to follow Nixon's act, and Carter doesn't either. He has a whole chain of ugly precedents to make him careful—Watergate, Vietnam, the Bay of Pigs—and I think he's very aware that even the smallest blunder on his part could mushroom into something that would queer his image forever in the next generation's history texts . . . if there is a next generation.

I don't think it matters much to Carter whether he's perceived as a "liberal" or a "conservative," but it does matter to him that he's perceived—by the voters today and by historians tomorrow—as a successful president. He didn't run this weird Horatio Alger trip from Plains, Georgia, to the White House, only to get there and find himself hamstrung by a bunch of hacks and fizzers in the Congress. Which is exactly what's beginning to happen now, and those people are making a very serious mistake if they assume they're dealing with just another political shyster, instead of the zealot he really is. Jimmy Carter is a true believer, and people like that are not the ones you want to cross by accident.

I'm not saying this in defense of the man, but only to emphasize to anybody in Congress or anywhere else who plans to cross Jimmy Carter should take pains to understand the real nature of the beast they intend to cross. He's on a very different wavelength than most people in Washington. That's one of the main reasons he's president, and also one of the first things I noticed when I met him down in Georgia in 1974—a total disdain for political definition or conventional ideologies.

His concept of populist politics is such a strange mix of total pragmatism and almost religious idealism that every once in a while—to me at least, and especially when I listen to some of the tapes of conversations I had with him in 1974 and '75—that he sounds like a borderline anarchist . . . which is probably why he interested me from the very beginning; and why he still does, for that matter. Jimmy Carter is a genuine original. Or at least he was before he got elected. God only knows what he is now, or what he might turn into when he feels he's being crossed—by Congress, the Kremlin, Standard Oil or anything else. He won't keep any enemies list on paper, but only because he doesn't have to; he has a memory like a computerized elephant.

Ron Rosenbaum: Did you ever have any ideology in the sense of being a liberal, a conservative . . . or were you an anarchist all along?

HST: I've always considered myself basically an anarchist, at least in the abstract, but every once in a while you have to come out of the closet and deal with reality. I'm interested in politics, but not as ideology, simply as an art of self-defense—that's what I learned in Chicago. I realized that you couldn't afford to turn your back on the bastards because that's what they would do—run amok and beat the shit out of you—and they had the power to do it. When I feel it's necessary to get back into politics, I'll do it, either writing about it or participating in it. But as long as it's not necessary, there are a lot better ways to spend your time. Buy an opium den in Singapore, or a brothel somewhere in Maine, I'd become a hired killer in Rhodesia or some kind of human Judas Goat in the Golden Triangle. Yeah, a soldier of fortune, a professional geek who'll do anything for money.

Ron Rosenbaum: You've received a lot of flak for your enthusiasm about Jimmy Carter's Law Day speech in Athens, Georgia. Do you still like Carter?

HST: Compared to most other politicians, I do still like Carter. Whether I agree with him on everything that's another thing entirely. He'd put me in jail in an instant if he saw me snorting coke in front of him. He would not, however, follow me into the bathroom and try to catch me snorting it. It's little things like that.

Ron Rosenbaum: In that Law Day speech, Carter quoted Bob Dylan. Do you really think Carter cares about Bob Dylan's music the way we do?

HST: I listened to Bob Dylan records in his house, but that was mainly because his sons had them. I don't think he goes upstairs to the bedroom at night, reads the Bible in Spanish while listening to *Highway 61.*

Ron Rosenbaum: Why haven't you written anything about Carter and the '76 campaign trail?

HST: I was going to write a book on the '76 campaign, but even at the time I was doing research, I started to get nervous about it. I knew if I did another book on the campaign, I'd somehow be trapped.

I was the most obvious journalist—coming off my book on the 1972 campaign—to inherit Teddy White's* role as a big-selling chronicler of presidential campaigns. I would have been locked into national politics as a way of life, not to mention as a primary source of income . . . And there's no way you can play that kind of Washington Wizard role from a base in Woody Creek, Colorado. I'd have had to move to Washington, or at least to New York . . . and, Jesus, life is too short for that kind of volunteer agony. I've put a lot of work into living out here where I do and still making a living, and I don't want to give it up unless I absolutely have to. I moved to Washington for a year in 1972, and it was a nightmare.

Yeah, there was a definite temptation to write another campaign book—especially for a vast amount of money in advance—but even while I was looking at all that money, I knew it would be a terminal mistake. It wasn't until I actually began covering the campaign that I had to confront the reality of what I was getting into. I hadn't been in New Hampshire two days when I knew for certain that I just couldn't make it. I was seeing my footprints everywhere I went. All the things that were of interest last time—even the small things, the esoteric little details of a presidential campaign—seemed like gibberish the sec-

* Theodore White was an American journalist and author known for chronicling the play-by-play details of presidential elections in his *The Making of the President 1960, 1964, 1968,* and *1972* series.

ond time around. Plus, I lost what looks more and more like a tremendous advantage of anonymity. That was annoying, because in '72 I could stand against a wall somewhere—and I'd select some pretty weird walls to stand against—and nobody knew who I was. But in '76, Jesus, at press conferences, I had to sign more autographs than the candidates. Through some strange process, I came from the '72 campaign an unknown reporter, a vagrant journalist, to a sort of media figure in the '76 campaign. It started getting so uncomfortable and made it so hard to work that even the alleged or apparent access that I had to this weird peanut farmer from Georgia became a disadvantage.

Ron Rosenbaum: You became a public figure?

HST: Thanks to our friend Trudeau.

Ron Rosenbaum: Did Garry Trudeau consult you before he started including you as the Uncle Duke character in *Doonesbury*?

HST: No, I never saw him; I never talked to him. It was a hot, nearly blazing day in Washington, and I was coming down the steps of the Supreme Court looking for somebody, Carl Wagner or somebody like that. I'd been inside the press section, and all of a sudden I saw a crowd of people and I heard them saying, "Uncle Duke." I heard the words Duke, Uncle; it didn't seem to make any sense. I looked around, and I recognized people who were total strangers pointing at me and laughing. I had no idea what the fuck they were talking about. I had gotten out of the habit of reading funnies when I started reading the *Times*. I had no idea what this outburst meant. It was a weird experience, and as it happened I was sort of by myself up there on the stairs, and I thought: What in the fuck madness is going on? Why am I being mocked by a gang of strangers and friends on the steps of the Supreme Court? Then I must have asked someone, and they told me that Uncle Duke had appeared in the *Post* that morning.

Ron Rosenbaum: So all this public notoriety was a burden in trying to return to the campaign?

HST: It was impossible because there was no way for me to stay anonymous, to carry on with what I consider my normal behavior, which is usually—in terms of a campaign—either illegal or dangerous or both . . . It was generally assumed that I was guilty—which I was.

Ron Rosenbaum: So eventually you found that refuge in a kind of band of brothers?

HST: What? No, I have never had much faith in concepts like "a band of brothers"—especially in politics. What we're talking about here is a new generation of highly competent professional political operatives and also a new generation of hot-rod political journalists who are extremely serious and competitive during the day, but who happen to share a few dark and questionable tastes that could only be mutually indulged late and night, in absolute privacy . . .

Because no presidential candidate even wants to know, much less have to explain at the press conference, why rumors abound that many of his speech writers, strategists and key advance men are seen almost nightly—and sometimes for nine or ten nights in a row—frequenting any of the two or three motel rooms in the vortex of every primary campaign that are known to be "dope dens," "orgy pads," and "places of deep intrigue."

They simply don't want to hear these things, regardless of how true they may be—and in 1976 they usually were, although not in the sense that we were running a movable dope orgy, right in the bowels of a presidential campaign—but it was true that for the first time, there was a sort of midnight drug underground that included a few ranking staff people, as well as local workers and volunteers, from almost every democratic candidate's staff, along with some of the most serious, blue-chip press people . . . and it was also true that some of the most intelligent and occasionally merciless conversation of the whole campaign took place in these so-called dope dens.

Hell, it was a fantastic luxury to be able to get together at night with a few bottles of Wild Turkey or Chivas Regal and a big tape deck with portable speakers playing Buffett or Jerry Jeff or the Amazing Rhythm Aces . . . yeah, and also a bag of ripe Colombian tops and a gram or two of the powder; and to feel relaxed enough with each other, after suffering through all that daytime public bullshit, to just hang out and talk honestly about what was really happening in the campaign . . . You know, like which candidate was fatally desperate for money, which one had told the most ridiculous lie that day, who was honest and who wasn't.

In a lot of ways it was the best part of the campaign, the kind of thing I'd only be able to do with a very few people in 1972 and '68. But in '76 we were able—because there were enough of us—to establish a sort of midnight-to-dawn truce that transcended all the daytime headline gibberish and I think it helped all of us to get a better grip on what we were really doing.

I could illustrate this point a lot better by getting into names and specific situations, but I can't do that now for the same reason I couldn't write about it during the campaign. We all understand that, and the very few times I even hinted at this midnight underground, I did it in code phrases—like "tapping the glass."

Ron Rosenbaum: Tapping the glass. I wonder if you could explain that?

HST: Well, that's one of those apparently meaningless code phrases that I use in almost everything I write. It's a kind of lame effort to bridge the gap between what I know and what I can write without hurting my friends—sort of working on two or three levels at the same time.

Ron Rosenbaum: So if you go back and read your stories, a scene where you talk about "tapping the glass" with Carter campaign staffer "X" . . .

HST: Right. That means chopping up rocks of cocaine on a glass coffee table or some mirror we jerked off the wall for that purpose—but not necessarily with one of Carter's people. The whole point of this wretched confession is that there were so many people tapping the glass in the '76 campaign that you never knew who might turn up at one of those midnight sessions. They were dangerously nonpartisan. On any given night you would meet Udall* and Shriver staffers, along with people from the Birch Bayh† and Fred Harris** campaigns. Even George Wallace was represented from time to time; and of course, there was always hardcore press dopers.

Ron Rosenbaum: That's amazing. You were covering this media-saturated presidential campaign during the day, and then snorting coke at night with all those hotshot politicos?

HST: They weren't very hotshot then.

Ron Rosenbaum: OK. But since we're talking about drug use during the '76 campaign, it's obvious we're talking about people who are now in the White House, right?

HST: Well . . . some of them, yes. But let's get a grip on ourselves here. We don't want to cause a national panic by saying that a gang of closet coke freaks are running the country—although that would probably be the case, no matter who had won the election.

Ron Rosenbaum: Times are definitely changing, eh? But since Carter won the election, let's focus on him for a moment.

---

* Morris King "Mo" Udall was a Democratic representative from Arizona. He ran for the Democratic presidential nomination in 1976.

† Birch Bayh is a former Democratic senator from Indiana. He ran for the Democratic presidential nomination in 1976.

** Fred Harris is a former Democratic senator from Oklahoma. He ran for the Democratic presidential nomination in 1976.

HST: Well, why not? Let's see how thin a wire we can walk here, without getting ourselves locked up . . . Indeed, and meanwhile let's rent a big villa in the mountains of Argentina, just in case my old friend Jimmy is as mean as I always said he was. Anyway, yeah, we're talking about at least a few people in the White House inner circle; not Cy* and Ziggy† and that crowd, the professional heavies who would have gone to work for anybody—Carter, Humphrey, Brown.** Shit, they'd even work for me, if I'd won the election.

Ron Rosenbaum: The inner circle of Carter's people are serious drug users?

HST: Wait a minute, I didn't say that. For one thing, a term like serious user has a very weird and menacing connotation; and, for another, we were talking about a few people from almost everybody's staff. Across the board . . . Not junkies or freaks, but people who were just as comfortable with drugs like weed, booze, or coke as we are—and we're not weird, are we? Hell no, we're just overworked professionals who need to relax now and then, have a bit of the whoop and the giggle, right?

Ron Rosenbaum: Weren't they nervous, or were you nervous, when you first started doing coke together?

HST: Well, I suppose I should have expected the same kind of difference between, say, the '72 and '76 campaigns as I saw between '68 and '72. When I went to New Hampshire in '68 I was a genuine unknown. I was the only person except for Bill Cardozo who would smoke weed, ever. I mean in the press. In '72 it was a revolution in that sense and people in the press openly smoked hash and did coke. So I should have expected it in '76, but I hadn't really thought of it. It stunned me a little bit in '76 that coke was as common as weed had been in '72 and almost right out in the open, used in a very cavalier fashion. As I say, in 1972 it was a fairly obvious consistent use of the weed by McGovern's people, in '68 it was McCarthy, but this time it was across the board.

Ron Rosenbaum: In a way, what you're saying is that it was kind of truth-telling substrata of drug users, and that's why you couldn't write stories about it.

---

* Cyrus Vance was the secretary of state during the Carter administration.

† Zbigniew Brzezinski served as a national security advisor during the Carter administration and currently is an analyst for various television networks. Hunter admired his intelligence.

** Jerry Brown is a former Democratic governor of California.

HST: Yes, for the first time I was really faced with the problem of knowing way too much.

Ron Rosenbaum: Was this a good or bad thing?

HST: I think it was good. It allowed people who would never under the circumstances have been able to sit down, get stoned and talk honestly about whether they should even be working there.

Ron Rosenbaum: People are always asking how did you get away with it. Why aren't you in jail with all the stuff you write about drugs on the campaign trail? Do you feel that the Secret Service was specifically tailing you after you started writing these articles about all the dope you had taken?

HST: No. I made my peace with the Secret Service in early '72 when I went to a party in the Biltmore Hotel here in New York after McGovern's primary victory, and there were about ten agents in a room. Three of them were obviously passing a joint around. The look on their faces when I walked in there . . . all of them turning to look when I walked in . . . it was a wonderful moment of confrontation. I didn't want to be there, they didn't want me in there. Immediately they just crushed the joint and tried to ignore it. But the room was obviously full of marijuana smoke.

Ron Rosenbaum: And everybody knew that you knew.

HST: Oh yeah, of course. But I decided not to write about it—at least not right away.

Ron Rosenbaum: Was there ever any kind of trouble with the Secret Service after that?

HST: No trouble at all, except when they tried to bar me from the White House during the impeachment thing. I called the guards Nazi cocksuckers or something, and in order to get in the White House I had to promise not to call anybody Nazi cocksuckers. I just waved my hand at the White House itself, you know, with Haldeman inside. I kind of got off that hook. And then I promised not to call anyone Nazi cocksuckers, and they let me in.

Ron Rosenbaum: Some of your fans wonder if you ever make up some of the bizarre incidents you describe. You've said that all the outrageous drugs you did and things you did in your Las Vegas book were true, except the notorious incident where you supposedly paralyzed yourself with adrenochrome extract from live human adrenal glands.

HST: If I admitted that it was true, it was tantamount to admitting that I was a first-degree murderer of the foulest sort, that somebody would kill a child in order to suck out the adrenaline.

Ron Rosenbaum: But in the book you didn't say that you killed the kid. You just said that you got it.

HST: That's right. I said that my attorney had gotten it from a client of his. What I was doing was taking what you normally feel from shooting adrenaline into the realm of the extremely weird.

Ron Rosenbaum: Have you ever had that feeling? Shooting adrenaline?

HST: Oh, yes. Whenever it was necessary. Sometimes nothing else works. When you really have to stay up for the fifth day and fifth night . . . and nothing will work not even black beauties. Then you shoot adrenaline. But you have to be very careful with it. First don't ever shoot it into a vein. That's doom. But even then, you've got to be very careful because you can drive yourself completely berserk, and I'm sure it would be just the way I described it in *Las Vegas*.

Ron Rosenbaum: I always thought you were talking in metaphorical terms when you said, "I like to work on the adrenaline."

HST: Yeah, but usually my own. I'm really an adrenaline junkie; I never get anything done without the pressure of some impossible deadline.

Ron Rosenbaum: How would you describe the adrenaline high?

HST: At its best it's one of the most functional of all the speed sort of drugs in that it has almost no rush unless you overdo it, and almost no crash. I never considered speed fun. I use speed as fuel, a necessary evil. Adrenaline is much smoother and much more dangerous if you fuck up. I fucked up one time in a motel in Austin, Texas. I was very careless, and I just whacked the needle into my leg without thinking. I'd forgotten the vein thing, and after I pulled the little spike out, I noticed something was wrong. In the bathroom the tile was white, the curtain was white—but in the corner of my eye in the mirror I looked down and saw a hell of a lot of red. Here was this little tiny puncture, like a leak in a high-powered hose . . . You could barely see the stream. It was going straight from my leg and hitting the shower curtain at about eye level, and the whole bottom of the curtain was turning red.

I thought, oh Jesus Christ, what now? And just went in and lay down on the bed and told the people in the room to get out without telling them why; then I waited twenty minutes and all I could think of was these horrible Janis Joplin stories: you know, OD'ing in a motel . . . Jim Morrison . . . Jimi Hendrix . . . needles. And I thought, oh fuck, what a sloppy way to go—I was embarrassed by it. But after twenty minutes nothing happened.

Then I really began to get nervous and I thought, oh God, it's going to come all at once. It's a delayed thing, like those acid flashbacks they've been promising all these years.

Ron Rosenbaum: When are we going to have them?

HST: I've been waiting for a long time.

Ron Rosenbaum: Once I asked a friend of yours why you are so attracted to Carter and this guy says, well, Carter's basically in a lot of ways a conservative good old boy and so is Hunter. Do you think that's true in some ways, or that you're a good old boy that's gone weird?

HST: That sounds better. Good old boy gone weird. That's a good line anyway. I wouldn't deny that I would just as soon admit it.

Ron Rosenbaum: You had a fairly straight upbringing in Louisville, Kentucky, didn't you?

HST: Well, I was a juvenile delinquent, but a straight juvenile delinquent. The kind that wore white bucks, buttoned-down Oxford cloth shirts, suits. It was a good cover to use to rob crowded liquor stores. I discovered then that it helps to have a cover. If you act as weird as you are, something terrible is bound to happen to you, if you're as weird as I am. I mean if I looked like I thought, I wouldn't be on the streets for very long.

Ron Rosenbaum: Were you ever busted?

HST: Yeah, repeatedly. I learned about jails a lot earlier than most people. On about ages fifteen through eighteen I was in and out of jails continually. Usually for buying booze under age or for throwing fifty-five-gallon oil drums through filling station windows—you know, those big plate-glass windows. And then I was expelled from school once—for rape, I think. I wasn't guilty, but what the hell. We were in the habit of stealing five or six cases of beer on weekends to drink. That night was the Friday night after my expulsion. We did our normal run and stole about five or six cases. We took one of them and put it on the superintendent of schools' lawn at one o'clock in the morning and very carefully put twenty whole bottles right through every pane in the front of his house. We heard them exploding inside, and they must have gone mad—you heard them in the bedrooms, in the living room, every window was broken. I mean, what kind of thugs would do that? Twenty-four hand-beer-bottle-grenades . . . to wake up and hear the whole house exploding! Which window is going to be hit next? We deliberately took about ten minutes to put them through there because we knew they'd never get the cops there in ten minutes.

Ron Rosenbaum: Makes you feel someone's out to get you. Twenty-four bottles of beer, that's heavy. So you were into overkill when making statements?

HST: That wasn't overkill. It was massive retaliation, the court of final resort. I was expelled for something I hadn't done or even thought about doing.

Ron Rosenbaum: What is your favorite drug experience?

HST: Well, there are very few things that can really beat driving around the Bay Area on a good summer night—big motorcycle, head full of acid—wearing nothing but a T-shirt and a pair of shorts and getting on that Highway 1 going 120 miles an hour. That's a rush of every kind—head, hands—it's everything put in a bundle. Because first of all, it's a rush, and also it's maintaining control and see how far I can go, how weird I can get and still survive, even though I'm seeing rats in front of me instead of cops. Rats with guns on . . .

Ron Rosenbaum: How do you handle something like that?

HST: I never know. It's interesting, always a different way. Mainly it's figuring out real fast whom you are dealing with, and what their rules are. One of the few times I ever got in trouble, I wasn't drunk or pumped up. I had a loaded .44 magnum in the glove compartment, a bottle of Wild Turkey open on the seat beside me, and I said, well, this is a good time to try that advice a hippie lawyer gave me once—to pull down the window just a crack and stick out my driver's license. So I started to do that. I was just getting it out, when all of a sudden the door on the other side opened. I looked around, and here was a flashlight glaring right in my face, and right beside the flashlight was a big, dirty .57 magnum pointed at me. They didn't give a fuck about my license. They jerked me out of the car and pushed me up against the side. I said something about my constitutional rights, and they said, "Well, sue us" or something and kicked my legs. So I gave it up and eventually I paid a $35 fine, because it's easier than arguing. I had just bought the car. It was a Saab. The night before I had pushed my English Ford off a cliff in Big Sur, 400 feet down to the ocean, to get even with the bastard for all the trouble it caused me. We filled it with gasoline and set it on fire just before it went over the edge.

Ever since then I have made it a point to be polite to the California Highway Patrol. I have a National Rifle Association sticker on the back windows of my car, so that any cop on the driver's side has to pass that and see it. I used to carry a police badge in a wallet, and that helped a lot.

Ron Rosenbaum: I reread *Fear and Loathing in Las Vegas* last summer. I loved it, but I felt it was really a sad book filled with regret for the passing of the San Francisco scene.

HST: No, not really. But I think almost any kind of humor I like always has a touch of melancholy or weirdness in it. I seem to be alone, for instance, in considering Joseph Conrad one of history's greatest humorists.

Ron Rosenbaum: Were you also down on the drug experience in that book?

HST: No. I kind of assumed that this was sort of a last fling; that Nixon and Mitchell and all those people would make it very soon impossible for anybody to behave that way and get away with it. It wouldn't be a matter of a small fine. Your head would be cut off.

Ron Rosenbaum: So it's a real exploration of terminal paranoia.

HST: Well . . . it was kind of a weird celebration for an era that I figured was ending.

Ron Rosenbaum: Maybe you can tell us the true story of the birth of Gonzo journalism. It was the Kentucky Derby story you did for *Scanlan's* magazine in 1969, right?

HST: I guess it's important to take it all the way back to having dinner in Aspen with Jim Salter, a novelist who had sort of a Continental style. It was one of those long European dinners with lots of wine, and Salter said something like, "Well, the Derby's coming up. Aren't you going to be there?" And I thought, well, I'll be damned. That's a good idea.

I was working at the time for Warren Hinckle at *Scanlan's* magazine. So I immediately called Hinckle and said, "I have a wonderful idea, we must do the derby. It's the greatest spectacle the country can produce." It was 3:30 in the morning or something like that, but Hinckle got right into it. By that time I'd learned to hate photographers; I still do. I can't stand to work with them. So I said we've got to get an illustrator for this, and I had Pat Oliphant in mind. Hinckle said fine, you know, do it.

In an hour's time the whole thing was settled. Oliphant wasn't available, but Ralph Steadman was coming over on his first trip to the U.S. and it was all set up that I would go to Louisville and do the advance work, and Ralph would meet me there later.

I think I took off the next day. The whole thing took less than twenty-four hours. I got there and of course found that the place was jammed, there were no rooms and it was out of the question to get a press pass. The deadline had been three months earlier. It took me about two days to get two whole press kits. I'm not sure exactly how I did it. I traded off the outrage, which was so gross, that somebody from a thing called *Scanlan's,* which we told them was an Irish magazine famous all over the world, was sending a famous European artist to illustrate the derby for the British Museum, weird stuff like that. They agreed to give me two of everything except passes to the clubhouse and the drunk tank—I mean the blue-blood drunk tank at the center of the clubhouse. That's where Goldwater* and all the movie stars and those people sit. The best seats in the house. They wouldn't give us those. So I think we stole those.

In any case, we got total access to everything, including a heavy can of Mace . . . Now this is bad, this is ugly. The press box is on the roof, directly over the governor's box. And I had this can of Mace, I'm not sure why . . . maybe for arguments; Mace is a very efficient way of ending arguments. So I'd been fondling the can in my pocket, but we couldn't find any use for it—nobody threatened me. I was kind of restless. Then just before the Derby started we were standing in the front row of the press box, up on the roof, and just for the hell of it I blasted the thing about three times about 100 feet straight down to the governor's box. Then I grabbed Ralph and said let's get out of here. Nobody Maces the governor in the press box. It's not done. It's out of the question. I have no idea what the hell went on in the box when the stuff hit because we took off. That was the end of the story.

About two days later, Ralph had all the drawings done, and I stayed on to write the story, but I couldn't get much done. That goddamned Kent State thing happened the Monday after the Derby, that was all I could think of for a while. So I finally flew up to New York, and that's when the real fear started. Most of the magazine was either printed or on the press out in San Francisco—except for my story, which was the lead story, which was also the cover story, and I was having at the time what felt to me like a terminal writer's block, whatever the hell that means.

I would lie in the bathtub at this weird hotel. I had a suite with everything I wanted—except I couldn't leave. After three days of not writing more than two pages, this kind of anxiety/depression syndrome builds up, and it really locks you up. They were sending copy boys and copy girls and people down

---

* Barry Goldwater was a senator from Arizona. He was also the Republican presidential nominee in 1964.

every hour to see what I had done, and the pressure began to silently build like a dog whistle kind of scream, you know. You couldn't hear it but it was everywhere.

After the third day of that horrible lockup, I'd lie in the tub for three hours in the morning drinking White Horse scotch out of the bottle—just lying in the tub, feeling like, "Well, I got away with it for awhile, but this time I've pushed it too far." But there was no alternative; something had to go in.

Finally I just began to tear the pages out of my notebooks since I write constantly in the notebooks and draw things, and they were legible. But they were hard to get in the telecopier. We began to send just torn pages. When I first sent one down with the copy boy, I thought the phone was going to ring any minute, with some torrent of abuse from whoever was editing the thing in the New York office. I just sort of sat back and watched TV.

I was waiting for the shit to hit the fan . . . But almost immediately the copy boy was back and wanted more. And I thought, "Ah, ha, what's this?" Here's the light at the end of the tunnel. Maybe they're crazy, but why worry? I think I actually called Hinckle in San Francisco and asked him if he wanted any more pages and he said, "Oh, yeah. It's wonderful stuff . . . wonderful." So I just began to tear the fucking things out. And sometimes I would have to write handwritten inserts—I just gave up on the typewriter—sending page after page right out of the notebook, and of course Hinckle was happy as twelve dogs. But I was full of grief, and shame. I thought this was the end, it was the worst hole I had ever gotten into. And I always had been almost pretty good about making deadlines—scaring people to death, but making them. This time I made it, but in what I considered the foulest and cheapest way, like Oakland's unclean touchdown against Miami—off balance . . . they did it all wrong . . . six seconds to go . . . but it worked.

They printed it word for word, even with the pauses, thoughts, and jagged stuff like that. And I felt nice that I hadn't sunk the magazine by failing to get the story done right, and I slunk back to Colorado and said oh fuck, when it comes out I'm going to take a tremendous beating from a lot of people.

But exactly the opposite happened. Just as soon as the thing came out, I started getting calls and letters. People were calling it a tremendous breakthrough in journalism, a stroke of genius. And I thought, what in the shit?

One of the letters came from Bill Cardozo, who was the editor of the *Boston Globe Sunday Magazine* at the time. I'd heard him use the word Gonzo when I covered the New Hampshire primary in '68 with him. It meant sort of "crazy," "off-the-wall"—a phrase that I always associate with Oakland. But Cardozo said something like, "Forget all the shit you've been writing, this is it; this is pure Gonzo. If this is a start, keep rolling." Gonzo. Yeah, of course. That's what I was doing all the time. Of course, I might be crazy.

Ron Rosenbaum: Is it sheer intelligence?

HST: Well, It's more than that . . . Let's not forget now I've had at least ten years of paying dues. I know I have some talent, whatever that means. Some people are good at money and some people are good at basketball. I can use words to my advantage, which is a great trick to have.

Ron Rosenbaum: Are there some things in your notebooks you can't put in your stories?

HST: All the best stories are unwritten. More and more I find that I can't tell the whole truth about events. I have one book I'd like to write, and the rest will have to be done to pay the fucking rent. That'll be the one where there'll be no question if anybody's lying. Well, there will be some question, but the truth is usually a lot weirder than anything you can make up. I'll make sure that it dooms as many people as possible—an absolutely true account, including my own disaster and disappearances. To hell with the American Dream. Let's write it off as a suicide.

Lecture at the University of Colorado (Boulder)—November 1, 1977

Interviewer: CEB an affiliate of UCSU is proud to present Dr. Hunter Thompson. (Applause)

HST: That's not enough. Did I apologize for being late?

HOST: We're very sorry for being late tonight . . . The plane was a little bit late.

HST: We're not in jail. Really, what the hell are they for? Who controls those things? Turn those [lights] off. (Lights turned off) Thank you.

HST: Oh, you're apologizing for being late?

HOST: Yeah, we're apologizing for being late.

HST: Some Nazi held us up at the gate down there. We had no permit to park and . . . we weren't on the list?

HOST: Yeah, we were on the list.

HST: They weren't there though. No, we were out there for 45 minutes held up by some local Nazi . . . (Looking at the host after a pause) You're supposed to get this thing going.

HOST: Oh, I see.

(Applause)

HST: In other words we're trying to determine the nature and the meaning of the crowd, as it were. If we start on the wrong subject it will take us a long time to get back to the right subject. Is there any dominant curiosity here that could deal with? . . .

You, yes?

HOST: We have some mics back there. Does anybody have a suggestion? Or a question?

Audience: OK, I'm not going to ask you what is reality now . . . OK. What I want to know is—Do you think that the authorities on earth, be they what they are, have been contacted by extraterrestrials, intelligent

creatures from another planet? (Crowd laughs) I really want to ask you this, man.

HST: Which authorities? Who?

Audience: Whichever ones are in charge. You know, depends on where you're at.

HST: Well, probably so.

Audience: Thank you.

HST: Why not? OK is that the subject we have to deal with tonight?

Audience: Have you ever, since *Fear and Loathing in Las Vegas,* do you think you've ever found the American Dream? You know, that disco you were looking for?

HST: I found it right there, that's a great American novel.

Audience: That's it?

HST: Yea, that's it.

Audience: You know, Hunter, a lot of the questions that we came up with is like . . . when you're writing about the American Dream in *Fear and Loathing,* we weren't really quite sure what you were talking about really.

HST: Well, what puzzled you, what bothered you?

Audience: Well the whole idea of the American Dream . . . is there really something out there that you were looking for? As college students here that's something we're all here to find out, you know. That's why we're all here, right guys?

HST: Well it's like the golden streets of heaven, and U.S. Marines that patrol them, or guard them. I was always going to ask a Jesuit why, if heaven was as fine and organized place as it's supposed to be, they need a bunch of goddamn Marines to guard the streets. Yeah, we've been taught, whole generations of people in this country; we've been taught that the American Dream is the sort of the guiding ethic for enterprise, democracy, honesty, truth, beauty, things like that. And if the myth exists it's like a rainbow, it's a worthwhile thing to chase. There are worse ways to spend your life than chasing the American dream. But once you've found it, like I did in Vegas, what's called the old Psychiatrist's Club, then it is kind of puzzling. You feel kind of naked and alone out there, because once you've found the dream, it is generally just a slab of burned-out concrete in Las Vegas called the old Psychiatrist's Club, then it's kind of hard to go on from there on the same. You don't have the same kind of dedication to journalism.

I flew out here from Chicago . . . Tex Colson,* our old friend from the White House who is . . . Apparently for the first time I listened to him for a few hours, and I think he probably is serious about Jesus. But he was framed sitting next to a guy, I noticed he was wearing a yellow French cuffed shirt and I noticed he had his presidential cufflinks on. And, as we got off the plane, I was going to tap him on the shoulder and say, "Those are nice cufflinks, I don't have any myself, but last time I saw the ones you're wearing, you bastard, you were pointing at me saying you were going to put me in jail for the duration." Which is true, the last time Colson spoke to me was the time he put me in jail for just being a degenerate bad person, ha. The record should show that, since then Colson's been in jail and I haven't. And I don't need Jesus yet, I might keep Jesus in reserve.† Did we answer that question? No we didn't. Yeah we did.

Audience: Dr. Thompson, are you still a bigger football fan than President Nixon?

HST: You know what, I used to think that was the only time Nixon spoke the truth to me. And from what I've learned since then I suspect he even lied about that. No, actually he gave me a serious crack back the first time I talked to him about football when he knew the name of a second-string Oakland flanker who played seven plays in one Super Bowl; never showed up again. Next I know, I knew who he was, what he had done, and I knew where he'd gone to college. I'm not sure what it tells us, except that at least he can tell the truth on that one thing. No, I guess that Nixon and I must share one thing in common, that we are serious football fans. There's no shame in that, that you have one thing in common with Richard Nixon. We both were adults, we spend American money. So it's eerie to find out that I could get along with Nixon and actually have a ho-ho conversation about football, because I was told he lied about everything; and that was the one thing he caught me on. But we caught him in the end, on a much bigger thing.

Audience: You know, earlier tonight you talked about Vietnam, and how you felt that more things should be said about Vietnam that haven't been said. Do you care to talk about this at all?

---

* Charles Colson is a former special counsel to President Nixon. Colson pleaded guilty to obstruction of justice charges during the Watergate scandal.

† While serving a seven-month prison sentence resulting from his role in the Watergate scandal, Colson became a born-again evangelical Christian. He later founded Prison Fellowship Ministries and has published prolifically on the subject.

HST: We were talking about books. The best books that I've read recently have been books on Vietnam. And they're not just good books about Vietnam, they're good books period. *Dog Soldiers** [by Robert Stone] has been out now for about two years, that's the best novel by an American writer that I've read in about ten years. And Michael Herr† (I think) who is a free-lance journalist who would write long things for say for *Esquire* [and other publications], has a book out just about now called *Dispatches,* which probably is the best book, not only about Vietnam, but the whole generation and the fixation that we all, in the end, had to have about the damn place. That's why I went over there, in the last two weeks of the war, the place had been causing so much trouble for ten years I thought I should see it, but I saw this fence.

Audience: In the end of one of your books, I think it was *'72,* when you went over to Vietnam for the final days there, you went to Cambodia and you said you experienced the fear and the loathing?

HST: No, Cambodia no. That went down about the time I got lost.

Audience: What?

HST: If I said I went to Cambodia, I lied.

Audience: I have a question up here.

HST: I can't answer any questions about Cambodia, I was not allowed to go there, the Khmer Rouge had taken over and they were vicious little bastards. Jacques Leslie, who works at the *LA Times,* is one of these [inaudible] "confirmed agent" freaks who cannot come back to this country, the culture shock has been too heavy.** To him New Delhi is home, and Hong Kong is sort of like what we think of here, it's his version of New York. To go from New Delhi to Hong Kong you're going to the big city. And a lot of people like that, correspondents who get so locked into Asia or places, they can't come back to this country. But Leslie, he carried magnetic chessboards, so the men will stick on the chessboard for . . . maybe until the next war. You can keep a game going when you're always in jeeps or on planes and in

---

* Robert Stone's novel *Dog Soldiers* won the National Book Award in 1975.

† Journalist and *Esquire* Vietnam War correspondent Michael Herr wrote his memoir *Dispatches* about his experience covering the Vietnam War. Thompson wrote "*Dispatches* puts the rest of us in the shade" as a promotional quote for the hardcover edition of the book. Herr later cowrote the narration for the Vietnam War epic *Apocalypse Now* and cowrote the screenplay for *Full Metal Jacket* with Stanley Kubrick.

** Jacques Leslie is a former Vietnam War correspondent for the *Los Angeles Times*. He was later dispatched to Hong Kong to write about the death of Chairman Mao Zedong. He resigned from the *Los Angeles Times* in 1977 to write as a magazine freelancer.

other . . . the chess would never . . . there's no way to knock them off. And . . . what was I saying. About Leslie? I don't recall. We get lost.

Audience: In your book *Hell's Angels,* you described a Hell's Angels gang-bang at a Merry Pranksters party up in San Francisco I think it was.

HST: La Honda.

Audience: La Honda, yeah. In Tom Wolfe's book, *The Electric Kool-Aid Acid Test,* he described a scene that was very similar.

HST: It wasn't just similar; I sent Tom my tapes, the exact . . . He asked if I would send him the raw data, it's a horrible phrase, I mean an ugly, vicious scene. And any similarity is explained by the fact that we both described them from my tapes.

Audience: Whatever happened to Tom Wolfe? Where is he now?

HST: Oh, you know, he's alive and well in New York. He's turning into a royalist of sorts. He thinks that I'm turning into a brain-damaged geek. Tom's idea of a progressive decade is: Camel hair coat in every closet and Guccis on every other foot. But he didn't really agree that the country is into what I call the grim slide; I think it is. But he's a good person, good writer; he doesn't hurt anybody. He gets by without causing the kind of damage that Colson does, or Nixon. I don't think people understand just how rotten and wretched and sick the trade of being a writer is. I would prefer to never run into him again, but since I'm not into crime deeply enough that I . . . There's nothing else that seems worthwhile doing except maybe hunting sea snakes in the Great Barrier Reef, I'd prefer to do that. Yea, I'll write when I must write, it's either that or I'd have to go to work. I haven't had a job in about twenty-one years. You pay dues in some odd ways when you have to entirely make up for not working for three or four years. It catches up with you, it hurts, it's hard. That's what I'm doing now.

Audience: Do you make enough money handing out talks at colleges like this than you would going on writing anyway?

HST: I could. I could make ten thousand dollars a month doing this. But you have to take this kind of thing very seriously and work at it. Like Julian Bond,* I saw him on Tom Snyder† the other night, saying that three months

* Julian Bond is a civil rights leader from Georgia and the chairman of the National Association for the Advancement of Colored People.

† Tom Synder was the host of NBC's late night television talk show *Tomorrow* from 1973 to 1982.

out of the year he goes out for 90 straight days. He probably makes about five thousand dollars a day off of that. I figure, if I can make two thousand a month at it, that pays for my cocaine. We keep a separate account for this; it's a very frivolous account. I think the money could be spent going out the same way it came in . . . for no reason at all. You want to talk again?

Audience: Yes.

HST: Go ahead.

Audience: Have you ever met Trudeau?*

HST: I've never met Trudeau. Every time he gets the chance to meet me, he gets sick. It actually happens once a year at the Norml† parties, the annual Norml convention in Washington. He sells cartoons to raise money, and I'm his national strategist on the extremist side. I actually am on the advisory board, the national advisory board, which is eerie. After being a criminal for twenty years to look down and see your name on the bottom of the stationery of the advisory board with the ex-director of the DEA [Drug Enforcement Administration] and the same people that have been trying to lock you up for eighteen of the last twenty years . . . you're now on the board of directors with, it's wonderful. I'm not sure who's using who in that situation.

The only constant reaction I have to it is it's very strange to be a cartoon character. When you're trying to get around in the world and still make a living and get by, and if you don't believe it, try it sometime or even try to find someone to ask what it feels like . . . there ain't none around. It's a very strange thing to be. And it happens all over the world, in Perth, Australia, in Mystic, Connecticut, anywhere that goddamn comic strip constantly pops up. Waco, Texas. It robs me of a very valuable human part of my life, which is, the progress you assume. Some people want to grow up and be firemen and some want to be president. Nobody wants to grow up and be a cartoon character. And there's no precedent, nobody tells you how to handle it, I might someday.

Never mind, let's get off the subject.

Audience: Will you ever run for an office again, say in Aspen?

HST: I would say no, unconditionally, an honest no. This is the closest I've been to being insane, except for maybe last summer, when I actually con-

---

* Garry Trudeau is a cartoonist and creator of the *Doonesbury* comic strip. Thompson is characterized in the comic strip as "Uncle Duke."

† National Organization for the Reform of Marijuana Laws.

sidered running for the Senate for Colorado. I seriously thought about it, and I feel full of shame and grief when I look back on it and realize that I was serious, but only for a while. My friend Gary* talked me out of it, we flipped a coin.

Audience: How do you feel about Carter?

HST: The same way I always did. I haven't changed my mind about Carter. What prompted you to ask that? Do you have any specific? . . .

Audience: We just wanted to get your general feeling.

HST: No, I feel the same way ever since I first met the man.

Audience: What's your opinion of David Rockefeller and the Trilateral Commission?†

HST: Well, let's see, we know first they're rich people. And second, they're powerful people because they're rich. They're not necessarily smart. And to me not necessarily dangerous. But they're just smart enough to be embarrassed about the kind of stuff that would make them dangerous . . .

Audience: They first interviewed Carter to see if he was acceptable for the Trilateral Commission.

HST: He was acceptable before that. He was acceptable back in '72 or '73. Why shouldn't he be? You know, when they're grey and liberal . . . what the hell? Or be a conservative that comes out a fascist libertarian, excuse me.

Audience: Did you say fascist libertarian?

HST: Well I'm just trying out phrases. I don't get a chance to use microphones that often and hear what it sounds like at home like this.

Audience: No, no, no. More along the line of the Trilateral Commission in West Germany, Japan, and America, and they are just trying to maintain capitalism.

HST: It's like the Bilderberg society,** it's sort of these boogeymen, like the communists, in a sense, say in South America, or among low-level American diplomats or soldiers, who attribute massive and unnatural strength to

---

* Gary Hart is a former Democratic senator from Colorado. He served as senator from 1975 to 1987 and sought the Democratic presidential nomination in 1984 and 1988.

† The Trilateral Commission is a private, nongovernment group encouraging constructive foreign policy decisions and economic cooperation between North America, Western Europe, and Pacific Asia. Billionaire David Rockefeller founded the commission in July 1973.

** The Bilderberg Group is an exclusive and mysterious secret society of powerful economic and policy leaders from around the world. The group annually convenes in secret to discuss international policy.

the enemy, in order to justify their own existence. I don't really hate the Trilateral Commission, those bastards can barely keep their banks afloat, much less . . . And for all the presidential candidates last time . . . And President Carter was not the choice of the almost pure establishment kind of people, who are and run the Trilateral Commission.

Audience: Yea, only because he didn't know.

HST: Well, they had all their own people, and [the] incumbent president [Gerald Ford]: you know, a dingbat Republican with no brains at all. You see . . . I don't think it was in the interest of David Rockefeller and those people to risk electing Carter when they had the choice, if they were smart enough to get them elected, of almost any of their own people.

Audience: I have a question. You keep mentioning cocaine, but I read an article you had where you called it a watered-down drug for the masses.

HST: Oh that's a treacherous, useless fact.

Audience: What did you say again? Do you remember what you said, something about going to a party and . . .

HST: I'm serious, just because you read something in a magazine that said I said it, it has no goddamn relation in the world to whatever I said.

Audience: Do you remember what you'd said in that article?

HST: Well, at first you hadn't mentioned the magazine, where . . . What are you talking about? Why don't you get your facts down and we will talk about whatever it is you want to talk about.

Audience: Never mind. It's just that you had an opinion about cocaine, that you would like to go to a party with cocaine users and give them methedrine, acid and saltpeter.*

HST: Since you don't recall where you read that, there's no point in my even thinking about why I might have said it. That's one of the luxuries of living this way, you can say whatever you feel like saying.

Audience: I just wondered something. Why is your name still on the staff of the *Rolling Stone* magazine when I read an interview that you expressed displeasure with it.

HST: I don't know why I did explain. I don't understand these things, I've got some weird friends. It's kind of fun to play around with them. I never asked that my name be taken off, I didn't see any point in that. And for some

---

* Saltpeter is a nickname for potassium nitrate, one of the oxidizing chemical compounds used for producing black gunpowder.

reason, I never thought about asking about it. I'm a firm believer in making life as easy as possible. And why should I have my name taken off of there. If he wants to keep it on, that's easy.

Audience: Are you planning on writing for them again?

HST: Well, I wasn't but right now I am. I'm not sure how it happened or why. I haven't slept now for . . . this is the fourth night. And we spent probably all last night at the offices over in Central Park, in the Plaza fountain. Jesus Christ, that's such a bizarre shift. Yesterday was the first time I've been in the offices and it actually intimidated me, it was weird. So we had a kind of celebration last night; for the first time Wenner not only had access to the best kind of sound equipment, but he understands it. Or he somewhat understands it, because his office is full of really elegant machinery. And last night we wired it all together and really cranked it on with the old Rolling Stones albums.

Audience: You know I think it's a real honor to have your name on their magazine. (Inaudible talking in the audience) Wouldn't you want the better city to be the winners in the World Series like Los Angeles?

HST: I think having a favorite baseball team is like having a favorite oil company.

Audience: Are the rumors really true that they have Rin Tin Tin's brain in suspended animation in Fresno?*

HST: I think so, why shouldn't they, what the hell . . .

Audience: Last time I heard you speak, you were talking, very vehemently opposed to what *Rolling Stone* was doing now; now you're talking about writing for them again. What changed your mind?

HST: What makes you think there's a contradiction in that? Well I used to . . . [inaudible] I don't write anymore in journals for anybody.

Audience: Weren't you good friends with Ken Kesey back in the early '60s?

HST: Yeah, have you heard rumors that we were no longer friends? . . . I think Kesey has done probably the most honorable thing a writer can do in this country, which is head out and retire and just refuse to say any more than he wants to say. Unfortunately his family has a dairy farm and mine doesn't. So I have to work for my money. There are no trust funds, there's

---

* Rin Tin Tin is a famous German Shepherd dog used in radio, television, and film productions, including ABC's *The Adventures of Rin Tin Tin*, which aired from 1954 to 1959.

nothing . . . If I had fifteen hundred dairy cattle, believe me, you'd never hear my name again except on *Doonesbury.* But Kesey, that's what he does. He told me in '66 or '67 that he was never going to write again because he thought it was a bad way to communicate. At that time we were all nuts and this sounded like one more piece of talk. But he sort of carried out his threat. Still, there are very few American writers that have written two books as good as the *Cuckoo** and the *Great Notion*†; those are two very good books. If you can get two out of two like that, you deserve to have dairy cows in return.

Audience: Hunter, can you tell us if there's anybody left in Washington as evil as Nixon? And if so, are they in a position of responsibility?

HST: If there was, I wouldn't be here, man. I'd be in Washington.

Audience: Do you name names?

HST: No! That's what I mean, there's nobody. That's one of the problems in writing about politics now, or even political journalism, you gotta have real ugly bastards to crank you up. Who are the boogeymen now? I would say that when I flew out from Chicago I was sitting next to one of the great boogeymen of our time as far as I'm concerned. A truly evil person, Colson. When he was in the government. He was the one said, "Once you get them by the balls, an election might as well follow." That's what he had above his desk in the White House.

Audience: This is not political, and it may sound really naïve, but how do you escape structure the way you do? You're incredible; you're wonderful in your degeneracy.

HST: I have a feeling that I didn't hear enough . . . I heard enough to know it's a dangerous question but not enough to answer it. You have to tell me again.

Audience: I'm impressed by your ability to escape structure the way I feel like I'm a prisoner of it. It seems in some of your writings you've been able to do that, you express yourself that way. I hate to use the word degenerate; it's the only word I can think of.

(HST joking with girl answering question . . .)

HST: Why do you feel like, I'm paraphrasing you, since I can live outside structure, that I must be degenerate or insane . . . You have to write real fast and never sleep much.

---

* Ken Kesey's landmark novel, *One Flew Over the Cuckoo's Nest* (1962).

† Ken Kesey's novel, *Sometimes a Great Notion* (1964).

Audience: I was wondering when and how you met Ralph Steadman, and also to what extent do you believe his pictures portray your views, do you feel they portray them accurately?

HST: I would generally endorse almost any artistic expression Ralph made. He was probably one of the most completely articulate people I've ever met and one of the best people in terms of his own head and his life. He does better with his pens and his paper than I do with a typewriter. Steadman, they should make more like him.

Audience: How did you meet him?

HST: It was a total accident; I was actually, when Pat Oliphant was here as a cartoonist for the *Post,* here in whatever this town is down here . . . When I decided that I should go cover the Kentucky Derby, it was all back to the land of my youth, that sort of thing, and dig up one more bone. I called Pat at night and said, "Look I don't want to work with photographers" and I wanted Pat, I knew he was a good artist, and at that time Pat was the best and closest person I could get. But he had it in his contract that he couldn't take outside assignments, and it was Warren Hinckel, who was the editor of *Scanlan's,* he had been the editor of *Ramparts* for a few years. He's run about seven magazines into the ground, and he's still the best editor to work for. As long as you don't have to pay him. But Hinckel got Steadman, well, that's one of my favorite developments in the story. He said, "I know a guy in England who is very good." Nobody had ever heard of him, including me, and there was really no choice, I just had to accept Hinckel's judgment, and he sent him to Louisville to meet me at some weird hotel on the outskirts of town. That's one of the best presents I ever had; it was a really a nice accident. He was kind of underground, not notorious but known in England at that time. Now he's almost as respectable as Oliphant is.

Audience: Where do you want to be when you're fifty years old?

HST: Down with the maggots, with the sharks. If I ever got to be fifty years old, I'd be so confused I'd probably have to go into EST or something. To have lived this long has seriously disoriented me.

Audience: What do you mean by Gonzo? What does Gonzo mean?

HST: Most people like you ask me questions like that in shock. I don't know, I really don't know. It was a good word that I liked at the time and it separated me from, say, the new journalist or . . . I didn't feel I was a part of any group or type of journalist and Gonzo was a good word. I could have called myself a sand nigger at the time you know.

Audience: What does that mean?

HST: Nothing, nothing at all. Well it means what I do, that's what I gather from people who've tried to do it. But it's the same reason I always insist on having my own weird corner, like National Affairs desk, or Global Affairs desk, or Foreign Manager; it's a perversity.

Audience: When Ken Kesey said that he thought the novel was not a good way to communicate, was that just an offhand remark, or did he think there was a better way?

HST: Apparently he was right because he hasn't written another one since then, and he's obviously capable of doing it. There's some people we have to take at face value; Kesey's one of them.

Audience: Does that mean that he's just given up trying to communicate or that he's trying in a different way?

HST: Umm, that's a heavy judgment. Kesey has appeared to have worked out a life for himself which is many jumps ahead of what I've worked out. I'm still . . . I think he's come to some kind of adjustment in his own world that I haven't. So that's why I said he's probably ahead of me. Just because he's quiet doesn't mean that he wants to talk. A lot of times it's a lot more fun to be quiet.

Audience: You said you liked to make life as easy as possible and you also said that for the past 18 or 20 years you've avoided going into jail. I was wondering if you could give any of us peons out here on how to avoid that unfortunate circumstance, you know, one or two things we could jot down on the back of our driver's license or something?

HST: That would be very dangerous to do that. Sure as hell whatever I told you would not work for you next time you tried to use it . . . Well, I could . . . There's no such thing as paranoia, but the menace is really worse than what people tell you it is, even your most paranoid friends. And I just never assume that anybody around me is anything but a potential menace. That goes for a lot of my best friends. Those people I know, my friends that have been busted, have been busted for that reason, was that they just got dumb about what they were doing. The minute I say that, I'll get busted tomorrow, probably in Steamboat Springs.

Audience: . . . Is your 50,000 dollar offer for Idi Amin's* head on a silver platter still in effect?

---

* Idi Amin Dada was a military dictator and president of Uganda from 1971 to 1979.

HST: That's a kind of thing to get me into journalism. I could get involved in a project like that, if you could combine it with journalism. I could get paid for the story and also paid for the head. But, I say that now and that is one more strike against me when I go out of the country. For the same money I'd actually prefer to go after Idi Amin's head than I would having to suffer writing another book.

Audience: I guess it's a lot easier to stay out of jail if we all had a three-hundred-dollar-an-hour lawyer around us all the time.

HST: Not if he's dead, which he is.

Audience: Oh excuse me. You mentioned earlier "the great American slide" and I'm wondering what you meant by that? America being in a slide . . . if you could be more specific.

HST: I think this was a nice idea we had in this country and a nice landscape to experiment with. But I think there comes a time in almost any experimentation or idea, where you have to evaluate it, maybe our time has come. In the context of the real world, not just the American world but all around, we haven't done too well. We are not a very good advertisement for the idea we represented.

Audience: Do you think there's a hope or are you pessimistic for us coming out of this slide or what?

HST: No. If you lose one wheel of the car, you might be able to get to the side of the road, and some freaks can make it on two, but if you lose three, man, you're in serious trouble. I think we've lost three.

Audience: So we might as well go out and snort as much coke as we can, right?

HST: I didn't say that.

Audience: Well it would be a good way to go down.

HST: Well shit, do you have any coke?

Audience: Inaudible question.

HST: When McGovern was beaten in '72 worse than any losing candidate since whoever first ran against George Washington. It's getting more and more painful for a lot of people to remember who beat him. His name was Richard Milhous Nixon, and he was a fucking rotten bastard and a dishonest pagan, and he got not nearly enough what he should've gotten. You talk about losing battles and degrading the system, nobody has done more to discredit the idea that democracy can work and that decent people can be elected and run it than Richard Nixon. He shamed us all. But not so much as that 62 percent of people in the country who did vote for him in '72. And those bastards have it on their consciences and they should.

Audience: It sounded disconcerting to hear you say that, with the removal of President Nixon, you feel that a lot of the big evil has been removed form Washington and you feel the same way about Carter . . .

HST: I didn't say that now, you people have a tendency here to kind of wander.

Audience: OK, say you feel the same way about Carter, which you did say and I believe the title of the *Rolling Stone* article was an endorsement with fear and loathing but endorsement.

HST: All that proves is that when a 12-point headline on the cover is worth 20,000 words inside . . .

Audience: I'm saying that shouldn't you be doing something more? It's fine that you've got a little circle of friends that, I'm sure, supply you with the best drugs possible, but for the person on the street getting arrested and put in jail.

HST: Calm down. You're getting excited.

Audience: Well it's fine for a national figure. But don't you feel you should be endorsing a candidate who, instead of . . . having a lot of people killed . . . that you should be endorsing somebody who [inaudible] in psychedelics.

HST: Pick one of your complaints.

Audience: I'm just saying that, instead of saying you're going along with Carter, it's fine with his policies against the big oil companies but shouldn't you be moving towards where everyone could use the drugs that you obviously have got so much out of?

HST: You're just a natural fool. At first you set yourself up for . . . I can't answer questions like that.

Audience: I just wondered if there was any substance behind the "have a good time, let's all get high"? It only gets us so far.

HST: Why are you people looking to me for a justification for what you want to do, anyway? Why don't you just go ahead and do it? My not endorsing that is a matter of self-defensive politics. No, I wouldn't tell anybody to go out and get into drugs or madness. But if you can handle it, it's a nice way to go sometimes.

Audience: You made a statement in your interview in *New Times* magazine that without the use of drugs, you would have the mind of a forty-year-old accountant. Do you really believe that and do you suggest it?

HST: Did I say that? Without the use of drugs I might be working for *Time* magazine perhaps, or the *New York Times.*

Audience: If you didn't say that then I have another question . . .

HST: Why do you believe everything you read in magazines, you must be crazy.

Audience: I was asking you, I don't believe it, that's why I came, to ask you.

HST: I don't know if I said that, it's possible but if I was wrong . . . I know what direction you're getting at. The part of the question was, What effect have these drugs had on your life? These kind of questions people are always asking me. And it's obvious, you can't maintain a total duality of lifestyles that would allow you to work as the managing editor of, let's say, *Ithaca Daily News* and also be an acid freak . . . somebody who steals airplanes at nights and zooms over Pittsburgh and comes home to his wife. No, if you're into drugs and you try to maintain a functioning role in society, yeah, they're going to be a factor. If only because people will make them a factor.

Audience: One more question. They have a picture of you passing a sobriety test by flipping your glasses off the back of your head and catching them. Can you really do that?

HST: Only under extreme pressure. Which I did then. I did that and I beat the CHP* twice in four nights. Both times I really should have been locked up. No, I shouldn't have, the evidence suggests I was as harmless as I claimed to be. I didn't hit anybody, I caused no trouble, but I was extremely drunk.

Audience: In 1977 we came down. Given your actions and your attitude as demonstrated here and reported in the media, I got one question. OK, to preface it: What I am talking about primarily is the way you acted when you first met Carter. You were drunk, you were loud, you were all those things.

HST: I was the same way I am now.

Audience: Exactly . . . How do you maintain your credibility and your contacts with people like Ted Kennedy, who introduced you to Carter, who was your ticket to Carter; how do you maintain your contacts with those people that you seem to have so much fun putting down, you seem to have so much fun taking apart?

---

* California Highway Patrol.

HST: They like me. That's an honest answer, I don't know. That is a fact, that Carter worries about me. He's told people that he thinks I'm a bad advertisement for the human race. But he thinks I'm salvageable. People all looked at my life and felt that way, that if I could just be brought to see that I would be different; but they were just dumb. I saw the light.

Audience: If I were to grant you three wishes right now, what would they be?

HST: One of them would be we would have to end this thing, quickly. That's not really a wish, I can do that. Let's see, Jesus. Someone says "dairy cows." Well, if you think of it they'd be a lot of trouble, dairy cows. I don't think we can have the mobility and whatever internal it'd take to just get into a degenerate lifestyle. I don't think . . . I'd get into a sort of white trash . . . trip just to make a fool of myself and not have to worry it will show up in *Time* magazine the next week.

Audience: You've got two more.

HST: Two more, that's it. Some sleep right now. I'd like to have . . . Shit I'm trying. I don't work for the Prison Fellowship Committee.* I wish I could answer your question. Think about that.

Audience: I'd like to know if that chain you have has any mystical significance to you, and I'd also like to know if you think fascism is doing well in America today.

HST: Better than ever. Fascism always does pretty well when people get lazy and pissed off. Almost any solution you come to when you figure, "Oh, fuck I'm tired of that . . . let's kill those bastards." Anytime things get the best of you, that's a natural drift into a fascistic kind of solution. So in a country where there are no solutions and many problems, I think it has a tendency to adopt fascistic solutions.

Audience: What would you do if you were 25?

HST: Just what I'm doing now except I wouldn't be getting paid for it . . . I was broke and not quite sane. I'm still broke and not quite sane, but the former has changed somehow . . . I was rejected and ejected, it's the only . . .

Audience: I just decided maybe I would ask you, is reality a pickle, a prune, or a 3.2 joke?

HST: That's the question I've been waiting for all night. What do you think?

---

* Prison Fellowship Ministries, founded by Charles Coloson.

Audience: Hunter, you seem to be kind of a basic hedonist like most of us. I imagine, is that a true statement to begin with?

HST: Well you said it seems that way and I would just leave it that way.

Audience: OK, just to get on with my last two-part question, I would like to know what you thought of the Grateful Dead, and what are six of your favorite things to do?

HST: The Grateful Dead has been for a long time one of my favorite bands and . . . Favorite things to do, I like to look at my watch, see to me it's 12 o'clock, that's what my watch says.

Commonwealth Times (Richmond, Virginia)—November 28, 1978

The Hunter Thompson Saga

BY S. M. JACKSON

PART I—DR. GONZO AND THE TRAVELING FLIM-FLAM BAND

Hunter S. Thompson, alias Dr. Gonzo, the mad wizard of baroque journalism, has finally been lured into the city of Richmond. He has not come, fair children, out of love for Virginia, nor from any altruistic concern for his fellow man; he has come dancing to the tune of $1,500—and if you cannot deal with that simple fact, then too bad for you. For as Hunter Thompson makes abundantly clear, idealism is a fool's profession when money is the only game in town.

And so he arrives, nestled in the back of a forty-foot Winnebago—cloistered to the rear like a dutiful nun while Nick the Creep wheels and deals, hunkered down over the steering column—redolent eyes flashing fire.

PART II—THE BANSHEE COMES TO RICHMOND AND SCREAMS NEVERMORE

General applause and whistles from crowd. He moves across the stage like a man on wooden legs, glances at the audience, then finds his chair and sits down. He has been drinking heavily all day, and God only knows how many hard drugs are in his system. But despite everything, he continues to function.

HST: Hello. Test. Let's see—it takes me a few minutes to calm down—in particular I've never done one of these things in daylight. And it seems unreal. And, well, it is—the whole thing is unreal. Yeah, you get out of some giant bus with strange windows, and see yourself in the comic strips, and coming here—and it's hard to really decide what you're doing. I have to catch a plane to L.A. and be at the Playboy Mansion in L.A. at 8:00. Yeah, life has become very strange. And maybe we should just talk about it. (Thompson looks to his left where a young student with long hair sits, obviously uncomfortable and confused.) Do you have any idea what we're going to do? (Scattered laughter from audience)

Now it's going to take me a few minutes to settle down. Or, I maybe never settle down. I may run completely amok, and begin to bleed from the mouth and gums—piss all over myself and have to be taken off. But that's the risk you run when you do public. (Light chuckles from crowd)

One of these days it'll probably happen. But we should have some sort of general attack at least, some rationale for being here—outside the fact that it's a wet and ugly day outside. What shall we talk about? Treachery? (Thompson glances at person on his left, who is sort of acting moderator for the occasion.)

Didn't you have a question . . . I could sit here and wander awhile. Or we could talk about herpes, or mad dogs—peacocks. But, would you . . .

Moderator: OK.

HST: I think we should have a formal start here so we have some sense outside—the only sense of reality we have right now is this blazing light on me, which I have done everything possible to cut down but I can't. So, let's focus on something here.

Moderator: OK. I'll open with a question, and after Dr. Thompson responds, if anyone else has a question, just feel free to ask. (Formal interrogation begins.)

You have said that great writers should be larger than life—and you've talked of the psychology of "edge work." In one of your books, you mentioned your own experience of going "over the high side" of a curve. You have written of the Hell's Angels and how they live on the thin edge of mortality, something Ken Kesey referred to as "Guts Balls." You seem to have lived in this manner all your life. Why do you believe in "guts-balls"; and does it get harder to play this game as you get older and more financially secure?

HST: No, it gets easier. It gets easier because I never figured that I'd last this long anyway. And "guts-balls" is really an ancient football expression. And I think it dates back to probably "let's win this one for the Gip." I sold a novel called "Guts-balls," which I never wrote. It's getting much more lucrative for me to sell ideas than it is to sell writing. That may say something about me or the market, I'm not sure. I'm not sure I like it, or if it's just that I've lived that way all my life. I mean, well there are different ways to do it. I thought I was fairly close to the state of the art until I talked to Muhammad Ali for awhile, and this was after he beat [Leon] Spinks the last time. That maniac was talking about losing the fight—losing the title again—just so he can win it the fourth time. Now, he's already pulled off a miracle. That is edge-work. That is almost a generic commitment to edge-work that will leave him battered, and bleeding, and wondering why the fuck he was ever there in the first place. He should have quit. But a man that crazy who would go out and lose a title and then win it again for the fourth time, after being the first man in history to do it for the third . . . that is edge-work. It's a commitment. And it's fun if you can get away with it. It's probably a better way to live than any other way I've lived. I was once committed to a life of crime . . . but then I found Jesus.

(General laughter and carrying on, etc., from audience)

Actually, I found jail for about 30 days. And it's interesting, but I don't want to go back. And I haven't [knocks on wood] been back. It's a hard thing to talk about. I seem to be advocating a kind of life that only one person in a thousand could probably live though, and then by luck. So, it's hard to talk about it without calling it almost an insane way to live, which it probably is.

But there must be something to it or I wouldn't be paid to sit here and answer questions about it. And I never did understand that either—to find myself in Richmond on a rainy afternoon explaining why I don't have any real sense for what, for money. It's just an odd way to live. I'm adjusting slowly. But I planned to die at the age of 27, and I've been confused ever since. And certainly when you think about being an American writer, and being successful, what it means opening up a paper anywhere from Perth, Australia, to somewhere in Finland and seeing yourself in the comic strips—there is no precedent for that. It may be a good thing. I have the feeling that it's sort of like an icebreaker wandering through fields that someone else will eventually make sense of.

And I only went into it because I can't do anything else. I'm too old to learn, and I make too much money to quit. I'd rather fight than change right now. So I'm stuck with it and so are you, for the moment. So, do we have any questions? Maybe some hostile and aggressive questions—something challenging almost everything I stand for, believe in or said.

Audience: What's your favorite color?

HST: My favorite color is puce.

Audience: Do you have any idea what the eighties might have in store for us?

HST: For you . . . or for me? (Big laugh from the crowd)

I would say, seriously, probably a general and overall prevailing condition of either war or imminent war and certain disaster following that, which will begin with a first-year recession, then depression, then several disastrous small wars, and then the king-hell bitch war that we've all been waiting for—it'll happen in Africa. I'm not sure we'll ever make it to the year 2000 and I'm not sure we should. I don't think we deserve to. But I think that, yeah, the eighties will hold massive and destructive war for us which is really our destiny, to be a very short-lived warrior state, and the only great piece of terrain in the world which nobody can afford to lose is Africa. There are a lot of people, at least half the people right now in the government, who figure we can afford to lose anything else, even a quarter of the side of some destroyer cruising the North Sea, so to lose Africa is out of the question. We must fight for Africa, and you know what is going to happen when we do that, don't you? No? What do you think? What would you guess?

Audience: California falls into the sea!

HST: That's guesswork, Africa is certain.

Audience: Civil war!

HST: In this country?

Audience: Yeah.

HST: Where you from? Think about civil war, the South shall-rise-again mentality. If you want it you'll have to battle over New York City or Boston.

Audience: You're just afraid.

HST: Afraid?

Audience: Tired.

HST: I'm not afraid. Goddamn it. I wouldn't get up . . . hold up your hand.

I just want to see—have a sense I'm talking to a moron. What do you think?

Audience: What do I think? You can't fight 'em.

HST: No, I'm curious. I really have come out of a completely different furnace than most of you people.

Audience: Industrial confusion.

HST: In what sense? What is going to happen is the labor force is going to shrink drastically and if we last ninety more years, the unions will run the country because we'll be shrinking in the amount of skilled workers . . . That's pretty broad, and that's pretty presumptuous. But I think you're probably right in a very rough, abstract way. One thing is, there's nothing that menacing and tangible to grab right now. I can recall almost all though the sixties, I'd wake up every morning in a black rage every time I saw a newspaper, and spending sometimes half the nights either throwing rats at things or running from cops, or sending telegrams to the White House threatening to slit McNamara's throat.* There was a sense, and I don't think it was just me in the sixties—not only was it very important to be right and to react, because there wasn't much time if you didn't react—but there was also a sense of being right.

If one and one made two, and you sensed that, and the president said one and one made three, then he was wrong. Now, we know better, don't we? That was a very off and I think a very rare time of only-once-in-every-generation to go for five or six years thinking that we really were the wave of the future, and that all we had to do was act in order to make it so. I think it was a very important illusion, and without it life sure has been and will be a lot duller. It was also a time when you had to react to get any sense of politics, when every time you turned around, the candidate you were counting on to save the world had his head blown off right in front of you. I'm not sure who would react right now if Carter was shot.

(Scattered applause)

I like Carter—but there's not that sense of Armageddon that we had almost every day in the sixties. You had just a little bit of rest before someone else was killed. And 1968 was a year, looking back on it now, that I'm sure it'll be five hundred years before another thing like that comes. It was like a war that lasted 365 days. But I think that it was the Vietnam War and the draft. By the way, I'm for reinstituting the draft, just in case anyone here wants to think about that.

Audience: Well, there's stuff going on right now that a lot of people would probably get crazy about.

HST: Well, what bothers you? What bothers you enough to—

Audience: Disco!

(Complete roar of approval—applause, cheering, wildness, etc. This remark obviously strikes the common spiritual denominator of the audience.)

---

* Robert McNamara served as secretary of defense during Vietnam War for the Kennedy and Johnson administrations.

HST: That's easy! That's like being bothered by herpes, or something. If disco bothers you, you can settle all your scores in one night. I'm not going to tell you how—and if you did it, I'd be indicted for some sort of conspiracy. But people have settled their scores with horrors in very unusual ways—usually involving gasoline. (Increased laughter)

I wouldn't advocate the burning of discos, but at least we got herpes and disco—but really, that is small. What would happen to you if you solved all your disco problems? It would take you about three days. What after that? Seriously.

Audience: When was the last time you tripped?

HST: I'm under the influence of LSD right now and have been for about three days. (Sympathetic applause, cheers)

I've learned to handle it. I think drugs are good for me, and, I say me—I don't mean that for most of you. I've found over a period of years that most people are dangerous to take acid with.

Audience: Dr. Thompson, on your travels with the Carter campaign, did you ever meet Peter Bourne,* and if so—did he ever write you a prescription?

HST: Dr. Bourne? You mean, Pete? No. Pete never wrote me a prescription. I never asked him for one. I never really trusted good ol' Pete like the others did. He was suppose to be our link with the White House and, you know, almost a fifth column—and then that freak goes in and does everything but write lude scripts for the secretary and also for Hamilton† [Jordan, Carter's chief of staff]—nothing should be given to Hamilton, even coffee. He's one of those people who should be kept on a diet of soup and speed. No, Bourne just causes a lot of trouble. He's set back marijuana reform legislation at least two years.

Hello? Is Peter up there? He's probably up there with a thirty-odd-six sighting down on me. No, we trusted the White House to be rational about marijuana, instead they hit us with that Paraquat policy. And Bourne, he's not a bad guy—a fool, but not a bad person—went along with it.

---

* Dr. Peter Bourne served as President Jimmy Carter's deputy campaign director and Special Assistant to the President for Health Issues. In 1978, Bourne was forced to resign after writing a fraudulent sleeping pill prescription for a White House aide. Bourne was later accused of using cocaine at a party hosted by the National Organization for the Reform of Marijuana Laws (NORML).

† Hamilton Jordan was President Jimmy Carter's campaign adviser and chief of staff.

Audience: Didn't Nixon decide Paraquat policy* before Carter in the war on drugs?

HST: Bourne worked for Nixon before he worked for Carter. Bourne tried to get me to work on a National Drug Abuse Council in about 1973 or '4. And here's a letter from the White House while he even worked for Nixon. And can you believe it said they needed input from unusual sources, or something like that? And I wouldn't go near that thing for a thousand dollars a day. Imagine, working for Nixon. Pat Buchanan said that the reason I—he's one of Nixon's primary speech writers for most of his political life—said that the reason I called the president a thieving pig-fucker and a lying swine and all that, was that I had a character defect. And that is possibly true, but I have to wonder how you explain what is wrong with a man who wrote speeches for Nixon for 10 years. And what the hell do you see when you look in the mirror in the morning. So, I can live with a character defect—I couldn't live with that. But Richard Nixon will be back, hopefully. And as long as that possibility exists, my work is not finished, and I can look forward to . . .

Audience: In *1984,* Winston Smith says that if two plus two equals four, then all else follows. You made a similar comment just a few minutes ago. Do you believe, in fact, that 1984 is already here, and that the entire 1960s were just a passing fantasy of Jimmy Carter's, a fabrication, e.g., Rockefeller's home plan?

HST: You mean the sixties was a, just a last great crash of illusion before this case of reality has come down to us?

Audience: No, they were just a passing fancy to please the masses.

HST: Last charge of the light brigade sort of thing: A doomed, but noble purveyor of chaos.

Audience: You just made that statement . . .

HST: I'm just trying to agree with you in some way. Are you asking a question or are we trying to define the sixties?

Audience: No. I asked you . . . I'm trying to define the 1984 of George Orwell. You just made . . .

HST: I think it was Mao Tse-tung who said all political power grows out of the barrel of a gun. And whoever owns that in 1984, if he says that two and two equal five, it will equal five.

Audience: What do you think of the Sex Pistols?

---

* "Paraquat Policy" refers to a drug enforcement method of eradicating cannabis plants by using a broad-leaf paraquat weed herbicide to destroy the plant.

HST: Uh, not much. (A sudden, one might say tremendous, response)

Audience: Did anything important happen politically in the last elections in November?

HST: You mean last week's? For me it did, yeah. I'm into local politics. We took on John Denver and a fascist sheriff in Aspen and beat them. But I think few candidates being beaten who probably deserved to anyway was to set up a really serious dumb nervous tension concerning 1980 because no one knows what's going to happen.

Audience: Do you think the Youth International Party, the Yippies, have any future, any role to play in our political protest?

HST: No.

Audience: Do you think the post-Watergate morality is just a façade and that you're just exploiting it, or are you just waiting around for something to happen again to someone and are you just sitting on the can?

HST: If I were exploiting anything at all, what would it have to do with the post-Watergate mentality?

Audience: Say that again!

HST: If I were guilty of exploiting or innocent, or could be proud of exploiting some things. But what does what I'm doing have to do with the post-Watergate mentality?

Audience: In that you helped shape the post-Watergate mentality by being the first to criticize the Nixon administration.

HST: Well. OK. At the time they called me a dumb fool and said I should leave the country or be locked up.

Audience: Tell that to your audience . . . that's your whole bag. You like to cut your own cake, I've seen you before.

HST: Well, my whole bag is being right. And if I'd been wrong about what I wrote in 1972, I wouldn't be either here or I wouldn't have written much after that.

Audience: You don't think there are things worth writing about?

HST: No. I have retired from that kind of journalism. I don't see how I can take it much further. I'm not retired from politics because I think, I know, it's a weapon I can use in self-defense. Journalism is, I think, was in a sense, a fad. So much beastly reality was laid on you every day in the newspapers and in the newscasts in the sixties . . .

Audience: Is your "doctor" a fad? Does that mean anything to you anymore?

HST: Gonder?

Audience: You are a doctor of journalism, is that right?

HST: A doctor of divinity. (Scattered laughter with a pervading sense of euphoria)

Audience: That's not what I understood before.

HST: Well, you get your facts, or at least your rumors, straight before you argue. I'll argue with you all you want, but it's really kind of hard to argue with somebody whose mind is wandering. Really, I'd love to know what, if I were guilty of criminal fraud, it would have to do with the post-Watergate mentality, which I assume you identify with in some way.

Audience: I just think that you're sitting back on your reputation, and just gathering the laurels.

HST: That could be, that could be. And if that's gathering laurels, I wish to hell it would happen to you some day, and you'll figure out—you'll never say that kind of thing again.

Audience: Are you working on a project now, and is it going to be on Gonzo-type journalism, or is it going to be straight fiction or fantasy, whatever?

HST: I'm working on two films now. One that's based on my life—and this is how strange things have become—which I imagine I'll end up writing a screenplay for. And, plus, I'm putting out a collection of my work to press. I feel like I'm almost embarrassed to be in the way of the myth. I think a lot of people would be much happier—everybody from Trudeau to my publisher, all my lawyers and probably my family too—if I were just to blow up in a puff of smoke some day, 'cause it is hard to walk around and have this legend following you. It's impossible for me to work at press conferences. I can't work with the normal journalists. This notoriety has gotten out of hand. And sure, there are some benefits to it, but there are tremendous disadvantages. One of them is that there's no precedent for it. I have to be very careful how I handle it. And now my judgment is that I should stop journalism.

I never understood what Hemingway meant when he said that journalism was good for a writer as long as he knew when to quit. Now I do. I think I have taken journalism way past what most people who get into it on an individual basis could have or would have taken it. And, there's not that much room. For good journalism, you need bizarre reality, and our reality has become very mundane right now.

Audience: Do you think that the street use of acid is on the increase in our society?

HST: Just hold your hand up so I can get a sense of . . . yeah, OK. Oh, it's you again. (Medium-brewed laughter)

Audience: Do you think the use of acid is on the increase in general in the United States today, and do you think the clandestine factor in the use of LSD is perhaps on the increase too?

HST: No, I think that LSD has become almost a connoisseur's drug now. Almost all psychedelics have become so out of style that they're not economic to make anymore. Really brutal downers now are what's in style. Yeah, like PCP, where you get down and fall. I've eaten PCP and I would not recommend it at all to anybody. It's a different kind of drug; it's one that takes you away from reality instead of heightening it.

Audience: Pig tranquilizers!

HST: Ah, it's a large animal tranq, yeah. Pig, if you want to call it that. Kytomine is a nice one. It's for, let's see, subhuman primates and small cats. If you're going to get into animal tranqs, it's probably better to get kytomine than it is to get PCP. You can probably run right through a Plymouth with a head full of PCP.

(Several questions are asked, overlapping one another in a blur of sound.)

Hang on for a minute. We have a man here who's fought for a mike. Charles Manson is going up for parole today just in case you . . . I wondered why you didn't want to complain about the news. I guess the papers are not down here yet. OK.

Audience: With party platforms between the Democrats and Republicans being pretty much the same thing—nebulous, politics in America seems to be sliding toward individuals, and not parties—such as, taking a party for convenience and not for the party's policy, just for elections. What do you think will be the outcome of this trend?

HST: Well, I think it's both inevitable and almost meaningless. Well, you see what the fate of someone like Michael Dukakis of Massachusetts* who rode that horse as fast as he could and has got suddenly knocked off for reasons as puzzling as the ones that put him where he was in the first place. That could happen to Jerry Brown. When there are no major ideological wars

* Michael Dukakis is the former Democratic governor of Massachusetts. He was the Democratic nominee for president in 1988.

going, it's much safer to run the politics on personality. And right now, it's very dangerous when personality becomes the governing factor of the failure or success of a politician's career.

Audience: Is Carter guilty of that?

HST: Yeah, I think much more so than I expected him to be. I thought Carter would take care of business just because I knew he was such an egomaniac that I figured he cannot afford to fail in his own mind.

Audience: Is he a Jesus freak as much as he pretends to be?

HST: That worries me, you know, because it just occurred to me the other day. I guess I was listening to some weird radio broadcast. Eighteen people had jumped off a balcony in Salt Lake City; those that survived the fall were eaten by bystanders, or something like that. And somebody said, "That's God's will"*—and it suddenly occurred to me that, my God, Carter may think that. And if there is a logic that's undeniable that a person believes very firmly—you know, a born-again Christian who believes that God controls everything for the greater good, then whatever happens is God's will. Well, that's a very spooky way of looking at the president—to think if he looks up at night, sees a giant rocket shooting overhead and heading for St. Louis, then he'll just go back to bed, and read the Bible in Spanish and figure it's God's will.

(Murmur of assent)

I don't think we should talk about that too much. Because the logic is there. I'm not sure of what Carter would say if he were asked to explain that. There's no way you can get around the fact that whatever happens is God's will, if you really believe that sort of thing.

Audience: You mentioned seeing yourself in the comic strips a lot. What do you really think of Trudeau and his kind of portrayal?

HST: I really don't know what the hell to think about it.

Audience: Have you ever met him?

HST: No. I've never run into him, never talked to him, never seen him.

Audience: Do you want to?

HST: Not particularly, because if I do I will set him on fire, just . . . (Big laugh)

---

* In 1978, Utah cult-leader Immanuel David told his followers he was God and proceeded to commit suicide. Three days later, his wife, Rachel, forced or threw her seven children from the eleventh-story balcony of a hotel in downtown Salt Lake City before jumping herself. The tiny cult defended the murder-suicides and remains intact today.

I really don't know what to think of it—it's . . . every once in a while it pisses me off; at first it baffled me. Every once in a while it amuses me. I will figure it out sooner or later, and, he's a very short person anyway. He may as well walk on his knees as his feet. So I'll just see about that when I talk to him. Maybe he has a good reason for it. I don't know what. But it really is a bad thing to have to cope with.

Audience: What do you think the world situation would be if Kennedy hadn't been assassinated?

HST: Which Kennedy?

Audience: John F. Kennedy.

HST: John Kennedy . . . different. No, I'm sorry—I don't mean to be flip there. I think that was the first shock at the time to the sixties generation that maybe things weren't going the way we thought they were, and yet—but when Kennedy beat Nixon in '60, it was a serious landmark in politics. And there was a feeling for several years, even things like the Peace Corps—apart from Kennedy's dealing with the Congress, he dealt really well with the people, and there was the feeling that he really was going to do something, and it was kind of nice to be an American. I think since then, that feeling has been diluted and dissipated and pretty rightfully put where it belongs. It's no longer an honorable profession to be an American.

Audience: In the Rolling Stone's tenth anniversary issue, you wrote an article entitled "The Banshee Screams for Buffalo Meat."* Whatever happened to Oscar Zeta Acosta, and can you tell us about any recent Brown Buffalo sightings?

HST: I think I can honestly tell you that Oscar was killed. He's dead.

Audience: From the cigarette boat?

HST: No. From a .45 slug in the stomach on a different coast.

Audience: I'm sorry to hear that.

HST: He was shot in the stomach in the Pacific rather than whatever that alleged story was. No one knows exactly for sure, or can say or will say what happened. I lose about two friends a year now, but Oscar was very special. And I think I can say, and I'm sorry to say it, but I think he's been killed. Matter of fact, I've been told that by people I would bet on.

Audience: By whom?

---

* Hunter S. Thompson, "The Banshee Screams for Buffalo Meat: Fear and Loathing in the Graveyard of the Weird," *Rolling Stone* #254, December 15, 1977.

HST: Oscar pissed a lot of people off. He never passed an opportunity to do it very quickly and in any circumstance. In his case, he was running drugs. And it's not a good thing to piss off four people in the middle of the Pacific if they're armed and you're not, and they can put you overboard, which they did. That's the kind of life he lived. He would not want to have died in an old age home. I'm not sure he would want to die from a bullet in the stomach, being kicked off a boat off of Mazatlan, eaten by sharks—but uh, those things happen pretty fast. I'm sorry to say—yeah, he's dead.

Audience: Dr. Thompson, do you yourself feel you're in danger from some kind of threat because you've revealed many problems in the system like "Strange Rumblings in Aztlan"* and later in "The Banshee Screams for Buffalo Meat" you were threatened?

HST: I'm always threatened, continually. Yeah, but I don't see what good it would accomplish by getting rid of me, but I'm not sure there aren't people who wouldn't feel better if I were cut in half or my head cut off or worse. Yeah, I think I would probably be nervous if I didn't feel that sense of menace; I think unless you stir something up somewhere, there's either something very suspicious about you or you're not doing your job. If everyone agreed with me or liked me I'd be very worried.

Audience: Dr. Thompson, what do you think of the media kind of manure where the Bee Gees are on the front of every cover?

HST: That's usually just a result of a very high-powered PR effort. When you happen to see Lily Tomlin† on the cover of *Time* or *Newsweek* at the same time or Bruce Springsteen, that's no accident, for the writers from *Time* or *Newsweek* did not all wake up one morning at four as some strange moonchild passed by the window, and recognized Bruce Springsteen as a great genius. It was because those things are organized and paid for very lavishly. In dull times—that's why *People* magazine is such a great hit—it tells you something when *New Times* folds and *People* magazine becomes a great hit or the *New York Times* starts a gossip magazine. So it doesn't really tell you anything but that there's a lot of really good PR people in this country. And with the right kind of handling just about anybody can get on the cover of *Time.* It takes a little more work to get on the cover of *Newsweek;* you have to have a

---

* Hunter S. Thompson, "Strange Rumblings in Aztlan," *Rolling Stone* #81, April 29, 1971.

† Lily Tomlin is an American actress and comedian who received an Academy Award nomination for her role in the Robert Altman film *Nashville.*

gimmick of some sort. I don't really know. It happened so fast, and there was no reason for it.

Audience: Why did *New Times* fold? There was no going-downhill sign about it.

HST: You know it was sold to one of those giant corporations, like MCA or something, about a year ago. And when they sold it, I think [George A.] Hirsch and [Jonathan Z.] Larsen, who started the magazine, promised bigger and better things. There was no reason at all to my knowledge for it to fold. I see the results of poor editing, and forget about that, it was one of the best political magazines in the country. I was very disappointed and shocked to see it fold. I imagine it was corporate economics—that's my guess.

Audience: You don't think they could have kept it going, though?

HST: Oh, sure they could have.

Audience: Well, that seems really stupid if . . .

HST: In any event, it was sold to one of those multinational things about a year ago. I'm not even sure who owned it—it wasn't the original people.

Audience: Do you think anybody will be able to replace it, you know—come up with something better along those same lines?

HST: Possibly. Good magazines seem to spring up in response to situations. And right now we don't have any situations that really generate the publishing of a daily newspaper, much less a new magazine. Perhaps it just made sense to fold *New Times.* Maybe the editors were more into its reality than the readers were. But it was a very good political magazine, and I'm sorry to see it go.

Audience: Dr. Thompson, you said in 1971 that one of the basic laws in politics is that action always moves away from the center—that the middle of the road is only popular when nothing is happening. Can you expand on that?

HST: My God, I have a feeling I've been doing that for quite a while. But I think that's the situation we're in now. I think that living right now . . . it's not a safe position to take, but in situations where there's either no necessity or—sometimes you just take a position 'cause that it's fun or you get pushed into it. But I feel that the basic arguments now are so hopeless—like how to deal with the dollar, or how to deal with the Arabs, whether to tear up the entire West for coal or for oil. It's hard to get these issues that are as clear-cut as they were in the sixties which boiled down to whether you were either going to be drafted and killed in Vietnam immediately, or maybe have your legs blown off for no reason at all; or get paralyzed by some cop's truncheon in front of a draft board. I'm not sure right now if I were forced to take a position, a terminal position against anything, which one I would choose. I would say yeah—just to hark back to a scab, if they would reinstitute the draft, that would probably pep up the political dialogue pretty quickly. But what it does is involve a lot of people who otherwise . . .

Audience: You're saying that moving away from the center means either taking one side or the other?

HST: Well, I think that only happens in situations where you or I are forced to take positions like Vietnam. It took a long time for even McGovern to take a position on Vietnam, but once you took that position, you were locked into it. There are very few things like that now. Energy is perhaps the most—well, the Panama Canal was probably the most volatile issue. And that was totally meaningless. It was like debating the size of marbles. But I think the reason we have that is because there are no issues that force you to say which side you are on. That time has come, it's just that we're not there now. I think we are in that condition of limbo. What do they call it . . . Malaise? Angst?

Audience: Why doesn't the *Rolling Stone* take a moderate politically active role? A la Patrick Buchanan.

HST: Well, that was a dumb goddamn article and it was my idea, but they blew that. What would you prefer to see *Rolling Stone* . . .

Audience: More consistency

HST: Well, what positions—anyone, would you prefer to see brought into some . . . give me one issue you would like to see them take on.

Audience: (Response inaudible)

HST: Well, the only serious editorial Wenner has written in five years was the one he wrote against Paraquat and Peter Bourne. *Rolling Stone* is not interesting even to the editors anymore.

Audience: Yeah, I was wondering, I think it was 1969 you ran for mayor of Aspen . . .

HST: 1970, yeah—

Audience: . . . on the Freak Power thing. I was just wondering how it went. What did you do for a campaign and who ran with you for office and whatever?

HST: We threatened to jerk the rug right out from under them, period. And we ran against the incumbent sheriff on a very serious ticket which got labeled "freak power"—well, yeah I suppose it was "freak power" when I had to sit next to the incumbent sheriff in debates like that and say "when we run your rotten corrupt ass out of office, we're going to sit in your office and eat mescaline on a slow night with the deputies." And you got to keep in mind that I won the town, that I won three out of six precincts with that program, and one of the points was to tear up the streets the next day—all the streets. And what I found out about two years later, it was not my program at all—it was the language. When we changed "tearing up the streets" to "malls," everyone thought it was wonderful. Now we have malls everywhere—too many malls. Once again, it was sort of an icebreaking thing. Two years later we won almost every office in the county which we've controlled ever since. And we almost lost two of them last week because we had gotten lazy and complacent. We had forgotten how it was when you could get arrested, locked up for ninety days, and fined $300 for blocking a sidewalk. That doesn't happen anymore.

Audience: There's a lot of research being done right now as far as alternative energy sources—sun power, wind power, breeder reactors. Obviously, the future in energy is not in fossil fuels. Do you see any other alternative source, or do you think that one of the sources I named would more apt to be feasible?

HST: I think we're going to stumble or be dragged into the ultimate realization that solar power is all that's going to save us. Unless we can figure out some way to make the ocean work. But as you say, when we run out of fossil fuels, we'll be out of them. Whoever has the most of them will be able to see it. That's why Africa is so important.

Audience: Do you think we'll find a way to make solar collectors and solar batteries more efficient than they are now?

HST: Oh yeah. But I'm not sure that's going to be consistent with a healthy economy because we've developed an economy that is a sort of a disease-ridden form of free enterprise, which involved price fixing and in total control, not just industry, but whole resources like energy. And you can see the kind of anarchy here, economic anarchy that would result when you get everybody using their own solar power. So I think we'll have that, but we'll have it in the middle of chaos.

Audience: Can we keep it out of the hands of cartels like VEPCO,* or Appalachian Power, so we don't get charged through the ass for what's coming down free?

---

* Virginia Electric and Power Company.

HST: If you want to you can, yeah.

Audience: How? What do we do?

HST: Eventually, they'll own it. I'm not sure how those bastards will figure out how to own the sun, but they will. They'll own the technology; they'll patent the technology of it somehow. Solar power is a very definite possibility right now—solar heat with a little imagination and a little money. It's easier than heating your house with propane.

Audience: Do you believe knowledge is being repressed by the oil industry—knowledge of free energy sources like the ocean and solar energy?

HST: By the oil companies? Wouldn't you be a little concerned about something that might put you out of business forever? I'm on your side, but let's face it, we're dealing with a very serious economic reality. Five generations of Mobil, and they're very unsettled by the idea that they can no longer pull the switch if they want to. And there's no real interest on their part unless they get a patent on some device using the sun and the sea. It's in their interest to shoot down the kind of technology and stop it. And they use lobbies for that in Washington.

Audience: Dr. Thompson, do you think there's any hope for a young person to feel that he's effective individually in a large society? Do you think he can be effective actually through a career or through his job . . . through drugs or astral travel?

HST: No, I think it's much harder to feel that you are effective or successful within the system now because nothing seems to be going anywhere. I think the bottom line on all that is that if you can get away in this life with doing what you want and be proud of it—that to me is effective. If nothing else, it tells one other person anyway that it's possible to live without having to get in line, or clip coupons. I think it's very important for people to successfully live in tense opposition to the system. As Dylan Thomas said at one point—"It's a writer's first duty to attack his country and assault everything it stands for." There comes a time when you can't do much else. There would be no way I could go back and work for *Time* magazine now, I mean, you really make your own bed after a certain period. And if the times are on your side, you're a hero—if not, you're a fool. Look what happened to Tim Leary. The tide came in and went out . . . and he went out with it.

Audience: Dr. Thompson, what are the main goals of your writing, and what is it that you've been trying to achieve throughout your career?

HST: Money.

(Applause—laughter and so on)

No, I don't want you to leave thinking I'm kidding. Because it's true. What would you think I'm trying to achieve?

Audience: Something besides money as your main goal.

HST: Like what? Look what fame has done for me. You can have the fame, and I'll deal with the fortune from now on. That confuses you, doesn't it? An answer like that.

Audience: Yes, it does.

HST: What did you expect me to say?

Audience: I didn't know. It's just that when you say your main goal is money, it sounds so contradictory.

HST: Why? What else is there?

Washington Journalism Review— November/December 1979

Interview by Jane Perlez

Jane Perlez, a reporter for the *SoHo Weekly News,* met with Hunter Thompson September 19th in New York while he was on a promotion tour for his recently published book of collected writings, *The Great Shark Hunt* (Summit Books). The interview in his suite at the Sherry Netherland Hotel was his first of the day, 2 p.m., Thompson's breakfast time. Six slices of uneaten French toast lay on the room service table. Thompson took to the iced Heinekens stashed away in his hotel bathroom. He wore a white t-shirt, white shorts, bare feet, and he talked for 90 minutes about Jimmy Carter, who he supported in 1976; Teddy Kennedy, who he is supporting in 1980; Hamilton Jordan, drugs and the upcoming political campaign. Known as the "craziest" journalist in America, this interview will surprise many who have never heard Thompson speak with such clarity. The interview is run in its entirety.

Jane Perlez: I thought I'd start by asking where you've been. You told Ron Rosenbaum of *High Times* magazine two years ago that you'd get back into politics when you found it necessary but that there were better things to do like buying an opium den in Singapore or a whore house in Maine. You haven't done either of those two things.

HST: No, Hollywood has taken care of that for me. I didn't realize you could also go to Hollywood. So I've been out there playing around for about a year. It's interesting to see what you can do there. I want to see if I want to stay with it or not. Seems that it could be fun to do. But on the other hand it's so different—you have to work with so many people and the politics are so weird, I'm not sure I could handle it. Then you figure, what the hell. There's a lot of money out of it.

Jane Perlez: More money than an advance for a campaign book?

HST: Another campaign book would be impossible. I don't see any point in doing that either. That would be backsliding.

Jane Perlez: Do you think that it is impossible for you, or do you think campaign books per se are a thing of the past?

HST: No, somebody should do it. But not me. You can sort of sneak up on them [the campaign people] like Teddy White in 1960. Then they know what you're doing, then either you become absorbed into it, you become a part of it, or else they get hostile. Or both. In my case, some people got hostile, and some people tried to absorb me.

Then when you go back to write another book, they're watching for you. The first time is nice, because they really don't know what you're doing at all. But once they know, you become trapped into playing the game. "You, the book writer, the chronicler," and they treat you like that. You get invited to things that you would have been put out of before and they know, for one thing, that the book doesn't come out until the campaign is over. So if you're writing a book, in theory, you have a lot more access than somebody who is writing for next week or tomorrow. There are a lot of crimes people will admit later on, but not during the campaign.

Jane Perlez: How much of the 1976 campaign did you cover? And why did you give up?

HST: I got through the Florida primary. I knew right away I wouldn't be able to make it all the way through. I was looking for enough so I could do one piece and then get out. The Florida primary seemed to me where Carter was clearly off and running. So I quit. Then by the time I wrote the thing, it was almost convention time.

Jane Perlez: In the decision to get out, how important was the fact that you felt crippled by knowing too much which you couldn't write?

HST: That's very inhibiting, something I'd rather not have to cope with again. It sneaks up on you, so that all of a sudden you know too much. It isn't as though they give you a choice of "Do you want to know too much?" and then you decided. All of a sudden you realize, "Ye gods, what am I doing here?" You've got two options. One, you can remind them by writing something or you can step all over them. Depends whether you like them or not. That's what it all comes down to: whether you like them.

Jane Perlez: Did you find that you liked the Carter people too much?

HST: They were the loosest. Like the McGovern campaign in 1972. Right away you find out where the fun is, where the dope is. People really try and enjoy campaigns. When you find the campaign so dreary, and then you find people you really like to be around—it hardly matters whether you like their politics. It gets so god-awful dreary, that anyone who can make you laugh is welcome.

Jane Perlez: How long ago do you think the Kennedy campaign started? When did the plot start?

HST: You mean when did the "train leave the station"? I'd say about six months ago. That's when it became visible. When it started would be two years ago, the minute Carter started looking weak and incompetent, the instant it appeared that Carter was not going to be able to handle it. You get interested, right, you get hungry, and the worse it gets, you think, "Mm, I've got a job." That's where it is now. Carter created the vacuum that sucked Kennedy into it.

Jane Perlez: Looking back on the Carter Law Day Speech in 1974, you went down to Atlanta for that speech in the company of Teddy Kennedy, which seems somewhat ironic. How do you look back on that day now?

HST: That strikes me, come to think of it, the day the plot started. Because Carter was so rude to Kennedy, deliberately. He got away with it that day. You hear rocks fly, and you hear things move, and I could tell that Carter was going to pay for that somehow. Kennedy the whole day was in kind of controlled funk. Carter first of all offered him his plane and then took it back, so Kennedy had to drive to Athens and was late for his speech. Little things like that got him really cranked up. Carter's paying for fucking with Kennedy.

Jane Perlez: You seem to have no doubt Kennedy will succeed.

HST: I'd be surprised if Carter survived the first three primaries.

Jane Perlez: But you were one of the first to tell us that he was a zealot and no one should underestimate his tenacity.

HST: Well, tenacity is one thing, but what I didn't realize was that he was incompetent. I'm surprised that he conned me on that point real badly. I have some tapes of him telling me—it's very sad, it sounded like a high school civics major telling you how he's going to run the country.

I've got eight hours of tape of him in '74, talking about worms in the ground and how the grass grows, driving around with him in a thunderstorm . . . I might even believe it again. Listening to the tapes, he sounds like a different person, the voice is different, he seems 20 years younger. I just thought it would be nice not to have to fight the White House for a while and have somebody mind the store. After 10 years of being gassed and all that shit, I was just tired of it. And then the choice comes down to Humphrey,

Ford, or Carter, then you can't hesitate too long. But he just proved to be an incompetent. He just can't do it.

Jane Perlez: Can you delineate the incompetence?

HST: It would be hard to separate the incompetence from everything else he does because they seem to be intertwined.

Jane Perlez: Do you think it's the people around him?

HST: Oh yeah, that's part of it.

Jane Perlez: Powell* and Jordan and Kraft?†

HST: Yeah, mainly that his advice comes always from the same people. They began paranoid, and now they're real paranoid. So when you get your advice from all those people, all the time, you get like Nixon. It's the bunker mentality. He doesn't trust people enough to consult people outside his inner circle.

Jane Perlez: How do you perceive Kennedy?

HST: I think he's a very able and effective senator. In terms of who's competent and who's not, Kennedy is demonstrably more so than Carter. Just as a general rule, Teddy has always had, I'd say, the best staff in Washington. To travel with Kennedy is almost like traveling with a very polished Presidential campaign, even though he's a senator going to make a weekend speech.

Jane Perlez: Are they fun to be with?

HST: The candidates are never fun to be with. The Kennedy people are all business. There wouldn't be much hanging out, getting stoned at night.

Jane Perlez: Looking back on it, don't you think the Carter staff were somewhat naïve?

HST: Yes, very. I think they thought that once they got into the White House they'd be immune, like Nixon, or like Nixon thought. I think once you win, you think: "We got past that." They didn't seem to learn much, once they got to the White House. They acted as though they were still running a campaign out of Georgia. As it turns out, getting elected President is pretty easy. It's being President that's tough.

Jane Perlez: Do you think Carter knew about the after-hour habits of his staff?

HST: Oh yeah. Remember, you're still working in a campaign at four in the morning. For Carter it worked out nicely that the most influential press

---

* Joseph "Jody" Powell served as White House press secretary to President Jimmy Carter.

† Tim Kraft served as President Jimmy Carter's assistant and chief coordinator.

people got along so well with his staff. Until it backfired it was good to have. It's been a plus until now.

Jane Perlez: How much do you think that the clubbiness between the blue-chip reporters and the blue-chip assistants helped Carter get the coverage he wanted?

HST: A tremendous amount. It gave Carter credibility. Once you're sympathetic to a candidate, it's easy to see why he might be better.

Jane Perlez: In the '50s and '60s, it used to be drinking. What's new, I suppose, is that it's people doing dope and coke.

HST: Don't ever forget sex in there. That would be a nasty can of worms to open. "Well, the coke ain't so bad, but man the sex, Oh, Oh!! Let me tell you about that." You could drop a few things that would make Chappaquiddick* seem too boring to talk about.

Jane Perlez: If you were going in to cover this campaign, what angle would you take, how would you go about it?

HST: You'd have to say what I was working for.

Jane Perlez: Let's start with a daily newspaper.

HST: You don't have much choice in those situations. The more often you have to publish, the more you're locked into the routine of the campaign.

Jane Perlez: Let's talk about pieces for, say, *Esquire*, which might be put into a book.

HST: That's an odd area, where you're writing stuff that appears during the campaign and you might also be writing a book, then people really don't know what you're going to do. Like Teddy White. He gets so much more access because he's not writing during the campaign. I'd go into this to write a book. First of all, there's a lot more money in a book. I thought about that last time. I wasn't going to write during the campaign. I was going to write a book.

Jane Perlez: But how would you approach the book?

HST: It all depends, you never know what's going to happen in a campaign. A campaign develops its own personality as it goes along, unless it's like a Nixon-Kennedy campaign, then you know ahead of time.

---

* Refers to the incident on Chappaquiddick Island off of Martha's Vineyard where Senator Edward Kennedy accidentally drove off a bridge, killing Mary Jo Kopechne, a campaign worker for his brother, Robert F. Kennedy.

Jane Perlez: Let's talk about the newspaper reporters. You've talked about the invidious situation that the reporters get into by knowing their sources so well, that they don't want to hurt them because they want to keep access. How do you get over that double bind?

HST: I don't know. First of all, you have to make sure you don't value friends in Washington. You should not live in Washington. If you live and work in Washington there's no way you can get over it. Sooner or later you're going to want something and they'll say, "You son of a bitch, remember that thing you wrote back in March," which gives them an excuse forever not to talk to you. So you really have to make your choice early. It works out if you make the right choice and humor the right people.

Jane Perlez: Things don't seem to change much. Already in New Hampshire there are reporters who've been covering campaigns the last three or four times.

HST: Five or six times for some. For a while there seemed to be a new kind of reporter covering campaigns. But they didn't appear much in '76. I don't know exactly what happened. I thought Timothy Crouse and I cut out in a whole new direction with the books we did in '72. But no one really picked that up.

Jane Perlez: You think Carter might take a vacation for four years?

HST: That'd be nice. He'd learn something about the economy and come back in four years and there might be this great reservoir of good feeling for this person who'd admitted he couldn't handle it. That might be a good calculated risk. Nobody tried that before. Teddy Roosevelt, maybe. It would be a ballsy move to decided that you needed a little bit more study and to promise to run again in 1984. And actually to plan for it. Campaign all around the goddamn world. I don't know who'd pay for that. It would be a real trip if he did that. People would be impressed.

Jane Perlez: He's always prided himself on ballsy moves, like Cabinet shakeups.

HST: He has to have a little more intelligence than to know that that's not enough and that you've got to have something more. Anyone can be ballsy. It's trying to make it work that's hard.

Jane Perlez: Let's talk about writing. You've said that Gonzo journalism is, in a way, simply first-draft journalism. If you'd done second drafts, how would they have been different?

HST: Quieter. I very rarely add crazier things in a second draft.

Jane Perlez: What have you done second drafts on?

HST: It's been a long time.

Jane Perlez: The *National Observer* pieces?*

HST: There may have been two drafts. The Vegas book was the last time I did a second, third, sometimes fourth, draft.

Jane Perlez: The Vegas book? Seems that's the book everyone perceived as being the most undrafted.

HST: That's why I liked the book. It's finely crafted in the way it's put together. There are only about 15 words in there that shouldn't be. I like that. Drafting is a very fine tool. I miss that. It usually makes it better, though you can worry a piece to death. It gives me a chance get out the craziness of the night before. I figure the night before, I can write it up, write anything, then the next day when I come back and look at it, I knock out parts that are too crazy.

Jane Perlez: It's interesting that the new piece by Norman Mailer in *Playboy* on Gary Gilmore is back to basics, and straight reporting. Have you read it?†

HST: No, but I heard that. Kind of flat, it sounded good.

Jane Perlez: Do you see that as a trend: Perhaps the interjection of the reporter in stories has run its phase?

HST: I don't see any real reason for it, either way. I think in Mailer's case and in mine, you get tired of doing the same thing after a while.

Jane Perlez: Isn't it a tremendous effort to keep yourself involved in the piece?

HST: I don't find that so much. It's just all first-draft stuff. The whole book [*The Great Shark Hunt*] is a collection of first drafts. I haven't changed anything since I put them in *Rolling Stone,* except for typos. It would all be about half as personalized as it is if I had time to do a second draft.

I've finished that one thing: being a Gonzo journalist—it was fun but it gets real old. I was a straight journalist for a while. So maybe what Norman is doing . . . maybe back to straight reporting.

If Mailer had time to do a second draft, or I had, neither one of our styles would be what they are now. I think what it comes from is trying to do too

---

* Between 1962 and 1964, Hunter S. Thompson wrote for nationally distributed Dow Jones Company newspaper, the *National Observer*. Thompson's tenure at the paper includes dispatches from Latin America as a foreign correspondent.

† Norman Mailer, "The Executioner's Song," *Playboy*, October–December, 1979.

much on a deadline that didn't allow for it. What it does is produce that crazy, frantic tone to it that if you don't do a second draft, it comes through in the writing. People call it Gonzo journalism, but it's carelessness, that's what it is.

Jane Perlez: Born out of the situation?

HST: Yeah, it's unavoidable. If I'd had more time, I'd probably have cured myself. I don't know what that would have done for it or for me.

But when you get on deadlines you can't get back to it the next afternoon. It has to go off. You pull it out of the typewriter, put it over the Mojo wire and bang, it's gone. I've even stopped editing pages, much less the writing. Put it in the typewriter and don't even bother to correct the typos. Try to call it in. Very slowly I'm getting around the typewriter and the printing pages. I believe sometime soon I'll be able to take it straight from babbling gibberish to some kind of photo display. I was one of the first journalists to use a tape recorder.

Jane Perlez: When?

HST: The Hell's Angels book. That was the first time they had cassette recorders. Before that you had to use the reel-to-reel stuff. But once they got it down to that size, I saw a whole new world beckoning.

Jane Perlez: The Hell's Angels guys weren't intimidated by it?

HST: They didn't see it. They saw the reel-to-reel stuff earlier and threatened to kill me. But this, I just wore in a shoulder holster, all of a sudden you don't have to write notes anymore. The worst thing about tape is listening to it.

Jane Perlez: How do you manage that?

HST: What I try to do is—I appreciate the remote pause—I try to be real conscious when I'm taping something that I'll have to listen to it, so I use the remote pause so that if you have five minutes of the waiter coming into the room, then I just cut it off. Listening to four hours of tape after listening to a candidate can be real interesting one day, but boy if you have to do it constantly, it can drive you mad. Most things you hear, they don't make any sense anyway. You have to separate the wheat from the chaff, and the more you have, the harder it is to do it. So what you end up doing is trying to edit on the spot. I used to put my mike in my watchband, down my sleeve so that it would be aiming out, so anytime you had your arm pointed at someone you'd pick it up. When you put your hand in your pocket you're in trouble.

Jane Perlez: When you're listening to the stuff at night, how do you write from the spoken word onto the typewriter?

HST: I usually go back over it and listen and write down the things that I like exactly as I heard them. You get to listen to it, write it down in legal pads, then you go over it and get totally accurate quotes. You'd be amazed how just about impossible—if you're going to listen to somebody in a volatile situation—to get say a five-minute, even a two-minute, quote right. From a tape recorder you can get all kinds of asides. If you tape it right and write down exactly what was said, it makes a big difference.

Jane Perlez: Do you think you could have written anything after Hell's Angels without a tape recorder?

HST: It would have been different. Because I saw what the tape recorder could do. I could just drive around in the car and keep the tape recorder out on the seat and you'd hear all of a sudden some horrible ripping sound, a fence being torn down, and you hear screams. There's no amount of memory that can bring it back to you that perfectly—that you can hear the sound of a fence being ripped out of the ground and hear what it sounds like. What I do is tape it on the smallest unit, but when I play it back I have 80 speakers in my living room so when I play it back I pick up everything. It's like being in the scene. There's no way that notes can bring that back to you. I have 20 speakers in every corner, so I can just sit in the middle.

Jane Perlez: So there is a reason why you go back to Colorado, aside from the mountains and the clean air. It's to be near your equipment.

HST: I've got so much equipment now I can't carry it around anymore. I used to be able to carry it with me.

Jane Perlez: Do you see Bill Cardozo [the *Boston Globe* editor who first called Thompson a Gonzo journalist]?

HST: He's out in San Francisco writing a book on some murder in Palm Springs. Some freak up in Boston invented the term, some eighth generation of street kid, but it was Cardozo who tied it to journalism. I thought: "that's a good word. I'll be one of those." It worked.

Rolling Stone College Papers—May 1980

Interview by David Felton

Felton: I have here a copy of your best-selling anthology [*The Great Shark Hunt*], and I notice above the title it says, Gonzo Papers, Vol. I. My question is, who's kidding who?

HST: What do you mean?

Felton: I'm wondering where Volume II is going to come from. I mean, I think it's generally agreed that you're pretty much washed up as a writer and a thinker and, to some extent, a human being.

HST: Hmmm . . . Jesus. Well, then there's really no point in doing this, is there?

Felton: Oh, I think there's a lot of point to it. For example, this anthology. It's probably the worst-edited and most self-indulgent book since the Bible. There doesn't seem to be any order. One-fourth of the book is either stuff that's been in previous books of yours or old, hack, pre-Gonzo stuff that reads rather flat and uninspired.

HST: That's the way I wanted it.

Felton: For what reason?

HST: I just thought it should be a permanent record. I thought it would be pretty fun to see the development from the air force to the Ali piece. It seems like I've been writing the same thing since I was eighteen years old. Looking back on it, I was surprised at the consistency of even the style, in terms of the attitude.

I never even thought about Volume II, frankly, I decided it would be nice to have Volume I on it.

Felton: I think you said earlier that at fifteen dollars, you thought the book was a good bargain.

HST: Yeah, I like it.

Felton: It just seems like the book was slapped together.

HST: Well, you're right.

Felton: I'm sure some people would say, well, so what? It's making a lot of money. But this is your textbook, this is what you'll go down in history with.

HST: I'll stand by this. It's messy, it's fucked up; it's not a bad book.

Felton: Well, let's talk a little about the *Buffalo* movie that's about to come out. How did you get involved in that?

HST: I got a call from Lynn Nesbit, my agent. She said there's this person who wants to buy the magazine article about the Brown Buffalo ["The Banshee Screams for Buffalo Meat," a eulogy for Oscar Acosta] for $100,000 and make a movie [*Where the Buffalo Roam*]. I thought, "Well, shit, that's wonderful."

They wanted to make a movie about whatever they perceived to be the relationship between these two characters. It was a weird idea. Actually, it was weird that it never occurred to me that it would be made.

Felton: But didn't it cross your mind that if the movie did get made, it would reflect on you and your legend or your personality?

HST: Probably. Yeah, if I'd thought about it. But, you know, I probably would have done it. I don't know why people are so concerned about my image. I'm an egomaniac. I should be the one concerned about my image! Why are you and Garry Trudeau so worried about this film hurting me? I'm not.

Felton: So at the time, without seeing a script, you signed the contract?

HST: I've been dealing with these yo-yos buying options on things for years. Options have been essentially paying the rent. The Las Vegas book has been optioned several times. So to me it [the Buffalo story] was just another option job. Then all of a sudden there was some moment of terrible horror when I realized they were going to make the movie. Last summer, when I actually saw the fucking set on the lot, I thought, "Whoa! Good God!"

Felton: But way before then, hadn't John Kaye, the scriptwriter, talked to you?

HST: Yeah, he seemed to understand a lot more than came through in the script. I was very disappointed in the script. It sucks—a bad, dumb, low-level, low-rent script.

Felton: Well, in this contract, do you have any kind of control or leverage?

HST: No. That was the first thing we agreed on. I just thought it would be safer not to have any.

Felton: I don't quite understand the reasoning, but . . .

HST: Well, if you have one percent leverage, you might be blamed for eighty percent. Since I have none, I can't be blamed for any of it. I signed away all editorial control at the beginning. I am executive consultant, which means I wandered around, fired machine guns on the set, drove a boat.

Felton: Yes, you can't be blamed for the script or the direction. Except that were you to say, at the beginning, "This is shit, I won't give my permission," then it couldn't be done, right?

HST: [Hunter bolts up and storms over to the fireplace, shouting.] Have you ever tried to deal with these mother-fucking lawyers and agents in Hollywood?

Felton: All you have to say is no.

HST: [Angrily, he pokes at the fire.] And you're sitting there telling me, broke as you are, that I'm fucking dumb for not getting more money or less money out of this?

Felton: No, I'm certainly not telling you you're dumb because you got more money or less money.

HST: I find it a little hard to take. At least I've cheated the fuckers out of $100,000. [He returns to his chair.] Well, that's not cheating at all; that's just routine for down there, another scam.

Felton: But regarding the Buffalo film, if it involved a character that might even be related to me, I think I would have checked to see who was behind it. I mean you already have a public image, and . . .

HST: Fuck yes! I've been in comic strips for years!

Felton: And for years you've been incensed about it.

HST: Well, I don't like it, no. I'm not incensed; I've gotten used to it.

Felton: Maybe incensed is too strong a word, but you've certainly been concerned with *Doonesbury,* with what you felt was Trudeau's invasion of your privacy.

HST: That was my original bitch with it. Then I began to realize how much money he was making off me, off my image.

Felton: Fine. But I think what we're really talking about is, either you are or you're not concerned about your image.

HST: I can't afford to be, man. I'd go mad. I don't even know what my image is. I have a feeling . . . it's always been bad. Ever since I was a teenage criminal, I've always been doomed, a person clearly headed for hell.

Felton: I wouldn't say that. You're admired by enough people to make your book a best seller.

HST: [Hunter refills his glass with Wild Turkey.] Look outside. Look around you. I have to take care of an eight-room house. I have five peacocks to feed. I spend maybe $10,000 a month on just simple fucking airfare. I have a huge ranch, another house, books, movies, weird gibberish happening. How in the hell could I afford to take the time to sit here worrying about my image?

I'm trying to think if I should be concerned. No, I don't think so. Why should I be?

Felton: Only because, as you've mentioned yourself, in the last year all this stuff's come down where your image is unavoidable.

HST: It's a nightmare, yeah. When at almost the same time your collected works are coming out, a movie's being made about you . . . And then you're in the comic strips . . . yeah, somewhere along there, I'm not sure where the line was, I became a public figure. I'm not admitting that legally. Legally right now it's quite critical if I'm a public figure. If I am not, Mr. Trudeau will be working in my yard for the next ten years, trimming the grass. But in a rough use of the word, I became a public figure. Somehow the author has become larger than the writing. And it sucks.

Felton: Do you think you've contributed to that in any way?

HST: Well, yeah, I probably have.

Felton: What kind of trouble was there recently at the College of Marin?

HST: Well, that was just a broken-down sound system and a bunch of loadies, very young—what I believe to be the second generation of Marin County. A grim comment; it chills you to see what the children of paradise look like.

Felton: What happened?

HST: Nothing. It was just chaotic. It was a low-rent operation. People were yelling at me, and the questions were weird, and kids were asking for whiskey. I never had kids come up and beg for drinks out of my Wild Turkey bottle.

Felton: Doesn't that give you the willies?

HST: Well, it didn't fill me with confidence. And the questions were so dumb that I just abandoned everything. When I start calling the crowd beer-hippies and thumb-fuckers and loadies and shit like that, it usually breaks down. I usually only lose my temper at schools of the rich.

Felton: A couple of years ago you appeared at NYU, and while you eventually answered questions, you spent the first half of the evening placing

bets with the audience that night. And at some point I yelled at you from the balcony, "How can you lower yourself to speak in front of a group of people that would pay money to watch you make a fool of yourself?"

HST: That's when I threw a piece of ice that hit you in the chest, right? Two hundred yards from the balcony.

Felton: That was a great shot, I won't quarrel with you on that. But you express disgust at people sucking your whiskey, yet it seems to me it's part of the same fan phenomenon. Do you feel any responsibility for that?

HST: [Suddenly cold and serious] No. Not the slightest. It's a problem, but I don't feel responsible.

Felton: Okay, well, let's try another image question. One piece in the anthology that disappointed me was "The Great Shark Hunt" itself. It seemed like a pale imitation of *FLLV,* but it was written several years later.

HST: Let's not compare this stuff to the Las Vegas book. Vegas was like four or five drafts. Probably the further back you go in time, the more rewrites we get in each piece. The newer stuff, almost without exception, is essentially journalism, as it was written on the day, sent in for a deadline, not edited, either then or now, and published. You tell me another journalist who would put his collected works in book form as he sent them in from some motel or wire desk in Zingaling, Missouri, Bangkok or Rio.

Felton: Do you think that's admirable?

HST: Yes, because it's taking an insane chance at being right an abnormal amount of the time—a high percentage.

Felton: Well, one charge is that in the last few years you've had a lot more trouble writing. And it's getting harder and harder until it's practically ceased.

HST: It's always been hard. But it rarely pays. And I never do it unless I'm broke. I've said that many times. Why should I work on deadlines? We're dealing with journalism. And it ceased to be fun. Just by answering my phone, I can make four times as much money as I do by writing all the time. Hemingway said that journalism was good for a writer if you knew when to get out of it. I think I stayed way too long.

Felton: Have you gotten out of it now?

HST: I hope so. But it's hard to get out of. I've always viewed it as a sort of a left-handed thing, sort of a ticket to ride. Journalism has always been my way of going to a place to see if I wanted to see what was going on. And you get addicted to that. It doesn't mean that writing the story interests me, I hate that.

I don't like to write. I don't care what happens after I write. Once I've gotten the story in my mind, the rest is just pain. And to cure the pain, we put it together between covers and call it *The Great Shark Hunt* and sell 100,000 copies at fifteen dollars apiece. It helps ease the pain.*

* *Rolling Stone College Papers* was a short-lived magazine geared towards a student audience. It was published between 1979 and 1980 by Jann Wenner and edited by his sister, Kate Wenner.

T.O. Magazine (Toronto)—November 1986

Thirty-Six Manic Hours in Toronto with Dr. Hunter S. Thompson, Guru of Gonzo Journalism

BY PAUL KAIHLA

We whip around Bayview Avenue where it drops into the Don Valley, only to come upon a police roadblock. I glance nervously at my passenger, but he seems oblivious to the law and annoyed at this unexpected inconvenience.

"I don't understand how a little bit of rain can completely paralyze a city of three million people," he mumbles through his sniffling.

It's 9:05 by the time we arrive at the Music Hall. Several ratty-looking fans are milling about menacingly outside. Six patrol cars are on call apparently because the police fear an all-out riot if Thompson fails to show a second time. Two unshaven kids in shorts drinking Budweisers greet us backstage. The audience is carrying on an aural riot beyond the curtains. Let's go! Thompson throws down his stuff, grabs an Upper Canada Lager and a whiskey out of the dressing room and steps out.

Applause. Thunderous, full house applause, screaming, and waving fists. It was as if the world's greatest rock band has just come on stage. Thompson is not just a writer to these people. He is something more: a living legend.

During the past several months Thompson has been working at San Francisco's notorious O'Farrell porn palace, doing research for his upcoming book, "The Night Manager." Thompson has always been drawn to outcasts, underdogs and the strange.

As strobes glitter and a nude albino woman puts on her seductive prowl a few feet away, I think about the strange relationship Thompson has with his fans. At the Music Hall show that night a pudgy, boyish man in his mid-twenties, stoned and pissed drunk, had seized the microphone. In a crude attempt to imitate Bill Murray's slapstick portrayal of Thompson in the film *Where the Buffalo Roam,* he wore a surgical vest and stethoscope. Later, he sat in the front row mouthing gibberish into a journalist's mini-recorder while

Thompson signed autographs 10 feet away. I wanted to explore this in the interview. I see an opening to ask my first question; Thompson's fixated on the albino.

HST: That guy at the hall was an asshole. But he didn't really bother me. I get used to it.

T.O.: Do you get upset at the way the media have portrayed you?

HST: Well, I don't mind being portrayed as a dope fiend or a sex fiend as long as there's something else in there. [He sighs wearily.] You know, I'm more concerned with the Supreme Court than I am about rock and roll—or with the war in Nicaragua* than I am about drugs.

T.O.: Can you have it both ways? Does it really surprise you, given the persona you project—writing about drugs, guns, and motorcycles—that you would be sensationalized as America's "outlaw journalist"?

HST: Looking back at it, it doesn't surprise me. But you don't expect that kind of attention as a journalist. All my professional life I've been used to standing at the back of the room. Even at the White House press conferences, I didn't want to sit down in the front with Dan Rather and those people. I viewed it from the distance, which gave me my ability to work with it. Once you're part of the club, you're locked in and they have you. It's when you don't owe them anything that you're dangerous.

But I noticed around the time of the Carter campaign that it had gone too far. I'd become a public figure, even by a lawyer's definition. During the primaries I was giving more interviews and signing more autographs than Carter was. I had become an actor in the drama I was supposed to be covering. That's why I quit covering politics.

T.O.: Have you been able to prevent your personal life from being consumed by the public image?

HST: That's why I live in Woody Creek, goddamnit. I can't keep them separate on the road. I used to figure that whatever I did myself was mine.

T.O.: But what else can you expect when you parade your private activities so much in your books?

HST: Well, I've slowed down on that. I've become quite self-conscious about including my personal life in my writing.

---

* The Contra War took place between 1981 and 1988. Led by President Ronald Reagan, the United States backed and armed rebel Contra forces to overthrow the Sandinista government. The conflict ended in a ceasefire in 1988.

T.O.: Is that a retreat from Gonzo journalism?

HST: I think it is. I think it takes an element of fun out of the writing for me and for other people. When you realize that any small thing you might do could turn up in *Doonesbury* the next morning, it takes all the fun out of it. When you realize that everything you write, like at four in the morning after you've been up for three days, will end up in libraries and your children will read it, it makes you much more cautious. It takes the fun out of it, being a perpetual public figure . . .

[Interview interrupted for signing of autographs]

"God, that girl at the show tonight . . . Did you hear her question about whether I'm the only person who seems to stand up and endorse this way of life?" he asks no one in particular as he empties a small pipe on an oak bureau.

T.O.: That's when the big moments of applause came . . .

HST: God, I haven't thought of it that way. [Thompson grins.] Then I started to think, I don't hear many people, you know, I see Frank Zappa down there fighting the rock-and-roll route.*

Yeah, I might be talking about survivors, rather than leaders of a movement. I hate to think I could be the last of the . . . what do you call it?

T.O.: Last of the counterculture?

HST: Goddamn. Me, be the last surviving dinosaur?! That's horrible! If it's true, they'll get me soon. [He roams the room, shaking ice through his sixth Glenfiddich.]

I've always thought of myself as basically the reasonable journalist. You know the others, they were the wild people. I got out of hand a few times, but only in the way I presented it. I don't go around advocating the use of drugs, particularly not now, goddamnit.

He suddenly turns nostalgic, talking about San Francisco and Haight-Ashbury. There is something charming and heroic about a man as roguish as Thompson who still remains faithful to the idealism of a nobler era.

---

* In September 1985, Frank Zappa testified in front of a United States Senate committee to defend artistic expression and free speech. Zappa decried what was perceived as censorship from the Parents Music Resource Center, which was coheaded by Tipper Gore.

HST: The whole definition of the drug culture was that we were in it together. If you got something nice, the instinct was to share it. You could live a million years in this country, or any other, and you would never have as much fun as you would have in San Francisco in the middle sixties. The sixties were a time when the clouds broke and people like Oscar Acosta [the Samoan attorney who appears in *Fear and Loathing in Las Vegas*] could actually get involved in the process. Christ, he'd have a hard time getting a job in a carwash today.

The crack dealers and street corner pushers have turned the drug culture into a mockery. The lack of honesty is shocking. The people who deal drugs now aren't survivors of the counterculture; they're a new generation.

T.O.: "The generation of swine"?

HST: Well, that's a provocative term. [smiles] I use that to make them jump. It's a generation epitomized by a poll *USA Today* did of college students: Eighty-seven percent thought that making money was the most important thing; seventy-nine percent thought it wasn't what you know, but who you know.

This is the time of fear and loathing, really. This is the generation we've been waiting for.

I-D Magazine—November 1987

Fear and Loathing: On the Trail of Hunter S. Thompson and Ralph Steadman

BY SIMON KEY

"What am I going to do, and is it going to be fun?" This is Hunter Thompson on the phone to Jacqueline Graham, his British press agent. "He's coming on condition he can play golf and shoot grouse," she tells me, "it's putting ten years on me." One week before he's due to turn up at the Edinburgh Book Fair to give a talk with Ralph Steadman he's having trouble renewing his passport.

I meet Jacqueline Graham and Sonny, a former Pan publisher, for a few drinks. It's obviously clearly on Sonny's mind that Thompson has a predictable tendency to behave in a quirky manner. "I don't know if I want to shoot grouse with Hunter, I might get killed."

Ralph Steadman doesn't play golf; I say I know a good golfer. "Is he weird?" asks Jacqueline Graham. Weird enough, I say. Apparently Hunter Thompson doesn't necessarily like people that are too strange, and the straight and the sensible keep him on track it would seem.

Saturday morning arrives, but Hunter Thompson doesn't. There is a big sign by the marquee in red ink about him missing the plane and I feel a bit of a dork, being loaded up with a microphone and tape and with a photographer due to arrive in 20 minutes.

Unsure of what to do to salvage my fast-sinking article I charge into the lobby of the Roxburgh Hotel and ring Jacqueline Graham's room to try and get Hunter Thompson's phone number. She sounds frayed at the edges, having been on the phone since two in the morning trying to piece together what went wrong. Over my shoulder I notice a large silver-haired man in a light plaid jacket talking to some drunks. I check this description with Jacqueline Graham and, sure enough, it's Ralph Steadman, so I plough through a couple of chairs and set up my bagful of equipment.

Ralph Steadman is very apologetic and very disappointed and speaks to me (largely in anecdotes) for an hour and a half.

"Hunter was on the phone negotiating for this trip for ages: 'Okay, Ralph, let's see what we've got now. We've got the suite in the Caledonian, right? We'll go to St. Andrews? It's worth coming just for St. Andrews . . . Well, that's two things, what else have we got? We got shooting? Definitely shooting? What is it, Ralph? Pigeons, rabbits or what?' Grouse. 'Grouse! Aha! I'll teach you to shoot your own meat, Ralph. You'll love it.' He was going to get this extraordinary bogus reference or something about his golf handicap so he could get into St. Andrews, so he's very serious about his golf . . . y'know . . . 'I'll bring my putter'."

So he was going to come?

"Oh, no doubt about it. That's why I can only put it down to this peculiar mental hang-up . . . you know, knowing that at the eleventh hour something will go wrong. In the back of his mind there's always this massive dragging of feet. He tried to come, he got out of the front door, he got in a car, a taxi albeit driven by a drunken taxi driver, made his way there as best he could . . . but it never happened. I mean, fancy getting a drunk cab driver?! Only Hunter could manage that. Typical! I hate being here on my own. I hate being the organ-grinder's monkey—he's always doing this to me! Whatever trips we've been on, he's always landed me in it somehow."

I ask about *The Curse of Lono*.

"It was really terrible getting him to work at the typewriter . . . he just wasn't interested once he got to Hawaii." Thompson and Steadman had been sent to Hawaii by *Running* magazine. A letter from Thompson is reproduced at the front of *Lono;* it states: "Dear Ralph, I think we have a live one this time, old sport. Some brute named Perry up in Oregon wants to give us a month in Hawaii for Christmas and all we have to do is cover the Honolulu Marathon for his magazine, a thing called *Running* . . .

But just how were you going to do the talk with Hunter?

"I was going to read the origins of Welsh humor, and play the bagpipes, but not now."

If you could put a percentage figure on how much of a book like Lono is anywhere near accurate . . .

"It was worse than the book, you know . . . it is reality . . . We did have those terrible stories when we did have rocks thrown at us out of the water; he did nearly tread on my little daughter's head coming to get the bloody TV set. It isn't always the way with Hunter, but that time the reality of the situation was more extreme than his written interpretation."

Were you involved in "Silkroad,"* one of Hunter's new books?

"No, he's only just told me about it. I read the synopsis of the book and it's basically about drug smuggling in the Gulf of Mexico. It's a weird idea, it's all politics. It's really a satire of current politics and the dope trade—and 'Silkroad' is a wonderful title for it. And this other book he's doing, the one about this sex club—apparently it's as full of lots of girls doing unspeakable things to each other. He told me the publishers have a problem with it because they think it's pornography. He also told me it's a way of paying the rent."

Would you say Hunter Thompson was afraid of anything in particular?

"Ah . . . Straights."

Really?

"I should think so. He's got a very noble side to him, has Hunter. . . . "

He's not scared of dying?

"Well, he thought he was going to die at 30 and so he says he's living on borrowed time. 'I figured it'd be over at 30 . . . but I lived on. I can't believe it!' But he probably wouldn't admit to that either."

So you're pretty angry he hasn't shown up?

"Yeah. I was on the phone, shouting at anyone who'd listen. I suppose Hunter's still with this drunken taxi driver somewhere between Aspen and Denver."

It's probably not worrying him though, is it? . . .

What are your favorite memories of *Fear and Loathing?*

"Hitting the fear, getting right to the edge. I think the same goes for Hunter."

Do you think he expected to become such a celebrity?

"I think it's inevitable that he became one being a man who does like to be an energetic force like being in a hurricane. I think he expected it, too, because he always wanted to be in the center of the hurricane, in the eye of the storm. It's a necessary part, otherwise he's asleep. 'It's a matter of movement,' he said, 'movement is energy, energy is life, that's all you need to know.' I remember him saying that on the road to Las Vegas."

Hunter Thompson is dealt with by those who know him as both a human sandstorm and a child. They are reluctant to give out his number, partly to punish him, partly, I think, because he's their friend.

---

* An excerpt of Thompson's "The Silk Road: Fast Boats on the Ocean at Night" was originally published in *Songs of the Doomed: The Gonzo Papers, Volume III*, Simon and Schuster, 1990.

I-D: I tell him that I was looking forward to seeing him play some golf at St. Andrews . . .

HST: So was I, that was one of the great disappointments of my recent life. I embarked, I took off, I thought I would be there. But you know, I got hijacked . . .

I-D: What happened? You got swept up by a drunken taxi driver, didn't you?

HST: How did you know that? I felt terrible then and I feel terrible now. I really let Ralph down, and he was very, very mean when I last spoke to him. He'll get me back I'm sure.

I-D: We weren't sure if you'd get a golf pass.

HST: I got a letter from the golf pro about my handicap. I did everything right except miss the fucking plane. I had gone 255 miles over the mountains to Denver and then back—it was a terrible ride with this vicious shit-eating fuck . . . You know, that's a long ride when you've missed the plane. Never trust a taxi driver.

I-D: Have you been to Scotland before?

HST: No, I never have. I was genuinely looking forward to it. It would have been fun.

I-D: Fear and Loathing in St. Andrews would certainly have made a good feature.

HST: Oh boy. Well, that was it last weekend. That was Fear and Loathing just trying to get to the airport. I don't like to think what would have happened if I would have gotten to Scotland.

I-D: What are you writing at the current moment?

HST: Well, what I'm writing and what I'm publishing is different. I've just done a book, it's called "A Generation of Swine." I don't want to go into it because if I do, it might not get published . . . if you see what I mean. (Thompson recently wrote in his *San Francisco Examiner* column, "Huge brains, small necks, weak muscles, and fat wallets—these are the dominant characteristics of the Eighties—the generation of swine.")

I-D: What do you make of the Reagan administration and this year's Irangate scandal?*

---

* In November 1986, the United States government under President Ronald Reagan's administration was found to be selling arms to the Iranian government in exchange for hostages held in Lebanon.

HST: Well, that's why I called the book "Generation of Swine." The Reagan administration is one of the worst we've ever had.

I-D: Worse than Nixon?

HST: To me, yes. Nixon was an outright criminal, a shameless beast. But he was a good character, somewhere between, you can't say King Lear, but you know, Iago, and not even that good. But Nixon had some character. These people are oily and greasy and way too smooth. They're worse than Nixon as all modern right-wing greedheads are. They're fascists and they get away with it, which is a strange, strange thing.

I-D: Who could take over at the White House?

HST: Well, almost anybody I'm afraid. Unfortunately I think it's gonna be George Bush—that would croak the hopes and dreams for a whole generation to have Bush follow after Reagan.

I-D: There are many conflicting stories about how much of *Fear and Loathing* actually happened.

HST: Well a lot of time has passed since it happened, but I reckon about 90 percent of it is true. I read it now and I think, my God, that was me, I did that.

I-D: Do you still live life at a fast pitch?

HST: Well people say I do, I guess, so I don't brag about it. I would probably rather live more calmly. I keep thinking, well, it's bound to slow down sooner or later.

I-D: There's that passage at the beginning of *The Great Shark Hunt* where you're in the hotel building, 24 floors up, debating whether or not to throw yourself into the fountain. So what keeps you going? Why didn't you jump?

HST: The truth is I don't know. You know, right now I'm being . . . I have to call a lawyer right now, because the sheriff's putting a restraining order on me. I'm all in the papers for shooting at golf balls with a shotgun.

I-D: I see. Due to your hedonistic misbehavior, do you find it hard to discipline yourself to write?

HST: Always, always. I hate to write. But you either do that or you get a job. I've been 25 years without a job and 23 without sleep. I'm quite proud of that. I'm a hillbilly from Kentucky. I'm lazy and I hate to write. I hate to work but you've got to do it.

I-D: Did you expect to become a cult figure?

HST: Hardly, what did I expect?

I-D: Well, you were the first journalist to put yourself center stage in your work, so do you think you're your own man?

HST: Well, I think it was really just laziness. That way I don't have to create a character. That's one less character I have to create. I really just try and get by and write what I can.

I-D: Did you much prefer America in the Sixties or America in the Eighties?

HST: Well, at the risk of sounding like an elderly termite or something . . . yeah. The sixties were a lot more fun and the reason it was a lot more fun is because people believed it was going to be fun. What we have now is a generation—that's what this political book is referring to—a generation of swine. I don't think it's too much fun to play the stock market. Maybe it is . . .

I-D: What do you think of the growth of Yuppies in America?

HST: Yeah, well you had a generation once full of angry young men, and their phrase was, "I've got mine, Jack." That's the same password that the Yuppies have. They're dull, they don't expect much; they don't expect the President to be honest, they don't expect him to be clever. It's two o'clock here, what time is it there?

I-D: It's about nine o'clock.

HST: Well, it's two o'clock here and the sheriff is coming back from lunch, so is my lawyer, I hope. I must make this connection. I just can't have police out here . . . it makes me feel real nervous. If you can figure out some way that I can make this up to your people, I wish you'd tell me. Ralph will figure out some way to get me back, but it'll be horrible, you know, to land upside down in a vat of scum. But that's what he'll do to me.

I-D: What's next for you, Hunter?

HST: Well, I'll have to write a column about the day, called "Last Taxi to Scotland." It'll be a very sad piece, a hideous piece, a very dreary, shoddy, shameful piece . . . Apart from that I don't know . . . maybe I can come over to London and star in a musical. Right now I'm going to star in jail unless I get my lawyer . . . I am sorry I didn't make it. I'll leave earlier next time.

Rolling Stone—November 25, 1987

Interview by P. J. O'Rourke for the 25th anniversary of *Rolling Stone* magazine

O'Rourke: A lot of people thought you were making your stories up as you went along, that Gonzo journalism was more fiction than truth.

HST: I'm a great fan of reality. Truth is easier. And weirder. And funnier. Not all the time, but you can fall back on the truth. You can't fall back on a story you made up, because then you start to wonder if it is good or funny or right. I'm lazy. If I have a fact, I don't have to worry about if I've made the right move or said it properly.

O'Rourke: You can safely embroider up on it.

HST: Exactly. If you don't have it down in the beginning, then you're just putting on a weird dance. The only way I can get away with the Gonzo thing is by telling the truth. Take Muskie in the 1972 presidential campaign—Muskie's weeping in New Hampshire, going crazy in elevators in Florida, bitching and whining. I happened to pick up a pharmaceutical newsletter. There was a report on Ibogaine.

O'Rourke: Ibogaine? What is it?

HST: Oh, it's a wonderful African drug. Natives in African use it when they want to sit by a watering hole and wait for beasts. It freezes you in a catatonic stupor. But it also makes you subject to sudden rages. This was what I'd been watching with Ed Muskie, and I thought, "By God, that's what he must have been eating." So I wrote that a mysterious Brazilian doctor appeared, and the word was that he had brought in some Ibogaine. Which explained all of Muskie's behavior. If I'm going to go into the fantastic, I have to have a firm grounding in the truth. Otherwise everything I write about politics might be taken as a hallucination.

O'Rourke: The fantastic with its feet in the truth. Is that your definition of Gonzo?

HST: I give the Ibogaine as an example of the Gonzo technique. It's essentially a "what if." If Ed Muskie's acting like this here's an explanation. But I had to have his behavior down—talking with his innermost staff people. They were telling me things they don't tell other reporters. Like "Ye gods, man, how did I ever get involved with this campaign?"

O'Rourke: Does it bother you that a lot of writers try to imitate you?

HST: You notice there are not a lot of Gonzo journalists working. I get all kinds of things in the mail, from journalism students, from kids trying to be Gonzo journalists. If it doesn't work, man, it's horrible.

O'Rourke: Isn't your writing different from the work of most other so-called new journalists? I thought they were trying to get inside other people's heads and use the techniques of fiction. But you don't do that. You're a participant in the story, as opposed to just some fly on the wall.

HST: I'm the only writer in Tom Wolfe's book about new journalism with two pieces in it.* I like Wolfe. We talked a bit on the phone. I asked him, "Just what is it, Tom?" I never did understand it.

O'Rourke: Not at all?

HST: It was a leap forward from the old wire-service type of journalism. Mark Twain, in that sense, was a new journalist.

O'Rourke: What you do is something like Twain's *Innocents Abroad.* He's there. He's part of it. He's telling the story like he would to his friends.

HST: See, Wolfe is not a participant. He's a hell of a reporter. But being a part of the story is critical to me. Because that's where I get my interest in it. Wolfe gets his interest from backing off. And I get my interest from the adrenaline that comes from being that close.

O'Rouke: When I do Lebanon or the Philippines, what I'm trying to do is what the regular grown-up journalists do at the bar at ten o'clock. I want to tell the readers what these people tell each other at ten o'clock when they've had eleven drinks.

HST: I have a theory that the truth is never told across a desk. Or during the nine-to-five hours. Even on the telephone. I call people at night.

O'Rourke: And if you were there, you have to tell what happened to you too.

---

* Tom Wolfe, *The New Journalism,* Harper & Row, 1973.

HST: That's what gets me into stories. When Wolfe did the book on Kesey [*The Electric Kool-Aid Acid Test*] he wasn't there for a lot of it. He re-created it. [Whistle of admiration.] I can't do that. It's too damn much work. It's easier to be there. Maybe it's more of a risk.

O'Rourke: Like when you got stomped in *Hell's Angels.* It's an amazing part of that book. What would the ending have been without your being beat up?

HST: I'd finished the book. Shit, the book was already in type. I didn't like the cover. I told Random House, "You fucking pigs, I'll go out and photograph it myself." It was a Labor Day run. I was showing the Angels the cover. They hated it. And I said, "Hey, I agree with you." I'm showing them the dust cover, and it said $4.95—whew, $4.95, that must have been a long time ago. And the Angels said, "Jesus, $4.95! What's our share? We should get half." And I said, "Come on." I was getting careless, see. I said, "It takes a long time to write a book. Nothing—that's your share." The next thing I knew, I was waking up in the back seat of a car, and my nose looked like putty. My head was the size of yours and mine put together. It was morning, and a cop was looking in the window. He said, "My God, what happened to you?" And I said, "I went to a Hell's Angels party last night."

O'Rouke: Every article I've ever seen about you, there's a lot of shit about how crazy you are. Why do you have to carry this freight around of being America's premier maniac?

HST: Well, it's that fucking *Doonesbury,* for one thing.

O'Rourke: What possessed Garry Trudeau to make you Uncle Duke?

HST: His other characters were kind of stupid, I guess.

O'Rourke: But I've never understood how your character was cast. You're actually pretty close to Trudeau's political opinions.

HST: People think it's a joke. Like I get paid for it or something. You know, me and Garry must be big buddies. Well, fuck that. I've never even seen the little bastard. All this stuff avoids coming to the point that matters, which is what I turn out. Funny, I almost never get questioned about writing.

O'Rourke: Okay, a question about writing: Why are you a journalist?

HST: I would not be anything else, if for no other reason than I'd rather drink with journalists. Another reason I got into journalism: you don't have to get up in the morning.

O'Rourke: I'd rather hang out with bad writers than good accountants.

HST: Exactly. Imagine hanging out with lawyers. Now everybody wants to be a lawyer or a banker.

O'Rourke: Jesus Christ, isn't that strange? Because that is all our generation didn't want. We wanted anything else but. I wanted to work on the railroad.

HST: I wanted to go to Brazil. Well, let's make one quick pass at this and not brag at all. What we both wanted, a long time ago, was to be happy, successful, crazy writers and get paid for it. Right?

O'Rourke: How old were you when you decided to write?

HST: About sixteen. That was all that really interested me. That's the main thing about journalism: it allows you to keep learning and get paid for it.

O'Rourke: Who were you reading when you were in high school?

HST: Well, this might sound trite, but I was immensely impressed by Faulkner, by Hemingway, by Fitzgerald. But I didn't read any of them in high school, really.

O'Rourke: You decided to be a writer at sixteen. There must have been somebody you were reading.

HST: I was a vicious JD. I used to cut class and read things like Plato's *Republic.*

O'Rourke: A weird kind of JD.

HST: We'd go out and read that stuff all day and drink beer and—

O'Rourke: Rob gas stations?

HST: Yeah. I talk about that in *Fear and Loathing on the Campaign Trail.* The arrogance of the criminal mind. *The Fountainhead* was one of the things that really impressed me. That was my politics. I've never really been a liberal. To me politics is the art of controlling your environment. If you don't get into politics, somebody else controls your environment, your world.

O'Rourke: Why do you think the Sixties were worth a shit? Did you have fun in the Sixties?

HST: Yeah. A lot of fun. I had fun in the Seventies. I have fun now.

O'Rourke: Do you think the Sixties actually meant anything, or was it just some bohemian aberration?

HST: Well, it meant something to me. It enabled me to begin what's turned out to be, like, twenty-five years without a job and twenty-three years with no sleep.

O'Rourke: A lot of shit to go through to make a living.

HST: In the Sixties, I learned it had to be done. You really have to participate in your life. That was the most powerful thing about the Sixties. If you wanted to run a president out of office, you could do it. But this generation today near college age—I miss in them the sense of possibility.

O'Rourke: They do have a crabbed outlook, don't they? If they don't get into dental school, it's the end of the world.

HST: A BMW and a wife who's a lawyer. Everybody's wife's a lawyer now. Five of the seven Democratic candidates have wives who are lawyers.

O'Rourke: They're going to be in trouble when it comes around to divorce time, aren't they? You've called the kids of today "a generation of swine." How come?

HST: You call them fruit bags, that doesn't work. You call them yuppies, that doesn't work either. I found that "generation of swine" makes them jump.

O'Rourke: Recently you told a college audience at Marquette University, "George Bush should be killed. He should be stomped to death, and I'll join in."

HST: Okay, that's two federal crimes of five years each.

O'Rourke: Will you get indicted now, because we put that on tape?

HST: No, no. I explained it all to the Secret Service. See, I know about guilt, and I know about politics, and as I told the students, the guiltiest man in politics today is George Bush. He's at the root of this whole Iran-Contra thing.

O'Rouke: How did the students react?

HST: Hey, they cheered! Then I called for a voice vote. It was two-thirds to stomp him. Meanwhile some fucking maniac recorded it and took it to the *Milwaukee Journal*. And the U.S. attorney in Milwaukee was about to indict me on two felony charges: five years for threatening the vice president and another five for inciting others to do it. I was on my way to cover the Iran-Contra hearings for the *San Francisco Examiner,* and I started getting calls from the Secret Service.

O'Rourke: Did you answer any of those calls?

HST: Not at first, because I thought they were cranks. If it was important, they'd leave a message. And then the Secret Service showed up at the *Examiner* and at my lecture agency. I realized they were serious. So I called the Secret Service guy in Denver, Larry Hoppe. And he was very nice. And I said, "What's going on here, man?" And Hoppe said, "Dr. Thompson, let me tell you one thing: I would advise you not to go to Washington without talking to me first." So I said, "Come on over. What the hell."

Well, we talked for a while, and by that time Hoppe knew it was a joke. I said, "Have times changed? I've threatened to drag people around Washington by their nuts behind Oldsmobiles at a hundred miles an hour. I've advocated the slaughter of all politicians. What are the guidelines now?"

He had a pretty good sense of humor. He said, "Well, you can't say that he should be strung up. If you say that to people, whap! Ten years. You can say he should be tarred and feathered." And I said, "Wait a minute. I don't grasp it. I would almost rather be strung up than tarred and feathered. What's the difference?" And Hoppe said, "I don't know. That's the way it is. Don't go out anymore and threaten to string George Bush up or stomp him to death."

O'Rourke: Now to what level of public figure does this extend? Take somebody I really hate, like Meese.* Meese is not an elected official. Can I say that somebody should slice Meese open and wrap his intestines around a phone booth?

HST: No, you probably can't. He should be flogged—just not to death.

O'Rourke: What if we said Meese should be fucked by an elk?

HST: That's apparently harmless as hell. I believe that Ed Meese—being a person without any honor, a fat bastard, really a congenital cheap pig in the style of and on the level of Richard Nixon—should be locked in a large concrete basement with an elk. And the elk should be ram-fed full of acid before he's put in there.

O'Rourke: An angry, horny, acid-crazed elk.

HST: Meese is naked, and the elk is huge, maybe 800 plus.

O'Rourke: Elks can be ugly customers.

HST: And once they're full of acid, and they're really horny—oh yeah, all night long!

---

* Edwin Meese served as attorney general during the Ronald Reagan administration. He held the office between 1985 and 1988.

Studio for Men—February 1989

Thompson on Thompson

INTERVIEW WITH JACK THOMPSON

**Note: This is not a complete transcription.*

Jack Thompson: You've been over here before, haven't you?

HST: Yeah. I had a good time. I really did. It was a crazy trip. I came down to make a speaking tour and suddenly found myself in the Sydney Town Hall. I've got a picture of it right across the room from me here—with organs around the stage. Then I went to Melbourne and did the same thing.

JT: You got a civic reception here?

HST: Then I went to Canberra and spoke to the National Press Club. Every place I went, the people were crazy as loons.

JT: Do you like that? Do you like people to be as crazy as loons?

HST: Well, I like to be the craziest man in the room usually. There's great comfort in knowing that nobody else is as crazy as you are. Let me ask you, what made you become an actor?

JT: What made me become an actor? It was the easiest thing to do.

HST: Actors have to get up really early in the morning, don't they?

JT: Yes, they do. When you're working on a movie it's like, a 10-, 12-hour day and then home. It's very monastic for a brief period of time . . . You have a lot of respect and interest in your fellow writers, your fellow craftsmen.

HST: I use quotes like little jewels. I steal from other writers but at least I admit it. I hope it shows my good taste. Well, we're just a very small band of brothers. Joe Conrad, Mark Twain, Sam Coleridge . . . oh, let me think now . . . Scott Fitzgerald, Hemingway. I like Hemingway, but I kind of worry about being identified with him.

JT: Why is that? Because you keep your prose refined? You know what I mean, minimal?

HST: Well, not nearly as clean as Hemingway did.

JT: No, of course, but nevertheless it's clipped, isn't it? Do you think that's true of your own writing?

HST: When I do it right, it is. On the other hand I just got the British version of *Generation of Swine* and one of the things I'm in protest of, is that in the introduction there's a paragraph about heaven and hell, and they've changed it. You know what it's like when you tell a writer how to write? As an actor you'd get the same thing. Anyway, this thing about heaven—they took out every piece of punctuation in the whole goddamned paragraph.

I've already lived a lot longer than I planned to . . . I'm 51 now, minus 27 . . . really, I've already lived 24 years past what I really planned to live. I thought I would die at the age of 27. Well, I planned to. I worked at it.

JT: And to your surprise you survived it.

HST: No, to my horror. Well, you can imagine what happens to you when you live 24 years past your deadline.

JT: Past what you were planning for. Does this affect your writing?

HST: Oh . . . to a certain extent, yeah.

JT: So you're more a romantic than a cynic, are you not?

HST: Uh huh. Jack? I think you went straight to the point there, yes. That's a problem. That's a horror. To be a romantic and you know what people say . . . only the good die young. Well, where does that leave me then?

JT: And me, since I'm about the same age.

HST: How old are you Jack?

JT: I'm 48.

HST: Well we're together then.

JT: We are indeed. We've been through about the same period of time. I didn't know how long I was going to live but I certainly set out from a very young age to live as long as I possibly could.

HST: Oh Jesus! I set out from a very young age to live as short as I possibly could.

JT: Well, where did it go wrong for you Hunter? (laughs) Why are you still living? You are enjoying life, are you not?

HST: Yeah, I'm enjoying it. The reason I live up here in the mountains at 8,000 feet, deep in the snow and woods, is because when I go out in life it's a confrontation at all times, it's a war.

JT: I understand that. I have a farm which is home to me. I'm in town at the moment doing some work but my home, like your home, your re-

treat, is a little farm about 1,800 feet above sea level and about 14 miles from the coastline, 300 miles north of Sydney.

HST: That's nice, one of the really elegant places in the world. I like Australia.

JT: It's a beautiful part of the world, the east coast of Australia. So maybe when you come back here we should get together and go look out over the Pacific Ocean from one of those beaches.

HST: I'm supposed to come down and write a book about Australia.

JT: Fantastic. Would you write your book about Australia? I was going to say the same as your other books, but that's an absurd question. You would write about Australia, whatever you observed of Australia. There's a thing that I'd like to ask you. I spend quite a bit of time in America and years ago when Nixon was impeached, I thought that maybe there would be a sense in which the office of the President itself is not infallible. And I just wondered, because it's not entirely clear from your writing, I just wondered how you feel about the fallibility of the office of President.

HST: With Watergate, what we took great pride in here was that it didn't really have much to do with the President himself, or the office. It was more the fact that the people, and the press, actually did run the country and that we could throw out a crooked President, and there was a great amount of pride in that, not that the President was infallible. We've had some real bastards and I'm sure you have too down there. We took great pride in that we could throw him out.

You know, chase the bastards out of Washington. And somehow there was a great celebration of the power of the people after Watergate. Hell, I did it myself; I was proud of all of us. And somehow that has not carried over. There was a great celebration but it was honored more in the spirit than the reality.

JT: Don't you think that whatever forces there were that you exposed simply closed their ranks?

HST: I'm not sure they closed theirs. I think we got lazy and we congratulated ourselves—"Goddamn, weren't we . . . "

JT: Yes, and "Now what are we going to do?"

HST: More powerful. It's hard to throw a goddamned President out. Hell, I participated in throwing two of them out. Three actually, if you count Ford. What we've lost in this country now, I think, is that sense. Being able to throw them out; chase the President in the White House if he's crooked.

JT: Yes, participatory politics.

HST: Well politics is a thing that everyone can participate in. Hell, I'm a politician. I hate to say that, but in a democracy, you have to be a politician.

JT: Yes. If the democracy is working, surely everyone is involved politically.

HST: What I've been really disappointed in here is that we had the first under–50 percent voter turnout this time since 1920. Less than half of the voters care enough to vote. And that doesn't work in a democracy.

Primetime Live (ABC News)—February 27, 1992

Down and Out in Aspen

INTERVIEW WITH JUDD ROSE

**Note: This is the raw, transcribed text from a conversation between ABC News reporter Judd Rose and Hunter S. Thompson. The final piece, titled "Down and Out in Aspen," aired on February 27th, 1992 and also included interviews with notable Woody Creek residents George Stranahan and Sheriff Bob Braudis.*

Judd Rose: Let me start off by asking you the sort of central question to all this: who do you like better: Negroes or Jews?

HST: Why would you ask me a question like that?

Rose: Because David Rosenthal told me too as sort of an icebreaker.

HST: [Laughs] Yeah. It figures. How about you?

Rose: Me? Well . . . Jews. I'm related to a bunch.

HST: OK. No comment.

Rose: That doesn't mean I like them . . . All right, let's at least get a little serious here.

Rose: Let me read you something I think you'll recognize. You wrote, "Aspen is a place where absentee greed-heads are taking over the town like a pack of wild dogs, reducing the once-proud local population to shame and degradation." Tell me about that.

HST: That pretty well says it.

Rose: What's the problem with Aspen? What's happened to it?

HST: Well, that's a long story.

Rose: I got time.

HST: I can blow my own horn and say that when we had the Freak Power uprising, I lost the sheriff's race—thank God—but, at the same time, we really won the control of the local politics. Politics is the art of controlling your environment. This is my environment, so I have to be into politics. Nationally, so does the Democratic Party. The *New York Times Magazine* last year blamed me for this outburst of 26-million-dollar homes on the hillside.

Rose: Blamed you?

HST: Yeah.

Rose: Why is it your fault?

HST: You should have done your homework. Because I, with my henchmen Joe Edwards and Dwight Shellman—there were only three county commissioners in those days and all you had to get was two of them—I wanted to be the lightning rod. I'd seen the hate vote the year before . . . that's politics. In two years, we had the sheriff and two of the three seats, so we held back development. They're blaming me for when the dike broke. But we held it back about 10 years. We preserved our environment to whatever extent you can in a jet-set booming glitz. Suddenly Aspen was Hollywood crazed. It's a resort now, not a town.

Rose: Meaning?

HST: People have second homes here. A friend of mine took his daughters through the West End, the elegant core of the old town and where all the new houses are. He could go for that whole block and there wasn't even one light on or one person at home all through 2nd Street, Francis, and Lake, because all these are second homes and nobody lives here. People do live here, but the second home crowd, like Prince Bandar* who looks down on George [Stranahan] when he milks his cows. You know George, he's not a dairy farmer. George and I have turned Woody Creek into a hell of an Alamo.

Rose: How do you mean "Alamo"?

HST: Well, it's pretty dark.

Rose: I mean . . . I get the historical reference.

HST: Goddamn, man. Yeah, right? I hadn't thought about it that way before. Is there a cigarette out there? Goddamn.

Rose: You wrote that Aspen had become a "service community." You said "a slavish service community of pimps and middlemen where the only real question in politics is 'How much money do you have?'"

HST: We try to keep it from becoming that. We had a reason to brouhaha about the elk. We had an incident recently where people with a lot of money

---

* Prince Bandar is a former Saudi ambassador to the United States. He held the position as ambassador from 1983 to 2005. In 1991, he completed construction on "Hala Ranch," a massive, 56,000 square foot mansion between Aspen and Owl Farm, Woody Creek.

tried to buy their way into the wildlife corridor, the part that makes the place a mountain place to live. People wanted a zoo here; we already have a zoo, which these bastards with the second homes wouldn't pay for. The football team didn't have enough money for jerseys. The town is underfunded because of second homes and the absentee landlord class.

Rose: They give nothing back to Aspen?

HST: When they want something, they do. Prince Bandar gave about a half million dollars, maybe more. Shit, if I had that kind of money, I could find a lot of things to do.

Rose: So Prince Bandar is one of the good guys?

HST: One of these days, one of these bastards will come along and propose to fund a zoo. We'll round up all the animals up here and put them in the zoo, two by two. And then the Hollywood rich can move into the animal territory, which they can't now. We just recently got a case where the planning and zoning commission was influenced a bit. You could say bought, yeah. Boss Tweed* went to jail for worse things than they did. But they tried to create an exemption and overrule the wildlife commission. So they became wardens and all that and said, "Well, that may be elk country, but who the hell will notice. Just this little bite."

(Other person in room): That's the Tony Yerkovich† deal you're talking about.

HST: It's funny you should mention that.

Rose: Why don't you tell us about the Yerkovich deal? This is a guy who's one of the Hollywood crowd.

HST: Yeah. He's an old friend of mine.

Rose: Oh, you're friends?

HST: Oh yeah. It makes things difficult. I introduced him to the community.

Rose: But you're feuding, right?

HST: Not feuding. He just happens to be the one who influenced the planning and zoning to overrule the wildlife officers—the guys who make the

---

* Boss Tweed was a Democratic representative from New York. He served political office from 1853 to 1855. He was found guilty on corruption charges for swindling an estimated 75–200 million dollars from New York City taxpayers between 1865 and 1871.

† Tony Yerkovich is producer of the American television shows *Miami Vice* and *Hill Street Blues,* and is the owner of the Buffalo Lounge in L.A. where Hunter often dined.

maps. I don't need any maps. You can look off the porch here on the hill almost any day and see it's an elk highway.

Here is what you call the "seeds of a story."

Rose: [Reads from newspaper] "The creator of *Miami Vice* and his Woody Creek neighbors have convinced planning officials to override a division of wildlife recommendation not to build in a designated critical elk habitat." In other words, they're going to despoil the natural environment.

HST: If you somehow persuaded the planning and zoning commission to make one exemption—one here, one there—the next is to make exemptions for whole subdivisions. I thought we should hold a line there.

Rose: Let's call it what it is. What's going on here sounds like Hollywood money is spreading all over Aspen and part of what's happening is they're buying their way into the natural environment and spoiling it.

HST: That's a very broad stroke, but yeah.

Rose: I'd like you to tell me in your words what is going on here. And not just in this case, I mean in general. Quoting again from your book, you said, "There are two types of people now in Aspen: the users and the used and the gap between them is getting smaller everyday."

HST: I wrote that about two years ago, three maybe—"Community of Whores," the [San Francisco] *Examiner* column. Boy, I miss that *Examiner* . . . that ability with a column. I'm going to have to do it again in an election year.* But it's wonderful to have the illusion of the weekend's news and be able to smack the bastards overnight and have it published on Monday and see it. God knows if it really changes anything. But it's no wonder that people . . . I mean, here I am . . . a column . . . I have all kinds of access to . . . media. The whole Elko thing began and I tried to influence CNN on a devious plug. But we got wandering off on that . . .

Rose: Tell me what you mean. "The users and the used and the gap is getting smaller."

HST: The middle class has been driven out and the people who really created this town, the ones who came here to get away. I came here on the way from San Francisco to New York. My first book was coming out and I was all "Hot damn! I'm on the way to New York. Gonna swim in the

---

* Hunter did begin his weekly column for ESPN in 1999 that ended with his last column "Shotgun Golf" a week before his death. His column covered sports along with the Bush presidency and afforded Hunter one the most prolific writing periods in decades.

Plaza fountain and all that crap." And I stopped here because the book was postponed for a few months cause *Esquire* ran a big excerpt. So I was stuck and I rented a house just down the road here for a few months and I got to liking it. That was about '67. I just stayed here, because it's a nice place to live.

Rose: You felt like you'd found your paradise here?

HST: I never have thought it was a paradise. I keep meaning to move on.

Rose: One of the reasons we wanted to talk to you is because, as you talk to people who lived in Aspen and Woody Creek for a long time, a lot of people say, for all your outrageousness, you are pretty much the soul of this area. But, walk down Main Street in Aspen and you see Peters,* Marvin Davis,† movie stars, rock stars, and captains of industry. They seem to be the heart of Aspen now.

HST: I think maybe it's like being the Ghost of Christmas Past in terms of politics and being able to control your environment. I get very angry that even a friend of mine would try to buy, influence, and work behind my back. The county commissioners felt they worked behind their back to the extent where they canceled the whole planning and zoning authority to make these exemptions.

Rose: So is everything for sale around here?

HST: Well not any longer. Not the elk territory. I appealed the Yerkovich exemption. We got the law changed because the county commissioners voted 5–0 to withdraw the power of these realtors who work with the planning and zoning.

This valley's not for sale. Little pieces of Little Woody are, ye gods. Boy, if the dike broke here, those bastards would figure out some way to build on this side hill over here, even though it slides every time you get a torrential rain. They'd still build and sell them spec houses over there. This is home. This is my fortress.

Rose: So the valley would be covered with homes if they had half a chance . . .

HST: Yeah. People buy homes here to come here for Christmas.

---

* Jon Peters is a Hollywood film producer.

† Marvin Davis was the billionaire owner of Davis Petroleum, Aspen Skiing Company, the Denver Broncos, and Twentieth Century Fox.

Rose: So Hunter, you say Don Henley's* a friend; Don Johnson's† a friend. Are we being fair in indicting the Hollywood crowd? Are they all bad guys?

HST: Well, there's a difference between friendships in the Hollywood sense. That doesn't mean I won't turn my back if they want to build in the elk corridor, and that was kind of a shock to Tony. Until yesterday, in fact, I was blackballed from all the Hollywood guest lists.

Rose: You were blackballed from which list?

HST: The Hollywood people, though not all the Hollywood people. Just the glitz level. I went over to Jack Nicholson's house on Christmas. He's a totally different breed. He's been here for years. He came here as a hideout and went skiing here. There were no Hollywood parties on Christmas. What does he make, like 30 million a year? Jimmy Buffett and Jack Nicholson used to be the richest millionaires in Aspen. What's happened now is the billionaires have moved in on top of the millionaires. I'm the white trash on this road here.

Rose: Do you ever go into Aspen?

HST: As seldom as possible. It's become a nightmare with the police presence . . . and the sheriff is one of my best and only friends.

Rose: You say this is your fortress, so I . . .

HST: Well it was until those bastards came in my house last year with a bogus warrant and meddled around in here for God knows how many hours with six people. Those stupid swine. There are some lines you have to draw, and that was one of them for me. I have a lawsuit pending against the county and the DA's office now for $22 million. This is a national situation. The police state mentality is brought on by 12 years of one-party rule, and things get pretty weighted towards one side.**

---

* Don Henley is an American singer, songwriter, and drummer in the classic rock band, the Eagles, and was Hunter's neighbor for many years.

† Don Johnson, also residing in Woody Creek, is a television actor famous for his leading roles in the series *Miami Vice* and *Nash Bridges* (which Hunter and Johnson created together in the Owl Farm kitchen one evening).

** In February 1990, porn producer and actress Gail Palmer-Slater accused Thompson of sexual assault after a visit to Owl Farm. The district attorney and six officers searched Owl Farm for 11 hours, claiming to find LSD, a tenth of a gram of cocaine, a few ounces of marijuana, and dynamite. Thompson declared that his Fourth Amendment rights protecting against search and seizure had been violated and supporters organized a legal defense fund. The case and all charges were later dismissed. Hunter wrote extensively about this in his memoir, *Kingdom of Fear*.

Rose: I assume you have no particular sense of affection for what Aspen has become, you probably don't spend any time there and probably avoid it at all costs, right?

HST: Yeah, it's become dangerous. The federally granted police funds have swollen all police forces in the country with federal grants and money they get back from seizing people. That's one of the problems. We have a hugely swollen bureaucracy here now. I think the DA's budget in this county alone is like 38 million. It used to be 2 million. I'm crying about the good ole days, but the police bureaucracy is around everywhere. This should be a haven from it. Yeah, I engage in politics here because this is my home.

Rose: Let me ask you. You ran for sheriff once. If you ran again, let's say you ran for mayor or you ran for sheriff, and you got elected, what would be the first thing you'd do?

HST: Probably go to prison. I ran on the Freak Power ticket and the only compromise I would make was my deputies would only eat mescaline on duty. We had a pair of stocks built that were going to be on display at the county courthouse for dishonest drug dealers, as well as real estate brokers and drunken people of any kind. That's where the Hollywood mentality went wrong here.

It's like drug dealers: drugs are no excuse and being a star and money is no excuse to move into the elk corridor. We have to be a little responsible. They kind of forgot that, and you have to draw a line somewhere.

As for George and the county commissioners, we've just paid attention to politics. When you don't pay attention here, or anywhere else, someone else does. And that is what's happening to the second-home crowd.

Huge money is here. Prince Bandar is one of the royal family from Saudi Arabia and an ambassador to the U.S. He has a fortress up here. He's a wonderful guy. I admire Bandar, and he's been a decent neighbor. But, nonetheless, he has radar tracking of all the roads around here for security, and the State Department is practically in his home. He's been here for a long time, as with another Arab—Prince Faisal. He's been a neighbor for 10 years, and he's been great. But when you get Prince Faisal and Prince Bandar, the place becomes a nexus.

For example, in '90, before the Persian Gulf War, Bush* and Thatcher† came out here with their brigades in Woody Creek for a multi-summit. I

* President George H. W. Bush.

† Margaret Thatcher was the prime minister of the United Kingdom from 1979 to 1990.

mean, here's George Bush coming out of the Woody Creek Tavern with a bullhorn, waving to people.

Rose: A black day in Woody Creek . . .

HST: Yeah. We had to stop for like 45 minutes while the Bush-Thatcher motorcade came up from the tavern. They made the same right uphill, turned by Henley's house, and went up to the meadows.

Rose: So they did not stop here?

HST: No. Their destination was a little below. But the Secret Service did not come here and sweep the neighborhood. That was a great tribute to my perceived responsibility. There was a gun freak holed up, right over here on this mesa with a posse right there by the Bush entrance, by his flight path, and what the Secret Service thought was inside was a maniac gun freak.

Rose: You have, for a long, long time, been an artist of the written word, but now you've gotten into a different kind of art now. Tell me about it. We saw some of the procedure out there tonight. What are you doing?

HST: Well, the same thing I've been doing for twenty years. I'm just getting paid for it now.

Rose: Which is what, shoot?

HST: Karmic-ly write. Shooting and Karmic-ly write.

Rose: So you've been doing this for a long time, and now you're getting paid for it.

HST: Exactly.

Rose: Give me an idea, though, of what it is you are doing. You're obviously shooting, but there's more to it than that. Just tell me what the process is. You shoot these posters.

HST: I should get paid to answer that dangerous bullshit question of "What does it all mean?"

Rose: You don't have to tell me what it all means.

HST: I'm not doing the same thing shooting posters that I am being a defender of the elk or running for sheriff.

(Waves a *Rolling Stone* issue) This is Judge Clarence Thomas . . .

Rose: You're a friend of Judge Clarence Thomas?

HST: Wellllll . . . You might say that.

Rose: You say in the article "old pals."

HST: It was one night. I hope you don't make all your friends that way.

Rose: Quite a night it was, I understand.

HST: Memorable indeed. Yeah, the judge was a sport. He was a warrior and he was fun. This is the judge in action a long time ago. And we've all done weird things in our past . . . and it wasn't just the judge.

(Rose begins reading from "Fear and Loathing in Elko.")

Rose: I want to get back to your artwork here for a second.

HST: Well, this is my artwork.

Rose: This is obviously art, but there is the art that people don't probably know very much about. You're shooting the posters out there and then you're painting them, and these are being sold for fairly astronomical sums.

HST: I've been on this parade for over 20 years. I've been shooting at Hoover and people like him for 20 years, in a lot of ways. And I think it is important that somebody does that.

(Rose is handed a statement to read.)

Rose: All right, this is a statement that you wrote.

"Some men see a smoking, splintered mural full of bullet holes and blood flecks and the charred, jagged edges of random bomb blasts in the groin or the brains or the teeth of a damaged human image with its hands blown off and ask, why? But I see it and ask, why not?"

That's almost Kennedy-esque.

HST: Yeah, that's art. There's a little bit of the art getting the camel through the eye of the needle. We're talking here about a sitting Supreme Court Justice, and no decent person would run for the Supreme Court if you could have your path examined, even if for one night, 10 years ago on the high desert in Elko, when you happen to run into a herd of sheep on the road and tumble your white Cadillac into the desert and I just happen to come along.

Rose: I understand.

(Reading from the statement:)

"That is the art, Mary, that is the crystallized vision. I am only the medium, the channel—a human lightning rod for all the smoking homeless visions and horrible acid flashbacks of a whole generation, which are precious if only as living savage monuments to a dream that haunts us all.

"In our secret dreams we were brutes. We wallow and murder in sodomy. But, we also wallowed in beauty and we knew that beauty was truth, even when it fried you to a cinder or blew off the top of your head. But we still

live in fear of these flashbacks, which come in the night without warning and cause us to scream in our sleep. 'Art is long and life is short and success is very far off.' Joe Conrad said that, and he suffered more grievous flashbacks on any given Sunday than most men will know in all their lives. That is why I must do my art, Mary. It is often cruel and splintered and primitive, but I have no choice. They are graven images. Foul outbursts of madness and brainless violence that will always remain unspeakable unless we make it art.

"Or music. Or bombs. Or anything else that blows up or burns or explodes in a meaningless fireball until we give it the dignity of resurrection, the shock of recognition and the wondrous glow of love. When the going gets weird, the weird turn pro—that is the dogma. That is all Ye know and all Ye need to know. Take it from me—I understand these things."

HST: Very good. Good reading. You should read on the next audio book album.

Rose: So I guess that pretty much sums it up. I feel like I should go out and buy one of these things now?

(Peacocks in the background)

Rose: Peacocks?

HST: No. It's babies getting eaten by wolves outside. Yeah. Those are peacocks. It's horrible. Have you ever seen *Midnight Express*? It's the screech of a peacock in the night.

Rose: Well listen, we'll just wrap this up by asking you . . .

HST: "What does it all mean?"

Rose: "What does it all mean?"

HST: It means . . . hmm, shit. It's all about fun, really. If you can't have fun, it is not worth doing.

Rose: Are you having fun?

HST: Yeah. From time to time.

Rose: You're having too much fun?

HST: No, no. Hey, hey—that's what I got busted for. The too much fun club. We used to say, "It's only rock and roll . . . "

Rose: And I like it . . .

HST: It's getting harder and harder to like it these days. And that's not really rock and roll to keep greed-heads from moving into your backyard. There's a standard that we have to pay some attention to, or else our entire behavior is debased or degraded.

Rose: Is it ever going to get so bad that you're going to leave Aspen?

HST: It could. It might. Well, it almost got pretty bad when they came in and searched my house. Due to the duo that came to help me—the National Association of Criminal Defense Lawyers, Goldstein, Killam, Haddon, Michael Stepanian—we beat them like dogs.

Rose: But things keep getting worse out there in Aspen. Do you see a day when you would pack up and leave?

HST: I'm not sure I would really pack up and leave. As Faulkner said in "Barn Burning," "Wood and hay can burn."

Spin Magazine—May 1993

Interview by Kevin P. Simonson

Hunter S. Thompson, the outlandish creator of Gonzo journalism, talks with Kevin P. Simonson about life, liberty, and the pursuit of a good editorial assistant.

The tape recorder was turned on at 4:10 a.m. in Thompson's dark kitchen.

Spin: Are you anybody's target?

HST: I'm in a weird position—I'm seeing films about me on television and people writing books about me. It's very eerie to live like that. I try to ignore it.

Spin: Tell me about your next book, *Polo Is My Life: Memoir of a Brutal Southern Gentleman.*

HST: *Polo is My Life* will be my final statement. It's a love story much in the manner of *Blue Velvet* or *Psycho.*

It is a bizarre story about a doomed and dangerous love affair between a journalist who also works for the CIA and a beautiful pure blond, polo-crazy heiress from Palm Beach who is hiding out in the Rockies because her "family" was somehow involved in the murder of John Kennedy. She had written a bad check to buy a chic nightclub in Aspen—so her younger brother, a failed priest, can play the jazz piano every night in public, like Eddie Duchin.*

It's a doom-struck tale for our time. A hopeless maze of sex, violence, and treachery that can only end in death.

Spin: For years I've been hearing about your book "The Rum Diary." Are you working on it and what are your ambitions toward fiction writing?

HST: I've always had and still do have an ambition to write fiction. I've never had any real ambition within journalism, but events and fate and my

---

* Eddie Duchin was a popular American bandleader and pianist during the 1930s and 1940s.

own sense of fun keep taking me back for money, political reasons, and because I'm a warrior. I haven't found a drug yet that can get you anywhere near as high as doing a little time on the Proud Highway.

"The Rum Diary" is currently under cannibalization and transmogrification into a very strange movie.

Spin: Any other movie projects in the future?

HST: I got *Fear and Loathing in Las Vegas* sold and launched into a movie project.

Spin: Are you doing the screenplay?

HST: Probably. We're still arguing about the ending. They say it's weird and not fulfilling for today's "escapist" movie audience . . . which may be true. The script ends with the hero snorting amyls and going crazy in a gift shop at the Denver airport, while trying to purchase stolen Dobermans. I told them I'd rewrite it to have a bomb explode at the end—the whole airport will explode—like in *Terminator.*

Spin: You once said that if the movie was ever made, you wanted Dennis Hopper to play you.

HST: He might direct it. I wanted James Woods and Anthony Perkins. I still think Dennis might be good playing my role.

Spin: Sounds like a good project for David Lynch.

HST: We talked about that. He wanted to do that, as a matter of fact, and then he got onto that *Twin Peaks* thing.*

Spin: Do you think the book's heavy drug and alcohol content would have to be toned down to appeal to today's audience?

HST: No. Times have changed, the pendulum is swinging back. There are millions of boozers and hopheads out there, but they lie about it. It's dangerous these days to whoop it up in public. You can get locked up for having fun. TWA and Pan Am go broke, but new jails are a growth industry. It's like Germany in 1937. The Nazis were all dope fiends. They just refused to admit it.

Spin: Do you still drive a Chevy convertible—"the Great Red Shark"—like you did in the Vegas book?

---

* *Twin Peaks* was a serialized television drama that aired on ABC. David Lynch and Mark Frost created and coproduced the series.

HST: You bet. Let's go to the garage. This is all trouble waiting to happen—two red cars, one a gift from the Mitchell brothers,* a new BMW motorcycle, the newest one, that will go 140 miles per hour.

Spin: What was your role as executive consultant on *Where the Buffalo Roam*?

HST: I was staying with Bill Murray that summer. We had a big house in the Hollywood Hills, and I had a red 450 Mercedes. We've been friends for a long time. It's a tribute to some strange kind of friendship that it can survive throughout shooting the movie. He did a good job. I refer to it as impersonation. But it's a silly movie. It's a cartoon. Bill and I did all kinds of rude scenes. I had pretty much free rein.

Spin: Some libraries classify *Fear and Loathing in Las Vegas* as a travelogue, some classify it as nonfiction, and some classify it as a novel. You refer to it as "a far-out experiment" in Gonzo journalism, yet many critics consider it a masterpiece. How much of the book is true and how would you rate it?

HST: *Fear and Loathing in Las Vegas* is a masterpiece. However, true Gonzo journalism as I conceive it should be rewritten.

I would classify it, in Truman Capote's words, as a "nonfiction novel" in that almost all of it was true and did happen. I warped a few things, but it was a pretty accurate picture. It was an incredible feat of balance more than literature. That's why I called it *Fear and Loathing.* It was a pretty pure experience that turned into a very pure piece of writing. It's as good as *The Great Gatsby* and better than *The Sun Also Rises,* but it is not a novel. It is a very strange piece of reporting; at least it seems very strange now. Almost creepy, and of course I would never do that kind of thing now. We are Nazis . . .

Spin: A while ago, the spotlight shifted from your writing to your personal life when you were accused of sexual assault and several other felonies. [After being accused of third-degree sexual assault, D.A. investigators showed up at Thompson's home and conducted a search, finding large quantities of drugs and illegal dynamite.] Did the experience change you?

HST: I couldn't have told you what the Fourth Amendment said until I got rolled over by that gang of white trash pigs that came out here to the

---

* Jim and Artie Mitchell are the owners of the O'Farrell Theatre strip club in San Francisco where Thompson served as night manager for two years. He dubbed the club "the Carnegie Hall of public sex in America."

house. You pay more attention to it when they come to get you. The "Victory or Death" stance that I took is really a difficult one for most people to take. [Thompson refused a plea bargain for two years of court supervision and chose to face a possible 16-year prison term. All charges were dropped.] Everybody is rolling over. This is an age of cowardice, fear, greed. You can fight city hall, you can beat the system. People are getting afraid to try.

Spin: Did the end result overcome the bad publicity you received?

HST: It was about as much fun as I've had in my life. I thought it was a huge, positive thing. A great victory, and I don't think it's a personal one-shot victory.

I think it's something people should do and be able to do. If more people could say: "Fuck you. You're the ones who broke the law. You came into my house." However, the law is changing so rapidly now that you really have to have the best lawyers to fight now.

Spin: Since the trial, have you had any more encounters with law enforcement agencies?

HST: I had a little problem at the Durango Red Lion Inn. I fell in love with a table that was sitting in the middle of the presidential suite, so I told the management that I wanted to buy it from them, but nobody had the authority to sell it to me. So I went down to the office and had a friendly talk with them. Finally, I said, "Shit, I should have just stolen the table. Here I am down here trying to be honest and asking you just to put it on my bill and you won't." And the catering manager said, "Yeah, you should have." And then I said, "Yeah, I'll do that." I had chartered a plane. About two days later one of the deputy sheriffs from here called and said, "There is a sergeant calling from Durango saying they are going to have to arrest you for grand theft unless you make some arrangements to pay for that table." So I had a buddy go down and pay for it—$509—I could have bought the same thing in Denver for $150. Evidently the maid had reported a big egg-shaped indention in the rug and the manager turned me in to the police.

Spin: Don't you have a pretty impressive collection of robes you've stolen from hotels around the country?

HST: I pay for those robes! They always go on the bill. They put them on there for $75 a piece.

Spin: Your use of drugs is one of the more controversial elements about you and your writing. Do drugs and alcohol play as big a role in your life now as they did in your earlier work?

HST: Obviously, my drug use is exaggerated or I would be long since dead. I've already outlived the most brutal abuser of our time—Neal Cassady. Me and William Burroughs are the only ones left. We're the only unrepentant public dope fiends around, and he's 78 years old and claiming to be clean. But he hasn't turned on drugs, like Timothy Leary—that big phony.

Spin: How have drugs affected your perception of the world and/or your writing?

HST: Drugs usually enhance or strengthen my perceptions and reactions, for good or ill. They've given me the resilience to withstand repeated shocks to my innocence gland. The brutal reality of politics alone would probably be intolerable without drugs. They've given me the strength to deal with those shocking realities guaranteed to shatter anyone's beliefs in the higher idealistic shibboleths of our time and the "American Century." Anyone who covers his beat for 20 years, and that beat is "The Death of the American Dream," needs every goddamned crutch he can find.

Besides, I enjoy drugs. The only trouble they've given me is the people who try to keep me from using them. Res ipsa loquitur. I was, after all, a Literary Lion last year.

Spin: How is your physical health?

HST: I am like a fawn.

Spin: Does the media portrayal of you as a "crazy" amuse, inflame, or bore you?

HST: The media perception of me has always been pretty broad. As broad as the media itself. As a journalist, I somehow managed to break all the rules and still succeed. It's a hard thing for most of today's gentleman journalists to understand, but only because they can't do it. The smart ones understood immediately. The best people in journalism I've never had any quarrel with. I am a journalist and I've never met, as a group, any tribe I'd rather be a part of or that are more fun to be with—in spite of the various punks and sycophants of the press. I'm proud to be part of the tribe.

It hasn't helped a lot to be a savage comic-book character for the last 15 years—a drunken screwball who should've been castrated a long time ago. The smart people in the media knew it was a weird exaggeration. The dumb ones took it seriously and warned their children to stay away from me at all costs. The really smart ones understood it was only a censored, kind of a toned-down children's book version of the real thing.

Now we are being herded into the '90s, which looks like it is going to be a truer generation of swine, a decade run by cops and wardens—a generation without humor, without mercy; dead heroes and diminished expectations, a decade that will go down in history as the Gray Area.

At the end of this decade no one will be sure of anything except that you must obey the rules, sex will kill you, politicians lie, rain is poison, and the world is run by whores. These are terrible things to have to know in your life, even if you're rich.

A doomsday kind of thinking has taken over the media, as it has business and politics: "I'm going to turn you in, son—not only for your own good, but because you were the bastard who turned me in last year."

Spin: How do you react when you see others mimicking or plagiarizing your individual Gonzo style?

HST: What others? Only a madman would want to be labeled "Gonzo journalist" in these weird and wretched times. I have not pioneered a growth industry. I never looked for gangs or crowds or followers . . . in the Tim Leary tradition. But it's nice to have friends. Nobody needs mimics.

Spin: Do you consider P. J. O'Rouke a worthy Gonzo associate?

HST: P.J. is an old friend. He is a monster. We have fought back to back with iron bars against people who wanted to kill us. We have spilled blood together. We have walked with the King. Shit, P.J. would stab you just for fun.

Spin: Sweet Jesus, why?

HST: Who knows? P.J. is a warrior. He stabs for his own reasons, and he's usually right. Any enemy of P.J.'s is an enemy of mine. So be warned. If he stabs you, so will I.

Spin: Did O'Rouke get his style from you?

HST: No. P.J. has a style all his own and an attitude of his own. P.J. doesn't need to imitate my style. He isn't trying to be a Gonzo writer. I first ran into P.J. when he was testing new cars for *Car and Driver.* He came out here and we did some driving. I performed some serious road tests on a new Chrysler—one that he'd rented for Jimmy Buffett's wedding. I ran it full bore on twisting roads with him in the back seat. Anytime you're in the back seat and somebody is really screwing it on it is totally terrifying. The driver has to think about what he's going to do next, but the passenger becomes increasingly fearful about what the driver is going to do next—or he's still weeping about what happened last time. But P.J. handled it well. He is very cool under fire and he's also a good driver.

Spin: Do you worry about plagiarism, Doc?

HST: No, I pride myself with having the wisdom and taste to steal from the right people: Conrad, Fitzgerald, the Marquis de Sade, Prescott, Isak Dinesen, Coleridge, Twain, Pee Wee Herman—that swine. Yeah, there's also Ed Bradley, Anne Rice, Ralph Steadman—these are all my friends. I learn from these people. Especially the dead ones.

Spin: Are there other authors you're partial to?

HST: Jim Harrison is one of the really good writers in this country. I like everything Harrison does.

Spin: What does your writing routine consist of?

HST: It's very unusual that you arrive here on the same day as my box [of X-rated tapes]. I use these things for mood setters to get in the rhythm of working. *Caligula*'s one of my all-time favorites.*

I think I've suffered a general dip in adrenaline production, and I'm addicted to my own adrenaline usually.

Spin: Do you still crank everything out on your typewriter or have you started using a computer?

HST: I don't like the little screen. It's good for short stuff, but I think in terms of tangible weight. If I could get a big screen and show ten pages at once, but that kind of defeats the purpose. I suppose if I really got into it, it would help, or if I thought Harrison worked on a computer or he persuaded me I should, maybe I'd try it. I really think computers are only as smart as the person who programs it, and I'd have to program the damn thing myself in order for it to meet my needs.

Spin: I understand you have a difficult time keeping your editorial assistants around.

HST: It's my eternal quest for an editorial assistant or assistants. I need a staff of about six. I need a staff and apparently it has become too onerous for people in this country. I've been interviewing people out here for I don't know how long.

I'm looking for a girl who is fast and vicious, she must be fun and smart. The real question is, of course: Can she type? We can narrow this down pretty quick.

* *Caligula* (1979) is a feature film about the tragic Roman emperor Caesar Caligula, starring Malcolm McDowell. Gore Vidal wrote the screenplay.

I've got a catalog of mail-order brides here I'm currently considering bringing over. Right now English isn't so important—I just need an assistant. It's a dating service, of sorts.

Spin: Why was your last David Letterman appearance canceled?

HST: Well, I've been on there two or three times. I hate to go over there to the studio and hang around for two or three hours. I get drunk and mean, pacing around for that long.

The producer called me up the day before I was scheduled and said, "Hunter, you're going to be a good boy? You're going to be nice this time?" And I said, "Yeah, Frank, don't worry about it, as long as I can go on first. That way you don't have to worry about my behavior later on." He said he'd try to do it, but I was scheduled for third. I replied, "Well, Frank, if that happens, you know I'll get drunk and mean. I'll bring four huge thugs over there and they're going to hold Letterman down while I shave his head on camera."

Letterman has never liked me—he loses control of the show. Letterman's kind of a chicken shit. I never even thought he was really that funny; he's just sort of a punk.

The next day I was informed nothing could be done so I said, "You know what's going to happen. I've been up all night and I'm nuts already. If I come over there and drink heavily, you know shaving the head might be all the humor I can find that afternoon." Later, Letterman abruptly canceled it, and he had to talk, shovel smoke for 20 minutes, rather than have me on there.

Spin: The *New York Times* called you a "bitterly disillusioned idealist." Do you agree with this assessment?

HST: Yeah. But so what? That comes with the territory, and it's not bad company. They could have called me a "rich and joyful cynic"—like Ivan Boesky* or George Bush. I take a certain pleasure in being a bitterly disillusioned idealist. It's not as bad as it sounds. Maybe I'm just a romance junkie born addicted to the love and adventure ethic—cursed and burdened and stooped all my life from carrying the albatross of the "Romantic Sensibility"—like Shelley and Keats and Lord Byron and Big Sam Coleridge and Keith Richards and Bob Dylan.

---

* Ivan Boesky is a former Wall Street investor. He was convicted in a massive insider trading scandal in 1986.

Spin: All those people went nuts, Doc. Is that what you're trying to say? That you're going insane?

HST: Not me, Jocko. I am a brutal Southern gentleman who somehow got into politics. There was no avoiding it, then or now. They are backing us out of our holes—and you know what happens to them.

Vanity Fair—September 1994

Proust Questionnaire

Gonzo journalism's granddad (and sole survivor), Hunter S. This month he casts a bleary eye on V.F.'s Proust Questionnaire.

Vanity Fair: Which historical figure do you most identify with?

HST: Marquis de Sade.

Vanity Fair: Which living person do you most admire?

HST: Richard Nixon—despite rumors of his death.

Vanity Fair: What is the trait you most deplore in others?

HST: Greed and dumbness.

Vanity Fair: What is your greatest extravagance?

HST: The money I spend on the physical love of animals.

Vanity Fair: What is your favorite journey?

HST: Racing the stoplights on Park Avenue in a fast car at four o'clock in the morning.

Vanity Fair: What do you consider the most overrated virtue?

HST: Moderation.

Vanity Fair: On what occasion do you lie?

HST: To the police.

Vanity Fair: What is your greatest regret?

HST: The destruction by greedheads of the once honorable Woody Creek Tavern.

Vanity Fair: If you could change one thing about your family, what would it be?

HST: To get rid of my evil son.

Vanity Fair: If you could choose what to come back as, what would it be?

HST: I have no choice (and neither do you). I have been here many times for many reasons and I will be here after you leave. I am Lono.

Vanity Fair: Where would you like to live?

HST: In the Place of Refuge on the south Kona coast.

Vanity Fair: What is your most marked characteristic?

HST: A tortured, honky-tonk smile.

Vanity Fair: Who is your favorite hero of fiction?

HST: Dracula.

Vanity Fair: Who are your heroes in real life?

HST: Hal Haddon [lawyer, Gary Hart's campaign manager], Morris Dees [civil rights activist], Nina Hartley [porn star], Jacques Cousteau [undersea explorer].

Vanity Fair: How would you like to die?

HST: Explode.

Vanity Fair: What is your motto?

HST: "Res Ipsa Loquitur."

NuCity Press (Albuquerque, New Mexico)—March 1, 1995

NuCity Goes Gonzo

BY ALMA GARCIA AND NORMA JEAN THOMPSON

He who makes a beast of himself gets rid of the pain of being a man.
—HST

Here Today, Gonzo Tomorrow.

It's all true: Dr. Hunter S. Thompson is an electric charge of almost superhuman wattage, and energizes as many people around him as he drains. Naturally, he's also as human as the next person—only perhaps just a whole lot more brutal, kind, macho and in need of nurturing than the average person, all at once.

It's difficult to capture him, in more ways than one. Our taped interview with him yielded hours of unintelligible mumblings, as well as impenetrable static, the roar of car engines, and a background soundtrack of television and loud music—much of it orchestrated by Thompson himself, depending on his interest in having certain information recorded, it seemed.

In any case, we were able to salvage a few of the Doctor's thoughts, some of them even pertaining to the subjects in which he is considered to be an expert. Dr. Hunter S. Thompson's fans may have to struggle to reconcile his myth to his manhood, but it's good to know that in this world of compromised lives, a life of Gonzohood can be lived with complete integrity.

AN INTERVIEW WITH DR. HUNTER S. THOMPSON

On President Clinton

Norma Jean Thompson: Do you ever speak with Bill Clinton? Does he know what you're saying about him?

HST: Oh, yeah. I got into the Clinton thing with the idea that we could influence people. Yeah, the rock and roll president. He stands for everything

I hate; violating the Fourth Amendment, search and seizure. I've said worse things about Clinton than I'm saying now. I think the worse thing I've ever said about him is that he has the redneck taste of a man who would go on a double date with the Rev. Jimmy Swaggart.* That's a nasty thing to say. I've also said he has the morals of a lizard. He's a hiccup of history.

NJT: You really don't like him. Do you feel a responsibility to the people who take your opinions seriously? Doesn't it just help people rally around the right when you put him down?

HST: That's no reason why I should spend another four years getting tangled up by a treacherous asshole like Clinton. There are limits. He's further to the right than George Bush.

On General Politics

Alma Garcia: You said in *Fear and Loathing on the Campaign Trail* that tradition liberalism is dying or dead. Is Clinton exemplifying that?

HST: They should have done some ethnic cleansing of the liberals a long time ago.

AG: What are the top three things that should be on the presidential agenda?

HST: Resignation.

AG: Aside from resignation, is there anything in particular you think should be at the top of the presidential agenda?

HST: It doesn't matter right now, because (Clinton) won't fight for it. If people rallied behind him and decided to get something done, some agenda he endorsed, he would abandon it. It's a no-win situation, a serious character flaw.

AG: Who are the politicians you like?

HST: Not many. I'd like Gore in the House. Clinton you really can't turn your back on. If the Gores stayed in the cabin (on Thompson's property), they'd fit it. I wouldn't have to worry about them stealing anything. Now if the Clintons stayed there.

AG: Who are the other bad politicians?

HST: Well, it's a crooked class.

AG: Who are the worst ones?

HST: Fewer and fewer good people are getting into politics.

---

* Rev. Jimmy Swaggart is a Pentecostal preacher and televangelist.

AG: Who would you like to see as president? Next election, if it were possible, even if it's not someone who could possibly have a chance?

HST: I think Muhammad Ali would be good.

AG: Anyone who's a politician?

HST: If you're interested in generality, Gore. He's pretty interesting. He's the only one I'd vote for.

AG: And then we would have First Lady Tipper.

HST: Well, that's realistic. What if Clinton got sick? Tipper's not that terrifying compared to the Clintons.

On the Right to Bear Arms

NJT: Do you think that our Constitution is aging in the sense that it is not appropriate to this time anymore? Particularly in regard to the right to bear arms. Do you think it had a different intention when it was originally written?

HST: Are you suggesting that we trade it in for something new?

NJT: No.

HST: No. I think it's pretty good.

NJT: You think the Constitution still holds up?

HST: Yeah.

NJT: Even through times like that?

HST: Yeah.

NJT: Even though the people who wrote it might have had something else in mind?

HST: Well, to answer a question like that, you have to take considerable options. So what would you have done?

NJT: Well, it's a real problem. Think about guns today in gangs and with 12-year-olds in school. I mean, that was not the original intention. Wasn't originally bearing arms the way of protecting the democracy?

HST: Yeah. Well-armed militia.

NJT: I was just wondering if there are aspects of the Constitution, then, that are aging.

HST: Well, probably so. It's more than 200 years old.

NJT: Well, you have said the next five years will be like 50 years passing, and we're still trying to use a system that . . .

HST: What do you have in mind? What program are you pushing? The Constitution's done pretty well . . . I'm just giving my opinion. You have a special agenda. You have a grudge against the Second Amendment.

On Life in the '90s

AG: If the '80s was the Generation of Swine (referring to Thompson's book by the same name), what is the '90s?

HST: The '90s is the '80s without money.

AG: Do you know what will come after the '90s?

HST: I can't really guess. Something will of course. But I don't foresee all of this. (Gestures at the world at large around him.) It's not my business to foretell the future anyway.

On Fear and Loathing on the Campaign Trail

AG: Are the people who were involved in, say, the '92 presidential campaign—the press people, the aides—are they still getting as trashed as they were in '72? Or is this now the age of restraint?

HST: (Standing up to plant a kiss on Garcia's cheek) Thank you so much for asking that question!

No. That was a different kind of campaign . . . The first campaign without sex was '88. That's when things changed. This one was no fun, if drugs and sex is what you're talking about.

AG: What brought about that different approach?

HST: I think AIDS.

AG: AIDS and the "Just Say No" age?

HST: Yeah. Clinton is more anti-drug than Bush ever was.

AG: Although this may be an obvious question, how is media coverage of that kind of stuff evolving?

HST: I think it's disgraceful. Political coverage is getting worse.

AG: If you were to do another campaign, like the way you did in '72, what would you focus on this time?

HST: I wouldn't. It's something you do once. I have more access than I ever did, but with this whole rock and roll thing, it's not the educational experience it was the first time. The presidential campaign from the inside, now that was an adult dose. And that was a different role, covering a campaign. I realize my role has changed. I sign more autographs now.

On Drug Legalization and Addiction

AG: Do you think that drug legalization will ever be a viable prospect?

HST: Yeah, it'll have to be.

AG: For everything, or just for certain substances?

HST: It should be pretty much across the board. Not in Clinton's time. He'd give up anything that had to do with his brother (alluding to Roger Clinton's drug convictions).*

NJT: Do you think of yourself as a sex addict? Like you're a drug addict and alcoholic?

HST: I don't really consider myself an addict of any kind.

NJT: Have you ever gone a single day without taking a substance of any kind?

HST: This is the first day in a long time I haven't had sex.

On His Work

AG: Are you writing pretty much what you want to write? Or is there something else that you haven't gotten to yet?

HST: I like the surreal part of a story . . . Now I want to see what it's like to follow a storyline.

AG: Are you interested in writing again something in the style of *Hell's Angels*?

HST: Yeah, I'm a professional—a hitman. I like to think of it that way from the start.

AG: Since you've done straight journalism, are you interested in doing something totally fictional?

HST: Yes. That's what *Polo Is My Life* is supposed to be. Characters are a problem. And I keep running into reality. It follows me.

AG: Is your approach to writing a book the same each time?

HST: Feels the same. The details are different.

AG: What's your favorite book that you've done?

HST: This one's my favorite now. (Holding up a copy of *The Curse of Lono*.) I don't know why.

AG: Norma Jean told me that you and Ralph Steadman (the artist who has collaborated with Thompson since 1971) are an incredible team. She said that he's very different from you—a very quiet little British man—but

---

* Roger Clinton is the half-brother of former President Bill Clinton. Roger Clinton served a year in prison for dealing and distributing cocaine while Bill Clinton was governor of Arkansas. Bill Clinton granted his half-brother a presidential pardon before leaving office in January 2001.

that his shadow expresses the same outrage and expresses the same beliefs as your active voice.

HST: Yeah. With Ralph, you can take anything on. He's incredible.

On Sex, Love, and Marriage

NJT: What is the attraction to girls between 18 and 23, since that seems to be your age of preference as far as sexual activity goes.

HST: Well, yeah, there are reasons . . . 22 is a very good age.

AG: How so? Physically?

HST: At 22 you can afford to fuck around a little bit . . . 22 years old is a nice resilient age.

NJT: Do you think a 22-year-old would be capable of understanding and loving you?

HST: That's a different thing entirely you're talking about.

NJT: You have a secret reputation as being a pretty sexy guy. Do you know about this?

HST: I didn't know I have that reputation. Well, I don't know what to say.

NJT: I think it's because you're sort of ultra-masculine.

HST: A right-wing Nazi . . .

NJT: Yeah, and you bring out the real feminine in women.

HST: This S&M kick is all my idea . . .

AG: Somebody in Aspen told us that you were getting married. To a 21-year-old cocktail waitress.

HST: (Snorting, chuckling) Well, that's interesting, isn't it?

NJT: Do you think you'll ever get married again?

HST: I suppose it's always possible.

NJT: Is it possible you could still father a child again and want to be the father of a young child?

HST: That would be hard. I'd have to be a little bit addled to do that.

NJT: From personal experience, I know you to be very romantic and committed with the right woman. Do you believe in monogamy, true love, staying with one person?

HST: (enthusiastically) Oh, yeah. It's a nice idea. Yeah. And I never inhaled. Never inhaled. Even Gore admitted he inhaled. I find the idea interesting.

On Being a Hawaiian God

AG: Are you Lono? (Referring to Thompson's insistence in *The Curse of Lono* that he is, in fact, the ancient Hawaiian god Lono.)

HST: Yeah. Oh yeah.

AG: Is there any way to qualify that at all?

HST: No. You're Alma, right?

AG: Yeah.

HST: Well, I'm Lono.

On "The Fear"

AG: Do you still get The Fear? (Referring to an emotional state Thompson frequently expresses in his writings) Is there a way to describe what it is? I know it seems pretty self-evident, but I wondered if you had another way to describe it.

HST: Fear is a sensation you recognize. People who've had it know The Fear.

On Good and Evil

AG: Since a lot of your writing seems to touch on these themes, what do you believe is true evil? What is true good?

HST: That's impossible. Interesting question though, in a shoddy sense.

AG: Are there any specific actions that you see as pure evil or pure good?

HST: I think treachery is pretty close to evil. Now we're getting back to Clinton.

AG: Treachery in terms of broken promises, false intentions?

HST: Yeah. Don't see much pure good.

On O.J.

NJT: Do you think that O. J. Simpson is going to get a fair trial?

HST: Yeah, I believe that in the sense of what passes for a fair trial, it'll be as fair as trials get, I suppose. I'm not concerned about the fair or unfair aspect.

NJT: What is the most interesting aspect of the case to you?

HST: Well, I'm not sure what happened and who did what. But if he could have done that double murder, got rid of the gloves, got rid of all the blood and appeared on a plane to Chicago an hour later, leaving no clues expect what the cops say he left . . . I'd be scared of him. I think it's impossible . . . If you kill two people, one of them being your wife, it gets the adrenalin moving in strange ways.

On the End of the World

NJT: You said that by the year 2000, the world would be unrecognizable as we now know it. Does that include an abolishment of government as we know it? Do you really have an apocalyptic vision of the year 2000?

HST: That's pretty clear. That has been my dictum.

AG: An actual physical apocalypse?

NJT: Like in the Book of Revelation?

HST: No, it won't come like that. But it'll seem to, for a lot of people.

AG: How do you think it will manifest itself?

HST: Oh, many ways. I can't qualify my statement. It stands by itself.

NJT: Is it an economic or a moral thing? I want to know if you really believe that five years from now it's going to be so radically different that it'll be like 50 years have passed.

HST: Yeah.

AG: And are the ways just too numerous to go into?

HST: Yeah. I'd have to make a list.

AG: What's at the top of the list?

HST: Let's go on to something else. If it's going to snow tomorrow, I don't think I want to sit around and list the 57 reasons why or maybe . . .

AG: Will people recognize it for what it is?

HST: Some.

On the Past (With or Without Regrets)

NJT: Do you remember that time in San Francisco on one of your lecture tours. There was this girl who was in charge of tending to your needs, and she was driving us around and she asked, "Is there anything you need?" and you said, "Yes. Bring me some fat children to fuck!" She was so horrified that she quit her job that day, and we never saw her again.

HST: That's not true. None of it. (Long pause.) That may have been true—given the tenor of the times.

NJT: You got arrested that trip. It was really bad.

HST: I don't remember that at all.

NJT: You don't remember being in handcuffs and tossing me your address book as you were being run out of the room and saying: "Think, bitch! Think!"? I was screaming because we were on acid and I was having so much fun—and a couple in the next room thought I was being murdered. The police thought I was a minor. They called through the door: "Are you all right, miss?" Then they came into the room with their guns drawn and they arrested you! And Sandy (Thompson's ex-wife) saw the report. And that was the straw that broke the camel's back. That was the beginning of the end for you.

HST: Sandy didn't see it. (The phone rings, and Thompson holds a brief phone conversation.)

HST: She just called. That was Sandy.

NJT: Is that her up there? (Pointing to a photo)

HST: Yes.

NJT: She's like your soulmate, isn't she?

HST: Weird question.

NJT: That's not a weird question. She was with you 20 years. If that's not a soulmate, then what is?

HST: I don't know. You've got your opinion, and you insist on raising your opinion.

NJT: (Sandy) actually really divulged a lot about you in Jean Carroll's unauthorized biography.*

HST: I didn't read it. It made my life much more peaceful.

NJT: (Carroll) did a pretty good job.

HST: Well, it passed as whatever it was. It was awkward having people talk to my friends, pursuing them.

NJT: I think she did a really good job of revealing, as a woman, more than just the "guy stuff" that so many people talk about with you. She viewed you in a more whole way. And Sandy's insights were so beautiful.

On Death

NJT: Are you afraid of death?

HST: No . . . No. There is no death.

---

* E. Jean Carroll, *Hunter: The Strange and Savage Life of Hunter S. Thompson*, Dutton, 1993.

Weekend Edition Sunday (National Public Radio)—November 24, 1996

This month marks the 25th anniversary of the publication of Hunter Thompson's groundbreaking book, *Fear and Loathing in Las Vegas.* Weekend Edition Senior Editor Greg Smith spoke with Thompson, as well as *Rolling Stone* Publisher Jann Wenner, artist Ralph Steadman and musician Jimmy Buffett about the reissue of the book (Random House/Modern Library) and a commemorative CD (Island Records), which features Buffett's music.

Liane Hansen, Host: This is *Weekend Edition.* I'm Liane Hansen.

Twenty-five years ago this month, we first hit the road with Dr. Hunter S. Thompson and his attorney via the pages of *Rolling Stone* magazine.

The articles then became the book *Fear and Loathing in Las Vegas.* Today, you can hear it on a commemorative CD featuring the voices of Harry Dean Stanton, Harry Shearer, Buck Henry and Laraine Newman. Jim Jarmusch stars as Thompson, and Maury Chaykin as Gonzo, his Samoan legal counsel.

The road Hunter Thompson is still on led to New York recently, where *Weekend Edition* senior editor Greg Smith caught up with the good doctor at his suite at the Four Seasons Hotel.

Greg Smith, *Weekend Edition* Senior Editor: I should explain first of all a couple of things about Hunter S. Thompson, self-styled Gonzo journalist. He's a night owl. He's partial to exotic expensive locations and to intrigue, which explains why he was registered at the hotel under the name Ben Franklin. And he has a tendency towards tangents.

Thompson says the legendary trip to Las Vegas and subsequent book mark the end of an era.

HST: It was a nice epitaph for the '60s. The '60s was like an attitude more than anything else—a state of mind, although brought on by—starting with the Kennedy/Nixon election—well then Kennedy's assassination, then murders of Bobby Kennedy and Martin Luther King. It was also Lincoln Rockwell* who was assassinated.

In the '70s, it was a different period. The '70s is really the people that survived the '60s. After Watergate had a feeling that they had won in the '70s. I don't recall there has ever ever been an atmosphere so ripe for the plucking . . .

LAUGHTER

Smith: In terms of journalism and expenses as the 1970s.

HST: Oh, yeah, it's really changed.

You know the bottom line was not the consideration then. You know the 1960s was war, warfare and the '70s—getting Nixon out, and then, electing Carter. Oh, yeah, it was, it seemed like huge progress finally after all the leaders had been killed and this ragged band of survivors that got beaten again with McGovern. It looked like it was in the '70s, we had taken over the White House, which we had.

Smith: In 1971, *Rolling Stone* publisher Jann Wenner saw the first draft of *Fear and Loathing* and ran with it. In jacket copy for the book, Thompson writes about what he calls the essence of Gonzo journalism—a style of reporting, he says, based on William Faulkner's idea that the best fiction is far more true than any kind of journalism, that the writer must be a participant in the scene while he's writing it.

Twenty-five years after he wrote *Fear and Loathing,* Thompson doesn't think much of what's come to be called public or advocacy journalism. He remains a very independent writer and still feels the need to be personally involved in his writing.

HST: Tom Wolfe has a different take on that. He backs off and probably sees it better than I do. What is it, the forest or the trees, who's the forest . . .

LAUGHTER

Yeah, I like to get among the trees. And then, hopefully you can see the forest, too.

But I don't—the advocacy is it has the look of that group journalism. It's, it's difficult for me because . . .

LAUGHTER

---

* George Lincoln Rockwell was the founder of the American Nazi Party. He was assassinated on August 25, 1967.

Well, for one thing, there weren't any, there weren't a lot of newspapers clamoring to adopt my style of journalism back then—not like the North Carolina experiment* where what they all covered, they pooled in coverage. Well, that's a tricky one because it's a different kind of advocacy, isn't it? It's almost like a fix.

Smith: A fix often supplied by Ralph Steadman who, for a quarter of a century, has translated Hunter Thompson's words into pictures. His weird pen-and-ink drawings give a strange tempestuous reality to the text.

* During the 1994 North Carolina governor's election, six of the state's major newspapers and nine broadcasting stations attempted a statewide citizen-journalism project to enhance campaign coverage. The goal was to include varied citizen sources in what was billed as a "Your Voice, Your Vote" effort for non-journalists to weigh in on the gubernatorial election.

Rolling Stone—November 28, 1996

Interview by P. J. O'Rourke

Fear and Loathing in Las Vegas was first published here in *Rolling Stone* 25 years ago. We, the times, the country and the world have changed. Dr. Hunter S. Thompson's book has. It was then and is now a perspicacious, seminal, nonpareil, virtuoso work, the kind of thing that sends you to the dictionary looking for a word that does it . . .

Atavistic adj. of or pertaining to a characteristic found in a remote ancestor, e.g., the velociraptor, but not in nearer ancestors . . . justice.

Fearing and Loathing in Las Vegas is also a sort of accident. It was a literary byproduct. In the midst of some international journalistic brilliance, Thompson had a happenstance of artistic genius. In 1971, Hunter was deeply and rather dangerously involved in writing about the killing of Chicano journalist Ruben Salazar. Hunter had a good source on the story, Mexican-American lawyer and political activist Oscar Acosta. But Oscar was surrounded by youthful hotheads paranoid of any connection to an Anglo, however sympathetic to the cause that the gabacho was supposed to be. So Thompson suggested that he and Acosta take a weekend jaunt to Las Vegas. They'd have time to chat in private on the drive.

The rest is history. Sort of. Physics, anyway. Chemistry, definitely. Abnormal psych, for sure. Plus PE and lunch.

Fear and Loathing in Las Vegas addressed the great themes of late-20th-century literature—anomie, being and nothingness, existential terror. But two things separate Hunter Thompson from the common herd of modern-lit angst peddlers. First, Thompson is a better writer. He flips Kafka over on his back like some big insect. He makes Genet sound like a children's book author—Buzzy Bunny and His Puppy Pals Blow Me. Compared with *Fear and Loathing in Las Vegas,* Albert Camus' *The Stranger* becomes a lame jailhouse whine, and all of Sartre is just some French doofus sitting around in a café, saying "Wherever you go, there you are."

Second, Thompson makes us laugh. This is something we're unlikely to do during performances of Samuel Beckett's *Waiting for Godot,* even if we're as high as Raoul Duke. Hunter Thompson takes the darkest question of ontology, the grimmest epistemological queries, and by his manner of posing them, sends us doubled over in fits of risibility, our sides aching from armpit to pelvic girdle, the tops of our legs raw from knee-slapping, beer spitting out our noses. We laugh so hard that at any given moment, we're almost as likely to vomit as the 300-pound Samoan attorney.

Read Beckett, Sartre, Camus, Genet and Kafka and you'll say: "Life is absurd, the world is meaningless, and all of creation is insane."

Read Hunter S. Thompson and you'll say: "Life is absurd, the world is meaningless, and all of creation is insane—cool."

THE UNERRING QUALITY OF DOPE LOGIC . . . WRITING IN FEAR AND THE WORSHIP OF RULES . . . THE DEMOCRACY OF DRUGS

O'Rourke: At the time you were writing *Fear and Loathing in Las Vegas,* you implied that things had gone wrong with the '60s, that it was a flawed era.

HST: Well, the truth of the matter was, there was Kent State,* there was Chicago, there was Altamont.† The '60s was about the Free Speech Movement long before it was about the flower children. I was more part of the Movement than I was of the Acid Club. But you knew that something was happening. You have to remember that acid was legal. [Ken] Kesey was a leader of the psychedelic movement. Berkeley was a whole different thing. The music was another thing. There was the Matrix [club], Ralph Gleason,** everything.

O'Rourke: I had the best time of my life in the '60s, and I rail and curse against it because I miss it. But when we really get to talking about it, and when I really get to remember what actually happened, I recall that it was a horrifying period.

---

* On May 4, 1970, Ohio National guard members opened fire on a group of student demonstrators at Kent State University. Four students were killed and nine students were wounded.

† On December 6, 1969, the Hell's Angels were hired as security guards for a free Rolling Stones concert at Altamont Speedway in California. The crowd and Hell's Angels became unruly and frenzied, resulting in an Angel stabbing a young African-American fan.

** Ralph Gleason was an influential American jazz and rock critic, as well as a founding editor of *Rolling Stone,* alongside Jann Wenner. He died in 1975 and his name remains in memorandum on the *Rolling Stone* masthead, alongside Hunter's name.

HST: I might quarrel with your interpretation of the '60s as meaning nothing, but then I've said since then that we really had an illusion of power—the illusion of being in charge. Which was quite liberating. We did drive one president out of the White House.

O'Rourke: What went wrong?

HST: Killing the leaders of it didn't help a lot—and Chicago in 1968, Kent State, Nixon being re-elected. But I would have one or two shades of disagreement with you about the '60s. It's to be expected. Yeah, in your assessment of the '60s, I think you'd call it a time of dumb sheep or when the goats sacrificed themselves.

O'Rourke: Well, there is that lemming-like quality to the '60s.

HST: I happened to see the '80s as that. And God knows what the hell the '90s are. They are just brazen with rules. Rules are worshiped—to the point where football and basketball referees are becoming celebrities. And the compulsion, the lust, to be on TV: it may be the governing instinct of our times. We're into a new world. We're at the decadence. I keep saying there will be no year 2000.

O'Rourke: You have given a pretty negative depiction of the effect of drugs in your work. Basically, nothing happy happens to people when they take drugs. Instead, it's Edge City. There's a lot of stuff that you've written that Nancy Reagan could have used—"Kids, this is what'll happen."

HST: Whether it's negative or not, the reality of it is you start playing with drugs, the numbers aren't on your side for coming up smelling like roses and being president of the United States. I did at some point describe the difference between me and, say [Timothy] Leary's concept—you know, that drugs were a holy experience and only for, you know, the drug church. I'm in favor of more of a democratization of drugs. Take your chances, you know. I never felt that, aside from a few close friends, it was my business to advocate things.

O'Rourke: Do you think there's anything interesting about drugs for making art?

HST: Yeah, totally interesting. But it took me about two years of work to be able to bring a drug experience back and put it on paper.

O'Rourke: And not make it sound like a script for *The Trip* with Peter Fonda?

HST: And to do it right means you must retain that stuff at the same time you experience it. You know, acid will move your head around and your eyes and whatever else you perceive things with. But bringing it back was one of the hardest things I had ever had to do in writing.

O'Rourke: You can kid about it. But to really put it down on paper, to be honest about it . . .

HST: Well, that's what *Vegas* is about. It's about the altered perceptions of the characters. To me, that's really the bedrock of the book—their responses to one another's questions. It's like in *The Three Stooges:* that story where they were out in the rowboat in a lake and it sprung a leak. And the boat was filling up with water. So they decided to bash a hole in the bottom of the boat to let the water out. Now that's drug reasoning.

O'Rourke: Is there any reason to distinguish *Fear and Loathing* from fiction?

HST: I remember one Friday afternoon it had to be decided for the *New York Times*—"A work of the imagination" was what [Random House editor] Jim Silberman came up with. Of course, it didn't stick. We went to "nonfiction," which led to it being categorized as "sociology."

O'Rourke: Ouch. Anyhow, the way you write is what replaced fiction. All these guys—Camus in *The Stranger*, Beckett in *Waiting for Godot*, Ionesco with all those imaginary rhinoceroses running around*—they are trying to construct a fictional world that makes points about the absurd nature of modern life. You were just writing what had happened and blew them out of the water. The reality of *Fear and Loathing in Las Vegas* gives it a power like Henry Miller that, to me, imaginary rhinoceroses and Ionesco just don't achieve.

HST: Well, we did have imaginary alligators in this one.

O'Rourke: But it was real imaginary.

HST: As far as I was concerned, I was writing what happened to me in Las Vegas. It was just in the Gonzo thinking, taking it one step further.

I wrote it deliberately as a cinematic treatment. But I was too ignorant to know that interior monologue doesn't work well cinematically. That's what makes it so hard to film.

O'Rourke: Which is why *Where the Buffalo Roam* didn't work in certain ways.

---

* Eugène Ionesco was an absurdist French-Romanian playwright. In his play *Rhinoceros*, the residents of a small French town are perceived by Bérenger, the protagonist, to undergo a metamorphosis into rhinoceroses.

HST: Just a bad writing job there. But I think more happens in the mind in *Las Vegas.* That's why we had so much trouble filming it. How do you film fear? And also a certain kind of psychosis?

O'Rourke: For that matter, how do you write about it?

HST: Well, you know, I wrote it in the process. I wrote it by hand at first, in notebooks.

O'Rourke: You started while you were actually there in Las Vegas?

HST: And in fear.

O'Rourke: Quite reasonably.

HST: Oscar had left me there with a pound of weed and a loaded .357 and some bullets in his briefcase.

O'Rourke: And no money.

HST: I couldn't pay the bill. And I was afraid. And I was waiting for the right hour to leave the hotel through the casino.

And earlier I'd slowly, you know, moved stuff down to the car, small amounts, in and out. But there was one big, metal Halliburton [suitcase] that there was no way to get out. I was trying to pick the right time to leave. I remember at 4:30 in the morning, a poker game was going on, nothing but poker games. I just walked though the casino nonchalantly carrying this big Halliburton.* I was afraid. I was afraid of taking off, you know, in a red car, on the only road to L.A.

O'Rourke: What was scarier: Oscar leaving you in this situation or Oscar being there?

HST: I'd have preferred to have him there. Just all of a sudden being alone in a situation where you had been abusing drugs [thoughtful pause]—but not intentionally; we had gone there to do a story.

O'Rourke: You went there to work.

HST: I was afraid the whole time. I was in bad enough condition as it was. And, you know, I'm jumping a hotel bill out in Las Vegas then trying to drive to L.A. in a red car.

O'Rourke: Not entirely sober.

HST: That's not your best way to go—a stolen gun, a pound of weed. There was this big bulletin board on the edge of Las Vegas: "Attention, 20 years for marijuana."

---

* Zero Halliburton is an extremely durable, hard-shelled briefcase with the ability to lock.

O'Rourke: For me, the key moment of the paranoia was the enormous, frightening sign outside the hotel window. Oscar wants to shoot it. But you say, "No, let's study its habits first."

HST: We're feeding off each other. There's a knock on the door, and somebody says, "Well, it must be the manager ready to shoot our heads off." And the response from the other person is to immediately get a knife, open the door, and slit the [guy's] throat.

Yeah, try this for dope logic: On *Las Vegas* cover, Oscar wanted: By Hunter Thompson and Oscar Acosta. He said, "I'm not some fucking Samoan," which I had written to protect him. I said, "Oscar, you're a fucking member of the California Bar Association. You're engaged in extremely public hearings protecting the guys who tried to burn down the hotel when Reagan was speaking." I put Samoan in there for a reason. God Almighty [displays the back of a hardcover copy of *Las Vegas* with a caption identifying Acosta], I wrote that. Yeah, I told him, "This is crazy." But he insisted on this photograph and being identified in the photograph.

O'Rourke: But can you be productive on drugs? I mean, we know that drugs definitely give you different viewpoints, looking at the world through a fly's eye and so on.

HST: Without the drugs, we would not have gone to Las Vegas. Well, we would have had completely different experiences. And the logic of the whole thing was drug logic: Here are Oscar and I in the middle of this weird murder story ["Strange Rumblings in Aztlan," *Rolling Stone* 8], and there are all these bodyguards around. "I can't stand it anymore." "These fuckin' spics." You know, half of them are threatening to kill me. The feeling was, "I can't even talk to you." The logic of, "Let's go to Las Vegas and dump them," which we do, that wouldn't have happened without drugs. It was the right thought. But drugs get to be a problem when the actual writing time comes, except just as a continuation of the mood.

ON A HELL-BOUND TRAIN . . . GATSBY VS. THE GOOPS . . . READING FOR POWER AND FITZGERALD'S LEVERAGE

O'Rourke: You're fairly aggressive. Journalism is a wonderful way to exorcise aggression.

HST: That is one of my main frustrations of not writing a column anymore.

O'Rourke: I just don't know of anything better in the world than the justified attack on authority figures that also uses humor. Is there anything that beats making fun of people?

HST: Not if they're the right people. I think the shared perception is huge in that. You know what works: If they jump, you know you got the right word. With readers, I was surprised, and still am, at the very solid and articulate mass of people out there who are extremely varied but really do like me and agree that I'm expressing their feelings. I believe that journalism and fiction have to do that. It's not just amusement.

O'Rourke: Fiction writers, even when they use interesting techniques, are often not audience directed. If you're a journalist, you have to be directed to your readers.

HST: Newspapers give you that connection with your reader. You've got no choice. You are fucked if you're not connected.

O'Rourke: So what do you tell people who say they want to become writers?

HST: Ye gods, that's a tough one. I think that one of the things I stumbled on early, as really a self-defense mechanism of some kind, was typing other writers. Typing a page of Hemingway or a page of Faulkner. Three pages. I learned a tremendous amount about rhythm in that way. I see writing really as music. And I see my work as essentially music. That's why I like to hear it read out loud by other people. I like to hear what they're getting out of it. It tells me what you see. I like to have women read it. If it fits musically, it will go to almost any ear. It could be that that's why children relate to it.

O'Rourke: And also you know if you're getting your reader to hear it the way you want it heard.

HST: I like to hear them getting it. Boy, that's when you know you're on the same fucking frequency. Without the music it would be just a mess of pottage.

O'Rourke: Did anybody read aloud to you as a kid?

HST: Yeah, my mother did. We were big on stories in the family—fables, bedtime stories. The house was full of books.

There was no wall in the house that didn't have bookshelves. It's like this house [points to rows of shelves]. The Library, to me, was every bit as much a refuge as a crack house might be to some gang kid today. You know, a library card was a ticket to ride. I read every one of those fucking things. My mother was a librarian for the Louisville [Ky.] Public Library.

O'Rourke: John Updike's mother told him that the whole Rabbit series read like an A student's idea of what a high school athlete's life is like . . .

HST: Wow. To have his mother say it: "I knew there was a reason I was always disappointed in you, my son." Imagine the struggle that my mother had to go through.

O'Rourke: How did she feel about your writing?

HST: For 10 years, the fact that I was a writer had little to do with the fact that I was seen merely as a criminal on a hell-bound train. My mother had to be down there on Fourth Street, at the main desk of the library, and had to have people come in asking for my book before she was convinced that I had a job.

O'Rourke: What was the first book, the first whole book, you read?

HST: Good lord, man—anybody who would remember that is probably in some kind of trouble or lying.

O'Rourke: No, they say that drug addicts always remember the very first time they had the drug, or alcoholics remember the first drink.

HST: [Pauses] Jesus, I think you're right.

O'Rourke: I think I am, too.

HST: Well, in my grandmother's bookcase there was a book called *The Goops*.* I was maybe 6, 7. It was a rhymed thing about people who have no manners—people who drooled. The Goops, they use the left hand; they chew all their soup. The Goops were always being punished for rudeness. My grandmother pulled it out for me to let me know that I was going against history. It was like a poem on every page, iambic pentameter definitely, and she gave me a sense of rules, and she managed to shame me for being a Goop—and being a Goop was like being a pig and lowlife. And it registered.

O'Rourke: What about the first grown-up book that you read?

HST: You've got to keep in mind that through high school, I was a member, actually, an elected officer, of the Athenaeum Literary Association, which really governed my consciousness. It started out at Male High [in Louisville]. We'd gather around on Saturday nights to read. It was a profoundly elitist concept. It ended up being a kind of compensation for cutting school. You know, "What have you got? Where were you yesterday, Hunter?" "Well, I was down at Grady's, on Bardstown Road, reading [Plato's] 'Allegory of the Cave' with Bob Butler and Norman Green, drinking beer." I don't know, it was fun. We were reading Nietzsche. It was tough, but when you're cutting school,

---

* *The Goops and How to Be Them* is a series of children's books published by artist and writer Gelett Burgess.

you're reading for power, reading for advantage. I've always believed: You teach a kid to like reading, they're set. That's what we did with Juan [Thompson's son]. You get a kid who likes to read on his own, shit, you've done your job.

O'Rourke: When you started reading on your own, who did you turn to?

HST: When I was in the Air Force, I went into a feeding frenzy. I read contemporary stuff—*The Fountainhead.* I had Hemingway, Fitzgerald, Faulkner, Kerouac, e. e. cummings. The thing that was important to me about Hemingway at the time was that Hemingway taught me that you could be a writer and get away with it. The example he set was more important than his writing. His economy of words I've paid a lot of attention to. The thing about typing other people's work was really an eye opener to me. I just started doing it. I had Dos Passos*—that's where I got a lot of my style stuff, the newsreels up at the beginning of his chapters. I came to Fitzgerald early. At 19 or 20, *The Great Gatsby* was recommended to me as my kind of book.

I've said before, *Gatsby* is possibly the Great American Novel, if you look at it as a technical achievement. It's about 55,000 words, which was astounding to me. In *Vegas* I tried to compete with that.

O'Rourke: I didn't realize *Gatsby* was that short.

HST: It was one of the basic guiding principles for my writing. I've always competed with that. Not a wasted word. This has been a main point to my literary thinking all my life. Shoot. I couldn't match 55,000 no matter how I chopped. I even chopped the ending off.

There are few things that I read and say, "Boy, I wish I could write that." Damn few. The Book of Revelation is one. Gatsby is one.

You know Hemingway's concept: What you don't write is more important than what you do. I don't think he ever wrote anything as good as *The Great Gatsby.* There are lines out of *Gatsby*—I'll tell you why it's so good: Fitzgerald describing Tom Buchanan. You know—athlete, Yale and all the normal stuff, and the paragraph ended describing him physically. Fitzgerald describing said about Tom Buchanan's body, "It was a body capable of great leverage." Back off! I remember that to this day, exactly. You finish *Gatsby,* and you feel you've been in somebody else's world a long time.

O'Rourke: You've said that you initially wanted to write fiction and that you saw journalism just as a way to make ends meet.

---

* John Dos Passos was an American novelist. He was the author of *Manhattan Transfer* and *Big Money.*

HST: Essentially to support my habit, writing.

O'Rourke: Do you still work with fiction?

HST: That brings us to *Polo Is My Life* [*Rolling Stone,* 697].

O'Rourke: Were you working on *Polo* from a sort of a *Fear and Loathing in Las Vegas* point of view, or was it a fictional construct?

HST: Both. I had to do it journalistically as serial coverage [for *Rolling Stone*], then adapt it, which is where the real mix came in. I was struggling with the fiction—the rats in the rafters over the pool were rumors that I tried to relate to the story.

O'Rourke: Rumor is a form of truth, after all.

HST: Remember the Muskie thing? That wasn't a lie. I wrote that there was a rumor that he had taken Ibogaine. ["Not much has been written about the Ibogaine Effect as a serious factor in the Presidential Campaign, but toward the end of the Wisconsin primary race—about a week before the vote—word leaked out that some of Muskie's top advisers had called in a Brazilian doctor who was said to be treating the candidate with 'some kind of strange drug' that nobody in the press corps had ever heard of." *Rolling Stone,* 108.] It started the rumor, but there was a rumor.

O'Rourke: It was a real rumor.

HST: With *Polo,* the journalistic aspect in covering events wasn't at all what I had in mind. After all, *Polo Is My Life* is a horrible joke, you know, a mean, wicked title. I became suddenly and deeply and intensely involved with a woman who was seriously into polo and planning to leave her husband. We were going to run away. This was a horsewoman, you know. About 5 [feet] 10 [inches]. I mean. A raging beauty. She had a two-goal rating. I met her one afternoon—bright sunlight. She had her horse tied up outside, and she said, "Well, I can't run away with you, actually. Who would take care of my ponies?" And I looked at her funny, and she said, "You don't understand, polo is my life." That's where the title came from. It had nothing to do, really, with polo. It was a love story. The polo-match coverage gave a body to it that was good for *Rolling Stone* for articles. But it got away from the original idea.

NEW AND RARE . . . TWO WEEKS IN LAS VEGAS . . . A LIGHT-HEADED FEELING . . . DRUNK, HORNY AND BROKE

O'Rourke: What is Gonzo journalism?

HST: I never intended Gonzo journalism to be any more than just a differentiation of new journalism. I kind of knew it wasn't that. Bill Cardozo—then working for the *Boston Globe*—wrote me a note about the Kentucky

Derby thing ["The Kentucky Derby Is Decadent and Depraved," *Scanlan's Monthly,* June 1970] saying, "Hot damn. Kick ass. It was pure Gonzo." And I heard him use it once or twice up in New Hampshire. It's a Portuguese word [actually, it's Italian], and it translates almost exactly to what the Hell's Angels would have said was "off the wall." Hey, it's in the dictionary now.

O'Rourke: Not many people get to add anything to the dictionary.

HST: That's one of my proudest achievements. It's in Random House [and many other dictionaries]. I'm afraid to quote it.

O'Rourke: Where did the phrase "Fear and Loathing" come from?

HST: It came out of my own sense of fear and a perfect description of that situation to me. However, I have been accused of stealing it from Nietzsche or Kafka or something. It seemed like a natural thing.

O'Rourke: I was never really sure how long you actually spent in Las Vegas.

HST: The chronology gets weird. There was a huge break between the Mint 400 motorcycle race—which we were all very excited about—and the DA's conference. I was there in early summer. What happened is, I came back here to Woody Creek [Colo.], then I went to San Francisco. The first half of it was clearly a story—we'd agreed on it. But I guess I got back here, and some mail had accumulated. At the time, I was a member of the International Association of Police Chiefs, since I was the chief magistrate of Woody Creek. And I would get all these magazines and propaganda and stuff, and invitations, and one of them was the National District Attorneys Conference, in Las Vegas. I guess I was thinking Vegas 2 already: "Hmm, this story's not finished, really."

O'Rourke: It needed more "research."

HST: Yeah, this was a breakthrough. So I called Oscar, and I said, "Hey, are you ready to go? We have another date in Las Vegas." He resisted at first, but he couldn't resist me. And this time he flew in, and I flew in. Our cover was absolutely essential. I had registered for the conference, sent in a check—it was $125 apiece—talked to Jann [Wenner]. I had told Oscar, "Don't tell anyone we're going to penetrate the deepest bowels of the enemy. This is not funny." I hadn't told anybody around here. Unfortunately, when I got on the plane, there is the Pitkin County [Colo.] district attorney, Jim Moore, whom I knew pretty well. He said, "Hi ya Hunter, where you going?" And I said, "Holy shit." We took separate seats, and for a while I wrestled with it. Maybe I said, "That's funny, I'm going to Las Vegas too." Maybe I got into the seat next to him; anyway, I confessed "I am going to this convention, and I'm going as Raoul Duke. I'm undercover totally, and unfortunately you know about it. I didn't mean for this to happen. And can I count on you to guarantee my cover?" "Uh," he said, "Yeah, I think so, yeah."

He ended up being very helpful; I don't think he ever blew my cover. He suffered through it the whole time, that entire week in August. In the book, the break's not really clear, but it went from June to August.

O'Rourke: It feels as if it could have happened in a week or a four-day weekend.

HST: It was two one-week blocks. The preparation before, in L.A., it was already a part of it. I knew what I was doing there, and I knew it was very dangerous. Oscar was an investigator. I was a magistrate. The story was still rolling.

O'Rourke: How did you do the actual work on "Vegas"? What was the drill?

HST: Right after Hemingway wrote *The Sun Also Rises,* he wrote a very small book, not much noticed. And I remember reading that he said, "I wrote that just to cool out after *The Sun Also Rises.*" I was working on Salazar, an ugly murder story. You know how you get. You get that, "Fuck, damn, where shall we go now?" You know, "Whose throat can I eat?" And when I got stuck out in that Holiday Inn near the Santa Anita racetrack, outside Pasadena [Calif.], I was there to work on this murder story. That was work, boy, that was blood. And, boy, that role got very, very, tough. That's why I went to Las Vegas. And when I came back from Las Vegas, I was still writing that story.

O'Rourke: So you'd work on *Vegas* as a break from the real assignment on hand?

HST: Yeah. I'd write from the notes I'd made all the way from before I left there. But it was really my notes . . . I stopped as often as I could. I was just an image on the freeway, a red convertible driving fast to L.A. on the 305. So I would stop and make these copious notes in these weird honky-tonk joints. I'd start out about dawn. I'm just thinking, "Ye gods, this is a story." The lead, I think, was the first thing I wrote. I don't think it was ever changed. And no doubt it came from a list somewhere: "We were somewhere around Barstow on the edge of the desert when the drugs began to take hold." And you asked me if books seemed to me like drugs, for fuck sake.

O'Rourke: It's extraordinary how different the two pieces of writing are.

HST: They were written at the same time, same hotel room. It was a 24-hour-a-day gig. I'd speed, and I would just write. I remember it was the spring meeting at Santa Anita, and I was surrounded by horse-people. Everywhere around me, all the other rooms were jockeys, tall blond women, owners, gamblers. I was the weird one there.

O'Rourke: Yeah, I suppose. What was the response when you filed this new story?

HST: The staff then was a pretty tight group. We had dinner down at some Mexican restaurant we used to go to a lot, to celebrate the bringing in of the great Salazar saga. That was the event. We sat at a booth—white Formica table—there were four of us in there: Jane [Wenner], Jann, me inside, and [former *Rolling Stone* editor] David Felton. I might have said something to Jann that afternoon like, "I got a little something extra."

But I remember sitting down there across from Jann—it was just the two of us at first—and I just said: "Hey, try this." I think the first day it was nine pages—somehow it went in nines. It was just my handwritten notes, which went on and on and on. That was the thing about *Rolling Stone* in those days: It was logical. Here I'd had one great triumph and said, "Hey, wait a minute, come over here, I got something better." And I knew somehow it was better. I knew it was special. It was a different voice. Jann read it. He was the one for a real judgment.

He made me an offer. Can you imagine anyone doing things that way now? But it was just entirely natural, and it's always been that way. It was, "Hey, hot damn, this is good. What else do you have?" I'd say, "this is a large thing; I'm full of energy here," and that energy meant finishing something. And he went right along with it.

O'Rourke: You don't get that too often.

HST: I've always appreciated that moment.

O'Rourke: I've never been able to decide what makes me most envious of you as a writer, whether it is the "I feel a bit lightheaded; maybe you should drive" or when Oscar turned to the hitchhiker and said, "We're your friend. We're not like the others."

HST: We happened to pick up this kid on another road, not on the road from L.A. to Las Vegas. I was driving; it was the first time around—the red car. I saw a kid hitchhiking. A tall, gangly kid. I said, "What the hell?" and I pulled over: "Hop in." "Hot damn," he said, "I never rode in a convertible before." And I said, "You're in the right place." I was really pleased. That was a true thing. I identified with him. I almost said, "You want to drive?"

O'Rourke: Which would have been a good idea in the event.

HST: But all those events, it's the attitude that really seems to meld them together. Granted, my behavior may be low-rent, but it was investigative journalism: "I'm new and rare."

O'Rourke: You were, after all, looking into things. Albeit those things didn't exist.

HST: It was my assignment. I had two assignments: I was there to cover the Mint 400, and I was there to cover the DAs' conference. What are people bitching about?

O'Rourke: It wasn't like you didn't write anything. That's the thing that usually pisses editors off.

HST: *Sports Illustrated* rejected the 2,500 words that I sent them; all they wanted was 250 for a caption. "Not acceptable for our format."

O'Rourke: I can see the layout problem they might have had. Was Ralph Steadman in Las Vegas during any of this?

HST: No, we sent it to him all at once when it was finished. When I went to Las Vegas, one of my jobs was to find physical art: things that we used, cocktail napkins, maybe photos—we didn't have a photographer. But that concept didn't work. I rejected it. It was a cold afternoon, Friday, on a deadline in the *Rolling Stone* offices, when I rejected [Art Director Robert] Kingsbury's art for the "Vegas" story. It was a real crisis. "What do we do now?" This is one of those stories that you read in bad books. I said, "What the fuck, let's get Ralph Steadman. We should have had him there in the first place."

We'd worked together on the Derby piece and also on the America's Cup nightmare. It never got published. *Scanlan's* had gone under. Ralph and I had become somewhat disaffected, estranged, because of his experience in New York—his one and only experience with psychedelics, with psilocybin. And he swore he'd never come back to this country and I was the worst example of American swine that had ever been born.

If I had had my way, Ralph would have gone with me to Las Vegas. It was some kind of accountant's thing: "Save on the art," you know. I didn't like the cocktail-napkins thing, but it wasn't that big a story, really. And you know, Ralph wouldn't do it unless he was paid $100,000 or something like that. But when the other art was rejected, I think Jann was there: "Let's call Ralph." The story was done. It was one of those, "How fast can we get it to him? How fast can we get it back?" And, you know, we got him on the phone. You know [British accent], "Thot bastuhd. Well, ah'll hav a luk at it. Ah, yes, I can probably do it." The manuscript was sent off. He'd never been to Las Vegas.

O'Rourke: I don't think it was probably necessary for someone to have been to Las Vegas to illustrate that story. I mean, the visuals were kind of "Internal."

HST: Yeah, but there was no more communication with him for, like, three days. We were all a bit nervous. And I would say, "Don't worry, he said he would do it." But his heart was full of hate. In about three to four days, a long tube arrived at the office. Great excitement. I was there when some messenger brought it in: a big, round thing. And we went to the art department. It was huge. Very carefully, we pulled the stuff out and unrolled it. And, ye gods, every one of them was perfect. It was like discovering water at the bottom of the well. Not one was rejected; not one was changed. This is what he sent.

O'Rourke: There was one year when there seemed to be a festival of biographies done on you. Have you read any of them?

HST: Were there three biographies in one year? I think they were all betting—you know, there was a pool betting on which day of the year I would die. But I never read any of them, no. I saw pieces here or there. But I didn't want to read them because I didn't want to get pissed off at my friends.

O'Rourke: You could write your own memoirs.

HST: Well, I've been working on these [collected] letters. It's an incredible thing, seeing my life unreeled in front of me. You don't know what the next box is going to hold when you review your life page by page. I don't know how many people would volunteer for that. Have it reviewed in public, you know, and publish it.

I've been humiliated, really, to see how much time I spent between haggling over small amounts of money and being broke. All that effort, it's a wonder anyone had any time to work at all.

O'Rourke: It's one of the mysteries of youth, isn't it?

HST: Yeah, drunk, horny and broke. Somehow, there were 48 hours a day and 18 days in the week. But the suffering of going through 10 years of it. "Free-lance journalism"—that sounds romantic now, right? But the desperation—teetering from one word to another.

EPILOGUE: ROAD MAN FOR THE LORDS OF KARMA . . . MR. NABOKOV WILL SEE YOU NOW . . . SEX AND GOD

O'Rourke: Here's a question: Are you religious? Do you believe in God?

HST: Long ago, I shucked off the belief that the people I was dealing with in the world, the power people, really knew what they were doing at all. And that included religion. The idea of heaven and hell—to be threatened with it—was absurd. I think the church wanted it to keep people in line. I've kind of recently come to a different realization that I'm in charge, really. That it comes down to karma. Karma is different things to different countries, but in the Orient, karma comes in the next generation.

O'Rourke: And ours comes in the mail.

HST: I've kind of updated Buddhism. In order words, you get your rewards in this life, and I think I'll be around again pretty quickly. Karma incorporates a measure of behavior, and in my interpretation, like everything else in this American century, it's been sped up—you know, the news, the effect of the news, religion, the effect of it. The only kind of grace points you get there is, they let you rest for a while sometimes. I may be sent back. I see myself as a road man for the lords of karma, and I'm not worried about my assignment. Of course, a lot of people have good reason to worry.

O'Rourke: I think I know several people who are probably walking around as bugs right now.

HST: Three-legged dogs on a Navajo reservation. Yeah, Pat Buchanan coming back as a rat on the great feeding hill in Calcutta. In Buddhism there is an acceptance of the utter meaningless and rottenness of life. I think Nixon got his karma in time.

O'Rourke: OK, check off God. How about sex? You don't often get graphic on us. Is writing about sex as hard as writing about drugs?

HST: It's difficult to do.

O'Rourke: Are there any writers who you think do it effectively, honestly, dirtily? And honestly.

HST: Well, I think that Nabokov could.

O'Rourke: A beautiful writer.

HST: Hell of a good writer. A friend of mine, Mike Solheim, was up in Sun Valley [Idaho] back in the early '60s. He told me that Nabokov used to come to the Sun Valley Lodge with an 11-year-old girl. He said it was weirder than *Lolita:* "It's very nice to meet your niece, Mr. Nabokov." Well, that goes back to the new-journalism question, about writing from experience.

O'Rourke: When you read it, you knew this was from real experience. This was not Thomas Mann writing "Death in Venice," which seemed to be a student's idea of what a hopeless crush would be, as if he'd observed someone go through it.

HST: And the reason for that is, Nabokov was up at Sun Valley Lodge with an 11-year-old-girl.

O'Rourke: I'm afraid *Lolita* strictly fits into the Gonzo framework.

HST: But, man, that's where the fun is. You know, why write about other people's experience?

The Book Report.com—June 1997

Interview by Sara Nelson

We were a little tense at The Book Report the other day. Would Hunter S. Thompson, famed author of *Fear and Loathing in Las Vegas* and the new bestseller *The Proud Highway,* really show up for his live interview? He is, after all, an unrepentant Dunhill-smoking, Patrón-swilling, walking chemical laboratory whose closest friends concede can be just a tad unreliable.

But Hunter said he'd come, and so he did. We agreed to let him keep his TV tuned to his beloved basketball playoffs. Our interviewer was TBR Executive Editor (Sara Nelson), aided by producer Sean Doorly (Sdoorly). Our unflappable host was Marlene T.

Marlene T: Hello, Sara and Mr. Thompson. Good evening!

HST: Good evening.

Sara Nelson: In your new collection of letters, *The Proud Highway,* edited by Douglas Brinkley, you said that you threw out 12 letters for every one that was published. When did you start saving your letters and why?

HST: Apparently so. I didn't really write a lot of letters until I went away from home. If I knew something about what was going to happen. But I haven't looked at any of them until now.

Sara Nelson: Did you know you were going to be a writer when you were 3 on your mama's knee?

HST: I knew pretty early on. By the time I got to high school I knew what I was going to do. Mainly because I looked around and saw there wasn't much else I was able to do. I was a criminal. I was a juvenile delinquent. I was charged with everything from rape to assault. I bit a woman on the back. I was the Marv Albert* of my time. I was a wild boy.

---

* Marv Albert is a former NBC sportscaster.

Sara Nelson: One thing I noticed from the letters—and this will surprise many people—that there is always a real politeness in your tone, even when you're yelling at someone. Where does that come from?

HST: I guess I'm just courtly until people get in my way. You'll find most Southerners are like that. I'm just thinking.

Sara Nelson: In the letters the people you correspond with are many and varied. How did you meet up with these people . . . did you stumble upon them?

HST: They just happened to be in the same line of work I was in. Given my calling I had to stumble across people who felt the same way. I was a young reporter. So was Charles Kuralt.* Wait till we get to Volume II, you'll really accuse me of name dropping. My neighbor Ed Bradley, all kinds of people. My greatest talent is in my ability to choose good friends. It's about as important as things get.

Sara Nelson: You said first impressions when meeting people are very important.

HST: The first impression is always the right one. I rarely change my mind upward about people. Sometimes you're fooled quickly. You want to be fooled. If you can't trust your first impression you're going to have a harder time than you should.

Sara Nelson: At the end of *Fear and Loathing,* you say "there will be no year 2000: not as we know it." What do you mean by this, and what are your plans for New Year's Eve 1999?

HST: It's hard to say what I meant by "as we know it." I'm not about to go up on a mountain on New Year's Eve and wait for the lightning to strike. But, the years after 2000 will be a monumental change in the way life is lived here. It will be harder and harder to relate to our children. I don't know what it's going to be. I don't plan to be around in the year 2000. I'll be taken away by the Sufi God.

Sara Nelson: What can you tell us about the *Fear and Loathing in Las Vegas* movie? Will there be any animation in it by director Terry Gilliam or perhaps Ralph Steadman? When is it due for release, how involved are you in it, any possibility you'd make an appearance?

---

* Charles Kuralt was an Emmy Award–winning television journalist for *CBS Evening News with Walter Cronkite.*

HST: I am a road man for the lords of karma. As far as I know, they start shooting in July. Johnny Depp just left here and went to see Terry Gilliam in Vegas.

Sara Nelson: Why did it take so long to make the movie?

HST: Lawyers have stood in my way. It's a very hard book to translate to film because there's so much interior monologue. The what-if factor. I tried to write it cinematically and let the dialogue carry it, but I forgot about the interior monologue. It's kind of hard to show what's going on in the head. I think we should do it like a documentary.

Sara Nelson: Do you read *Doonesbury?* What do you think?

HST: I don't read any comic strip.

Sara Nelson: What writers do you enjoy reading?

HST: Oh. Sins of omission. Jim Harrison* is someone I always enjoy, one of the great contemporary writers. I like Tim Ferris' Big Boom Theory.† I'm getting into a different kind of reading, not straight novels. I've been reading a lot about the Hellfire Club** . . . the original was elegant and very serious.

Sara Nelson: Hi Hunter—I have always enjoyed your work. How is your health? Are you still a walking science project? If you are doing well it's an inspiration! Thanks, Melissa in South Carolina.

HST: I'm doing all right, all things considered. For an elderly dope fiend out in the wilderness all by himself.

Sara Nelson: Dr. Thompson, Is it true that you are the real Keyser Soze?††

HST: I've been accused of that. It's a good question. Say, yes. The guy from that movie is going to play Oscar in the Vegas movie. That's a very intelligent question and I compliment the person who asked that.

Sara Nelson: Looking back . . . do you feel Richard Nixon was really the enemy to our generation?

---

* Jim Harrison is an American novelist and poet. His books include *Legends of the Fall, The Road Home*, and *The Theory and Practice of Rivers.*

† Hunter's good friend Tim Ferris is a science writer and the former New York bureau chief of *Rolling Stone*. His books include *The Whole Shebang, Seeing in the Dark*, and *Coming of Age in the Milky Way.*

** The Hellfire Club was an exclusive gentleman's club in London. The club was infamous for drunkenness, Satanism, and sexual debauchery.

†† Keyser Soze refers to the mysterious identity of a fictitious criminal in 1995 film *The Usual Suspects*, starring Kevin Spacey and Benicio del Toro.

HST: Yes. He personified the enemy. He stood for everything that was wrong and rotten. We were lucky to get it all rolled up into one person. It was Nixon who drove a very serious spike into the American dream. Nixon was the first president to be so massively and publicly exposed as an evil bastard. A lot of people knew U. S. Grant was a monster, or Harding—but a lot of people in those days was 200 or 500. Now, with even a rumor—44,000 people know it the next morning. Watergate shocked people.

Sara Nelson: What do you think about Clinton? Where does he come in in the hierarchy of bad presidents?

HST: Well, we still have a few years to go. Clinton already stands accused formally of worse things than Nixon would have been impeached for. I think Clinton is every bit as crude as Nixon. But maybe he is. I mean: Paula Jones?* "Come over here, little girl, I've got something for you"!? It's almost embarrassing to talk about Clinton as if he were important.

I'd almost prefer Nixon. I'd say Clinton is every bit as corrupt as Nixon, but a lot smoother.

Sara Nelson: What was the hardest part about writing *The Proud Highway?*

HST: I never really laid a hand on any of those letters. They were paraded before me and read to me by my son and Douglas Brinkley and total strangers, the editor of the local paper, Don Johnson and others. And that was very hard to deal with. I'm a very private person. To have your life read out to you one page at a time: It was a bizarre experience. It was like watching the raw video of your life.

What if all the letters had proven me to be a hideous lying monster who was wrong about everything? I would have burned them rather than let a horrible tale unfold. I don't see that I was much different than I am now. I was kind of relieved with the way the book came out. It's beyond an autobiography or a biography. I never knew what was going to come up next.

Sara Nelson: Were there some things in there you were sorry to see . . . or were upset by?

HST: Yes. I got tired and embarrassed by the constant poverty of those years. I told Doug this is really going to be a horrible downer of a book if all

---

* Paula Jones is a former Arkansas state employee who filed a sexual harassment lawsuit in 1994 against President Bill Clinton. She alleged that Clinton exposed himself to her while he was the governor of Arkansas. The lawsuit was later dropped and settled for $850,000.

it's going to be is about being broke. I didn't like being reminded of desperation at all times.

HST: Gotta check the game's score.

Sara Nelson: What's the score? Who did you bet on?

HST: 8–5 Chicago. I bet on Utah and 6 points.

Sara Nelson: Thompson, is there a drug now, or has there ever been, to which you would just say no?

HST: Let's see . . . I don't think I've ever seen a drug I wouldn't try or want anyway. Yeah. PCP, I would tend to avoid that in the future. I've always thought it's better to try things. Jimson weed: that's a bitch. Everybody should do jimson weed—once. I only did it twice.

Sara Nelson: Do you think drugs should be legalized?

HST: Yes. Across the board. It might be a little rough on some people for a while, but I think it's the only way to deal with drugs. Look at Prohibition: all it did was make a lot of criminals rich. Should be legalized for a matter of sanity.

Sara Nelson: Is your legal contest with the Aspen police resolved? If not, may justice be with you.

HST: Almost resolved. Nothing's ever resolved. I figure I'll be under arrest for the rest of my life for one thing or another. Some of my best friends are police—but not that many of them.

Sara Nelson: Will Ralph Steadman perhaps illustrate another book of yours sometime?

HST: Oh well I don't know. I might be executed tomorrow. Right now I'm doing an introduction for one of Ralph's books. He's doing something called *Gonzo: The Art.* I think he's stealing from me. I like Steadman and his coattail abilities. Ralph is better at business than I am. He has always managed to get free whiskey.

Sara Nelson: Can you comment on the passing of two of your friends—Allen Ginsberg* and Townes Van Zandt?†

HST: Yeah. Allen was a particular friend, one of my heroes, really. I knew him almost as long as I've been writing. I didn't know Townes that well: he's a really good friend of Lyle Lovett's. He was really good. I was once arrested

* Allen Ginsberg was an American poet and founding member of the Beat generation. He died in April 1997.

† Townes Van Zandt was an American singer and songwriter from Dallas, Texas. He died in January 1997.

with Ginsberg. He was a big help to me. He was one of the few people who read unknown writers' work. Maybe he was just hustling me. He liked to flirt, Allen. They called him a monster but he was only falling in love.

Sara Nelson: How do you reconcile your liberal politics with gun ownership? Is that not a contradiction?

HST: I think George Washington owned guns. I've never seen any contradiction with that. I'm not a liberal, by the way. I think that's what's wrong with liberals. I believe I have every right to have guns. I just bought another huge weapon. A lot of people shouldn't own guns. I should. I have a safety record. Guns are a lot of fun out here.

Sara Nelson: As somebody who likes guns and has taken part in his share of violence and anarchism, what do you think of Timothy McVeigh?

HST: Oh boy. Well, if he did that—apparently the jury has spoken—if I were him, I'd prefer the death penalty. If he blew up that building and killed that many people, we have to accept that, just like we had to accept that O. J. Simpson was declared not guilty. I'd rather be hung or shot or executed than spend my life in prison. If he did that he deserves to die. I can't conceive of doing that kind of damage.

Sara Nelson: You can't imagine that much violence?! Wow. You seem so mellow . . . how come you are so mellow? Have you just become an old softie?

HST: I was always a softie. But it always helps to win. To be right. You can afford to be a little more mellow.

Sara Nelson: It was a real pleasure . . . get back to your game . . . Thanks for coming by The Book Report.

Sara Nelson: Thank you, Hunter.

HST: Thank you.

All Things Considered (National Public Radio)—August 7, 1997

Hunter S. Thompson

INTERVIEW WITH JACKI LYDEN AND LINDA WERTHEIMER (WASHINGTON, D.C.)

Jacki talks with "gonzo journalist" Hunter S. Thompson.

Linda Wertheimer, Host: This is *All Things Considered.* I'm Linda Wertheimer.

Jacki Lyden: And I'm Jacki Lyden. In 1959, a decade before he became the great Gonzo journalist of contemporary American nonfiction, Hunter Thompson was broke, evicted, drinking hard and had just been fired from an upstate New York newspaper.

He wrote to someone in Puerto Rico that he needed a newspaper job—a someone who turned out to be William Kennedy, the future Pulitzer Prize–winning author.

Their correspondence was insulting, two-fisted, and the beginning of a beautiful friendship.

For more than 40 years, Hunter Thompson, an author known for his love of guns and narcotics, has been a compulsive letter writer, keeping a carbon copy of every letter he ever wrote—20,000—to Joan Baez, LBJ, Ken Kesey, Charles Kuralt, and dozens more.

The first of three volumes of his letters has just been published. It's called *The Proud Highway, Saga of a Desperate Southern Gentleman.* We spoke to Thompson about his letters and asked him the details of that story about his fight with William Kennedy.

HST: I was working for the *Middletown Daily Record* and I got in a fight with an advertiser, gentleman who ran a giant restaurant across the street because of the quality of his lasagna, I think. And I kicked in a candy machine because it wouldn't pay off in, you know, candy bars.

(Laughter)

HST: Yeah, I was fired.

Lyden: And did the next logical thing, applied for a job in Puerto Rico? Would you read a little bit from this letter. You can start at the top?

HST: Ah, what do you want to hear . . .

Lyden: "Dear Sir, I hear you need a sports editor . . . "

HST: All right. "If true, perhaps we can work something out. The job interests me for two reasons, the Caribbean location, and the fact that it's a new paper. The salary would be entirely secondary. It is as if I would not be here in our Rotarian democracy."

Lyden: You asked this publisher in Puerto Rico to give you a job, telling him that's you'd been fired and that you kicked in the candy machine. And I thought the letter that you got back a few days later was pretty fantastic. Tell us who this letter is from please.

HST: Oh, it's from William J. Kennedy, who was then the managing editor of the *San Juan Star.*

Lyden: And would later become the Pulitzer Prize-winning author of *Ironweed.*

HST: It's addressed to me in Louisville. "Dear Mr. Thompson, after giving careful consideration to your application, we've decided that for several reasons you would not be happy with us.

"First, our publisher is a member of Rotary. Second, your literary accomplishments would not really say you write as offbeat since three of our staff members have also finished novels and one is a playwright.

"We feel you had best return to your novel, perhaps even start another. You could build the plot around that bronze plaque on the *Times Star.* You should always write about something you know intimately.

"Too bad we couldn't get together. Lots of people go shoeless down here. You would have liked it.

"We're keeping your application on file. If we ever get a candy machine that needs someone to kick it in, we'll get in touch with you.

"Yours in Zen, William J. Kennedy, Managing Editor."

Lyden: How did you feel when you got that letter, of total snide, rejection?

HST: Well, I felt like beating his teeth in, frankly. It came in the same mail I think as a rejection letter for my novel. It was a bad day.

Lyden: You wrote back to William Kennedy. "Your letter was cute, my friend. And your interpretation of my letter was beautifully typical of the Cretan intellect responsible for the dry rot of the American press.

"But don't think that lack of an invitation from you will keep me from getting down that way. And when I do, remind me to first kick your teeth in, and then jam a bronze plaque far into your small intestine.

"Give my best to your literary staff, and your Rotarian publisher. If they're half as cute as you are, your paper will be a whomping success.

"I think also that I need not point out the folly of your keeping my application on file.

"Cheers, Hunter S. Thompson."

Wow.

HST: Wow, yeah. Well, you can see now why I was unemployed for most of those 10 years. Unemployable, actually.

Lyden: How did you guys become friends after that? You became friends for what, some 37 years?

HST: Well, I went down to Puerto Rico anyway and had a job on a magazine that was described to me as a new *Sports Illustrated* of the Caribbean.

Lyden: I thought it was called "The Puerto Rico Bowling News."

HST: Well, that's what I called it. It was called *Sportivo*, but it got me down there. And I went to see Kennedy and we arranged a truce, and I went over to the paper. We went out and drank. And he said, I have a good idea, why don't we continue this out at my house? And he called his wife and said he was bringing Hunter Thompson home, and she cried.

(Laughter)

HST: Begged him not to. Yeah, it was a very awkward moment, but we've been friends ever since.

Lyden: A lot of these letters that you write, and you write to Norman Mailer. You write to William Styron.* You write to the heads of major newspapers, influential newspapers like the *Washington Post*. And your tone . . .

HST: And they wrote back to me, yes . . .

Lyden: . . . your tone in all these is so brash. These guys write back to you. Phil Graham, then the owner and publisher of the *Washington Post*, answered your really intemperate letter to him.

HST: Intemperate?

Lyden: It was intemperate.

---

* William Styron is an American writer and novelist. His novel *Sophie's Choice* won the National Book Award in 1980.

HST: Well, it was a little . . . *Newsweek* had done a very dumb article on South America. And I was just calling it to his attention. Yeah, I guess it is a little brash. And it certainly explains why I was not hired.

(Laughter)

HST: The thing is . . .

Lyden: Well, actually, what strikes me, Hunter, is that you very nearly were hired. Instead of ignoring you, he wrote you back and basically said why don't you stop by in Washington the next time you're here.

HST: Well, I did. I liked him.

Lyden: But why do you think that these people answered someone who was basically making fun of them, cussing at them? Why did they answer?

HST: I was right, for one thing. And I don't know, they were good people.

Lyden: Were you serious about what you had to say to these publishers and to these newspaper owners and editors? Or were you sort of just trying to get a rise out of them?

HST: Hey, I was a freelance writer, period. And I had to live on what I sold. You bet I was serious.

Lyden: With all the volumes of letters that you now possess, is there one letter that you haven't written, that you wish you had?

HST: You mean, my priest begging for forgiveness?

Lyden: Exactly.

HST: No. No, I usually, I was of a mind to whenever I felt like writing a letter, I would sometimes unfortunately write it.

Lyden: Well, in fact a lot of these letters are just written pell-mell at 4:00 in the morning. And you know most of us would take that letter and put it under our pillows and say I'll sleep on it . . .

HST: Yeah . . .

Lyden: . . . and then I'll think about sending it out.

HST: Oh, but that's the fun of it, to know what's going on. What the hell, if you know you can change it. It's no fun to, you know, there goes all your adrenaline.

Lyden: Were you ever tempted to change it or did you ever have second thoughts?

HST: Yeah, yeah. Not often. Once you start taking your words back, or having second thoughts, usually you're going to get in your own way. So, I just figured what the hell. It's pure this way.

Village Voice—August 19, 1997

The Godfather of Gonzo Defends His Oeuvre and Stomps on His Enemies

BY TOM MCINTYRE

The Good Doctor, Hunter S. Thompson, seems to be in need of some medical attention himself as I enter his hotel suite in San Francisco's St. Francis Hotel. He sits on the couch, rubbing his left thigh. "This goddamn sciatica is burning down my leg. Good thing it hasn't worked its way to the other one yet." Thompson is discussing his back pain with science writer–former East Coast editor of *Rolling Stone* Timothy Ferris.

Even while he shifts around in obvious discomfort, pleading for someone to bring him muscle relaxants, Thompson, at the age of 60, is still an imposing physical force. He's in town to promote the release of *The Proud Highway: Saga of a Desperate Southern Gentleman.* I mention to him that I also am originally from Louisville.

"Goddamn! It's like an old homecoming. Colonel, you should come in here. We've got another Kentucky boy here."

The Colonel, Thompson's bartender, is a young, slightly built gentleman wearing a blue mesh T-shirt. He walks over to me, shakes my hand, and introduces himself simply as "Johnny." He then hands Hunter a drink, asking me if I would like one.

"Do you have something like Chivas Regal?" I ask.

Thompson and Ferris laugh. "We don't have something like Chivas Regal. We have Chivas Regal." When Johnny returns with the drink, I ask him where he comes from in Kentucky. "I'm from Owensboro originally, but I also lived in Frankfort and Lexington." The drink is exquisitely made, and I make a mental note to leave him a generous tip. As he starts to walk away, however, I realize that there is something oddly familiar about him, Johnny Depp, soon to be starring as Thompson's alter ego Raoul Duke in Terry Gilliam's screen version of Thompson's *Fear and Loathing in Las Vegas.*

But back to the original Hunter. During the hour that we chatted in his hotel room, he was calm, fairly lucid, and genuinely friendly. Perhaps it was just the muscle relaxants, but he showed no evidence of his legendary explosive temper.

McIntyre: I was reading some of your letters from the early 1960s to William Kennedy and Paul Semonin [a high school friend of Thompson's]. You were really despondent after the Kennedy assassination. Do you think his assassination was the beginning of the end of politicians we could trust?

HST: Well, I think it might have been the end of politicians we thought we could trust who were president. George McGovern remains a good friend and the best person I've ever met in politics. This is a pure quality person. But he got beat by 22 points. Jack Kennedy won and there was a great sense of empowerment that came with that. When I wrote to Lyndon Johnson applying for the governorship of American Samoa, I knew I wasn't an automatic choice, but I felt like we had taken over from those harsh years with Eisenhower and Nixon. Beating Nixon [in 1960] remains one of my great accomplishments. You see, I call it an "accomplishment." Like I did it.

McIntyre: You were one of the journalists who really kicked Richard Nixon before everyone else did.

HST: Yeah. I kicked him when he was up [laughter]. You know, in my mind, voting for Nixon is like having a permanent red N on your forehead.

McIntyre: You've said before that you thought J. Edgar Hoover was behind Kennedy's assassination. Is that what you still believe or do you think it was someone else, like the CIA?

HST: Well, I will say that I think J. Edgar Hoover was probably the most pernicious and damaging influence on the consciousness of a whole generation. That son of a bitch was head of all law enforcement in this country for like 50 years. He spanned five or six presidents. He was just a fucking monster, an utterly degenerate bull fruit who danced around at parties wearing a red pinafore calling himself "Miss Mary" and meanwhile persecuting all the gays. To allow that freak to be the head cop certainly turned my head about what cops were all about. I've been a criminal all my life. Speaking of that, I wonder where that pipe is [laughter]. I elected to grow up as a criminal, and Hoover made sure of that.

McIntyre: In his foreword to *The Proud Highway,* William Kennedy mentions that for years you have been starting different novels and not fin-

ishing them. And he states that *Fear and Loathing in Las Vegas* actually is your great fictional work. Do you think of it in those terms?

HST: Let's get one thing straight here now . . . [he calls across the room to Ferris and Depp] Tim, you may want to hear this. I'm about to bring the gong down on Kennedy. You too, Colonel. Kennedy said that I'm a writer of fiction. [Looking toward Depp] Last week, out at the house we pulled out a giant box, right? And it was incredible: we found every fucking note . . . all the handwritten scenes in notebooks [from *Fear and Loathing in Las Vegas*]. It had the fucking cocktail napkins from the Flamingo. When I finished with the story, I just put everything in a box and packed it and sealed it up. I was astounded. There are scenes and dialogue written in a notebook on the run that are word for word, that are in the book now. It was astonishing. I had no idea how true it was. It's down to incredible little details. I'm not sure what was made up there.

Depp: That was the shocking thing that I saw. I went through the manuscript and the notes and cocktail napkins and all kinds of material. And it really shocked me because I thought, "Oh my god. It's all true [laughter]. It's all real. It all happened!"

McIntyre: [To Depp] I know that you're going to be starring in *Fear and Loathing*. Has that been shot yet, or are you doing research for it now?

Depp: No, we're going to start shooting on July 21. It's directed by Terry Gilliam.

McIntyre: Really? So it's going to have some of those great hallucinatory passages made real.

Depp: Oh yeah.

HST: [Laughing] Not with my shit, they won't.

McIntyre: Are you going to be in the movie?

HST: I have no plans to. But I've always been a professional. For enough money, I'll do anything. I mean, the difference between the Hell's Angels and shark research out by the Farallons was immaterial to me. If an agent had wanted me to go out and get to know the sharks, I'd have gone out there and done that instead.

McIntyre: I want to finish up by asking you something that's always intrigued me about your relationship with Richard Nixon. You had one opportunity in 1968 to talk directly with Nixon sitting in the back of a car.

You guys talked about football. Why didn't you just go for the jugular right then and tear his mask off?

HST: There were two possible reasons. One is that I was chickenshit and didn't have the courage of my convictions. The other is that it was 20 below zero on the Massachusetts Turnpike that night.

Nixon had finished his last speech. He was going to win the New Hampshire primary, a horrible development, and he was going to leave Manchester that night. We were all in Keene, down on the Massachusetts border. And it was an hour and a half, maybe two, back to Manchester where Nixon had his Lear jet waiting. And the boss wanted to talk football. So he sent Patrick Buchanan out to find somebody in the press bus who could talk football. Well, I had been all but barred from the press bus because I was with Nixon and Buchanan and a few other people when the Tet offensive was on TV. You talk about going crazy! But they knew exactly where I was. And Buchanan worked the press corps looking for somebody to talk football with him, and Nixon was known to be quite a knowledgeable fan. And nobody would do it. We're talking about Johnny Apple* and that crowd.

It never occurred to me that I would be included in the search, and I wasn't at first. Buchanan really overlooked me as he was canvassing the press corps. I got to laugh after a while because nobody was volunteering. And I said, "Well, shit. I can." And he said, "Fuck you." I was out of the question.

So he went back over to this yellow Mercury. You see, Nixon had no Secret Service at the time. All he had was a state trooper, the driver of the car, and Patrick. They were desperate. The boss wanted to talk football. So finally, he came back over to me and said, "All right, Hunter. You're it. I'll be in the car. If you mention tear gas, if you mention Vietnam, if you mention anything except football, the car's going to stop and your ass is going to be out on the turnpike."

McIntyre: How long did you and Nixon actually talk in the back seat of that car?

HST: Oh fuck. It went on for three or four hours. So to answer your question, I could've gotten after him about what he'd done with the Cambodians, but not for long.

---

* Raymond "Johnny" Apple was a political correspondent and associate editor for the *New York Times* and covered the 1972 presidential campaign.

McIntyre: What did you find him to be like at that moment? Was he a personable guy?

HST: He was fun: just another sports fan. Talking football with Nixon was . . .

McIntyre: Serious business.

HST: Oh, you bet. We went back to the hotel, then we went to his plane and he took me on a tour of the Lear, which is a very small tour. He was amazed that it didn't have a bathroom in it: [as Nixon] "This thing, it has no crapper! No crapper! Well, let me tell you a secret: this thing goes so fast you don't need a crapper! That's the genius! That's the American way!"

Atlantic Unbound—August 26, 1997

Writing on the Wall: An Interview with Hunter S. Thompson

BY MATTHEW HAHN

The aim of every artist is to arrest motion, which is life, by artificial means and hold it fixed so that a hundred years later, when a stranger looks at it, it moves again since it is life. . . . This is the artist's way of scribbling oblivion through which he must someday pass.

—WILLIAM FAULKNER, interview with *Paris Review*, 1956

The interview took place at Thompson's home on the evening of July 15, extending into the early hours of July 16, 1997. Both the transcript and audio excerpts have been edited for clarity and length. At times they do not correspond.

MH: The Internet has been touted as a new mode of journalism—some even go so far as to say it might democratize journalism. Do you see a future for the Internet as a journalistic medium?

HST: Well, I don't know. There is a line somewhere between democratizing journalism and every man a journalist. You can't really believe what you read in the papers anyway, but there is at least some spectrum of reliability. Maybe it's becoming like the TV talk shows or the tabloids where anything's acceptable as long as it's interesting.

I believe that the major operating ethic in American society right now, the most universal want and need is to be on TV. I've been on TV. I could be on TV all the time if I wanted to. But most people will never get on TV. It has to be a real breakthrough for them. And trouble is, people will do almost anything to get on it. You know, confess to crimes they haven't committed. You don't exist unless you're on TV. Yeah, it's a validation process. Faulkner said that American troops wrote "Kilroy was here" on the walls of Europe in World War II in order to prove that somebody had been there—"I was here"—and that the whole history of man is just an effort by people, writers, to just write your name on the great wall. You can get on [the Internet] and all of a sudden you can write a story about me, or you can put it on top of my name. You can have your picture on there too. I don't know the percentage of the Internet that's valid, do you? Jesus, it's scary. I don't surf the Internet. I did for a while.

I thought I'd have a little fun and learn something. I have an e-mail address. No one knows it. But I wouldn't check it anyway, because it's just too fucking much. You know, it's the volume. The Internet is probably the first wave of people who have figured out a different way to catch up with TV—if you can't be on TV, well at least you can reach 45 million people [on the Internet].

MH: Let's talk about your inclusion in the Modern Library. You are now sandwiched in between Thackeray* and Tolstoy.† What does that mean to you? *Fear and Loathing in Las Vegas*, twenty-five years after it was published, is in the Modern Library.**

HST: That's a little faster than you'd normally think it could occur. You know, most of those people in [the Modern Library] are dead. No, I'm not surprised to be there. I guess it's a little surprising to be here still walking around and shaking people's hands. It tells me the Modern Library's catching up. But everything has sped up now. Instant communication. Instant news.

MH: When you were starting out, when you were eighteen and you started writing these letters in *The Proud Highway,* did you think your work would ever be considered classic?

HST: I never sat down and thought about it and stared at it. Obviously, if you read *The Proud Highway,* I was thinking somewhere along those lines. I never lobbied the Modern Library to include more living writers. I've always assumed it was for dead writers. But what I did assume at that time, early on and, shit, every year forever after that, was that I would be dead very soon. The fact that I'm not dead is sort of puzzling to me. It's sort of an awkward thing to deal with.

---

* William Makepeace Thackeray was an English novelist and author of the satirical novel *Vanity Fair.*

† Leo Tolstoy was a Russian novelist and author of *War and Peace* and *Anna Karenina.*

** The Modern Library is a series of influential and world-renowned books published by Random House. In 1996, *Fear and Loathing in Las Vegas* was issued in the Modern Library.

MH: You wrote in 1977, in the introduction to *The Great Shark Hunt* [a collection of HST's journalism], "I have already lived and finished the life I planned to live—(13 years longer, in fact). . . . " Thirteen years earlier would have been around the time you wrote *Hell's Angels.* Now it's twenty years since you wrote that introduction. Do you still feel the same way? What was behind writing that?

HST: Oh, sitting alone in an office in New York, the day before Christmas Eve, editing my own life's work—the selection, the order—because I couldn't get anybody else to edit it. Somebody pulled out because he wouldn't publish that poem, "Collect Telegram from a Mad Dog." I guess he was using that as an excuse. So I ended up having to do it myself. It was a little depressing, sitting up there having to do it myself. One of the advantages of being dead, I guess, is that somebody else can edit all this. For quite a while there I had to assume that I would never be in anything, much less the Modern Library.

MH: How is your health? How are you feeling now?

HST: I haven't started any savings accounts . . . I tell you, you'd act differently if you thought you were going to die at noon tomorrow. You probably wouldn't be here doing this. I just figured, "Bye, bye, Miss American Pie, good old boys drinkin' whiskey and rye, singin' this'll be the day that I die." Yeah, I just felt that all along.

MH: Live every day like your last, because you don't know what tomorrow's going to be like?

HST: Well, there's no plan for it. It's like going into the 27th inning in a baseball game. You're like, what the fuck am I doing here, man?

MH: There's a lot happening for you these days: *Fear and Loathing,* the movie; the Modern Library; twenty-five years of *Fear and Loathing: On the Campaign Trail.* Can you compare this time with anything prior—the excitement, maybe, of running for sheriff, or covering Nixon—now that you are sitting here looking back on it all?

HST: I got more of a kick out of running Nixon out of office than I have with these author parties.

You know, Gonzo Journalism is a term that I've come to dislike because of the way it's been cast: inaccurate, crazy. And in a way it might sound like, "what am I complaining about?" But there's a big difference. What I called Nixon is true—just a little harsh.

MH: If you were doing it again today, do you think you would go at it the way you did?

HST: Would I do it again, is that what you mean? I'm talking about the word "Gonzo." Yeah, I'd do it again. And that's the test of everything in life. You know, the way you look back on it. I use this a lot, a great measuring stick. I'd like a good war, a good fight. I get lazy when there's not one.

In journalism, one of the reasons I think I get the pleasure is the political factor. It's the effect you can have, with journalism. It's like writing a poem in the woods . . . you know that old thing about if a tree falls in the woods—

MH: If nobody heard it, did it happen?

HST: Yeah. Technically, no, there's no sound unless it's heard. [With journalism,] it's the effect, it's the sound, you know, when it's heard.

MH: It's the effect? And in that context you would call yourself—

HST: Successful. I don't need any prizes or parties to shore up my self-esteem. When I see Nixon getting on a plane, then I'm there. And he's headed west and I'm not.

MH: So that was it? Nixon getting on the plane?

HST: Yeah. That might have been the peak of effectiveness.

MH: What were you doing that day? Do you remember?

HST: Absolutely, man. I was in the White House Rose Garden. I was at the end of a red carpet that stretched from the stairs to the helicopter, which landed on the lawn. There were some Marines to my left, but I was the last human being in the line. Annie Leibovitz* was right beside me. And yeah, just being there and watching him get on, it was—not total victory, but it gave me a sense of being very much a part of not just my reality but everybody else's. There's a big difference between railing against some oppressor for twenty years and then ending up in the Bastille, or fighting a twenty-year war and watching the enemy vanquished.

MH: What were your thoughts when you saw him getting on the helicopter?

HST: I felt sorry for him. He hit his head. Right after he did this thing [makes the v-for-victory sign] at the helicopter door, he turned and lashed his head on the top of the rounded door, staggered sideways, and he was so—in some jurisdictions we might have called it "luded out"—he was tranquilized. There's a civilized word for it: sedated. He was almost led up the stairs.

---

* A friend of Hunter's, Annie Leibovitz is an American portrait photographer. She is the former chief photographer of *Rolling Stone* from 1970 to 1983. She is currently a featured photographer for *Vanity Fair* magazine.

Yeah, I felt sorry for him. Can you imagine that ride west? Jesus Christ, they flew to Andrews Air Force Base, I guess, on the helicopter, and then they had like a six-hour flight to San Clemente. Whew. That must have been a really dark flight.

MH: Did you have a relationship or correspondence with him after that?

HST: No. I was urged to, and I thought about it, but no, I didn't. I guess that's a political technique: the war's over, the game's over. I don't want to make it into a game, although I guess it is in the same sense that getting elected President can be seen as a game. It's a deadly serious game. It's a very mean thing.

I don't know why people think that the Mafia is merciless and badder than you know—and yet they don't assume that the President of the United States is in a position of such power, and that of course he's going to use the same fucking tools as the Mafia.

MH: The last we heard from you on politics was in *Better Than Sex,* and that was a couple years back. What do you think about the state of politics today?

HST: I would say that I am more into politics now than I was in '92. Yeah, I was mesmerized a little bit by the access [Clinton] offered me—like total access. "Come on down," you know? "Go out drinkin' with Hillary." Yeah, they did a good job on me. But I was set on beating Bush. I thought we were going to beat Bush at the Iran-Contra hearings, and I worked overtime. He was guilty as fifteen hyenas, and he got off, and it really bothered me. So I would have been for anybody in '92, just to beat Bush. And that's a dangerous trap to fall into—you know, the lesser of two evils.

MH: There's a lot of apathy today. People don't want to go out and vote.

HST: And why should they? I felt that way, and I didn't vote for Clinton in '96. I voted for Ralph Nader. There's a terrible danger in voting for the lesser of two evil because the parties can set it up that way.

MH: What do you think about the current two-party system here?

HST: I don't think it is a two-party system. And I think the reason Clinton was re-elected is that he understands the same thing. He took the crime issue away from the Republicans, and now he's taking the tax issue away. He's proposing a lower capital gains tax than the Republicans already had. So now the Democrats are champions of big business. He's an extremely skilled fucking politician. The Clinton people all had e-mail, beepers . . .

MH: They were wired in.

HST: Yeah, as opposed to the [Bush] White House. [The Clintons] moved into the White House, and it was like they moved into a cave. [A good friend] called me—a photographer, very close to the Clintons—telling me, ye gods, we move in here, and they still have a phone system that Abraham Lincoln would have appreciated.

MH: Clinton had wanted to be JFK. That's who he talked about in his campaigns.

HST: You tell Mr. Bill there's a reason that Jack Kennedy was shot, and he hasn't been.

MH: What's that?

HST: There's no reason to shoot Clinton. They didn't hesitate when Kennedy seemed to be going against them. They shot him. And they shot Bobby.

MH: They?

HST: They. If you are going to shoot the President of the United States, plan it and do it, you must be extremely well connected and smart and organized. Anybody who can organize a three-position, triangulated shooting at the President of the United States is very good.

MH: Your theory on the JFK assassination is what?

HST: That it was carried out by the Mob but organized and effectuated by J. Edgar Hoover.

MH: If popular culture holds up JFK as something good that could have been—and Nixon is seen as the opposite extreme—where does Clinton fall on the spectrum between JFK and Nixon?

HST: Well, Clinton will be lucky if he rates above Ulysses Grant or Warren Harding on the great scale. And he will, as long as the economy's good. [James] Carville was right—it's the economy, stupid.* And Clinton finally took that to heart. I think there are only three occasions in the history of American presidential elections when people have not voted obviously with their wallets.

MH: What are those?

HST: Oh, boy. I walked into that one, didn't I? I believe one was the JFK election, in '60. I can't scan it back that fast now. But in every case there

---

* James Carville is an American Democratic strategist and consultant. Carville was an influential strategist behind President Bill Clinton's 1992 successful campaign against the incumbent George H. W. Bush.

was—Woodrow Wilson may have been one—there was an instant, passionate issue. How the fuck Kennedy ever made Nixon a bad guy in 1960 is beyond me. That was real politics. A crazed Catholic playboy from Massachusetts, rich father supported the Nazis in 1940—I was against [JFK] at first.

MH: *The Proud Highway* contains some letters you wrote on November 22, 1963 [the day JFK was shot], to your friends Paul Semonin and William Kennedy. In the one to Kennedy you wrote, "There is no human being within 500 miles to whom I can communicate anything—much less the fear and loathing that is in me after today's murder. . . . No matter what, today is the end of an era. No more fair play. From now on it is dirty pool and judo in the clinches. The savage nuts have shattered the great myth of American decency." According to the book it was the first time you wrote the words "fear and loathing."

HST: I was amazed that it went back that far. I was not aware that I was accused of stealing it from Kierkegaard. People accused me of stealing "fear and loathing"—fuck no, that came straight out of what I felt. If I had seen it, I probably would have stolen it. Yeah, I just remember thinking about Kennedy, that this is so bad I need new words for it. And "fear and loathing"—it defines a certain state, an attitude.

MH: Clinton had a vision for a Great Society when he was elected. What do you think has happened since then?

HST: Well, the things that Clinton has been accused of are prima facie worse than what Nixon was run out of office for. Nixon was never even accused of things like Clinton is being accused of now. Bringing the Chinese into the political process, selling out to the Indonesians, selling the Lincoln bedroom at night, dropping his pants, trying to hustle little girls in Little Rock. God, what a degenerate town that is. Phew.

MH: How will history remember Bill Clinton?

HST: I don't know about history. I don't get any satisfaction out of the old traditional journalist's view—"I just covered the story. I just gave it a balanced view." Objective journalism is one of the main reasons American politics has been allowed to be so corrupt for so long. You can't be objective about Nixon. How can you be objective about Clinton?

MH: Objective journalism is why politics have been corrupt for so long?

HST: If you consider the great journalists in history, you don't see too many objective journalists on that list. H. L Mencken was not objective.* Mike Royko, who just died.† I. F. Stone was not objective.** Mark Twain was not objective. I don't quite understand this worship of objectivity in journalism. Now, just flat-out lying is different from being subjective.

MH: If you found yourself teaching a journalism course—Dr. Thompson's Journalism 101—what would you tell students who were looking to go about covering stories?

HST: You offering me a job? Shit. Well, I wouldn't do it, I guess. It's not important to me that I teach journalism classes.

MH: But if you did, what would your reading list be?

HST: Oh, I'd start off with Henry Fielding.†† I would read writers. You know, I would read Conrad, Hemingway, people who use words. That's really what it's about. It's about using words to achieve an end. And the Book of Revelation. I still read the Book of Revelation when I need to get cranked up about language. I would teach Harrison Salisbury of the *New York Times.* All the journalists who are known, really, have been that way because they were subjective. I think the trick is that you have to use words well enough so that these nickle-and-dimers who come around bitching about being objective or the advertisers don't like it are rendered helpless by the fact that it's good. That's the way people have triumphed over conventional wisdom in journalism.

MH: Who's writing that way today?

HST: Oh, boy. Let's just say, who's been arrested recently? That's usually the way. Like in the sixties you look for Paul Krassner,*** I. F. Stone. I don't think that my kind of journalism has ever been universally popular. It's lonely out here.

---

* H. L. Mencken was an American journalist and columnist for the *Baltimore Sun* from 1906 to 1948. Mencken is known for his expressive style and acerbic political analysis.

† Mike Royko was an American journalist and Pulitzer Prize–winning columnist for the *Chicago Tribune.*

** Isidor Feinstein Stone was an American investigative journalist. He self-published *I.F. Stone's Weekly* in the 1950s and 1960s.

†† Henry Fielding was an English satirical writer and humorist. One of his most popular novels is *The History of Tom Jones.*

*** Paul Krassner is an American satirical writer, journalist, and counterculture figure. He published the counterculture magazine, *The Realist*, from 1958 to 1974. Krassner cofounded the Yippies with Abbie Hoffman and Jerry Rubin in the 1960s.

A lot of times I recognize quality in the enemy. I have, from the very beginning, admired Pat Buchanan, who's not even a writer. He knows how to use words. I read something the other day, and I totally disagreed with him. But you know, I was about to send him a note saying, "Good!"

MH: If you were going to start a paper, and you were editor, who would you hire on? Who'd be on your writing staff? Living or dead.

HST: Whew! That would be fun. We're thinking of starting a paper here. These are not abstract questions. If I were to surround myself with experts, I'd hire P. J. [O'Rourke], Tom Wolfe, Tim Ferris. I'd hire Jann Wenner, put him to work.

MH: For this publication you're thinking about putting together now, what would be your mission?

HST: I can't think in terms of journalism without thinking in terms of political ends. Unless there's been a reaction, there's been no journalism. It's cause and effect. [A bottle of Wild Turkey is introduced.] Aw, man. I drank this like some sort of sacrament for—I mean, constantly—for I think fifteen years. No wonder people looked at me funny. No offense. This is what I drank, and I insisted on it and I drank it constantly and I liked it. Jesus. I laid off it for six months and went back to it—an accident one night, in a bar—and it almost knocked me off the stool. It's like drinking gasoline. I thought, what the fuck? . . . He Was a Crook [At HST's request, a cardboard placard is brought into (*Rolling Stone,* June 16, 1994) the room, bearing HST's obituary of Richard Nixon for *Rolling Stone,* dated May 1, 1994, and entitled, "He Was a Crook."]

HST: Here's one of the things I'm proudest of. It's about time you read something. Why don't you read that for us? This will be a lesson for you. Start at the beginning. If you haven't read this, it might explain a little more. Take it from the top. Headline and all.

[MH proceeds to read aloud the entire scathing obituary.]

MH: "'He Was a Crook.' By Hunter S. Thompson. Memo from the National Affairs Desk. Date: May 1, 1994. Subject: The Death of Richard Nixon: Notes on the passing of an American monster . . . He was a liar and a quitter, and he should have been buried at sea . . .

But he was, after all, the President. "Richard Nixon is gone now, and I am poorer for it. He was the real thing—a political monster straight out of Grendel—"

HST: Slow down, slow down, slow down. I've learned this the hard way. You gotta read slower, bite the words off.

MH: Okay. Okay. [Slowly] "Richard Nixon is gone now."

HST: Good

MH: "And I am poorer for it."

HST: Good.

MH: "He was the real thing—a political monster straight out of Grendel and a very dangerous enemy. He could shake your hand and stab you in the back at the same time."

HST: That's good.

[The reading continues. HST stops MH numerous times, telling him to reread lines that MH hasn't delivered to the author's satisfaction. Several times HST laughs out loud. HST soon becomes distracted and digresses, and MH puts the placard down on the couch.]

HST: Don't put that away! All the way to the end!

MH: All the way to the end?

HST: You bet. It's a lesson for you. You'll learn from this. I guarantee it. You're going to be happy at the end.

MH: A happy ending?

HST: Have a drink here, first, since you've already fucked up. You may as well have a drink.

[A glass of Wild Turkey and ice is placed before MH, and he continues reading to the end.]

MH: What inspired you to write this?

HST: I don't know if inspired is the right word. It's like tapping into a vein, I guess. But the history of this is instructive.

As it happens I was sitting in a house in New Orleans with Nixon's biographer, Steve Ambrose. He's a friend. And we were watching the last hours of Nixon. And Ambrose in his wickedness, in his self-serving skill, got me into one of these weepy, you know, "Well, he really was a nice guy . . . " Yeah, the death of Nixon: I either had to die or write it. I was staying at the Ponchartrain Hotel at the time in New Orleans. And I tried to react to it there. And after maybe two days, total failure. I couldn't. I was not up to the majesty of the event. I set such a high standard—H. L. Mencken's obituary for William Jennings Bryan, which then ranked as the most savage and unnatural thing ever said on the death of a famous or any other person. Mencken is a person I'd hire. But, with that being the standard, the target being so high, it was like being asked to run the three-minute mile. And, fuck, I tried for like two weeks. I failed in New Orleans, and I got back here, and I failed again. I despaired several times. I had Jann and Tobias* frantic on the other end [at *Rolling Stone*]. But I wouldn't let it go unless it was right, and it was nowhere near right.

MH: What was it that gelled it for you?

HST: Ah ha, thank you. It was watching his funeral on TV. It enraged me so much. It was such a maudlin, ruthless affair. I was thinking about going, but I wouldn't have seen the clarity of it as I did watching it on TV here. It was such a classically—you're talking about your objective journalism?—it was one of those things . . . speak no evil of the dead. Well, why not? What the fuck? Nixon goes out as a champion of the American dream and a hero. It enraged me. So it was the rage that tapped the vein.

MH: You say "Gonzo Journalism" is a term that you're not so fond of anymore, because it's been cast as inaccurate, crazy. Has anyone written Gonzo besides you?

HST: Is that [the Nixon obituary] Gonzo in your mind? Signed and shot by the author.

MH: No. I guess when I think of Gonzo, I'm thinking of your story "The Kentucky Derby Is Decadent and Depraved" [*Scanlan's Monthly*, June, 1970]. You throw yourself into the middle of a story and write your way out of it. Has anybody else done that?

HST: Oh, yeah, there are some good ones. Very few, but there was a novel called *Snow Blind,* in the seventies, about the cocaine trade.†

MH: Why has the term "Gonzo" fallen out of favor with you?

HST: Well, maybe because of what I just asked you. Since the Random House Dictionary defines "Gonzo" as sort of whatever I write or do, and I ask you, Does that Nixon obit seem like Gonzo Journalism to you? And you say no, then I have to wonder, right?

MH: How do you compare Gonzo to the New Journalism? Do you see them as separate or intertwined?

HST: Intertwined, in that it is no accident that Gonzo is in Tom Wolfe's book *The New Journalism* [1973].

---

* Tobias Perse was an assistant editor at *Rolling Stone*.

† American author Robert Sabbag's semiautobiographical novel, *Snowblind: A Brief Career in the Cocaine Trade*, was originally published in 1976.

MH: When you were writing in this way, did you feel that you were part of a movement, the New Journalism, or did you feel like you were just doing your own thing?

HST: No, I felt like I was just a journalist on assignment, really.

MH: In an early letter to William Kennedy you spoke of the "dry rot" of American journalism. Tell me what you think. What's the state of the American press currently?

HST: The press today is like the rest of the country. Maybe you need a war. Wars tend to bring out the best in them. War was everywhere you looked in the sixties, extending into the seventies. Now there are no wars to fight. You know, it's the old argument about why doesn't the press report the good news? Well, now the press is reporting the good news, and it's not as much fun.

The press has been taken in by Clinton. And by the amalgamation of politics. Nobody denies that the parties are more alike than they are different. No, the press has failed, failed utterly—they've turned into slovenly rotters. Particularly the *New York Times,* which has come to be a bastion of political correctness. I think my place in history as defined by the PC people would be pretty radically wrong. Maybe I could be set up as a target at the other end of the spectrum. I feel more out of place now than I did under Nixon. Yeah, that's weird. There's something going on here, Mr. Jones, and you don't know what it is, do you?

Yeah, Clinton has been a much more successfully deviant president than Nixon was. You can bet if the stock market fell to 4,000 and if four million people lost their jobs there'd be a lot of hell to pay, but so what? He's already elected. Democracy as a system has evolved into something that Thomas Jefferson didn't anticipate. Or maybe he did, at the end of his life. He got very bitter about the press. And what is it he said? "I tremble for my nation when I reflect that God is just"? That's a guy who's seen the darker side. Yeah, we've become a nation of swine.

MH: In *Fear and Loathing in Las Vegas* you were looking for the American Dream. What is there for people to find in 1997?

HST: Do you think we were surprised [in *Fear and Loathing*] to find that the American Dream was a nightclub that had burned down five years earlier? That we were surprised to find when we tracked it down that it had been the old Psychiatrist's Club? Prior to that its name had been the American Dream. Do you think that we were surprised to find that? No. I went out there looking to reaffirm Horatio Alger. I knew what was happening.

That's what the book is all about.

MH: From what I've read and from people I've talked to, the thing that people find most impressive about *The Proud Highway* is that from the age of seventeen or eighteen, you knew what you were going to do—

HST: Fifteen.

MH: People are impressed with your sense of destiny. I know that you say you got in trouble and journalism or writing was the only thing that was there for you, but at seventeen, eighteen—or even fifteen—plenty of things were open to you.

HST: Right, the world is your oyster. I guess I found out early on that writing was a means of being effective. Well, you can see the beginnings of that in *The Proud Highway.* I grew up thinking that, despite the obstacles presented by the swine, I would be successful no matter what I did. I guess that's one of the things about growing up in the fifties, it never occurred to me that you wouldn't be at least as successful as your parents. Now it's a minority position to believe that you might be even as successful as your parents.

MH: There's a letter in *The Proud Highway* [from 1965] **in which you said, "I should have quit journalism . . . and hit the fiction for all I was worth. And if I'm ever going to be worth anything I honestly think it will have to be in the realm of fiction." What if you had stuck to straight journalism? What do you think would have been the outcome?**

HST: It might have all hinged on Phil Graham's suicide in 1963, I guess. He was the publisher of the *Washington Post.* [HST had struck up a correspondence with Graham.] It's a wild thought—we'll have to wrap this up before I get really wild and start thinking out loud—but by now I could have been the editor of the *Washington Post.*

Contra Costa Times—August 30, 1997

God of Gonzo: Hunter S. Thompson Still Railing After All These Years

BY LYNN CAREY

I begin by mentioning seeing him at University of California–Davis.

Contra Costa Times: How does it make you feel when people are throwing baggies of stuff at you? Would you rather they were throwing, say, verse?

HST: No. I'll take the baggies.

Times: You're a hero to generations of fans.

HST: Why is that, I wonder?

Times: So, are you starting to feel like you're approaching 60, in a few weeks?

HST: That's nonsense, I'm approaching 23. (He chuckles.) But it does seem like one long year, since 22.

Times: What do you think is the biggest misconception people have about you?

HST: That I'm a nice person. (Laughter all around.) It's that comic strip (Garry Trudeau's *Doonesbury* has a character named Uncle Duke that looks and acts remarkably like Thompson). I don't read comic strips, but every morning. It's kind of difficult wandering around the world for I don't know how many years. You try being a comic strip character for 25 years.

Times: Aren't you flattered a little bit?

HST: Not at all. I think that's responsible for the largest single misconception. That the character he swears has nothing to do with me. I don't follow it, so I don't know what Duke does. But it might have something to do with bridging the age gap. When I have a nine-year-old boy come up to me speaking very articulately. And asking me to autograph a copy of *Fear and Loathing in Las Vegas.* Very polite. In a tavern. I wouldn't sign. I don't sign autographs when I'm trying to drink. All of a sudden I'm confronted with this nine-year-old boy talking knowledgeably about the book.

Times: A nine-year-old reading *Fear and Loathing in Las Vegas.* What does that tell us?

HST: I've wondered about it. I can only guess it had to do with getting away with it. It seems to me there's not too much you can get away with these days. (Pause) Where am I?

Times: Who's your hero now, Hunter?

HST: God, almighty. Heroes. Dr. Kevorkian comes to mind. Morris Dees, from the Southern Poverty Law Center. He's been a civil rights lawyer almost as long as I've been a journalist. I used to have three heroes. Muhammad Ali, Bob Dylan and Fidel Castro. I don't have any reason to change that.

Times: Do you ever feel like some of the people who hang around you, you could ask them to do anything and they'd do it, for free?

HST: Are you offering to do something?

Times: That depends. But the people in Woody Creek (his home, a "fortified compound" in Colorado), do they still flock to you like you're the Dalai Lama?

HST: I'm still intensely active in local politics. I think politics is the art of controlling your environment. It's important to me who's sheriff and who's mayor. It probably should be important who's president.

Times: What's your legacy?

HST: Being a writer in America is very hard. A freelance writer. I'd like a monument to me indicating that you can do it. If you don't lie.

Times: If you don't lie?

HST: Yeah. That's a tricky thing to say. Yeah. I've been pretty honest, I guess, with what I've written. The only thing that would hurt me would be to be accused of some really horrible, the kind of crimes I jump on people for. Lies, treachery. If it came out I was working for Scientology all this time.

Times: Do you ever get tired of the word "Gonzo"?

HST: Yeah. I just did that to differentiate myself from the "new journalists" that were cropping up. I don't know why I did it. It seemed like a good idea at the time. But since then, we don't have any generations of Gonzo journalists, it's more than going out and getting drunk and pushing people around in public places. It's in the Random House Dictionary as whatever I do. "As defined by the work of Hunter S. Thompson," something like that.

Times: That's great.

HST: Yeah, but it's kind of lonely.

Times: And kind of a lot to live up to.

HST: I'd like to pass it on to more people. But it isn't something like the key to the kingdom that you are given. (He gestures to *The Proud Highway.*) I'm shocked at all the 10 years of agony in there. I didn't really do the cutting (Douglas Brinkley is the book's editor), I just objected to the poverty (described in the letters). Particularly to the weird sums that are given. It just proves that it wasn't so easy. But it looks like fun, doesn't it?

Times: Yep!

At this point the author escort is frowning and pointing to her watch. In the spirit of Gonzo journalism, she is ignored.

Times: What do you think was your proudest moment?

HST: I get these big, huge questions. Any time you can beat city hall.

Times: So it's not like when one of your books came out, your proudest moment. Like, *Hell's Angels.*

HST: That was close. I was never surprised to be published. I just thought it was overdue. And going back to Louisville (he received the key to his hometown in December). That large event. Getting my mother there. She had a wonderful time, drinking whiskey. She and my aunt were in the front row, in Memorial Auditorium. I was proud of that.

Times: Did you have any say in having Johnny Depp portray you?

HST: We're both from Kentucky.

Times: Had you seen his movies?

HST: No. We met in a bar in Woody Creek. I didn't know who he was. I had no idea he was going to play me in a movie. He's getting nervous, now.

Depp: I already told Hunter that if I even do close to a good job of portraying him, he'll probably despise me for the rest of my life. That's why I figure we'll hang out now.

HST: While we can.

Times: Were you a fan? Is that why you went to Woody Creek then?

Depp: I've always been a fan. But I needed advice.

Times: On what kind of gun to buy?

Depp: No, no, I'd always been a fan.

Times: So, you had read his stuff?

Depp: Oh, yeah, I'd read a lot of his stuff.

HST: I thought he was just a homeboy, being brought up to the house by a friend. I was a little puzzled by the fact that his girlfriend (superstar model Katc Moss) was traveling with her mother and a bodyguard. But I adjusted to it.

Times: Are you a grandpa yet, Hunter?

HST: No! No I'm not. I forced my son's wife to have several abortions.

Author escort: You can't print that.

Puritan Magazine—1998

Interview with Hunter S. Thompson

BY PHOEBE LEGERE

Hunter pulls out an enormous gun.

Legere: How long is that barrel? Is that an 8 inch barrel?

HST: 8 and three quarters

Legere (nervous): That's powerful.

HST: Uhuh. It can knock a fingernail off of that thumb there.

Legere: What kind of gun do you use—for the paintings?

HST: .45? There's no safety on it.

Phoebe screams, he brandishes the gun.

HST: You never know.

Legere: Wait wait! I want to get a picture.

(Two shots out the window.)

HST: I missed it all right. Well tomorrow I guess my job is to pull letters.

Legere: You're very good in bed—did your dolls teach you how to have sex? How did you learn your way around the female genitalia?

HST: I know nothing of the female genitalia.

Legere: Ya . . . you do something.

HST: I don't know anything about it . . . it's a totally foreign subject to me.

Legere: One of the things that I love the most is your inclusion of Steadman right with you all the time and your use of those beautiful drawings. How did you get the idea to put drawings—illustrations—into your books when nobody else does that? Nobody even picked up on it. It didn't become a trend. It's sort of unique to you.

HST: That was a time in '70, '71, '72, when I actually had the luxury of choosing whether to have Annie Leibovitz or Ralph Steadman illustrate my work. Annie's such a bullheaded monster of a photographer and she's the best at what she does and so is Ralph. It was a real luxury to be able to choose between them and I just figured that Ralph—I could try Ralph more. Anyway, photographers are always working . . . there are kinds of friction between photographs and words. It's hard to work with photographers and Ralph's hard to work with, but he kind of sees the work farther than I do. So I just figured rather than argue with Annie, I'd fight with Ralph.

Legere: Well they're so beautiful, and the readers just love your relationship with Ralph.

HST: Did you see that one? (Hunter indicates Steadman's *Goddess of Polo Players*—the female horse with four eyes and big bosoms.)

Legere: Yes. You gave me a copy from the original and I have it hanging in my house. Now, who taught you about the female body? How do you know? Most men don't even know where the clitoris is—let alone the labia. You have a way of stimulating the labia which is really where it's at. How'd you learn that?? Some whore must have told you.

HST: It's hard for me to comment on.

Legere: Could you talk about being engaged politically in service of the environment?

HST: Politics is really the art of controlling your environment. The airport—these greed-heads are destroying my environment. We've got to step up the grassroots organization (against) industrial tourism. That's the Aspen Skiing Company you know—it's a company. The ski company wanted to enlarge the airport. They want to bring in more and more people. It worries me. That's what was wrong with them and we beat it.

Legere: Did you grow up in the country or city?

HST: Well it was probably city but in a very green area called the highlands—Cherokee Park—middle class. Relatively artsy, chic section of Louisville. Oh I felt so dull and so dumb and I went to many jazz and blues places I . . .

Legere: I'm just wasting time here.

The interviewer is overwhelmed. He looks so adorable.

Legere: What was the name of the air force base where you learned to fly planes and drop bombs on people and where you learned about naval warfare?

HST: Eglin Air Force Base. Eglin. It's in the news everywhere (indicating the NY *Times*).

Legere: Oh I'm so glad your reading the *Times*!

HST: Ha ah oh yes (sarcastic). Thanks to you I'm catching up.

Legere: Would you like to comment on the front page? I'm dying to hear your take on Bob Dole!* And, by the way, no one is going to see this. It's just for Flypaper, a little online newspaper.

HST: You've been lying all along!

Legere: Have you ever played Russian Roulette?

HST: In the head? No.

Legere: If madness runs in your family . . .

HST: It doesn't run in my family . . . No one ever said I was crazy. You perhaps . . . You're nutty as a fruitcake. Yeah, madness ran in my wife's family. Its always the . . . Sonny, excuse me, Sonny is a stripper.

Legere: But your son is so normal. Where did she go?

HST: She's not my wife.

Legere: Who could leave you? You have Eleanor throw them out.

HST: That's right.

He starts to rip my blouse off. I repel him using a judo defense maneuver—pinning his arms behind his back. He tries to rip my thumb off.

HST: I don't really want to touch you at all, because I think you present a very aggressive, mocking point of view.

I release him and hug him tenderly.

Legere: You have never been interviewed by anyone who loves you more than I do?

HST: I didn't say—you've discussed that—I was talking about your aggressively mocking situation on the heterosexual landscape (fake laugh).

Legere: Well I can't even follow that.

HST: . . . A pretty aggressive political viewpoint.

Legere: I love your flowers. Did you grow them yourself? Are you into horticulture?

HST: Yes I am.

Legere: I picked you some flowers in the forest . . . the devil's paintbrush. Who killed Bobby Kennedy?

HST: We . . . this is kind of a jump for me but we'll get to it . . . people in collusion with elements of the Los Angeles Police Department and the LA County Sheriff's Department—LAPD, LA County—the LAPD.

Legere: Who were they working for?

---

* Bob Dole is a former Republican senator from Kansas and the 1996 Republican presidential nominee. Dole served in the senate from 1969 to 1996.

HST: Ya well, that's like saying who was Oswald working for?*

Legere: Who was Oswald working for?

HST: I believe J. Edgar Hoover essentially . . . trace that back I think Hoover did it.

Legere: OK. Now I wanna know about Jimi Hendrix. And Janis Joplin and all those folks. And . . . and Kurt Cobain.

HST: I can't do it all now. These are research projects.

Legere: OK. Can you just say a few words about Hillary?†

HST: Hillary is one of my favorite people.

Legere: Is she great?

HST: No she's a monster.

Legere: She's a top, right? Because she's gay, right? Did you have sex with her?

HST: Yah.

Legere: I would love to fuck her.

HST: She's probably the most unsexual person I've ever . . . She hates me.

Legere: She comes across very cold.

HST: She hates me personally.

Legere: Why? How could anyone hate you? How could any woman hate you? How could anyone with a brain hate you?

HST: She calls me that horrible Hunter Thompson.

Legere: And what do you think of Lyndon Johnson? Was he in on it?

HST: He was Hoover's neighbor . . .

Legere: Where did they live?

HST: In Arlington, Virginia. They were next-door neighbors.

Legere: Tell me how you've changed. How you've matured. It seems like when you were 21 you were nice, romantic, sweet, kind. Now you've just turned into a kind of rotten caricature of a sadist. Can you talk about that?

HST: It has a lot to do with who I was exposed to in that period of time. The people who shaped my psyche and my life . . . and you.

Legere: What did they do to you? It seems like you were so nice before.

HST: I was nice last week. I just thought that the flogging . . . that your . . .

Legere: OK. Here's what I want to know . . .

HST: You want to be flogged as a civil right?

---

* Lee Harvey Oswald was the convicted assassin of President John F. Kennedy.

† First Lady, at the time, Hillary Rodham Clinton.

Legere: Here's what I want to know. Among the Muslim people, men are allowed to have 4 wives. It seems like you have at least 5 or maybe more.

HST: What makes you think so?

Legere: Maybe 50 but 5 sort of formal . . .

HST: That's an absurd statement! It's like something out of Mars. I don't know what would make you say that.

Legere: In 1958 when you wrote that letter which we read tonight, it seems like you were experiencing some kind of urban romance that we just don't feel anymore. Could you say anything to the kids about life? Something for the kids?

HST: Do you want that letter?

Legere: They seem to be more completely brainwashed by mass media; more conforming. They seem to be completely controlled by radio and television. Was it that way in 1958? What were you reading? Were you reading Kerouac?

HST: I was.

Legere: Were you into the Beat thing? Ginsberg?

HST: Yes.

Legere: And it seems like you decided to be a genius before you were 21. You decided. Is your mother a genius?

HST: She's the head librarian of the Louisville Public Library System. She's a very smart woman.

Legere: And what about your dad? You never talk about him.

HST: He was pretty smart.

Legere: I'm not here to rape you intellectually. I'm only here to spread the good news about your talent.

HST: Yes.

Legere: And character.

HST: Indeed.

Legere: Do you have a stun gun?

HST: Yes.

Arena Magazine (United Kingdom)—September 1998

Vegas Stripped: Guns, Drugs and Johnny Depp. Hunter S. Thompson Has Waited 25 Years for His Warped Vision to Hit the Screen

BY TOBIAS PERSE AND TAD FLORIDIS

Arena: Why did it take 25 years to turn *Fear and Loathing in Las Vegas* into a film?

HST: Well, I was in no hurry to have it made. It has been optioned many times. I've gone to LA and New York to meet all these people and it went on and on. Hal Ashby [director of *The Last Detail, Shampoo,* and *Coming Home*] spoke about doing it—that he considered doing the film was a real honor. Ralph Bakshi [director of *Felix the Cat* and *Lord of the Rings* (cartoon)] wanted to do it in animation. I talked to Jack Nicholson and Dennis Hopper at some point. They were going to be the pair. There have been a lot of other people. But I haven't been in a rush.

Arena: So how did it finally happen?

HST: There was kind of a landslide of activity where it went from low-budget, kind of a weird, lame little art project that had hovered in limbo to all of a sudden, "Ye gods, well, well, well." Yeah, [Terry] Gilliam is a big-time director, and he upped the budget considerably. And Johnny Depp and Harry Dean Staton, and Gary Busey and Benicio del Toro. Yeah there's a decent confluence of talent on this.

Arena: When did you first meet Depp?

HST: A few years ago, a friend of mine who lives here in Woody Creek called me down to the Tavern to meet Johnny Depp and his girlfriend. It was ten o'clock at night. I was going to do some bombs out back, but I went down there. It was fine. It wasn't until we left the Tavern and came back here that I realized there were three other people with us: Kate Moss's mother and two bodyguards. We did a little shooting.

Arena: Was Depp a good shot?

HST: Johnny responded well to my instruction. I pride myself as a shooting instructor. I can teach anyone to shoot—well, not anyone, there are exceptions, as always. I have a whole different method, and it worked that night. First shot, whack, Johnny hit this prepared canister of gasoline. We have a movie of this which Kate took. Her mother and the bodyguards were terrified. Here's this daughter, this franchise, a billion-dollar face filming a wall of fire.

Arena: How much time did he spend in Woody Creek preparing for the role?

HST: A lot more than he would have if he weren't a friend. Johnny's a gem, a warrior really. He was not coddled. He stayed downstairs, in the basement, in the Depp suite, and would rummage through boxes of stuff that I'd collected in Las Vegas and would walk up with old Circus Circus cocktail napkins, matchbooks, notebooks . . .

Arena: The letters which you had archived since you were a teenager were recently published in the collection *The Proud Highway.* Keeping all this documentation seems like part of some kind of grand plan, as if you knew their worth from the beginning.

HST: It's more and more apparent that I knew all along. That's going to be the indictment: he knew. There were no mistakes.

Arena: At what point did it become clear that your plans for solitude and concentration on the commissioned story of the murder of Ruben Salazar, the Chicano journalist, were being sidetracked into the course of events which ended up becoming *Fear and Loathing*?

HST: After a few days, Oscar had to go back on the plane to deliver a brief in court for the Biltmore hotel trial, a huge headline case. There was no time. I took him to the airport, drove right up to the plane. At the last second, Oscar handed me this leather lawyer's attaché case and asked me to bring it back. When I finally looked in it, there were no documents, no papers at all. It was just a big bag of marijuana and a Colt—not loaded—and a box of bullets. I thought, you fucker. Do I throw the gun away, throw that pound of weed away? Of course, it would have been smart. But let's face it, this was 1971. (Pauses) What would you have done with it?

Arena: I probably would have dropped it into a rubbish bin and moved away from it all as quickly and quietly as possible.

HST: Yeah, the instinct to throw it into the nearest trash barrel might have been there. But I figured, what's wrong? I'm a respectable journalist. I'll just hide it in the trunk and get back to LA without any troubles. Why should I have any troubles? That was the logic of the time: well, let's see. I'm smart. I know what I'm doing. I have a red car. Las Vegas.

Arena: He may have been your attorney but in the book of *Fear and Loathing in Las Vegas* Oscar seems like something of a liability . . .

HST: Oscar may have been a liability, but he was also a huge asset. He was more than a friend; in some hideous way he was really a brother. Oscar would take it one notch on anybody. You always had to be ready with Oscar, because he would not back off. And he had a fine sense of fun. With Oscar leaving, yesterday's fun becomes today's uh-oh.

Sports Illustrated had turned the story down, I had no money. I had this Carte Blanche card, it had been taken and cut in two right in front of me when I was trying to buy Juan [Thompson's son] a shirt or something. I had to flee this utterly horrible hotel by myself, skip out on the bill with a pound of weed, a weapon, a box of bullets. I'm in this red car on the only road back to Los Angeles. There was that constant fucking pressure.

Arena: How about working with Benicio del Toro. Did you have to give him any direction as to how Oscar behaved?

HST: Benicio took a lot of abuse from me. He swelled fifty pounds, and he got bigger and more menacing than Ralph ever was. This thing did not go through peacefully. It was high-wire work.

Arena: A lot of people read *Las Vegas* and ask, is this fiction?

HST: If people knew how real this is. It happened.

Arena: How important were Ralph Steadman's illustrations to the story?

HST: Ralph has always been a godsend. Without Ralph my life as a writer would have been very different. He is utterly critical. I saw early on that I could use him as a prism, a sounding board. If I was horrified at something and I confronted Ralph with it, he would be more horrified. Not only would he give me art, he would give me words, copy. His sense of shock was high energy for me. He can do all kinds of things—stamps for the Queen, his books—but he needs to be challenged. That's when he does his best work. And I challenge him.

Arena: A lot of people are protective of books they like. Were you worried that the film adaptation would not live up to the experience of reading it?

HST: I really can't see how there's a downside to this, except you suggesting it might shame my legacy and replace the book. I don't think so. But now that you've raised the question, yeah, maybe Depp did deliberately sandbag me—maybe this is going to be a rotten, evil joke on me. Yeah, maybe we should bring him in on this. (Thompson calls Depp on his mobile phone. Depp's voice mail picks up, and Thompson begins to talk into the speaker phone's mic.) I'm asking for a little help here because I'm being led down the garden path by some journalist who's asking me about the movie. It may be better if you gave me a ring back. You know how I roam far afield if I don't have any direction. Punctuality may help. Thank you very much (Clicks off).

Arena: Do you think the presence of drugs in the story made *Fear and Loathing* an unpalatable movie to shoot?

HST: Definitely. There was something like a ten-year hiatus when the subject became very un-hip and dangerous. The Nancy Reagan idea of Just Say No. Hollywood took that very seriously. I didn't get the full meaning of that until years later.

Arena: This is probably not a film Nancy will enjoy.

HST: Oh, Christ no. The book talks about drugs. It is not, however, about drugs. This story is not about drugs, and I don't think the film is. But when you get into boycotts and lists, you get Las Vegas was on it.

Arena: Did you and Terry Gilliam talk about the book's themes?

HST: We did. I was with Gilliam and Depp and Benicio at the Chateau Marmont, and the question came up, "Well, what's this all about?" It was not a question I wanted to waffle on. I waited a few beats—one, two, three, any more than that would have been dangerous—and I said, Hope. This is a story about hope. At which point, Benicio bursts out laughing and slid down on the garden tiles. After the *Hell's Angels* book, Random House was paying my expenses for the next project. They didn't know what it would be. I packed all kinds of research into it and decided on the death of the American Dream. It has been a constant theme for me. What's *Las Vegas* about? What I was doing and what I wrote about was looking for the death of the American dream.

Esquire Magazine (London)—November 1998

Night of the Hunter

BY BILL DUNN

The Doctor Will See You Now . . .

I Got Rhythm . . .

As the night wore on, it became apparent that the Doctor doesn't like doing straight interviews; he has to get to know someone first—drink with them, study their habits. But we eventually settle down in the kitchen where he gives me an impromptu writing lesson by making us read pieces of his work out loud and conducting with his hands from his high stool, beating the air rhythmically and occasionally intoning, "Slower!" or encouraging, "That's it!" and, "Sixteen lines straight; no punctuation. That's four times longer than Joyce was ever able to do."

HST: Reading aloud is a necessity—it's amazing how what you wrote comes back to you through a filter. I love to hear women read my work. I explain it in terms of music.

ESQ: When you were learning, you used to type passages from other authors' work . . .

HST: You've never done that? Take a page of my work, Conrad's, whoever, and type it out. It's pretty difficult because everyone uses different rhythms. This is a basic tenet—this is where it starts.

ESQ: It reminds me of Ginsberg's "Howl."

HST: Yeah? Well, different rhythm. Allen and I have been together on many a fight. We were there at Kesey's [Ken, LSD evangelist and author of *One Flew Over the Cuckoo's Nest*] when the cops were arresting anyone who left. Allen and I went out like the Lone Ranger in a little Ford Anglia to challenge them in the name of journalism. My son Juan was lying in the back seat—he was eight months old. The cops said, "What have you got in there? Is that an infant?" I said, "Of course it's a child, I'm a working journalist!"

All the time in the background Ginsberg is going, "OM . . . OM . . . OM . . ." trying to ward them off.

ESQ: I thought they'd have slapped him in cuffs for being weird.

HST: [Laughs] No, actually did it. He said they gave off bad energy, hence the humming. When Allen died, I was supposed to go to LA to the memorial—a big dinner for about 2,500 people. I suffered here for a whole week—I just could not write a nice sentimental thing about Ginsberg. Then I said Johnny Depp would be there to read it. I very seldom give up, but I did—I sent Depp a fax saying, "Good luck—you're on your own, I've failed." And when I quit it was quitting. People ran. I was screaming, "OK I've failed, you can shoot me now!" I'd failed everyone—Depp, Allen, all my friends. It depressed me so much I took two Halcions, which should knock you out for about 12 hours, and went to bed. Maybe two hours later I got up and, in a mumbling fit, I sat down at the typewriter pouring this greasy sweat and wrote this thing. Johnny got it about two hours before he was due to go on. I'd have been a very different person today if I hadn't done that. [He plays the video of the memorial. The atmosphere is pretty funereal, when suddenly Depp appears and reads this touching yet irreverent tribute. Thompson describes Ginsberg as "A dangerous bull-fruit with the brain of an open sewer and the conscience of a virus. . . . " and later . . . "he was crazy and queer and small. He was born wrong and he knew it." Not a dry eye in the house.]

ESQ: You still type your work. You seem to have every other conceivable gadget—why not a word processor?

HST: There's a certain negative force when you use a typewriter that conspires to make you think. Sometimes I deliberately use single-line spacing because I can't make a mistake.

ESQ: You've invested so much time in the page?

HST: Exactly. I do use a word processor—*The Rum Diary* was put on disk—but it's usually after the fight. And I've yet to read a really good book that's been written on a word processor.

ESQ: Do you have a special inner calmness that enables you to take hallucinogenic drugs and operate fairly normally?

HST: Well, I happened to run across acid earlier than most people—in Big Sur in 1960. I was afraid of it. They told me, "You are too violent to eat LSD." That's quite a trip to lay on you to start with.

ESQ: You might turn into this Mr. Hyde character . . .

HST: Yeah—the minute you get out of control you might turn into something you've never seen but always dreaded? Wow! I stayed away from it for years. Finally I was at Ken Kesey's. Hell's Angels were gang-raping and clubbing people. I went up to Kesey and said, "All right, never mind what I've said before. This is too weird—I need some acid."

ESQ: Most people would have stayed straight to avoid the violence.

HST: Well, there was no other solution except leaving, and that was out of the question because there were cop cars waiting outside. I was meant to be writing the same kind of book that Tom Wolfe wrote [*The Electric Kool-Aid Acid Test*]. I never wrote it—I was just starting on the Hell's Angels book at the time.

ESQ: Who would be your chosen outlaws if you were starting out writing today?

HST: It's kind of hard to deal with today—everyone's getting rich writing gossip. Well, not writing the gossip rich. Fees for writers have actually gone down over the years. If I was starting to write today, I'd be appalled at the prices—it's made a freelance writer as rare as a five-toed sloth. It's mainly a matter of survival in a world where you have to use what you can do best.

ESQ: Hence Gonzo?

HST: That was just pure commercial journalism: if there is no story and you want to be on the front page, you'd better fucking well get a story! Basically that's it—you know, "There was no riot until we created one . . ."

ESQ: It was only after the success of *Hell's Angels* that your mom finally realized you had a "proper" job.

HST: Yeah [laughs]. Finally!

ESQ: Well, at least you weren't borrowing money from her anymore.

HST: I tended not to dwell on the bill collector and the wolf at the door. But it is a terrible part of the freelance writer's life.

ESQ: The philosophy coming through from your work is very liberal, but mixed with anarchy and fierceness . . . let people do what they want—up to a point.

HST: But just beware!

ESQ: . . . Which was the Angels' attitude?

HST: Yeah: massive retaliation—instantly. It was always a possibility.

ESQ: Like when they stomped you?

HST: Oh, I should have known. I violated all my own rules. It was hubris. I'd finished the book . . .

ESQ: Do you think society is less violent now?

HST: It's the cops who are doing the beatings these days. And Clinton is behind it. He's the most punishment-orientated American president ever—and that includes Nixon. At least he was specific about his enemies.

ESQ: Has Clinton replaced Nixon as your Satan?

HST: Clinton is white trash, and he has the specific gravity of white trash, which is mainly to clog up the fucking filters and stop it coming to surface. Yeah, you're right. I'm just warming up.

MOJO—April 1999

None More Gonzo

> *Regarding Ralph, his all-time favorite album is Jim Morrison (and The Doors)* American Prayer *because "it's wonderful to hear this suicidal singer giving it all in a concert in L.A. It's suicidal because you could kind of tell that he wasn't going to make it."*
>
> —HUNTER S. THOMPSON

MOJO: What Music are you currently Grooving to?

HST: My own album. Can I say that? For pleasure. And I've been listening to a Ry Cooder album made in Cuba called Buena Vista Social Club. I'm going to go down to Havana pretty soon—as an American, you have to come in from a third country; it's routinely done. Clinton is about to relax the economic embargo—I've heard stories of a horrifying avalanche of teenage prostitution and whoremongers down there.

MOJO: What, if push comes to shove, is your all-time favorite album?

HST: When I went to Washington for the first time, rented a house and all that, I turned on the FM radio looking for a good station, and the first song I heard was Sam Stone from that first John Prine album, the one with "Angel from Montgomery"; it had just come out. So, John Prine. And a Rolling Stones greatest hits.

MOJO: What was the first record you ever bought? And where did you buy it?

HST: Stole would be a better word. We all used to shoplift those little 45 rpm vinyl discs when I was a child in Louisville, Kentucky, in a music store downtown where we'd go after school. It had those booths where you could listen to any record you wanted. You'd choose which one you wanted to buy, and which two or three you wanted to steal. I was into rhythm and blues back then, and the first one I stole was "Work With Me Annie" by Hank Ballard. I also picked up Howlin' Wolf's "I Smell a Rat." Little Richard, one of my heroes for a long time . . . I don't know . . . my mind is hazy right now.

MOJO: Which musician have you ever wanted to be?

HST: The first time I heard that Chuck Berry tune "Maybelline" I was in the air force at a desert base. Here I was in a tin-box cantina and I thought, Boy, that guy Berry's having a good time—things are happening here!

MOJO: What do you sing in the shower?

HST: I don't sing, man. I think dark thoughts.

MOJO: What is your favorite Saturday Night Record?

HST: The theme from *Caligula*. A lilting love song, as I recall.

MOJO: And your Sunday Morning Record?

HST: "Will the Circle Be Unbroken" by the Nitty Gritty Dirt Band.

The Paris Review—Autumn 2000

Hunter S. Thompson: The Art of Journalism No. 1

BY DOUGLAS BRINKLEY WITH CONTRIBUTIONS FROM TERRY MCDONELL AND GEORGE PLIMPTON

The Paris Review: Reading *The Proud Highway,* I got the impression you always wanted to be a writer.

HST: Well, wanting to and having to are two different things. Originally I hadn't thought about writing as a solution to my problems. But I had a good grounding in literature in high school. We'd cut school and go down to a café on Birdstown Road where we would drink beer and read and discuss Plato's parable of the cave. We had a literary society in town, the Athenaeum; we met in coat and tie on Saturday nights. I hadn't adjusted too well to society—I was in jail for the night of my high school graduation—but I learned at the age of fifteen that to get by you had to find the one thing you can do better than anybody else . . . at least this was so in my case. I figured that our early. It was writing. It was the rock in my sock. Easier than algebra. It was always work, but it was always worthwhile work. I was fascinated early by seeing my byline in print. It was a rush. Still is.

When I got to the Air Force, writing got me out of trouble. I was assigned to pilot training at Eglin Air Force Base near Pensacola in northwest Florida, but I was shifted to electronics . . . advanced, very intense, eight-month school with bright guys . . . I enjoyed it but I wanted to get back to pilot training. Besides, I'm afraid of electricity. So I went up there to the base education office one day and signed up for some classes at Florida State. I got along well with a guy named Ed and I asked him about literary possibilities. He asked me if I knew anything about sports, and I said that I had been the editor of my high-school paper. He said, "Well, we might be in luck." It turned out that the sports editor of the base newspaper, a staff sergeant, had been arrested in Pensacola and put in jail for public drunkenness, pissing against the side of a building; it was the third time and they wouldn't let him out.

So I went to the base library and found three books on journalism. I stayed there reading them until it closed. Basic journalism. I learned about headlines, leads: who, when, what, where, that sort of thing. I barely slept that night. This was my ticket to ride, my ticket to get out of that damn place. So I started as an editor. Boy, what a joy. I wrote long Grantland Rice–type stories. The sports editor of my hometown *Louisville Courier-Journal* always had a column, left-hand side of the page. So I started a column.

By the second week I had the whole thing down. I could work at night. I wore civilian clothes, worked off base, had no hours, but I worked constantly. I wrote not only for the base paper, the *Command Courier,* but also the local paper, the *Playground News*. I'd put things in the local paper that I couldn't put in the base paper. Really inflammatory shit. I wrote for a professional wrestling newsletter. The Air Force got very angry about it. I was constantly doing things that violated regulations. I wrote a critical column about how Arthur Godfrey, who'd been invited to the base to be the master of ceremonies at a firepower demonstration, had been busted for shooting animals from the air in Alaska. The base commander told me: "Goddamn it, son, why did you have to write about Arthur Godfrey that way?"*

When I left the Air Force I knew I could get by as a journalist. So I went to apply for a job at *Sports Illustrated.* I had my clippings, my bylines, and I thought that was magic . . . my passport. The personnel director just laughed at me. I said, "Wait a minute. I've been sports editor for two papers." He told me that their writers were judged not by the work they'd done, but where they'd done it. He said, "Our writers are all Pulitzer Prize winners from the *New York Times.* This is a helluva place for you to start. Go out into the boondocks and improve yourself."

I was shocked. After all, I'd broken the Bart Starr story.

The Paris Review: What was that?

HST: At Eglin Air Force Base we always had these great football teams. The Eagles. Championship teams. We could beat up on the University of Virginia. Our bird-colonel Sparks wasn't just any yo-yo coach. We recruited. We had these great players serving their military time in ROTC. We had Zeke Bratkowski, the Green Bay quarterback. We had Max McGee of the Packers. Violent, wild, wonderful drunk. At the start of the season McGee went AWOL, appeared at the Green Bay camp and he never came back. I was somehow

---

* Arthur Godfrey was a national radio and television personality from the 1930s to the 1950s.

blamed for his leaving. The sun fell out of the firmament. Then the word came that we were getting Bart Starr, the All-American from Alabama. The Eagles were going to roll! But then the staff sergeant across the street came in and said, "I've got a terrible story for you. Bart Starr's not coming." I managed to break into an office and get out his files. I printed the order that showed he was being discharged medically. Very serious leak.

The Paris Review: The Bart Starr story was not enough to impress *Sports Illustrated?*

HST: The personnel guy there said, "Well, we do have this trainee program." So I became a kind of copy boy.

The Paris Review: You eventually ended up in San Francisco. With the publication in 1967 of *Hell's Angels,* your life must have taken an upward spin.

HST: All of the sudden I had a book out. At the time I was twenty-nine years old and I couldn't even get a job driving a cab in San Francisco, much less writing. Sure, I had written important articles for *The Nation* and the *Observer,* but only a few good journalists really knew my byline. The book enabled me to buy a brand-new BSA 650 Lightning, the fastest motorcycle ever tested by *Hot Rod* magazine. It validated everything I had been working toward. If *Hell's Angels* hadn't happened I never would have been able to write *Fear and Loathing in Las Vegas* or anything else. To be able to earn a living as a freelance writer in this country is damned hard; there are very few people who can do that. *Hell's Angels* all of a sudden proved to me that, Holy Jesus, maybe I can do this. I knew I was a good journalist. I knew I was a good writer, but I felt like I got through a door just as it was closing.

The Paris Review: With the swell of creative energy flowing throughout the San Francisco scene at the time, did you interact with or were you influenced by any other writers?

HST: Ken Kesey for one. His novels *One Flew Over the Cuckoo's Nest* and *Sometimes a Great Notion* had quite an impact on me. I looked up to him hugely. One day I went down to the television station to do a roundtable show with other writers, like Kay Boyle,* and Kesey was there. Afterwards we went across the street to a local tavern and had several beers together. I told him about the Angels, who I planned to meet later that day, and I said, "Well,

---

* Kay Boyle was an American poet, novelist, and journalist. She published numerous collections of short stories, novels, and poems, including *A Frenchman Must Die* and *Thirty Stories.*

why don't you come along?" He said, "Whoa, I'd like to meet these guys." Then I got second thoughts, because it's never a good idea to take strangers along to meet the Angels. But I figured that this was Ken Kesey, so I'd try. By the end of the night Kesey had invited them all down to La Honda, his woodsy retreat outside of San Francisco. It was a time of extreme turbulence—riots in Berkeley. He was always under assault by the police—day in and day out, so La Honda was like a war zone. But he had a lot of literary, intellectual crowd down there, Stanford people also, visiting editors, and Hell's Angels. Kesey's place was a real cultural vortex.

The Paris Review: Did you ever entertain the idea of writing a novel about the whole Bay area during this period, the sixties, in the vein of Tom Wolfe's *Electric Acid Kool-Aid Test*?

HST: Well, I had thought about writing it up. It was obvious to me at the time that the Kesey action was on a continuum with the *Hell's Angels* book. It seemed to me for a while that I should write a book, probably the same one that Wolfe wrote, but at the time I wasn't really into it. I couldn't do another piece of journalism.

The Paris Review: Did you connect at all with Tom Wolfe during the San Francisco heyday?

HST: It's interesting. I wanted to review Wolfe's book, *The Kandy-Kolored Tangerine-Flake Streamline Baby.* I'd read some of it in *Esquire,* got a copy, had a look at it and was very, very impressed. The *National Observer* had taken me off politics by then, so book reviews were about the only thing I could do that they didn't think controversial. I had wanted to cover Berkeley and acid, and all that, but they didn't want any of it. So I picked up Wolfe's book and wrote a glowing review and sent it in to the *Observer,* and my editor, Clifford Ridley, was pleased with it. About a week went by and I hadn't heard anything. Then my editor called me up and said, "We're not going to run the review." It was the first one they ever said no to; up until that point my reviews had been full-page lead pieces, like in the *Times Book Review,* and I was shocked that they would turn it down. I asked, "Why are you turning it down? What's wrong with you?" The guy obviously felt guilty, so he let me know there was an editor at the *Observer* who had worked with Wolfe somewhere else and didn't like him, so he had killed my review. So I took the review and sent it to Tom Wolfe with a letter saying, "the *Observer* won't run this because somebody there has a grudge against you, but I wanted you to get it anyway since I worked real hard on it, and your book was brilliant. I thought you should have it even though they won't print it." Then I took my carbons of that letter and sent them to the *Observer.* They said I'd been disloyal. That's when I was terminated. I just felt it was important not only that Wolfe knew about it, but that the *Observer* editors knew that I had turned them in. It sounds kind of perverse, but I'd do it again. But that's how Tom and I got to know each other. He would call me for directions or advice when he was working on the *Acid* book.

The Paris Review: Did that friendship and Wolfe's journalism have much of an impact on your writing?

HST: Wolfe proved that you could kind of get away with it. I saw myself as having a tendency to cut loose—like Kesey—and Wolfe seemed to embrace that as well. We were a new kind of writer, so I felt it was like a gang. We were each doing different things, but it was a natural kind of hook-up.

The Paris Review: Wolfe later included you in his book *The New Journalism.*

HST: I was the only one with two entries, in fact. He appreciated my writing and I appreciated his.

The Paris Review: As you explored the acid scene did you ever develop a feel for Timothy Leary?

HST: I knew the bastard quite well. I ran into him a lot in those days. As a matter of fact I got a postcard invitation from something called the Futique Trust in Aptos, California, inviting me to attend the fourth annual Timothy Leary Memorial Celebration and Potluck Picnic. The invitation was printed in happy letters, with a peace symbol in the background, and I felt a burst of hate in my heart when I saw it. Every time I think about Tim Leary I get angry. He was a liar and a quack and a worse human being than Richard Nixon. For the last twenty-six years of his life he worked as an informant for the FBI and turned his friends into the police and betrayed the peace symbol he hid behind.

The Paris Review: The San Francisco scene brought together many unlikely pairs—you and Allen Ginsberg, for instance. How did you come to know Allen during this period?

HST: I met Allen in San Francisco when I went to see a marijuana dealer who sold by the lid. I remember it was ten dollars when I started going to that apartment and then it was up to fifteen. I ended up going there pretty often, and Ginsberg—this was in Haight Ashbury—was always there looking for weed too. I went over and introduced myself and we ended up talking a lot. I told him about the book I was writing and asked if he would help with it. He helped me with it for several months; that's how he got to know the Hell's Angels. We would also go down to Kesey's in La Honda together. One Saturday, I drove down the coast highway from San Francisco to La Honda and I took Juan, my two-year-old son, with me. There was this magnificent cross-breeding of people there. Allen was there, the Hell's Angels—and the cops were there too, to prevent a Hell's Angels riot. Seven or eight cop cars. Kesey's house was across the creek from the road, sort of a two-lane black top country compound, which was a weird place. For one thing, huge amplifiers were mounted everywhere in all the trees and some were mounted across the road on wires, so to be on the road was to be in this horrible vortex of sound, this pounding, you could barely hear yourself think—rock 'n' roll at the highest amps. That day, even before the Angels got there, the cops began arresting anyone who left the compound. I was by the house; Juan was sleeping peacefully in the back seat of the car. It got to be outrageous: the cops were popping people. You could see them about a hundred yards away, but then they would bust somebody very flagrantly, so Allen said, "You know, we've got to do something about this." I agreed, so with Allen in the passenger's seat, Juan in the back sleeping, and me driving, we took off after the cops that had just busted another person we knew, who was leaving just to go up to the restaurant on the corner. Then the cops got after us. Allen at the very sight of the cops went into his hum, his om, trying to hum them off. I was talking to them like a journalist would: "What's going on here, Officer?" Allen's humming was supposed to be a Buddhist barrier against the bad vibes the cops were producing and he was doing it very loudly, refusing to speak to them, just "Om! Om! Om!" I had to explain to the cops who he was and why he was doing this. The cops looked into the backseat and said, "What is that back there? A child?" And I said, "Oh yeah, yeah. That's my son." With Allen still going, "Om," we were let go. He was a reasonable cop, I guess, checking out a poet, a journalist, and a child. Never did figure Ginsberg out, though. It was like the humming of a bee. It was one of the weirdest scenes I've ever been through, but almost every scene with Allen was weird in some way or another.

The Paris Review: Did any other Beat Generation authors influence your writing?

HST: Jack Kerouac influenced me quite a bit as a writer . . . in the Arab sense that the enemy of my enemy was my friend. Kerouac taught me that you could get away with writing about drugs and get published. It was possible, and in a symbolic way I expected Kerouac to turn up in Haight-Ashbury for the cause. Ginsberg was there, so it was kind of natural to expect that Kerouac would show up too. But no. That's when Kerouac went back to his mother and voted for Barry Goldwater in 1964. That's when my break with him happened. I wasn't trying to write like him, but I could see that I could get published like him and make the breakthrough, break through the Eastern establishment ice. That's the same way I felt about Hemingway when I first learned about him and his writing. I thought, Jesus, some people can do this. Of course, Lawrence Fernlinghetti influenced me—both his wonderful poetry and the earnestness of his City Lights bookstore in North Beach.

The Paris Review: You left California and the San Francisco scene near its apex. What motivated you to return to Colorado?

HST: I still feel needles in my back when I think about all the horrible disasters that would have befallen me if I had permanently moved to San Francisco and rented a big house, joined the company dole, become national affairs editor for some upstart magazine—that was the plan around 1967. But that would have meant going to work on a regular basis, like nine to five, with an office—I had to pull out.

The Paris Review: Warren Hinckle was the first editor who allowed you to write and pursue Gonzo journalism—how did you two become acquainted?

HST: I met him through his magazine, *Ramparts.* I met him even before *Rolling Stone* ever existed. *Ramparts* was a crossroads of my world in San Francisco, a slicker version of *The Nation*—with glossy covers and such. Warren had a genius for getting stories that could get placed on the front page of the *New York Times.* He had a beautiful eye for what story had a high, weird look to it. You know, busting the Defense Department—*Ramparts* was real left, radical. I paid a lot of attention to them and ended up being a columnist. *Ramparts* was the scene until some geek withdrew funding and it collapsed. Jann Wenner, who founded *Rolling Stone,* actually worked there in the library—he was a copy boy or something.

The Paris Review: What's the appeal of the "outlaw" writer, such as yourself?

HST: I just usually go with my own taste. If I like something, and it happens to be against the law, well, then I might have a problem. But an outlaw can be defined as somebody who lives outside the law, beyond the law, not necessarily against it. And it's pretty ancient. It goes back to Scandinavian history. People were declared outlaws and they were cast out of the community and sent to foreign lands—exiled. They operated outside the law and were in communities all over Greenland and Iceland, wherever they drifted. Outside the law in the countries they came from—I don't think they were trying to be outlaws . . . I was never trying, necessarily, to be an outlaw. It was just the place in which I found myself. By the time I started *Hell's Angels* I was riding with them and it was clear that it was no longer possible for me to go back and live within the law. Between Vietnam and weed—a whole generation was criminalized in that time. You realize that you are subject to being busted. A lot of people grew up with that attitude. There were a lot more outlaws than me. I was just a writer. I wasn't trying to be an outlaw writer. I never heard of that term; somebody else made it up. But we were all outside the law: Kerouac, Miller, Burroughs, Ginsberg, Kesey; I didn't have a gauge as to who was the worst outlaw. I just recognized allies: my people.

The Paris Review: The drug culture. How do you write when you're under the influence?

HST: My theory for years has been to write fast and get through it. I usually write five pages a night and leave them out for my assistant to type in the morning.

The Paris Review: This, after a night of drinking and so forth?

HST: Oh yes, always, yes. I've found that there's only one thing that I can't work on and that's marijuana. Even acid I could work with. The only difference between the sane and the insane is that the sane have the power to lock up the insane. Either you function or you don't. Functionally insane? If you get paid for being crazy, if you can get paid for running amok and writing about it . . . I call that sane.

The Paris Review: Almost without exception writers we've interviewed over the years admit they cannot write under the influence of booze or drugs—or at least what they've done has to be rewritten in the cool of the day. What's your comment about this?

HST: They lie. Or maybe you've been interviewing a very narrow spectrum of writers. It's like saying, "Almost without exception women we've interviewed over the years swear that they never indulge in sodomy."—without saying that you did all your interviews in a nunnery. Did you interview Coleridge? Did you interview Poe? Or Scott Fitzgerald? Or Mark Twain? Or

Fred Exley?* Did Faulkner tell you that what he was drinking all the time was really iced tea, not whiskey? Please. Who the fuck do you think wrote the Book of Revelation? A bunch of stone-sober clerics?

The Paris Review: In 1974 you went to Saigon to cover the war . . .

HST: The war had been part of my life for so long. For more than ten years I'd been beaten and gassed. I wanted to see the end of it. In a way I felt I was paying off a debt.

The Paris Review: To whom?

HST: I'm not sure. But to be so influenced by the war for so long, to have it so much a part of my life, so many decisions because of it, and then not to be in it, well, that seemed unthinkable.

The Paris Review: How long were you there?

HST: I was there about a month. It wasn't really a war. It was over. Nothing like the war David Halberstam† and Jonathan Schell** and Philip Knightley†† had been covering. Oh, you could still get killed. A combat photographer, a friend of mine, was killed on the last day of the war. Crazy boys. That's where I got most of my help. They were the opium smokers.

The Paris Review: You hoped to enter Saigon with the Vietcong?

HST: I wrote a letter to the Vietcong people, Colonel Giang, hoping they'd let me ride into Saigon on the top of a tank. The VC had their camp by the airport, two hundred people set up for the advancing troops. There was nothing wrong with it. It was good journalism.

The Paris Review: Did you ever think of staying in Saigon rather than riding in on a Vietcong tank?

HST: Yes, but I had to meet my wife in Bali.

The Paris Review: A very good reason. You're famous for traveling on assignment with an excess of baggage. Did you have books with you?

HST: I had some books with me. Graham Greene's *The Quiet American* for sure. Phil Knightley's *The First Casualty.* Hemingway's *In Our Time.* I carried all these seminal documents. Reading *The Quiet American* gave the

---

* Fred Exley was an American essayist and writer of the novel, *A Fan's Note.*

† David Halberstam was an American Pulitzer Prize–winning war correspondent, sports journalist, and historical nonfiction author of *The Best and the Brightest* and *The Fifties.*

** Jonathan Schell is an American journalist, professor, and nonfiction author of *The Village of Ben Suc* and *The Military Half* about the Vietnam War.

†† Phillip Knightley is an Australian journalist and nonfiction author of *The First Casualty* and *The Second Oldest Profession* about international espionage, propaganda, and war.

Vietnam experience a whole new meaning. I had all sorts of electronic equipment—much too much. Walkie-talkies. I carried a tape recorder. And notebooks. Because of the sweat I couldn't write with the felt-tip pens I usually use because they would bleed all over the paper. I carried a big notebook—sketchbook size. I'd carry all this stuff in a photographer's pack over my shoulders. I also carried a .45 automatic. That was for weird drunk soldiers who would wander into our hotel. They were shooting in the streets . . . someone would fire off a clip right under your window. I think Knightley had one, too. I got mine from someone who was trying to smuggle orphans out of the country. I couldn't tell if he was on the white slave or the mercy market.

The Paris Review: Why only a month in Saigon?

HST: The war was over. I'd wanted to go to Saigon in 1971. I'd just started working for *Rolling Stone.* At a strategy summit meeting that year of all the editors at Big Sur, I was making the argument that *Rolling Stone* should cover national politics. Cover the campaign. If we were going to cover the culture, to not include politics was stupid. Jann Wenner was the only person who half-agreed with me. The other editors there thought I was insane. I was sort of the wild creature. I would always appear in my robe. For three days I made these passionate pitches to the group. At the end of it I finally had to say, "Fuck you, I'll cover it. I'll do it." Dramatic moment, looking back on it.

Well, you can't cover national politics from Saigon. So I moved lock, stock and barrel from here to Washington. Took the dogs. Sandy, my wife, was pregnant. The only guy willing to help me was Timothy Crouse, who at the time was the lowest on the totem pole at *Rolling Stone.* He had a serious stutter, almost a debilitating stutter, which Jann mocked him for all the time, really cruel to him, which made me stand up for him more and more. He never had written more than a three hundred word piece on some rock 'n' roll concert. He was the only one who volunteered to go to Washington. "Okay, Timbo. It's you and me. We'll kick ass." Life does turn on so many queer things . . . ball bearings and banana skins . . . a political reporter instead of a war correspondent.

The Paris Review: Crouse eventually wrote a bestseller about the press and the campaign—*The Boys on the Bus.*

HST: He was the Boston stringer for *Rolling Stone.* He had graduated from Harvard and had an apartment in the middle of Cambridge. Strictly into music at the time. He was the only person who raised his hand in Big Sur. We covered the 1972 campaign. I wrote the main stories and Tim did the sidebars. Then there was that night in Milwaukee when I told him I was sick, too sick to write the main story. I said, "Well, Timbo, I hate to tell you this but you're gonna have to write the main story this week and I'm gonna write the sidebar." He panicked. Very bad stuttering. I felt I had to deal with that. I told him he had to stop stuttering. I told him that it's not constructive. "Goddamn it, spit it out!"

The Paris Review: "Not constructive?" Easy for you to say.

HST: Well, I saw that he lacked confidence. So I made him write the Wisconsin story, and it was beautiful—suddenly he had confidence.

The Paris Review: In your introduction to *A Generation of Swine,* you state that you spent half your life trying to escape journalism.

HST: I always felt that journalism was just a ticket to ride out, that I was basically meant for higher things. Novels. More status in being a novelist. When I went to Puerto Rico in the sixties William Kennedy and I would argue about it. He was the managing editor of the local paper; he was the journalist. I was the writer, the higher calling. I felt so strongly about it that I almost wouldn't do journalism. I figured in order to be a real writer, I'd have to write novels. That's why I wrote *Rum Diary* first. *Hell's Angels* started off as just another down-and-out assignment. Then I got over the idea that journalism was a lower calling. Journalism is fun because it offers immediate work. You get hired and at least you can cover fucking City Hall. It's exciting. It's a guaranteed chance to write. It's a natural place to take refuge in if you're not selling novels. Writing novels is a lot lonelier work.

My epiphany came in the weeks after the Kentucky Derby fiasco. I'd gone down to Louisville on assignment for Warren Hinckle's *Scanlan's.* A freak from England named Ralph Steadman was there—first time I met him—doing drawings for my story. The lead story. Most depressing days of my life. I'd lie in my tub at the Royalton. I thought I had failed completely as a journalist. I thought it was probably the end of my career. Steadman's drawings were in place. All I could think of was the white space where my text was supposed to be. Finally, in desperation and embarrassment, I began to rip the pages out of my notebook and give them to a copy boy to take to a fax machine down the street. When I left I was a broken man, failed totally, and convinced I'd be exposed when the stuff came out. It was just a question of when the hammer would fall. I'd had my big chance and I had blown it.

The Paris Review: How did *Scanlan's* utilize the notebook pages?

HST: Well, the article starts out with an organized lead about the arrival at the airport and meeting a guy I told about the Black Panthers coming in; and then it runs amok, disintegrates into flash cuts, a lot of dots.

The Paris Review: And the reaction?

HST: This wave of praise. This is wonderful . . . pure Gonzo. I heard from friends—Tom Wolfe, Bill Kennedy.

The Paris Review: So what, in fact, was learned from that experience?

HST: I realized I was onto something: maybe we can have some fun with this journalism . . . maybe it isn't this low thing. Of course, I recognized the difference between sending in copy and tearing out the pages of a notebook.

The Paris Review: An interesting editorial choice—for *Scanlan's* to go ahead with what you sent.

HST: They had no choice. There was all that white space.

The Paris Review: What is your opinion of editors?

HST: There are fewer good editors than good writers. Some of my harshest lessons about writers and editors came from carrying those edited stories around the corridors of Time-Life. I would read the copy on the way up and then I would read it again after the editing. I was curious. I saw some of the most brutal jobs done on the writers. There was a guy there, Roy Alexander, a managing editor . . . oh God, Alexander would x-out whole leads. And this was after other editors had gone to work on it.

The Paris Review: Did anybody do that to your copy?

HST: Not for long. Well, I can easily be persuaded that I'm wrong on some point. You don't sit in the hotel room in Milwaukee and look out the window and see Lake Superior, which I've written by mistake. Also, an editor is a person who helps me get what I've written to the press. They are necessary evils. If I ever got something in on time, which would mean I'd let it go from this house and liked it . . . well, that's never happened in my life . . . I've never sent a piece of anything that's finished . . . there's not even a proper ending to *Fear and Loathing in Las Vegas.* I had several different endings in mind, another chapter or two, one of which involved going to buy a Doberman. But then it went to press—a two-part magazine piece for *Rolling Stone.*

The Paris Review: Could you have added a proper ending when it was published as a book?

HST: I could have done that but it would have been wrong. Like rewriting the letters in *The Proud Highway.*

The Paris Review: Would it help if you wrote the ending first?

HST: I used to believe that. Most of my stuff is just a series of false leads. I'll approach a story as a subject and then make a whole bunch of different runs at the lead. They're all good writing but they don't connect. So I end up having to string leads together.

The Paris Review: By leads, you mean paragraphs?

HST: The first paragraph. The last paragraph. That's where the story is going and how it's going to end. Or else you'll go off in a hundred different directions.

The Paris Review: And that's not what happened in *Fear and Loathing*?

HST: No. That was very good journalism.

The Paris Review: Your book editor at the time of the earliest states of what was to become *Fear and Loathing in Las Vegas* was Jim Silberman at Random House—a lot of correspondence between the two of you.

HST: The assignment he gave me to do was nearly impossible: to write a book about the Death of the American Dream, which was the working title. I looked first for the answer at the Democratic National Convention in Chicago in 1968, but I didn't find it until 1971 at the Circus-Circus Casino in Las Vegas. Silberman was a good, smart sounding board for me. He believed in me and that meant a lot.

The Paris Review: What about Raoul Duke? How did the alter ego come about, and why and when?

HST: I started using him originally in what I wrote for *Scanlan's.* Raoul comes from Castro's brother, and Duke, God knows. I probably started using it for some false registration at a hotel. I learned at the Kentucky Derby that it was extremely useful to have a straight man with me, someone to bounce reactions off of. I was fascinated by Ralph Steadman because he was so horrified by most of what he saw in this country. Ugly cops and cowboys and things he'd never seen in England. I used that in the Derby piece and then I began to see it was an extremely valuable device. Sometimes I'd bring Duke in because I wanted to use myself for the other character. I think that started in *Hell's Angels* when I knew that I had to have something said exactly right and I couldn't get any of the fucking Angels to say it right. So I would attribute it to Raoul Duke.

The Paris Review: Are the best things written under deadlines?

HST: I'm afraid that's true. I couldn't imagine, and I don't say this with any pride, but I really couldn't imagine writing without a desperate deadline.

The Paris Review: The lead to *Fear and Loathing in Las Vegas,* "We were somewhere near Barstow on the edge of the desert when the drugs began to take hold . . . " When did you write that? Did you write that first?

HST: No, I have a draft . . . something else was written first, chronologically, but when I wrote that . . . well, there are moments . . . a lot of them happen when nothing else is going right . . . when you're being evicted from the hotel a day early in New York or you've just lost your girlfriend in Scottsdale. I know when I'm hitting it. I know when I'm on. I can usually tell because the copy's clean.

The Paris Review: Most people . . . losing a girl in Scottsdale or wherever, would have a drink somewhere and go crazy. It must have something to do with discipline.

HST: I never sit down and put on my white shirt and bow-tie and black business coat and think, Well, now's the time to write. I will simply get into it.

The Paris Review: Can you describe a typical writing day?

HST: I'd say on a normal day I get up at noon or one. You have to feel sort of overwhelmed, I think, to start. That's what journalism did teach me . . . that there is no story unless you've written it.

The Paris Review: Are there any mnemonic devices that get you going once a deadline is upon you—sharpening pencils, music that you put on, a special place to sit?

HST: Bestiality films.

The Paris Review: What is your instrument in composing? You are one of the few writers I know who still uses an electric typewriter. What's wrong with a personal computer?

HST: I've tried. There is too much temptation to go over the copy and rewrite. I guess I've never grown accustomed to the silent, non-clacking of the keys and the temporary words put up on the screen. I like to think that when I type something on this [pointing to the typewriter], when I'm finished with it, it's good. I haven't gotten past the second paragraph on a word processor. Never go back and rewrite while you're working. Keep on it as if it were final.

The Paris Review: Do you write for a specific person when you sit down at that machine?

HST: No, but I've found that the letter form is a good way to get me going. I write letters just to warm up. Some of them are just, "Fuck you, I wouldn't sell that for a thousand dollars," or something, "Eat shit and die," and then send it off on the fax. I find the mood or rhythm through letters, or sometimes either reading something or having something read—it's just a matter of getting the music.

The Paris Review: How long do you continue writing?

HST: I've been known to go on for five days and five nights.

The Paris Review: That's because of deadlines, or because you're inspired?

HST: Deadlines, usually.

The Paris Review: Do you have music on when you write?

HST: Through all the *Las Vegas* stuff I played only one album. I wore out four tapes. The Rolling Stones' live album, called *Get Yer Ya-Ya's Out* with the in-concert version of "Sympathy for the Devil."

The Paris Review: At one point, Sally Quinn of the *Washington Post* got after you for writing about specific events, but only 45 percent is actually the truth . . . how do you reconcile journalism with that?

HST: That's a tough one. I have a hard time with that. I have from the start. I remember an emergency meeting one afternoon at Random House with my editor about *Fear and Loathing in Las Vegas.* "What should we tell the *New York Times*? Should it go on the fiction list or non-fiction?" In a lot of cases, and this may be technical exoneration, but I think in almost every case there's a tip-off that this is a fantasy. I never have quite figured out how the reader is supposed to know the difference. It's like if you have a sense of humor or not. Now keep in mind I wasn't trying to write objective journalism, at least not objective according to me. I'd never seen anybody, maybe David Halberstam comes closest, who wrote objective journalism.

The Paris Review: You can write anywhere, can't you? Is there a place you prefer?

HST: Well, this is where I prefer now. I've created this electronic control center here.

The Paris Review: If you could construct a writer, what attributes would you give him?

HST: I would say it hurts when you're right and it hurts when you're wrong, but hurts a lot less when you're right. You have to be right in your judgments. That's probably the equivalent of what Hemingway said about having a shockproof shit detector.

The Paris Review: In a less abstract sense, would self-discipline be something you would suggest?

HST: You've got to be able to have pages in the morning. I measure my life in pages. If I have pages at dawn, it's been a good night. There is no art until it's on paper; there is no art until it's sold. If I were a trust-fund baby, if I had any income from anything else . . . even fucking disability from a war or a pension . . . I have nothing like that, never did. So, of course, you have to get paid for your work. I envy people who don't have to . . .

The Paris Review: If you had that fortune sitting in the bank would you still write?

HST: Probably not, probably not.

The Paris Review: What would you do?

HST: Oh . . . I'd wander around like King Farouk or something. I'd tell editors I was going to write something for them, and probably not do it.

George Magazine—December/January 2001

Q&A: Hunter S. Thompson

BY JOHN PERRA

Hunter S. Thompson has made a career out of working on the wild side. His second collection of letters, *Fear and Loathing in America*, spans the turbulent years between 1968 and 1976, when he was "chasing" Richard Nixon, threatening to "jam fence posts up the asses" of editors, and trying to finish an elusive book on the death of the American dream. It's an autopsy the 63-year-old writer has been conducting ever since.

George: Why are you publishing your letters?

HST: I kind of like them and I didn't get paid for them when I wrote them. I kind of carried a grudge. It starts off with the late sixties. It is shocking to have to be faced with my history day by day.

George: But you had to have something like this in mind because you saved all your letters. Was that part of cultivating the image and icon Hunter Thompson or the writer? Or are the two the same?

HST: I never have understood the whole development but I noticed in *The Proud Highway* that at the age of nineteen or twenty I was telling people I would publish my letters before I died rather than after. That I was the new F. Scott Fitzgerald. I was bragging to girls about that. I'm not sure what the hell possessed me—I guess it was kind of a certainty that I was going to be a writer. Period. And by that time I realized I couldn't do much else. You know, once I got a job with a newspaper and I realized that you don't have to work nine to five or get up in morning . . .

George: Scares you?

HST: Not appealing. Oh I settled into this life early. I just took it for granted. And I guess if I took it for granted that I was going to be a writer. I remember I thought—well, I might as well be the best.

George: Do you think you're the best?

HST: No. I don't think I'm the best writer. I'm just thinking what I had to be thinking then. You know, why would I drag all these fucking letters all over the world for all this time. It makes me feel a little strange but now it makes perfect sense.

George: The letters are not only your history but a sort of history of that time in America.

HST: Yes I think that's true. I've always been kind of—well we might call it lucky—being at the right place at the right time.

George: What about that time. You seem to be so identified with it. And with all these things happening to you—like the inclusion in the Modern Library, the publication of the so-called lost novel and now your letters—I don't know how you're going to take this but it seems like all these things could've been done posthumously.

HST: Oh yeah, I'm sure that's what I was thinking at the time. I never expected to live this long.

George: Are you surprised that you're alive?

HST: Oh yeah. Very much.

George: So you got some extra time.

HST: Yeah. I don't know whether that's a punishment or reward. I think it's one of these gods with a sense of humor. There's not much humor in the Christian god or the church. I don't think there's any, is there?

George: I can't think of anything very funny off hand.

HST: Yeah. A lot of religions have, you know gods of good times and pleasure. Kind of outlaw sort of gods. Yeah. And this religion—there's no room for any of that.

George: Are you a practicing Christian?

HST: No—well, a small 'c' christian yeah. No—the Church of the New Truth was the last church I was a member of. And I haven't missed church. And I don't miss religion. What church are you of?

George: I was raised Catholic.

HST: Uh-oh. That's a horrible time right off. You got that guilt right away. Catholics kind of handle it pretty well. You're guilty but you know it's not going to ruin you. You just kind of have to pay for it.

George: Yeah. What do think about guilt? What do you feel guilty about? Or do you?

HST: (Laughs) Oh boy . . .

George: Or is there not enough time?

HST: (Laughs) Yeah—well I haven't had the time to worry about guilt. If I had failed or fucked up in some way or somehow induced my son to be put in prison—I'd feel guilty about that. But I've never had the time to feel guilty about it. That's the only question I ask myself: would you do it again?

George: Would you?

HST: Yeah. Absolutely.

George: Everything the same way?

HST: You don't get that option. If only I had known what I know now of course, I'd change strategies here or there. But you don't get that option to guess again.

George: Well what do you know now that you didn't know then?

HST: (Laughs) I often wonder about that.

George: What do you know for sure?

HST: I know that I'm a good writer and managed to make a living at it for a long time and that's pretty tricky.

And I have faith in my instincts after this much time. And that's one of the reasons I would do it again. Because it makes me feel a lot more comfortable to think that my instincts really are right. I don't know if I'd join Alcoholics Anonymous or some kind of a group where in order to be accepted you have to admit that your life up to now was all wrong. Holy fuck, that would really be horrible. How old are you?

George: Thirty-three.

HST: That's an interesting year thirty-three. It's like twenty-two, thirty-three . . .

George: Forty-four?

HST: Yeah. Yeah, you know I think maybe twenty-two is the best year. Thirty-three was a good one though.

George: What do you remember from being thirty-three?

HST: Fuck, I was running for sheriff and chasing Nixon around. I was deeply involved in things when I was thirty-three. I kind of thought, I guess, that well, you can live forever or die at any minute. I had no real sense of time at thirty-three. Even less at twenty-two. At twenty-two, looking back, you can see that a twenty-two-year-old can afford to fuck up. I mean at that age you can bounce. It gets a little harder at thirty-three.

George: Yeah, that's right.

HST: And forty-four. Yeah you're kind of stuck with your life at forty-four. Yeah but thirty-three's a good one. I [began to run] amuck for about seven years when I was thirty-three and it wasn't bad.

George: I've read your obituary of Nixon.

HST: Oh yeah? Oh good. Yeah. I'm very proud of that.

George: What is the work that you're proudest of?

HST: Oh Christ, it would be counter-productive to start thinking that way.

George: What jumped into your head immediately?

HST: Immediately? Well it goes back to—well I'm proud of myself [for] making it as a writer, I guess—you have to be one to how hard that is. I read myself now, and I find stuff that I've forgotten that I wrote; some of it bad, some of it elegant. I'm glad that I sort of worked on you know my tool. My craft.

George: I recently read that you stopped drinking.

HST: (Laughs) You did? No, I never stopped drinking. Yeah. Look what happened to George Bush when he stopped drinking.

George: He started making plans to run for president, I think.

HST: I guess so. But I have the feeling that he never really wanted to be president, and he still would just as soon be back partying somewhere.

George: Years ago, you got in trouble by saying that then Vice President George H. W. Bush was so evil that he should be stomped to death. Do you still think George Bush is evil?

HST: Yeah I think he's a rotten bastard, yeah. He got away with the Iran-Contra affair. That was worse than anything Nixon or Reagan ever did. That was one of the great unpunished crimes of the century.

George: George H. W. Bush, Dick Cheney, and James Baker* have been very powerful—in and out of office—for almost thirty years.

HST: Yeah, well it's Texas oil power. And now we got this little fart coming in, continuing it. That was a powerful crowd. He [George H. W. Bush] was head of the CIA. He was everything. Ambassador to China. He's a well-rounded man as they say. He and Baker, and the others out of Texas. That's almost like a different country.

George: Evil takes a lot of time to cultivate?

---

* James Baker served as the secretary of state under President George H. W. Bush and secretary of the treasury between 1985 and 1988 under President Ronald Reagan. Hunter wrote about James Baker rescuing "the goofy child president" with a plane full of lawyers during the 2000 hanging-chad controversy.

HST: Yeah, I think so. And one has to practice it at the levels of power. I don't think Gore or Bush Jr.—or whatever it is—the third? These are just punks. They wouldn't rank with any of the pure evil people. Nixon was almost pure evil, I think. He didn't even know how to hide it. But [George H. W.] Bush has developed that patina, that gloss. And Nixon never quite learned that. I was lucky to have Nixon around for that period.

George: How about someone to admire? A good politician.

HST: I think Bill Clinton is the best politician around.

George: But you mean that—

HST: In a mechanical way. Yeah. The main reason I supported Nader was because I think that we need another voice in the whole heart of this country or mind or soul—it doesn't have any voice. And the deals are from the same people, same companies, same interests and that amounts to a one party system. We certainly can't get anything like, say McGovern and Nixon. That was definitely a two-party system.

George: So when did it stop being a two-party system?

HST: Oh boy. Interesting question. Interesting as in the ancient Chinese curse that says may you live in interesting times. It stopped being a two-party system—boy let's see . . . Clinton came in. He came out of that conservative [Democratic Leadership Council]. That worked and it made it easy for him.

George: Well, he's sort of just gifted that way anyway right?

HST: Oh yeah. He was born in a vat of snake oil. Yeah, he's good. Clinton, I figure, is one of the worst products of a political system that is increasingly geared to putting up that kind of product. And in order to be president you got to be like Bill Clinton.

George: Is there a counter-culture anymore?

HST: No, I think what we see rather than counter-culture now is that old cop-out of working within the system. Rather than working against it. There are no revolutionaries. We felt in the sixties that we were definitely part of a revolution. You know the movement . . .

George: Do you think that now?

HST: Certainly not. No, I feel pretty lonely now. In a way, you could say there's no enemy. No visible enemy. I think about this a lot, with this corporatization of everything. In the corporate culture, as it turns out, nobody's really responsible. The stockholders are the boss and you can't get hold of anybody. You can't fix on any human target. My book [*Fear and Loathing in America*] is full of these things where I would single out a person. I would attack a company. I would find out who was the president and write these letters. When you wanted to blame somebody there was somebody to blame. I was able to take my complaints straight to Nixon.

George: What was your idea of "president" thirty years ago?

HST: I think maybe I kind of grew up believing H. L. Mencken's axiom that the only way for a journalist—writer—to look at a politician is down. You know, they're all contemptible swine. And the JFK murder had a huge effect on me and a lot of other people of that generation. And then you got Bobby Kennedy and Martin Luther King. It was a generation that was having all its leaders murdered right in front of their eyes. And that's why 1968 stands out in my mind as maybe the worst and weirdest year than anything I can remember in history. I still believe that and I can still feel that when I read these [*Fear and Loathing in America*] . . . well, it's not a journal is it? I'm not sure just what it is.

George: What do you think about letter writing now? We don't write letters anymore, we write email.

HST: Somebody I was talking to the other day said that he was sure that these letters of mine here [*Fear and Loathing in America*] will be the last book of letters. It's obviously a form that's just going out of practice. Imagine the collected emails! It doesn't feel personal, and it doesn't feel private, and it doesn't feel special.

George: Is there a letter in this collection that you would change if you had the chance?

HST: Take back a letter? I've sent a lot of letters that I kind of regret and wish I could get out of the box. But I can't. So what the hell, you know. I figured: take the ride. There are some letters I hid in this book that I'm not particularly proud of. I've written a lot of letters in a fever of rage to reporters or Jann Wenner or other editors and agents. Dared them to come to New York and I'd jam a fence post up their ass and slit their eyes out and cut their stomachs and you know, they were [telling people] "he killed an editor." I think that some editors have lived in fear that I would. It's good for them.

George: You mentioned earlier that it's lonely now—

HST: Yeah. You know I used to be invited to a lot of weddings, now I go to a lot of funerals. That's the physical reality. I remember meeting some freak—in the best sense—you know, a doper—I hadn't seen for a long time, and I asked him about some people I had known in some commune and I said where are those people now? You never hear from them. And he said, they're all either dead or in prison. Now, I don't know if I am an outlaw or if I've been classified as that—I don't think it's really by my choice. Well shit this is too complicated. Yeah one of my best friends here is a sheriff and I'm comfortable with it. But I've learned to bounce a lot you know in my career and wanderings. You got to be resilient.

I also learned early on—a very important thing to learn—that you take the book reviews and articles about you—if you believe them when they're good and complimentary you're trapped into believing them when they're bad. I've been careful not to take the you know the nice stuff too seriously. And so I'm protected against the ugly stuff.

George: In his foreword [in *Fear and Loathing in America*], David Halberstam says, I think his work is "touched by genius and transcends mere journalism." Did you set out to transcend mere journalism? Was that in your mind or were you just doing what you were doing?

HST: Well, for one thing it was fun to push the envelope in ways that I did. I would worry about it sometimes. Nixon, of course, loved campaigns and Hunter Thompson—same way—Oh I understood Nixon. When I met him we talked football. Period. That was the only reason he would talk to me. And he was good at it. I enjoyed talking football with him. But you can't forget the other things . . .

George: I think it's interesting that the word "Clintonian" refers to style and not to policy. How do you think he's changed the presidency?

HST: Well, politics now—the idea of getting into it with a future—there's no way that any decent person could do it. Yeah, you'd have to be—I'm probably the cleanest person in the country. I could be in politics; I've got nothing to hide. I have no dark unexplored periods in my life or things that I was thinking about that would be, you know, scarred by scandal. God everything I've done I've already admitted and been paid for. That sounds (Laughs) funny . . .

George: That is funny.

HST: (Laughs) But I couldn't run for anything, I'd just be pestered by all manner of . . . I feel that way anyway. Other than a relentless dope fiend and stuff like that—the book *Fear and Loathing in Las Vegas* could be held against me . . .

George: Do you think that this idea of a dangerous Hunter Thompson is a persona or is that real? If I say Hunter S. Thompson to you, what do you think?

HST: I guess, I see a nice guy with a slight smile. But I'm not dangerous. And I think, like recently when I totally accidentally, you know—shot my secretary. It was regrettable and she accidentally opened the door and wandered into a piece of shot from a four-ten. But of course, you know, it makes—it excites people to hear that I shot somebody. But there's a good side to this—I haven't been in the papers for any kind of accused violence and dangerous outrage for quite a while so that's good; it'll keep some of these freaks away from the house. And I believe that's one of the reasons I've lived in relative peace for some time.

George: What does Gonzo mean to you now?

HST: It's never really meant anything to me. That was just a word I picked up at a time when I was, I don't know just thinking that—when the New Journalism was very big—I didn't think I was necessarily a New Journalist like these others. I mean I see more of myself in Mark Twain than most of the New Journalists then, and that was the cream of the crop. It [Gonzo] was just a differentiation. Just sort of you know—a little fun, a little fear. I never expected it to last this long. Christ, there's Gonzo beer, Gonzo grapes—maybe people just liked the word. You think it's all me every time I see Gonzo in the papers? It is true but I no longer feel guilty for it.

George: So it's just a word to you?

HST: Yeah. I like words that cut and bounce. And that one definitely does. But when it happened back with the New Journalism—which was good stuff, good writers, and I respected all of them more or less. I wasn't trying to put them down.

George: What do you think of the Internet? It seems like everyone can be a writer now.

HST: Well everybody is.

George: Do you think that's true?

HST: Well . . . a writer . . . yeah boy I guess it's about time we had to make a distinction whether you say that with a capital "W" or not. With the Internet—none of these people could be published in any magazine that I'm aware of during my life. Yet they seem to feel that there's no difference between them and David Halberstam.

George: Do you think that's a good attitude in a way?

HST: No I don't think so at all. No, I think you have to learn the craft and learn to respect it before you set out to break all the rules. In fact, I used to read Joseph Conrad a lot, and I knew what good writing was. You know, I realize that Conrad did not write many things like my epitaph for Nixon.

George: What about it that offends you?

HST: Well actually there's not much about that that offends me but I think that's probably generational—there's not much that can shock or offend now.

George: And wouldn't you expect Hunter Thompson to write that?

HST: Well, maybe not as eloquently as this one is written. In many cases, I have to have somebody to compete with and in that case, one of things I really admired—all my life—is H. L. Mencken's obituary for William Jennings Bryan.

George: You had that in mind when you wrote the Nixon?

HST: Oh yeah. Absolutely. And I guess I was trying to set the bar a little higher. There are not too many things that I'm afraid to compete with; well, the Book of Revelation is one.

George: What is the American dream? Or was there ever an American dream?

HST: Jesus Christ . . . well I identified it as a junk nightclub that burned down. And there's more to that than just flip. I've considered that a lot. I've felt that in some ways I've lived the American dream. Let's just leave it at that because it's different for everybody. And as I say, I feel it sometimes. Yeah, each could possibly—aw never mind that's too arcane . . .

George: No, go ahead.

HST: I've been through this before as you can tell from reading this stuff. And I never have figured some of the most basic things out—like what is Gonzo journalism and what is the American dream. And shit, I still can't spell "sheriff." I think sometimes I really never learned anything much since I was fifteen. I know I have, but I haven't changed much. And maybe I'm either an example of integrity in a person or the dumbest person around. I haven't learned anything since I was fifteen.

George: Is that good or bad?

HST: (Laughs) Jesus man, maybe sometime I'll get a chance to grill you on your central meaning.

George: Anytime.

HST: That thing we said—would you do it again? It's good in that sense. Yeah, I'd do it again. And I tell you going through all your letters for all those years—it's merciless. And have other people doing it. Yeah, my son helping out a little bit. Editors editing. That's quite an experience. And I came out of it a lot better than I thought I would. I couldn't have done it myself. You know, going down there in the basement, reading all my letters. So in that sense, yeah—I don't have long or huge or long things that I feel shame about . . . we're in unfamiliar territory here . . . but ah . . . yeah, somethings I can't explain—By god! One thing we have not mentioned is Timothy Leary.

George: What would you like to say about Timothy Leary?

HST: Well, one thing I definitely regret is that I wrote an obituary for one of those special edition books. And yeah, I kind of reappraised him. He called me about every night for about two weeks before he died asking for forgiveness. I am on record as saying a lot of bad things about him. And so, you know—what the hell? It's not important to kick him one more time while he's dying. But now I wish I had because recently I found out that he was an FBI informant for the last twenty or twenty-five years of his life.

George: Timothy Leary?

HST: He turned everybody in. Everybody around me. I mean he was worse than Nixon.

George: I didn't know that.

HST: It's true. Check the recently released FBI files. Oh yeah—that's a fact. I wouldn't be telling you—I mean talk about betraying a whole generation. I want to make a point of righting that one wrong and that was I essentially forgave him. Yeah, said he was a warrior. But he was an asshole. He was a vicious goddamned treacherous . . . a . . . a . . . informant? I don't know—I'm still looking for the right word. . . . ah . . .

George: Pigfucker?

HST: No, that's mild. No, we're talking about lying, treachery, betrayal. This is solid hardcore stuff.

Yahoo! Internet Life—August 2001

A Twisted Wired Guy: Thc Original Gonzo Returns to the Spotlight to Fight the Good Fight Online and Settle Some Old Scores

BY HUGO PEREZ

Y-Life: Some people will be surprised to hear you're writing for ESPN.com. But you seem to have a lot of flexibility there—and a forum to talk about political issues.

HST: Absolutely—as much as I had at the [San Francisco] *Examiner*. I have very few frictions. Avoiding religious talk is one of them. Like using the comment, "Jesus, what a fool," or something. On several occasions, some editor has cut it to "Geez," which is maddening. There aren't too many places that my excesses are permitted and encouraged. Yea, "bastard," people have gotten used to that. "Swine of the week." "The whole Bush family should be boiled alive in hot oil in a pot." There are a lot of examples. The main thing, like with any other column, is to get it in. What was the old show-business axiom? "Ninety-five percent of the show is just being there on time." I wouldn't write much without a deadline. I've made 24 consecutive deadlines with ESPN.com.

Y-Life: You've made a lot of references to using technology as a journalist. Before the widespread adoption of the Internet, you used fax machines to send in your copy as late as possible.

HST: It was a fax machine that you would carry around, and this was in the days when people who had electric typewriters were ahead of the game. I could pull into a gas station—a closed gas station in South Miami, anywhere at all—and I used to carry a 50-foot extension cord, so I could plug it into the side of the building over by the rest rooms. And as long as I had a phone that I could get a quarter into, the machine would run, and I could transmit from any phone booth anywhere in the world. It enabled me to work on that deadline schedule. I knew that I could go a long way further than the people at the magazine expected, certainly. I didn't make any real friends in the production department. I was a huge luxury. I once sent a story to the *New York Times Magazine* by fax, and they were baffled by it. They wanted it on a telex, or whatever their chosen method was. I sent them my fax, and I had to tell the guy at the op-ed page, and he bitched about it. Then he found like 40 fax machines in the basement that he didn't know existed. All the correspondents had this option. I think the Internet's a little bit like that.

Y-Life: Recently you've used your ESPN column to spotlight the case of Lisl Auman, a woman you feel has been unjustly convicted in connection with the death of a police officer because she was in custody at the time. What made you decide to get involved?

HST: Are you familiar with Edmund Burke's dictum that the only thing necessary for the triumph of evil is for good men to do nothing? The first time I heard that, I think, was from Bobby Kennedy in 1968, and it just stuck with me. The other thing is that I got a letter from her, out of the blue. I was aware of the case. I had followed it in the newspapers, and I knew it was an outrage. I can't take on every outrage, but at least I'm not doing nothing. It's going to be a hard battle. I think we're halfway there, by getting the best legal talent in the country. You couldn't pick a more difficult case, really. You know, convicted, sentenced, murder of a cop, all the wrong buzzwords.

Y-Life: Could this case bring the kind of attention that could get this law off the books?

HST: Oh, boy. It's a drastic, vicious law—made for cops, made for prosecutors, a catchall. They don't have to prove anything. The felony murder statute and its application, it's a big one. That's why the NACDL [National Association of Criminal Defense Lawyers] is coming in. And I've got Morris Dees of the Southern Poverty Law Center involved, but unofficially. He just busted all those Nazis up in Idaho. He's a wonderful lawyer and a really good friend. And then I've got some appeals lawyers in Denver. I have an admirable network.

If there's one certain thing that I've learned from my own lifelong battle with the criminal justice system, it's that you can't fight the thing alone. You've got to have serious help. I would have been in the system 10 years ago if I hadn't had major rescue support, or cavalry over the hill. You can't do better than the legal team we have now. I think it's changed the whole nature of the case. She really was put on trial for being an undesirable person. Nobody ever even accused her of committing the crime.

Y-Life: Do you think that the Internet is effective at getting attention for this and building this kind of network?

HST: Christ, it has made a gigantic difference to her and her family, who were fighting a lonely fight. She has a Web site, Lisl [lisl.com]. Her parents maintain one, which had something like 5,000 hits a year for the first two years. The first time I discussed it in the column, they got 140,000 hits in a day, and they were astounded. They thought the machine was screwed up. It was a huge support thing.

Yeah, I think the Internet is made for situations like this. The case was languishing from lack of attention and interest. My job is to make it an issue, without making myself the issue. I'm trying to get the news to cut the word Gonzo from my identification. That's what the cops think they have a handle for: "Oh, yeah, Gonzo, I know the guy." If I let them turn it into a Gonzo case, it's not going to carry me too far in the appeals court process. I never have known what the hell Gonzo means anyway.

Y-Life: So how did Gonzo journalism come about?

HST: It was really born of innate laziness—which, quite frankly, I'm proud to have overcome, and nobody's even complimented me on it. I'm a monument to the triumph of laziness, because I just took the notebooks really and typed them up. I was trying to compete with photographers and illustrators. Whenever Annie Leibovitz would finish a story, she'd just send her film in. But I'd be left with the empty pages to slave over, so I thought, Well, I can do that too. One of these days, I'm going to put my notebooks in a film bag. They used to send them in a little fishnet bag with Press written all over it, and when I was working, I was trying to throw my spiral notebooks in that bag to New York. So I was trying to write on the run. You oughta see my notebooks. They will teach you something.

Y-Life: What prompted you to publish your letters? How do they fit in with the rest of your work?

HST: I think that this is a perpetual motion machine that I've invented for my tribe—my people, the freelance writers of the world. I've made a new highway to riches for all of this. I'm just being paid for the work that I did then that I wasn't paid for. What this also makes clear is that I somehow lived for 10 years on no money. I don't know how that happened. My income one year at Big Sur was $780, and that was a good year. I would sometimes write three or four letters a day. I had a lot of energy in those days that I wasn't putting to use.

Y-Life: Many of us believe that the cultural revolution of the '90s was driven by money and greed, but some idealist thought that technology could help the common man get together and win social causes. Do you see any correlation between the '90s and the '60s?

HST: No. I still have yet to see that the computer revolution, or the existence of computers, has really done anything truly good for me. And it's also given huge advantages to authorities—police agencies, militaries. I can certainly do without that. In fact, I paid little attention to it until I saw that I could make money on it. The Internet is not oriented to paying for content, and it's dangerously loaded with gibberish.

There are a few Web sites that are useful—of course, the *New York Times* and some others. But hell, I get the *Times* every day anyway, and I've just become habituated to reading the paper.

The Internet's good for research sometimes, but there's too much information, really. And there's very little screening process, like there is built into the educational system. You never know what the hell is true or pertinent. It's been very good for people who just want to vent and go public with their screeds. It might have been good for me at some earlier point in my career.

Y-Life: If you had had access to the Internet back when you were running for sheriff of Aspen in the '70s, do you think that might have helped your campaign?

HST: I couldn't have done any better than I did. We had world-wide media coverage all the time. We had the *New York Times,* and the BBC, and the *Village Voice, L.A. Times.* It was a huge help, and a bit of a hindrance. You couldn't walk anywhere in the Hotel Jerome without tripping over cables, and they were literally in the door of the hotel, and up the lobby and the stairs to our headquarters on the second floor. It was a big help, but I still believe that all politics is local. Still, it's good to have national attention and awareness. It jacks up the level of attention paid to any one thing.

Y-Life: You once said that journalism is not much fun unless there's a war going on. In the Lisl Auman case, do you feel you are waging a war?

HST: Well, war is the wrong word. Let's say campaign or issue. It definitely raised the level of adrenaline and commitment and concentration. I've always seen journalism as a political act.

Australian Broadcast Corporation—August 29, 2002

Interview with Mick O'Regan

O'Regan: Unlike Walter Cronkite, Hunter S. Thompson is a stirrer, a deliberately provocative commentator and a freewheeling iconoclast, infamous for his relentless critique of the American government and military.

He lives in the Rocky Mountains of Colorado and that's where I found him to ask his opinion of the state of the U.S. media.

HST: Well let's see, "shamefully" is a word that comes to mind, but that's not true in the case of the *New York Times,* the *Washington Post,* but overall American journalism I think has been cowed and intimidated by the massive flag-sucking, this patriotic orgy that the White House keeps whipping up. You know if you criticize the President, it's unpatriotic and there's something wrong with you, you may be a terrorist.

O'Regan: So in that sense, there's not enough room for dissenting voices?

HST: There's plenty of room, there's not just enough people who are willing to take the risk. It's sort of a herd mentality, a lemming-like mentality. If you don't go with the flow you're anti-American and therefore a suspect. And we've seen this before, these patriotic frenzies. It's very convenient having an undeclared war that you can call a war and impose military tribunals and wartime security and we have these generals telling us that this war's going to go on for a long, long time. Maybe not so much the generals now, the generals are a little afraid of Iraq, a little worried about it, but it's the civilians in the White House, the gang of thieving, just lobbyists for the military-industrial complex, who are running the White House, and if to be against them is to be unpatriotic, then hell, call me a traitor.

O'Regan: Do you think that most of the American media, or say most of the influential American media, has bought that patriotism line, and as a result are self-censoring themselves?

HST: There you go, self-censorship, yes, that's a very good point. Yes, I would say that. Now there are always exceptions to that but there've been damn few.

O'Regan: So is it the White House laying down what they think is appropriate journalism, or is it the news media outlets deciding that they have to be patriotic, that they're under some sort of undeclared duty at the moment, to somehow reflect the patriotism of the American public?

HST: Well it goes a little deeper than that, because this Administration is well on the road to seizing power, and Tom Daschle,* the Senate Democratic leader, the other day accused Bush of trying to seize dictatorial powers. Now that was a big breakthrough, and I'm starting to sense that the tide may be turning against the President; we have to beat this bastard one way or another. And the American government is the greatest enemy of freedom around the world that I can think of. And we keep waving that flag, freedom, yes, these people are flag-suckers.

O'Regan: What about the language that's being used to describe the so-called undeclared war? I mean there have been criticisms in the mainstream press in Australia that journalists have too readily taken up the language of politicians and bureaucrats, that they have uncritically declared the war against terror without really thinking it through; what's your assessment of the situation in the States?

HST: Well I'm glad to hear that—you're talking about Australian journalists?

O'Regan: Yes.

HST: Yes, well that's good. Congratulations, boys. There is not much of that in this country yet. This over here is the most paranoid, most insecure United States that I've ever lived in. I mean it's the worst this country has been since I have ever seen it.

O'Regan: Do you feel like there's a restriction of media freedom at the moment? Is there a restricted space for media freedom?

HST: I wouldn't say it's a restricted space, but it's a dark and dangerous grey area to venture into. Several journalists have lost their jobs, Bill Maher on ABC, but some people were made an example of early on. The media

* Tom Daschle is former a Democratic senator and majority leader from South Dakota. He served as senator from 1987 to 2005.

doesn't reflect world opinion or even a larger, more intelligent opinion over here, it's just this drumbeat of celebrity worship and child funerals and hooded prisoners being led around Guantánamo. No I'm very disturbed about the civil rights implications of this, and everybody should be.

O'Regan: So just on journalists who may have lost their jobs, are you saying that people who came out and were fearless in their critique of the government or the government's policy, that those people actually lost their jobs as journalists?

HST: Well I can think of two that come to mind right in the beginning. I haven't heard of any since. But I think Bill Maher, there was some kind of rave after 9/11 that all these people, cowards, you know these dirty little bastards, who snuck up on us and pulled off what amounts to a perfect crime really, no witnesses, very little cost; talk about cost-effective, that was a hell of a strike. I'm not sure I'd call them cowards, but that's what Bill Maher said on TV and he said he considered our missile attacks on unseen victims, wedding parties etc. that that was cowardly. Whacko. Well that brought a huge tidal wave of condemnation that came down on him. And that was the ABC, yeah.

O'Regan: So at the moment people don't want to hear that sort of criticism, they want people to rally round the flag and support the military?

HST: I think that's right, and I think the reason for that is that they don't want to hear it because, boy, that's going to be a lot of agonizing reappraisal, as they say. What reality is in this country and the world right now. Yes, popular opinion in this country has to be swung over to "the White House is wrong, these people are corporate thieves. They've turned the American Dream into a chamber of looting." It would take a lot of adjustment, mentally.

O'Regan: At the moment, even in Australia, the media is preparing for the first anniversary of the attacks in a couple of weeks from now. How is the American media preparing to sort of commemorate the first anniversary of the September 11th attack?

HST: You would never believe it, it's so insane. This is a frantic publicity. Every day on television the President's on TV at least once a day, and celebrations of the dead, the patriots, exposés on Al Qaida, it's just relentless, in fact 25 hours a day, of just how tragic it was and how patriotic it was, and how much we have to get back at these dirty little swine, and I wouldn't be at all surprised for as hideous and dumb as it sounds, an invasion of Iraq on September 11, yeah I'll get out and take a long shot bet on that.

O'Regan: That you think that the occasion might actually be used as a way of using that popular fervour or that popular patriotism as an appropriate day to launch an invasion?

HST: Well it seems like that to me, because that's their only power base really, is that frenzy of patriotism, and it's our revenge strike, you know, Uncle Sam gets even. If that's going to work at all, there would be no time when it would work better when everyone in the country is cranked up into emotional frenzies. I myself am getting little teary-eyed like watching some CNN special. This reminds me exactly of the month after the attack when there was just one drumroll after another after another. But there is some opposition now popping up in this country, a lot of it.

O'Regan: Could I take you back to September 11th? What I'd really like to know is your reactions. And I know you said you were writing a sports column for ESPN when the planes hit the towers, but could I get you to tell that story of when you found out about it and what you were doing and what your reaction was?

HST: I had in fact just finished a sports column for ESPN. Here it is: "It was just after dawn in Woody Creek, Colorado, when the first plane hit the World Trade Center in New York City on Tuesday morning. And as usual I was writing about sports. But not for long. Football suddenly seemed irrelevant compared to the scenes of destruction and other devastation coming out of New York on TV."

O'Regan: You went on to say in that article, which I have in front of me, that "even ESPN was broadcasting war news. It was the worst disaster in the history of the United States." Do you think that the event completely transformed the way in which Americans see themselves and their own vulnerability?

HST: No, the event by itself wouldn't have done that. But it was the way the Administration was able to use that event. Even use it as a springboard for everything they wanted to do. And that might tell you something. I remember when I was writing that column you sort of wonder when something like that happens, Well who stands to benefit? Who had the opportunity and the motive? You just kind of look at these basic things, and I don't know if I want to go into this on worldwide radio here, but—

O'Regan: You may as well.

HST: All right. Well I saw that the U.S. government was going to benefit, and the White House, the Republican administration, to take the mind of the public off of the crashing economy. Now you want to keep in mind that every time a person named Bush gets into office, the nation goes into a drastic recession, as they call it.

O'Regan: It seems a very long bow to me, but are you sort of suggesting that this worked in the favour of the Bush Administration?

HST: Oh, absolutely. Absolutely. And I have spent enough time on the inside of, well in the White House and you know, campaigns and I've known enough people who do these things, think this way, to know that the public version of the news or whatever event, is never really what happened.

O'Regan: Well let me just ask you on that. I mean you've pioneered a form of journalism called Gonzo journalism, in which it's almost like there's no revision. What you see and feel is what goes down on the page, and it's that first blush, that first image that hits the readership. Does that mean that in a way it's hard for you to appear credible within the U.S. media because people would say, Oh look, that's just another conspiracy theory from a drug-addled Gonzo journalist like Hunter S. Thompson?

HST: Yeah, that's a problem. I'm not sure if it's my problem or their problem. I've been right so often, and my percentages are so high, I'll stand by this column that I wrote that day, and the next one. So what appears to be maybe Gonzo journalism, I'm not going to claim any prophetic powers, but . . .

O'Regan: Well one of the things you do say in that first article you wrote, you say, "It's now 24 hours later, and we're not getting much information about the 5Ws of this thing." Now by the 5Ws I'm presuming you mean the Who, the What, the When, the Why and the How. Is that still how you feel, that a year later those key questions haven't been answered?

HST: Absolutely. It's even worse, though. How much more do we have than we had a year ago? Damn little, I think.

O'Regan: Hunter Thompson, will you be at home watching the commemoration programs on 11th September? Will you be among the audience, which I imagine will number tens of millions of people who watch what happens in New York?

HST: That's a good point, that's a good question, and yes, it's soon, isn't it? No, I won't. I think I'll grab Anita and take a road trip. We'll just go off and have a little fun. Why sit around and watch that stuff?

O'Regan: U.S. journalist, Hunter S. Thompson with a very personal and idiosyncratic view of September 11.

KDNK Community Radio (Carbondale, Colorado)—January 2003

Interview with Mary Suma

**Note: Interview transcript taken from the February 23, 2005, broadcast of* Democracy Now!

Amy Goodman: Today we pay tribute to one of America's best-known journalists and authors. . . . We hear Hunter S. Thompson in his own words talking about President Bush, Iraq, and much more. He was interviewed on community radio station KDNK in the Roaring Fork Valley in Colorado in January 2003. Former KDNK station manager Mary Suma began by asking Thompson about him, saying that "the idea of war is not just wrong but borders on insanity." This is Hunter S. Thompson.

HST: Of course, it depends on which vantage point you look at the war from. If you are the president of a huge oil company, no, it's not insane at all. The war would be quite justified.

Mary Suma: How do you feel—I've read that you were in the streets in the Chicago riots back at that convention? Do you think that we can elicit that sort of passion as it builds? I mean, it really seems to be building up there, the antiwar faction.

HST: Yes, it does. But look at this. I don't recall, anyway, a massive depression, economic collapse, at that time, 1968. I was going to say, "Do you?" But what we have now is a collapse of the economy and a totally unjustifiable war, irrational really, except from the point of view of the oil industry.

Mary Suma: Did you watch the State of the Union the other evening?*

HST: Oh, boy, I did.

Mary Suma: What did you think?

HST: I was horrified. It was a nightmare of a thing to go through. He rattled off all these "pie in the sky" ideas in the beginning, none of which are

* President George W. Bush's State of the Union address was delivered on January 28, 2003.

going to either work or be funded. He knows that. As a matter of fact, the *New York Times* today said that already they see that even Republicans are admitting that the Medicare—he was talking about the Medicare plan, the $400 billion plan—

Mary Suma: Right.

HST: Is impossible. Members of both parties expressed doubts about its feasibility today, forcing the administration officials to reconsider important elements of the package. So, none of the domestic issues he talked about are feasible. I don't even think he can get the tax cut through, which is insane. Cut taxes in a time when the country is going broke. It's not just the war that's wrong. I can't imagine any justification for just going over to Iraq and bombing the place back to the Stone Age like we did before.

Mary Suma: Why does it seem a good portion of the country is buying into this?

HST: That is a really—that's a disturbing aspect of it.

Mary Suma: Can we believe the polls? I mean, certainly the applause the other evening, they always say that you can sort of gauge the popularity of a president by the applause at the State of the Union. I don't know if that's true or not. But it seems like we're living in two separate countries.

HST: Well, remember, that Bush's popularity and the popularity—or the support for the war and two months ago when it was much higher. But these are just daily. These are things that change every day. But I remember writing in—I don't know, it might have been at least five years ago—it was I think, ABC, some serious poll, several of them came up with the findings that the American people, overall, favor giving up some of their freedoms in exchange for more security.

Mary Suma: Mm-hmm.

HST: They would rather be secure than free, in other words.

Mary Suma: Right.

HST: That really is shocking.

Mary Suma: It is shocking, and more so today, maybe.

HST: That's the answer, I think, for your question why is the public buying into it. Another reason is that the fear which I—that's why I tried to address or at least rave about in the book. Fear is an unhealthy condition, living in fear. And as we clearly have been for two years now, it makes the population more obedient, particularly if they're willing to give up their freedom for security. More obedient, more easier to control, and it's, well, it is very much like Nazi Germany.

Mary Suma: Mm-hmm.

HST: Remember the old good German syndrome.

Mary Suma: Mm-hmm.

HST: We used to ridicule it, the good Germans who just went along with it because that's what the Fuehrer* wanted.

Mary Suma: You've said the president has destroyed the country, the economy and our relationship with the rest of the world.

HST: Well, I believe that's true and even the countries that allegedly go along or support us, our allies going into this war, popular opinion in most of those countries, I can't say this for sure, but in England, certainly, the English people, as a whole, are strongly opposed to the war and to going along with whatever George Bush says. Democracy is on its last legs in this country, and freedom, you know, the Free World?

Mary Suma: Mm-hmm.

HST: We're defending freedom? We'll fight to the death for freedom? That's absurd. This country is no more a capital or bastion of freedom now than Nazi Germany was in the 1940s. This country is a rogue nation in a way, but worse than a rogue nation. We're a war-crazy, war-dependent, really, nation and that leads right to the oil industry. It is ridiculous. And particularly in the media; with the media I noticed. To not discuss the connection between oil and bombs in Iraq is disgraceful. Winston Churchill said, "In times of war, the first casualty is always the truth." Truth is the first casualty of any war.

Mary Suma: In lieu of fear.

HST: You see, I'm a little bit cranked up and fanatical about it.

Mary Suma: That's the age group, isn't it, Hunter, that we want to really—

HST: Yeah. This is—I mean, if you want to live in a Nazi nation, I wouldn't want to be 20 years old now.

Mary Suma: I wouldn't either.

HST: I fear for what's coming and for the welcoming committee of kids that's going to meet it, saying come on in. No, it's just ignorance, and well, the media, we're being deprived of the real news.

---

* "Fuehrer" was the title Adolf Hitler used to declare his supreme rule of Nazi Germany.

Mary Suma: Again, you're going to be at Paepke Park* on Saturday afternoon (for an anti-war rally). Do you know what your topic is yet? We know the topic, but do you know what—can you give us any preview of what's going to be said, or do you just stand up there and let it—

HST: Yeah. I usually just take a—just wing it, freefall, just like I did today. I had no idea what I was going to say today. This is really a disgraceful moment in history and just thinking about the war, or attending the peace rallies, going out in the street, voting with your feet, as they say.

Amy Goodman: Hunter S. Thompson speaking with KDNK's Mary Suma in January of 2003. She then asked him about his book *Kingdom of Fear: Loathsome Secrets of a Star-Crossed Child in the Final Days of the American Century.*

HST: It started off—it's supposed to be a memoir; I think it started off as memoirs. You know, it just sort of—a very quick and active story about how I got to be what I am today, at different key adventures in my life. Mainly it is fun. Yes, I could use a little bit more editing, but everything could. It's a fun read. It's a pretty savage one. And it's clearly, not anti-Bush, but anti-war. See, I don't hate Bush personally. I used to know him. I used to do some drugs here and there.

Mary Suma: Is that true, Hunter? What about, I didn't know that you were an unofficial adviser to Jimmy Carter.

HST: Yeah. Weird things happen here and there. I got to know him early, two years before he ran, and he just looked like a pretty good bet to me, because I was a gambler, and I wanted to win. It was important to win at that time.

Anita Thompson: Evan Dobelle, who was, among other things, Carter's Secretary of Protocol, he held a dinner in Hawaii about two months ago and Hunter was a guest of honor and he stood up to say and thank Hunter because Jimmy Carter would not be president if it wasn't for Hunter Thompson.

Mary Suma: Really?

Anita Thompson: Yes.†

Amy Goodman: Anita and Hunter Thompson. Anita, Hunter Thompson's wife, again, speaking with Mary Suma of KDNK in January of 2003.

---

* Paepke Park is a public park on Main Street in downtown Aspen.

† By the time Hunter and I were married, I relentlessly reminded anyone who would listen, whether it was on the air or not, of Hunter's influence on politics and readers.

Finally, Mary Suma asked Hunter Thompson about his upcoming trip to New York.

HST: What I'm going to New York to do is stir up trouble. I'm not going to change hats, yeah, Saturday in the park, Sunday in New York City, Monday night, Conan O'Brien, or something like that. I just believe in this. I'm offended and insulted by the slope of the American people, and that means us. That means these bastards who just sit around—

Anita Thompson: We're getting there.

HST: Let's keep hitting on this because I doubt that George Bush is going to go away before the next two years anyway. He should be run out of office. He should resign right now, in my opinion. I did call for his resignation, but I don't think we would have a groundswell immediately for that. There will be a lot of people who agree with me.

Mary Suma: Down the road?

HST: Well, no, in a year. I mean, the—

Mary Suma: Will we be at war in a year, Hunter?

HST: I think so, without a doubt. Like I said, we've been at war for 13 years. We've been bombing that country that long and we've cut off everything, all their food, books, we've cut off all imports of books over there.

Mary Suma: Have you ever been there?

HST: No. I don't really know Iraq. I made a point of getting to know it a lot better. It was a very advanced, progressive country. It had, what, 90-percent literacy, healthcare for the whole entire population. They were doing well; a prosperous nation with a high literacy rate. Many more book stores per capita in Iraq than there are in this country. Many. We bombed their children. We killed their husbands and wives and we bombed them, . . . and we're going to do it again. Just random killing like that, mass killing to force a population to get rid of Saddam so we can move in and take over and control the oil, God damn it, if that's not evil, I don't know what would be.

You know, Bush, he's really the evil one in here. Well, more than just him. We're the Nazis in this game, and I don't like it. I'm embarrassed and I'm pissed off. Yeah. I mean to say something and I think a lot of people in this country agree with me. A lot more never say anything. We'll see what happens to me if I get my head cut off in the next week by—it's always unknown Bush [inaudible] strangers who commit suicide right afterward. No witnesses. They have a new kind of crime.

Mary Suma: Is that the CIA kind of crime?

HST: Oh, absolutely. Anyone who's a successful criminal has got a crime. Absolutely no witnesses, no records. We can go on and on. I have to be restrained on the subject.

Amy Goodman: The late Hunter S. Thompson, speaking two years ago in an interview on community radio station KDNK in the Roaring Fork Valley in Colorado, speaking with then station manager Mary Suma. Hunter S. Thompson died of an apparent suicide this weekend; shot himself Sunday night at his home in Woody Creek, Colorado. His latest book, a collection of his essays called *Hey Rube: Bloodsport, the Bush Doctrine, and the Downward Spiral of Dumbness.*

Razor Magazine—January 2003

Bedtime for Gonzo

BY J. RENTILLY

The first time you speak with Hunter S. Thompson, it's 4:30 in the afternoon and he's waiting for his breakfast, trying to wake up. On the phone from Owl Farm, his acres-large ranch in Woody Creek, Colorado, just south of Aspen, the 63-year-old Thompson comes exactly as advertised: a grouchy, mumbling, flatulent, Dunhill-smoking, Patrón-gulping chemical laboratory who plays disoriented when it suits him, maintains a nocturnal lifestyle, and gets by despite—or because of—the "foul and odd temperament" to which he confesses this afternoon. This is the writer, after all, who once suggested that the only way to kill the pain of being a man is to become a beast.

Then there's the second phone call, the one that comes pre-dawn from Thompson's live-in companion, Anita Bejmuk. "Taking care of me is a job that requires a hell-of-a-lot sometimes," says Thompson. "And I try to take care of her, too." Early this morning, Bejmuk announces that Thompson will be ready to talk later in the day. The day passes without a word from Thompson. So does the next. Thompson is promised, then fails to appear. Icons, apparently, are frequently indisposed. And then you finally get him on the line.

Rentilly: Mr. Thompson. How are you?

HST: I'm not done waking up and I'm not very, uh, awake and I'm watching this World Series game.

Rentilly: Is this a bad time for you?

HST: Uh, it's not a good time. I really don't feel very smart. But what do you want to talk about?

Rentilly: I want to talk about the new book, *Kingdom of Fear,* and . . .

HST: I tell you, I could do this a lot better if, . . . goddamnit . . . if I could wake up and feel a little better.

Rentilly: You want to pick another time?

HST: Let's say something like. Oh, I don't know . . .

And suddenly you feel it all going south again, and fast. Thompson wants to finish the ball game, and you figure after that it'll be something else and then some other thing again. With deadline approaching, you're left to ponder the possibilities of writing a story about Hunter S. Thompson, father of Gonzo journalism, the legendary counterculture, anti-authoritarian figure, who has forged a career and a reputation guzzling drugs, haggling broads, rattling cages, naming names, shucking convention and etiquette, digging up bodies, and shitting on all things sanctimonious and false in seminal works of non-fiction like *Fear and Loathing in Las Vegas, Fear and Loathing on the Campaign Trail '72,* and *Hell's Angels,* and in unrefined, hard-boiled fiction tomes like *The Rum Diary* and *The Curse of Lono.*

If deadline comes to shove, you can always make easy jokes about how Woody Creek, Colorado, is 8,000 feet above sea level and so Thompson, the notorious, self-professed dope fiend, is always quite literally "high." You can paint a picture of Thompson's famous peacocks roaming freely around Owl Farm amid the buckshot. Thompson, an avid gun collector, occasionally unloads into the nighttime, an existential acting-out abetted by artillery. You can report on the giant American flag Thompson says hangs from his front porch to keep away the Nazis and—simultaneously, perhaps ironically—the Wagner music he claims to blare into the wilderness through a sound system that boasts more than 80 speakers. You can pontificate on the pages Thompson has recently written, wherein he refers to the current Presidential administration as the Fourth Reich run by "a goofy child-President," and wherein he laments that we "are about to start paying for the sins of (our) fathers and forefathers, even if they were innocent . . . " and that "we are down to our last cannonball."

But none of it's right. None of it could be right. At least not entirely right. Trying to imagine the "real" Hunter S. Thompson is like trying to imagine the American Dream itself, which Thompson in his writing has alternately embraced, defined, redefined, and utterly annihilated. In Thompson's new book, *Kingdom of Fear: Loathsome Secrets of a Star-Crossed Child in the Final Days of the American Century* (due from Simon & Schuster, January 21, 2003), a collection of some of his most recent and perhaps greatest writing, Thompson describes himself as "a professional journalist and a writer of books about life in the weird lane."

Maybe. But beneath the gruff, inaccessible exterior—the beast that conceals the pain of being the man—Thompson hides a sincere and noble heart, even if it is dosed with a bit of Percocet. The truth about Thompson: he is a Romantic in the grand, old-school tradition of the word. A man who in his writing and his lifestyle has perpetuated a larger-than-life persona, a loud and sometimes fearsome, apocalyptic but ultimately truthful voice and attitude and philosophy. Like Lord Byron or William Blake before him—political activists, incorrigible in their passions, who pushed life to the outer limits where most people become terribly uncomfortable or at least very, very afraid.

As Thompson writes in *Kingdom of Fear:* "It may be that every culture needs an Outlaw God of some kind, and maybe this time around I'm it. Who knows?" *Razor* found out when Thompson finally opened up during a savage journey to the heart of the American Dream.

Rentilly: You're a tough man to track down. I was beginning to think you just don't like doing interviews. That couldn't be the case, could it?

HST: Oh, no, no. I'd just rather not do some sort of negative junk, but I don't know. I'm just not in a very . . . I'm not in an articulate mood. My tongue hurts and it's hard to talk.

Rentilly: When we first spoke a couple weeks ago, you were fairly preoccupied with blow-up dolls and hashish. Are these truly at the forefront of your thinking these days, or is that just a way to tell a journalist to get fucked?

In your new book, *Kingdom of Fear,* you write about "adding up the score" on your life. I thought that kind of self-inventory and soul-searching was best left for old guys and dying men.

HST: I don't know. I've been adding up the score all along. I've been keeping score.

Rentilly: What is the score for Mr. Thompson?

HST: Well, I'm comfortable. See, I noticed something being forced to put something on paper for this book for what's been almost two straight years now. Try being my age and being forced, more or less, to take your life for—not for granted, but—the confrontation that it's been. Anyone in their sixties or seventies—hell, anyone in their forties—has to confront themselves I suppose. But this writing—this book—is doing it intentionally. This is a forced march through everything in my life. I have storyboards all over my house with big pictures of me in different times of my life. I'm so tired of myself. I'm having to explain all these pictures, all these episodes in my life. I have to explain me somehow.

Rentilly: Does mortality have much to do with what you're up to in a day? *Kingdom of Fear* is taking account of where you've been and what you've done.

HST: That's not my inclination. But it was the publisher's. Things like memoirs always seem easy. Everybody's got a couple good stories about themselves, don't they? But the unsettling part of this is the examination of your life, the real voluntary articulation of it, talking about people, talking about things you've done and maybe the wrong way. It's always been my cover, keeping it all under tight wraps and only explain myself when I really had to.

Rentilly: In your writing you've always seemed like a man who has moved straight ahead. It must be strange looking back as much as you do in the new book.

HST: Well, what I've noticed is that, I'm either the most steadfast, reliable man, with a natural level of integrity and loyalty or . . . I guess that sounds like gibberish, but you know what I'm saying: I'm either good, wise, brave, strong, all that. Or I'm just the stupidest man who's ever lived. I haven't learned anything since I was 15 years old. My positions and my basic stances are the same.

Rentilly: Your values, principals.

HST: Yeah. I can't see that I've really changed anything. I guess a man likes to think he's changed, but I just don't see it. I don't change much.

Rentilly: You write a lot of about your juvenile delinquent childhood, about pushing a Federal mailbox into the path of an oncoming school bus and other sundry peccadilloes from your youth. In the new book, you write: "I was cursed with a dark sense of humor that made many adults afraid of me, for reasons they couldn't quite put their fingers on."

HST: Yep.

Rentilly: How do you think that's informed your writing, being a rotten kid?

HST: Oh, I think it's a pretty strong factor. Gave me a kind of, I don't know, an anti-authoritarian kind of position. Which I think has worked out pretty well for me.

Rentilly: Anti-authority? Yeah, that seems to have panned out for you.

HST: Yeah. I've done all right, considering you can get put up against the wall and executed at any minute in this country for so much less than I've done in my lifetime.

Rentilly: Hunter Thompson might get away with it, but most of us don't dare to question authority too much these days.

HST: Yeah. This is turning into one of the most dangerous regime governments in the world—anywhere in the world—since Adolf Hitler.

Rentilly: It is a frightening time. I'm 31. I've got two little boys. Just getting through a day is scary sometimes.

HST: Well, Man, I don't envy you where you're at. See, you're part of the first generation that's going to do worse than your parents did. And your kids, probably worse than you. I would be feeling very unhappy if I were 31 and had two kids.

Rentilly: You say we're having kind of a "national nervous breakdown." You've referred to yourself as Dr. Thompson. Is there a prescription for this?

HST: Well, I usually have one. I don't have one right now. We're obviously going in the wrong direction. And, I go back and forth between wondering if there really are more Nazi bastards out there now on any city block in America than there used to be. And I wonder: if everybody in America voted would we have the same government we have now? I have a feeling that barely a 50 percent turnout at the polls is a large factor in who ends up controlling the government.

Rentilly: Not being able to count those ballots doesn't help, either, does it?

HST: These Nazis have created this system. They've very slowly built a very relentless, merciless system.

Rentilly: By "Nazis," are we talking about the current administration only, or the Republican Party in general? That may be an important distinction.

HST: Yeah, it's been a Republican fact of life since Nixon, I guess. Reagan is really where it started. Those same people were in there with Nixon and Reagan, some of them. And they brought Reagan in; he didn't bring them in. That's where it's all began.

Rentilly: Reagan actually said in 1985 that "this may be the generation that will have to face the end of the world."

HST: Yep.

Rentilly: I know you're no fan of Baby Bush, but I have to ask: Do you think the enemy is any more clearly defined or identifiable today than it was in the 1970s?

HST: Are we talking about the "sand niggers" over there or the Nazis at home? Look out for all of them.

Rentilly: We used to be told that there was nothing to fear but fear itself. Now I wonder, what isn't there to be afraid of?

HST: What isn't there? Well, let's see . . . Well, you can watch the World Series without fear of who's going to win or lose the games. No, every development internationally, in politics or in this continuing war, is nothing to be optimistic about. I don't see anything to be optimistic about. I'm not sure what all these politicians are afraid of. I know what you're afraid of, what I'm afraid of. But what could they possibly be afraid of when they spend all their time talking about having total war everywhere?

Rentilly: What do you think about war in Iraq? Is sending off 200,000 boys with rifles really the answer to our international problems and the victory to this so-called War on Terror?

HST: It'll help us out, sure. There's real strategy there, probably. I've been giving this some thought. The basic reasoning for this foreign war fetish is, basically, it's better to fight a war on the other side of the world.

Rentilly: Don't shit where you eat, in other words.

HST: Yeah. That's kind of a cynical way to explain it. It doesn't really cheer the people whose sons and daughters and parents and all that are routinely butchered over there, but it is over there.

Rentilly: At least it's not our skyscrapers coming down.

HST: Yeah. Right.

Rentilly: According to some of the books you wrote in the '70s, we're on borrowed time anyway. In *Fear and Loathing in Las Vegas,* you suggested we wouldn't even be around in 2000.

HST: Well, boy, what I did say is "there will be no year 2000 . . . "

Rentilly: " . . . Not as we know it."

HST: Well, that's almost right on, right there.

Rentilly: Did you really see any of this coming—the Elections, 9.11, this utter madness?

HST: Well, yeah. I mean I'm not some kind of warlock. I don't get my wisdom from piles of dead animals that I put up in the kitchen area. There's just a terrible logic to it all.

Rentilly: The subtitle of *Kingdom of Fear* references the end of the American Century. The century closed . . .

HST: The century's done. It ended with the election (in 2000). The numbers are right in front of our face. So the century's over. All done. But boy, I didn't expect the door to slam shut like a bank vault, like some mechanical door. Just a giant clang gone slamming shut on us. That's what the book's about. It's been kind of necessary to define wherever the American Dream was at the end of the last century. Because it's certainly not going to be like it was—not ever again.

Rentilly: I can't even imagine how to describe the American Dream right now. Can you?

HST: God, this is a horrible conversation for me to be dealing with right now . . . You must have a naïve faith that right will prevail, that it could succeed.

Rentilly: It's faith, ultimately.

HST: Naïve faith.

Rentilly: Relationships sometimes take that kind of faith, too. You've had some amazing friendships in your life. You've said that your "most amazing talent is your ability to choose good friends."

HST: I don't know if I'm deserving of it, but I do have some good friends. That's one of the most valuable things in life. Unimaginable pleasure I get from the friends I have.

Rentilly: I bring up your friendships because, very prematurely and unexpectedly, many of them are slipping away. Ginsberg left us a few years ago. Warren Zevon is one of the great, underrated musical artists ever, and a good friend of yours, and he could very well be dead by the time this interview is published.

HST: Warren is what being a good friend is all about. Oh, yeah. Warren has flown across the country at his own expense to back me on political rallies and all that. He makes public stands on issues that I've chosen to be involved in myself. He's high risk. You can count on Warren. I already miss him. He is hanging on, I guess. I just treat it like a bad phase, you know. He may go tomorrow, I don't know. It's a day-to-day basis for all of us. I'm very amazed that I'm still bumming around and having a good time.

Rentilly: I think you sell yourself short when you refer to yourself as "an elderly dope fiend off in the wilderness by himself." You've put out this image that betrays the heart you truly hold.

HST: Well, I always try to understand how somebody's parents would look at me. For example, Anita's mother when she heard that her daughter went off with a truly dangerous brute. It would not be my first desire or choice to have my daughter run off into the mountains with a . . . I don't know, what would you call me, Anita?

Anita: A teenage girl trapped in the body of an elderly dope fiend.

Rentilly: At 63, do you still get as loaded as you used to? You've been rattling around with a bottle of Percocet as long as we've been on the phone. But have you slowed it down a little?

Anita: (laughs)

Rentilly: What's in the pillbox for today's consumption?

HST: Oh, I'm not called a doctor for nothing.

Anita: Fresh-squeezed orange or grapefruit juice every morning. And his cholesterol is better than his doctor's.

Rentilly: Excellent. Is there anything to which we should "just say no"?

Anita: Warm beer.

HST: Cheap whiskey. Uh, let's see, I still enjoy a visit with just about anything.

Rentilly: I'd like to close by talking about something from the new books that's really stuck with me the last couple of days: "Morality is temporary. Wisdom is permanent."

HST: What the hell is that?

Rentilly: You wrote it.

Anita: Yeah, you did.

HST: Yeah. I don't really know how to respond to that.

Rentilly: Can you give me an example of what you mean by that?

HST: Did I really say that?

Anita: Yeah.

Rentilly: I know. Sometimes . . .

HST: Let's see, I guess morality is present-tense thinking. It's current. Wisdom is the luxury, perhaps, of hindsight.

Rentilly: It's that, "if only I'd done it another way." Is that wisdom?

HST: A lot of it is exactly that. Wisdom is more like, "Jesus Christ, that was dumb." You do something and you know you shouldn't have. You should've stuck with your instinct. Basically, that's one of my most important things, going on instinct.

Rentilly: Is there anything you'd take back?

HST: Take back?

Rentilly: Anything you'd do differently? Regrets, I mean.

HST: Oh. The question is: would you do it again? That's the reality. You can underline that one. Would you do it again? That's the test, maybe the final test, looking back on anything. I've been saying that for many years. That's the aging fruit of the aging person. That's about the only rule I've found that I can put on things is that question: would you do it again? Let's try one right now. Let's see, uh . . . I don't know you that well, your station in life . . .

Rentilly: Something from my life?

HST: An example for you. See, I know nothing about you or what your proclivities are.

Rentilly: See we could go very basic and ask, "Would I get married again?"

HST: That's a good one. Would you?

Rentilly: Yes.

HST: Okay. Okay, that's a good one. But when I ask, "Would you do it again?" it comes with a rule. The rule is, "Would you do it again, not knowing what you know now, not knowing what the outcome will be." There's none of that. You know what you know now and life's a safer bet all the way around. So you've got to ask the question like this, "Would you get married again even if it meant getting beat bloody three times on various occasions by the police?" or something like that.

Rentilly: I'll just go on the record and say that I'd get married again no matter what it took. I've got a good woman and I'm a very, very lucky man.

HST: Oh, well you are blessed. Love. That's a very valuable thing.

Rentilly: Yeah.

HST: Not everything pays off immediately. I'm often flogged. Risk is not just a four-letter word. It's something where bad things can happen. Love is like that. You get behind the wheel at 150 miles per hour in the night. Things might happen there that wouldn't happen, maybe, if you were at 75 miles per hour.

Rentilly: Sometimes it's just waking up in the morning.

HST: Yeah. You can't expect everything to go all right, but it all does balance. I just look at it like this: if I wouldn't do it again, it means that I wasted that time.

Rentilly: Doesn't seem like you've wasted a lot of time in your life.

HST: Oh, I feel like I've wasted a lot of moments. Yeah. I'm a pretty horrid taskmaster. I've been to jail a few times. I'd do that again. There are probably a few things I would rather not do again, but overall if I've got the feeling that I'd take something back or that I'm full of regret over something, it means that I was wrong. It's like Alcoholics Anonymous and you have to confess you're a hopeless alcoholic for the rest of your life and that your life was wrong for as long as your remember and that it always will be. You have to say you're wrong, that your life was fucked up all the way along.

Rentilly: You've never been through AA.

HST: No. But I get asked all the time to help people through. I've been personally involved here and there, counseling people who are prone to turning their backs on whole periods of their lives. You can't throw yourself on the mercy of other cripples who are also living wrong. You just can't do that. I've had a couple of moments where I've wished I never started drinking gin or that it was a terrible mistake to get into drugs, but I don't regret it. I've occasionally had some difficult times with them, but that just goes with the territory. Yeah, this is how I look at it: if it produces pages, it has to be right.

Rentilly: That sounds like a final word.

HST: I see it like this: whatever you're doing, even if it's crazy, if you get paid for it, well that can't be insane. There's insane that's functional, and there's insane that's dysfunctional.

Publishers Weekly—January 13, 2003

Fear and Loathing in the New Millennium

PW: Is your new book, *Kingdom of Fear,* all new material?

Hunter S. Thompson: It's totally new. It's supposed to be a memoir. I'm not sure what a memoir is; I had to look it up. I've got the definition up on the wall.

PW: What is it?

HST: Shit, it seems to be gone. Now that I've finished writing the book, I'm trying to take down the machinery of it. I have huge storyboards all over the walls. I work off of those boards.

PW: Do you write on a computer?

HST: No, I write on an IBM Selectric. I don't really take a screen as seriously as a page. I guess it's my newspaper background. Unless it's black and white on a page, it ain't written.

PW: True. You can't erase it as easily.

HST: Exactly. I've tried it. I have all the Apple equipment.

PW: So why did you write this book?

HST: Why? Because I'm a writer! This is not one of those autobiographies or "confessions of." I never really intended to do that. Shit, all my work is autobiographical, in a way. I like the book now. But I've never sent a book in that I liked when I sent it off. It's always, "Dear God, let's just get rid of this fucker."

PW: I guess that's what editors are for.

HST: Yeah, my editor at S&S is a good friend, and she's a good editor. But figuring out what classification it is has been a problem all along. What do we tell the *New York Times* bestseller list? Is this a novel? "Fiction" and "nonfiction" are 19th-century terms.

PW: Well, book publishing is kind of old-fashioned.

HST: Part of that's nice. But those kinds of roles and lines are not going to last forever; they never do. What was Mark Twain? A novelist or a journalist?

PW: Both, I think.

HST: Yes. Well, I'm a writer.

PW: What do you think about your work being taught in journalism school?

HST: I like it, but I'm not sure how it's being taught. I'd like to sit in on a class sometime and wear a wig or something. My impression of journalism school is that it's basically something that teaches the publishing side of writing.

PW: I think the schools would like to think that they teach writing. But of course, a lot of people don't think journalism school is even necessary. What kind of writers do you think should be taught in j-school?

HST: Hang on, hang on, there's some kind of animal outside. Good God, what's happening? Get out of here, you bastards! Okay. So you're in New York?

PW: Yes. It's a good place to be for writing. Do you feel removed, living in Colorado?

HST: Not really, because, shit, it seems I'm always on the phone all over the world all of the time. I'm not sure how it would've turned out if I had stayed in New York. I figured if I was ever going to beat New York or conquer it or whatever, I'd have to move out of New York. I can't conceive of writing a book in New York now.

PW: Why?

HST: I know too many people. I got the book today, by the way.

PW: How's it look?

HST: The first time you hold a copy of a book you've been working on all this time in your hands, it's hugely gratifying. It looks good. You haven't seen it, have you?

PW: No, but I've got a galley, which I enjoyed reading. For a memoir, it's got a lot about Bush, September 11 and terrorism.

HST: I think it'll get some people going. But I'm curious. I like to hear something come back at me about what I've written. I think the country right now is in the worst trouble it's been in anytime that I've been alive.

Time Out New York—January 30, 2003

Oh, Loathsome Me: Hunter S. Thompson Checks in from Woody Creek and Rants Nostalgic About a Life Lived in Fear

BY COREY SEYMOUR

Dismiss Dr. Hunter S. Thompson as simply a countercultural literary bad boy running on (admittedly) high-octane fumes, and you're in for an ass-whopping, either literal or metaphorical. You'll also miss the point. For over 30 years, Thompson has been insightfully limning politics, culture, and sports, as well as what's left of the American Dream at the turn of an apocalyptic century. He has also redefined the very nature of commentary and reportage in such books as *Hell's Angels, Fear and Loathing in Las Vegas,* and *Fear and Loathing on the Campaign Trail '72,* among many others. His collected letters so far number two thick volumes, comprise a stunning and massive record of a singular life lived in the passing lane. As his newest book, *Kingdom of Fear: Loathsome Secrets of a Star-Crossed Child in the Final Days of the American Century,* was about to hit the shelves, the 65-year-old Gonzo Godfather spoke with TONY by telephone from the comfort of Owl Farm, his "fortified compound" near Woody Creek, Colorado. True to form, Thompson answered some straightforward questions in his rope-a-dope, seemingly Faulkneresque fashion, with pit stops along the way to read a bit of Coleridge, fiddle maddeningly with his remote ("You dirty bastard") and pontificate on the dream-enhancing capabilities of multiple nicotine patches. Oddly enough, his first words to use were, "Hold on . . . my priest is leaving."

Time Out New York: Your new book is being billed as "a definitive and inimitable memoir."

HST: [chuckling] Oh God, yeah.

Time Out New York: It seems like you've always put yourself in the middle of the story. How is this book different?

HST: I've grown a little tired of discussing artificial categories. How long do I have to argue with this goddamn line between "is this fact, is this fiction"? Shit, it's what I say it is. I'm a writer. Fiction and Nonfiction are best-seller terms created by the best-seller list. I guess memoir is the word that seemed to be . . . the publishers were more enthusiastic about it than any other type of book from me.

Time Out New York: Can you look back to one particular moment in your past when it occurred to you that you were different, or just not like other people?

HST: Jesus. In terms of life-or-death rapid learning, I would say it was when I had to suddenly go into the military. I flew down for basic training and I remember being just wild drunk, like two days and nights with my friends in Louisville, just barely making the plane, and having no idea what I was doing or where I was going. I'd brought a flask on the plane, and some other guys had a pint of gin. I then actually passed out on the runway down there, where we were met by drill sergeants, and I was lying in the sun and vomiting and being herded through a maze of events—getting your head shaved, and just stumbling from place to place, marching in squads. I was able to cope with and even thrive in a radical change of cultures that a lot of people wouldn't adjust to and don't really learn from. What I learned was how to get along with power, I think, and authority, and to work maybe independently of it yet still within it.

Time Out New York: Why did you "have to" go into the military? Were you drafted?

HST: No, no . . . it was a long summer of driving a truck for this Chevy agency in Louisville. I wrecked a truck in late morning and drove it back to the . . . well, I just put a slice down the side. But at lunchtime, I figured that this was so bad—I'd taken one chance too many. I went across the street and volunteered.

Time Out New York: How many times have you been arrested, and how do you avoid being arrested more often?

HST: I don't commit crimes! I have a very clean rap sheet. Being detained and then fucked with by cops, that's a whole different game. But actually arrested and put in jail—oh, three or four times. Now, if we're talking courtrooms, we're talking in the thirties and forties and fifties. But I'm innocent, and I believe that! There have been lapses in my wisdom, and I have done things that . . . well, shit, I'm smoking marijuana—I'm a criminal! But that doesn't seem wrong to me in a larger sense. I consider myself . . . and I am . . . a Road Man for the Lords of Karma. I can't have a vicious criminal record. I can't go around hurting people.

Time Out New York: You've inspired a million imitators—every college freshman with a bit of literary sensibility and a bong seems to think they're going to write like you. Was there one numb nuts out there, on a pilgrimage to see Dr. Gonzo, who was particularly memorable?

HST: Oh, uh . . . Yeah, there's been violence . . . I also get these manuscripts. There's one by some woman in Florida titled "What It's Like to Be Mentally Ill and in Love with Hunter S. Thompson." About 150 pages of single-spaced typed, all caps.

Time Out New York: What about people actually showing up at your place?

HST: There are always those. I get a lot of weird shit left down at the gate; people are afraid to come up to the door. The bartenders at the tavern make a lot of extra money giving false directions here. It's a serious crime to reveal my address. I've been here 30 years and I've been a credit to the neighborhood. I'm a good neighbor. A good friend.

Time Out New York: Didn't you blow your neighbor's house off its foundation once?

HST: Oh . . . that's right. [Chuckling] Yeah. Well, it wasn't that bad. It cracked his swimming pool. A huge bomb in the Jeep went off. The tailpipe was blown about 250 yards into the road . . . big hunks of metal everywhere.

Time Out New York: So you've got your writing, reading, news, football, guns and explosives. Are there any esoteric interests that people don't know about?

HST: Well, I've developed a serious interest in fat young boys. Let's see . . . fixing chairs?

Time Out New York: Ever think of trademarking "Fear and loathing" like Phil Jackson trademarked "threepeat"?

HST: Jesus! No, I haven't. It's used all the time—I should be paid for it. I'll look into it. I'm just very busy. This ain't no rest home out here.

Salon.com—February 3, 2003

Hunter S. Thompson: The godfather of Gonzo says 9/11 caused a "nation-wide nervous breakdown"—and let the Bush crowd loot the country and savage American democracy

BY JOHN GLASSIE

February 3, 2003: He calls himself "an elderly dope fiend living out in the wilderness," but Hunter S. Thompson will also be found this week on the *New York Times* bestseller list with a new memoir, *Kingdom of Fear: Loathsome Secrets of a Star-Crossed Child in the Final Days of the American Century.*

Salon.com: Your new book, *Kingdom of Fear,* is being called a definitive memoir—although almost all of your books seem to be autobiographical in one way or another. What's the difference between the written accounts—of drug use, run-ins with the law, sex, fast cars, guns and explosives—and real-life events?

HST: I don't really see any difference. Telling the truth is the easiest way; it saves a lot of time. I've found that the truth is weirder than any fiction I've seen. There was a girl that worked for me a long time ago, who graduated third in her class from Georgetown Law School, and was from some kind of uptown family in Chicago, and instead of going to work for some big-time firm, she came to Aspen and ends up working for me out here in the wilderness. A year or so later her mother or father were coming out to visit. I've had some understandable issues with parents—really all my life. And I'd be worried about my daughter, too, if she'd run off with some widely known infamous monster. And so I asked her—just so I could get braced for this situation, meeting the parents and having them come to the house: "Given what you know about me and what you hear about me, which is worse?" She finally came out and said there was no question in her mind that the reality was heavier and crazier and more dangerous. Having to deal with the reality is no doubt a little more traumatic.

Salon.com: Indeed, your author blurb says you live in "a fortified compound near Aspen, Colorado." In what sense is it fortified and why does it need to be?

HST: Actually, I live in an extremely pastoral setting in an old log house. It's a farm really. I moved here 30 years ago. I think the only fortification might be my reputation. If people believe they're going to be shot, they might stay away.

Salon.com: Yes, I understand you're a gun enthusiast, to put it euphemistically. But do you support more restrictive gun laws? Do you support a ban on assault weapons?

HST: I have one or two of those, but I got them before they were illegal. In that case, if I were sure that any tragedies and mass murders would be prevented, I'd give up my assault rifle. But I don't really believe that. Do I have any illegal weapons? No. I have a .454 magnum revolver, which is huge, and it's absolutely legal. One day I was wild-eyed out here with Johnny Depp, and we both ordered these guns from Freedom, Wyo., and got them the next day through FedEx. Mainly, I have rifles, pistols, shotguns; I have a lot of those. But everything I have is top quality; I don't have any junk weapons. I wouldn't have any military weapon around here, except as an artifact of some kind. Given Ashcroft* and the clear blueprint of this administration to make everything illegal and everything suspicious—how about suspicion of being a terrorist sympathizer? Goddamn, talk about filling up your concentration camps. But, yeah, my police record is clean. This is not a fortified compound.

Salon.com: So, just to clarify, how do your views stack up with the NRA's?

HST: I think I'm still a life member of the NRA. I formed a gun club out here, an official sporting club, and I got charter from the NRA. That made it legal to have guns here, to bring guns here, to have ammunition sent here, that sort of thing. I've found you can deal with the system a lot easier if you use their rules—by understanding their rules, by using their rules against them. I talk to a lot of lawyers. You know, I consider Pat Buchanan a friend. I don't agree with him on many things. Personally, I enjoy him. I just like him. And I learn from Pat. One of the things I'm most proud of is that I never had anybody busted, arrested, jailed for my writing about them. I never had any—what's that?—collateral damage.

---

* John Ashcroft served as the attorney general under President George W. Bush from 2001 to 2005.

Salon.com: But speaking of rules, you've been arrested dozens of times in your life. Specific incidents aside, what's common to these run-ins? Where do you stand vis-à-vis the law?

HST: Goddammit. Yeah, I have. First, there's a huge difference between being arrested and being guilty. Second, see, the law changes and I don't. How I stand vis-à-vis the law at any given moment depends on the law. The law can change from state to state, from nation to nation, from city to city. I guess I have to go by a higher law. How's that? Yeah, I consider myself a road man for the lords of karma.

Salon.com: In 1990, you were put on trial for what you call "sex, drugs, dynamite and violence." Charges were eventually dropped. Since then, you've been outspoken on Fourth Amendment issues: search and seizure, the right to privacy. I assume you've taken a side in the civil liberties debate that's come up in the aftermath of 9/11?

HST: It's a disaster of unthinkable proportions—part of the downward spiral of dumbness. Civil liberties are black and white issues. I don't think people think far enough to see the ramifications. The PATRIOT Act* was a dagger in the heart, really, of even the concept of a democratic government that is free, equal and just. There are a lot more concentration camps right now than Guantánamo Bay. But they're not marked. Now, every jail, every bush-league cop can run a concentration camp. It amounts to a military and police takeover, I think.

Salon.com: Well, as some have pointed out, Lincoln suspended habeas corpus during the Civil War. Is some suspension of civil liberties ever appropriate or justified in a time of war?

HST: If there's a visible, obvious threat like Hitler, but in my mind the administration is using these boogeymen for their own purposes. This military law is nothing like the Constitution. They're exploiting the formula here: The people are afraid of something and you offer a solution, however drastic, and they go along with it. For a while, yeah. My suspicions are more justified every day with this manufacturing of dangerous killer villains. The rest of the world

* The USA PATRIOT Act is legislation that was ratified by Congress and signed into law by President George W. Bush in 2001. The acronym stands for Uniting and Strengthening America by Providing Appropriate Tools Required to Intercept and Obstruct Terrorism. The PATRIOT Act increases law enforcement's authority to access, search, and intercept records and intelligence on U.S. citizens, immigrants, and foreigners suspected to be involved in terrorism-related activities and allows officers to detain suspects.

does not perceive, I don't think, that some tin-horn dictator in the Middle East is more of a danger to the world than the U.S. is. This country depends on war as a primary industry. The White House has pumped up the danger factor because it's to their advantage. It's to John Ashcroft's advantage. There have always been pros and cons about the righteousness of life in America but this just seems planned, it seems consistent, and it seems traditional.

Salon.com: What do they get out of it?

HST: They get control of the U.S. economy, their friends get rich. These are not philosopher-kings we're talking about. These are politicians. It's a very sleazy way of using the system. One of the problems today is that what's going on today is not as complex as it seems. The Pentagon just asked for another $14 billion more in the budget, and it's already $28 billion. [Defense spending in the 2003 budget rose $19.4 billion, to $364.6 billion.] That's one sector of the economy that's not down the tubes. So, some people are getting rich off of this. It's the oligarchy. I believe the Republicans have never thought that democracy was anything but a tribal myth. The GOP is the party of capital. It's pretty basic. And it may have something to do with the deterioration of educational system in this country. I don't think Bush has the slightest intention or concern about educating the public.

Salon.com: Many people would say you're un-American and unpatriotic.

HST: I think I'm one of the most patriotic people that I've ever encountered in America. I consider myself a bedrock patriot. I participate very actively in local politics, because my voice might be worthwhile. I participate in a meaningful way—not by donations, I work at it.

Salon.com: Well, what do you prescribe? What do you advocate?

HST: All the blood is drained out of democracy—it dies—when only half the population votes. I would use the vote. It would seem to me that people who have been made afraid, if you don't like what's happening, if you don't want to go to war, if you don't want to be broke, well for God's sake don't go out and vote for the very bastards who are putting you there. That's a pillar of any democratic future in this country. The party of capital is not interested in having every black person in Louisiana having access to the Ivy League. They don't need an educated public.

Salon.com: So what took place during this past election?

HST: I believe the Republicans have seen what they've believed all along, which is that this democracy stuff is bull, and that people don't want to be burdened by political affairs. That people would rather just be taken care of.

The oligarchy doesn't need an educated public. And maybe the nation does prefer tyranny. I think that's what worries me. It goes back to Fourth Amendment issues. How much do you value your freedom? Would you trade your freedom for some illusion of security? Freedom is something that dies unless it's used.

Salon.com: This is coming from someone who's described himself as "an elderly dope fiend who lives out in the wilderness" and also as a "drunken screwball."

HST: A dangerous drunken screwball.

Salon.com: Right. Sorry. So why would anybody listen to you?

HST: I don't have to apologize for any political judgments I've made. The stuff I've written has been astonishingly accurate. I may have been a little rough on Nixon, but he was rough. You had to do it with him. What you believe has to be worth something. I've never given it a lot of thought: I've never hired people to figure out what I should do about my image. I always work the same way, and talk the same way, and I've been right enough that I stand by my record.

Salon.com: But is there a sense in which your views are, by definition, going to be seen as fringe views—views that can just be discarded?

HST: That is a problem and I guess *Fear and Loathing in Las Vegas* might have colored the way people perceive me. But I haven't worried that people see me as "dope fiend," I'd rather get rid of the "elderly" rather than the "dope fiend."

Salon.com: You have famously attached yourself to the word "fear" since you wrote *Fear and Loathing in Las Vegas.* Now you've written *Kingdom of Fear.* Will you explain?

HST: This country has been having a nationwide nervous breakdown since 9/11. A nation of people suddenly broke, the market economy goes to shit, and they're threatened on every side by an unknown, sinister enemy. But I don't think fear is a very effective way of dealing with things—of responding to reality. Fear is just another word for ignorance.

Salon.com: You write in *Kingdom of Fear* about the passing of the American century—

HST: That's official, by the way. The American century was the 20th, so sayeth Henry Luce.* And when it ends, Christ, you can't avoid thinking: "Ye Gods!"

Salon.com: To whom or what is the 21st century going to belong?

* Henry Luce was an American publishing magnate who founded *Time, Fortune,* and *Life* magazines.

HST: That's something I have not divined yet. Goddammit, I couldn't have told you in 1960 what 1980 was going to be like.

Salon.com: You've also referred to your beat as the "Death of the American Dream." That was the ostensible "subject" of *Fear and Loathing in Las Vegas.* Has it just sort of been on its deathbed since 1968?

HST: I think that's right.

Salon.com: A lot of people would argue with you about that anyway, and believe that the American Dream is alive and well.

HST: They need to take a better look around.

Salon.com: But in a way, haven't you lived the American Dream?

HST: Goddammit! [pause] I haven't thought about it that way. I suppose you could say that in a certain way I have.

Salon.com: You said back in 1991 that you were "as astounded as anybody" that you were still alive. Still drinking, smoking and doing drugs?

HST: I guess I'd have to say I haven't changed. Why should I, really? I'm the most stable neighbor on the road here. I'm an honest person. I don't regret being honest. I did give up petty crime when I turned 18, after I got a look at jail—I went in there for shoplifting—because I just saw that this stuff doesn't work. There's a line: "I do not advocate the use of dangerous drugs, wild amounts of alcohol and violence and weirdness—but they've always worked for me." I think I said that at a speech at Stanford. I've always been a little worried about advocating my way of life, or gauging my success by having other people take up my way of life, like Tim Leary did. I always quarreled with Leary about that. I could have started a religion a long time ago. It would not have a majority of people in it, but there would be a lot of them. But I don't know how wise I am. I don't know what kind of a role model I am. And not everybody is made for this life.

Salon.com: In fact, you've experienced more than your share of dangerous situations. You've been beaten by the Hell's Angels. You were in the middle of the 1968 Democratic Convention riots. You've been shot at. What's going on with that?

HST: By any widely accepted standard, I have had more than nine lives. I counted them up once and there were 13 times that I almost and maybe should have died—from emergencies with fires to violence, drowning, bombs. I guess I am an action junkie, yeah. There may be some genetic imperative that caused me to get into certain situations. It's curiosity, I guess. As long as I'm learning something I figure I'm OK—it's a decent day.

Salon.com: Is there anything you regret?

HST: That goes to the question of would you do it again. Would I leave my Keith Richards hat, with the silver skull on it, on the stool at the coffee shop at LaGuardia? I wouldn't do that again. But overall, no, I don't have any regrets.

Marty Beckerman Interview—February 3, 2003

My Chat (and Hash-Smoking Session) with Hunter S. Thompson, Gonzo Journalism Legend
Interview for www.martybeckerman.com

HST: Nixon looks like a liberal compared to this guy.* I never thought I'd say that. It's a horrible thought.

MB: [Legendary White House reporter] Helen Thomas called him the worst president in American history a couple weeks ago. Would you agree with that assessment?

HST: That's what I said to Charlie Rose today. Easily the worst.

MB: You write passionately about the 1968 Chicago Democratic convention. Was that the death of the American Dream for you? [Protests against the convention were met with unprecedented police brutality.]

HST: No, it was just the beginning of the fight. I would say right about now, boy, we're losing. They've got this country turned into a police state. I'm not sure how that term would resound with you, but a police state is a heavy situation.

MB: Well, Bush just authorized the U.S. military to kill American citizens overseas if they're suspected of being terrorists. ["THE ASSOCIATED PRESS, Dec. 4, 2002—American citizens working for al-Qaida overseas can legally be targeted and killed by the CIA under President Bush's rules for the war on terrorism, U.S. officials say."]

HST: Yes, suspected of terrorism. It's not so bizarre that our conversation tonight could be seen by someone in the police station as sympathy for terrorists. What's going on here? Valhalla. All you have to do is keep moving west, and you'll still get arrested.

MB: Bush Sr. has been very quiet these days. Do you think he's still running the show?

---

* Then-President George W. Bush.

HST: The answer is yes, but I wouldn't go out looking for a boogeyman. He's running it in the figurehead sense that his son is the president. I still remember the night, that horrible night I watched the Bush family [on the evening of the 2000 election], the old man laughing like a hyena. I believed Gore could win, and when they called—the whole family, gathered together in Texas—they looked like little piggies, and then the old man and that horrible laugh . . .

MB: The Bush family history is terrifying. They've been in business with Hitler, Saddam, Osama . . . [George W. Bush's grandfather, Prescott Bush, had his stocks in Nazi steel manufacturing removed by Congress in 1942 under the Trading with the Enemy Act.]

HST: And they're Jesus freaks on top of it. Carter was one and I loved Jimmy Carter—we're still good friends—but this is a stupid Jesus freak. Carter deserved the Nobel Prize.

MB: Do you believe the end of the world is coming?

HST: Yeah, it is the end of the world. What, do you think it's going to come on a TV show, right on schedule? Shit. They've been digging this for a long time. Read the Book of Revelation . . . The end of the world is not just coming; it's here. Until Bush came in it was still possible to be successful, happy. That was two years ago, but now the wheel is turning and I don't think what we're in now will possibly get any better.

MB: So are you excited to be here for the apocalypse at all? Of all the generations in human history, we might be the ones around for the end.

HST: It's not going to happen like a thunderclap. I would like that, really. Why not? A gigantic thunderclap . . . Yeah, the floods, the nightriders, the marauders . . . It's going to be pretty grim.

MB: Do you think there'll ever be another draft after Vietnam?

HST: Oh God . . . Jesus, I hope so. The draft was a disaster. The Army has become a pack of vicious, predatory, mercenary hired killers, and a draft would democratize the Army as it always has. That's why Vietnam turned out to be a victory for our side—for the antiwar folks. You think jail's better than going into the Army? If you don't like it, then you don't enlist. Enough people felt that way, and lo and behold.

MB: *Kingdom of Fear* is your first book of new material in ten years. What have you been up to in the last decade?

HST: Oh, the same old thing, I suppose . . . Yeah, I've worked the same stories.

MB: In *Kingdom of Fear* you claim that *Fear and Loathing in Las Vegas* is as good as *The Great Gatsby* and better than *The Sun Also Rises*. That's quite the claim.

HST: [Laughs] In a moment of hedonism, yeah. It's better than *Sun Also Rises,* better than *Gatsby.*

MB: It's studied in colleges now. You're part of the canon of American literature.

HST: Yeah, that's good.

MB: Why do you think *Las Vegas* is the book that resonates the most with people over the years? When people think you, they think that book.

HST: Oh God . . . I know, I know. Why do I think it resonates over and over again with different aged people? Well, I'll play with you on that. I don't really know. I could say it's fun, but it's more than that. Why do you think it is? Why do you think it's true?

MB: Well, the book's a ride. On the surface it's this cartoonish, ether-chugging adventure, but then there are all these darker themes—the death of the American Dream, instant gratification, how Americans find happiness—all that's underneath. So it's like a thrill ride to read the book, but then you pick up other messages along the way.

HST: [Laughs] Yeah, well, that's good enough for me. Weird. It's like *Huckleberry Finn* or something like that, you know? Travel journalism. I just wrote it down in my notebook . . . There's still that controversy whether Mark Twain wrote fiction or not.

MB: Do you ever feel pressure from your fans to live up to the cartoonish image you projected in the old days?

HST: What do you mean I projected? You mean [*Doonesbury* creator Garry] Trudeau. I don't even know Trudeau. I was never looking for publicity and said, "Hey Garry, why don't you put me in that strip of yours? That's a pretty good idea."

MB: Let's talk about *The Rum Diary* for a minute. Was it weird to put something out 40 years after you started it?

HST: Well, I like the book. If I thought about it much, it might be weird. Yeah, I didn't worry about it. You can't afford to worry about it.

MB: Was the novel complete before it was published, or did you do touch-up work on it?

HST: [Laughs] Cut out everything. There were scenes in there that the American public isn't ready to handle, to put it lightly.

MB: There was that famous fax you sent to a woman executive overseeing the *Rum Diary* movie in which you threatened to chop off her hands if things didn't get rolling. How'd that turn out?

HST: Oh yeah . . . Whoop! Whoop!

MB: [Rolling Stone founder] Jann Wenner is notably missing from the *Kingdom of Fear* "Honor Roll." What in God's name happened to *Rolling Stone* magazine?

HST: God . . . This is the same thing Bob Dylan and I were talking about recently. What happened? I don't know. Goddamn.

MB: Are you ever going to write for Rolling Stone again?

HST: I doubt it. As a gambler, I'd probably say not likely.

MB: How does it feel to have multiple biographies written about you? Flattering? Terrifying?

HST: Well, there are three or four out there, right? Of course, it's like reading reviews. With Jean Carroll's book [*Hunter*], what happened was every old friend of mine had been contacted—friends I'd forgotten about—and I got calls from all my friends telling me this lady had come by trying to get quotes for her book. My ex-wife called me a wife-beater and a thief. People I hadn't heard from in 30 years called me to ask if it was okay to talk to this lady, and some didn't even call me. I didn't want to say, "No, you can't." But, that crazy bitch.

MB: You're becoming an elder statesman of the counterculture. What's that like?

HST: I have no idea what it's like.

MB: Have you ever overdosed on anything?

HST: [Laughs] Vitamin A. I did beta-carotene and—I'm trying to think of the others—I did a super-overload of like thirty-five or -six vitamin tabs. I'd been up for two days working on this story, on deadline and I'd almost finished it, and I was definitely tired and worn-out. So instead of drugs I did vitamins. I thought, well, fuck—I'm too tired to do speed; it would be too dangerous. Why not go healthy, you know? So I starting eating these vitamins—C, D, E—and I figured if vitamins are good for you in an emergency, why not just double-up, quintuple-up? And I ate vitamins by the handful for like two minutes without stopping, thinking these would pump me up. And if vitamins are good, the more the better . . . Holy shit. I was turning beet-red, sweating, paralyzed—it's a little bit like hashish, actually.

MB: In the new book you admit you secretly pray to God.

HST: No, this is far beyond God.

MB: God can't save us now?

HST: There is no God.

MB: A lot of the figures from the '60s have passed on in the last 10 years—Ginsberg, Leary, Kesey—how does it feel to see that era fading away?

HST: You morbid little bastard . . . Yeah, how does it feel to be the last buffalo? Fuck, I don't know. I don't think anybody knows . . . When you talk about the '60s, you're talking about people who were scared out of their senses, trying to get the feeling for what the fuck was going on.

[Thompson suddenly screams for his assistant to turn the television volume up to eardrum-shattering levels. The History Channel is airing former U.S. ambassador Adlai Stevenson's Oct. 25, 1962 address to the United Nations General Assembly, demanding that the U.S.S.R. immediately withdraw its nuclear warheads from Cuba. The address on behalf of JFK is widely credited as having prevented the Cold War from going nuclear.]

"This one always gets to me," Thompson says wistfully, captivated for the entire duration of the speech. "You know, it haunts me that I never pursued the 'who killed Kennedy' story. I believe it's the one story I consider a failure. Yeah, I failed, and now the assumption is that obedience is normal—the president is king."

CNBC—February 8, 2003

Interview with Tim Russert

Author Dr. Hunter S. Thompson talks about his childhood, political background and his new book, *Kingdom of Fear*.

Tim Russert: Good evening. Welcome again. Tonight, we talk to one of America's best-read authors. This is his 13th book. You've read about Gonzo journalism. This is the father of Gonzo journalism. With us, the one, the only Dr. Hunter S. Thompson. Welcome.

HST: Welcome.

Russert: You have a new book out.

HST: Yep. Yep.

Russert: And—and I was—it's a m—a memoir of sorts. But the other interesting thing I was reading in the papers the other day is that you were in Aspen, Colorado, part of an antiwar demonstration. And I want to talk a little bit about that.

HST: Definitely.

Russert: Tell me why you oppose the war against Iraq.

HST: Well, it seems like not just dangerous but insanely dangerous for us. I don't even think it's our war. I think it's Mr. Bush's war. And I think it's just like they say about the Civil War, that's Mr. Lincoln's war. But it just seems incredibly stupid to go off—here's a man who's taken the country in two years from a prosperous nation of peace to a broken nation of war. That's kind of hard to see that the people keep voting for him. That's what baffles me about the American people now.

Russert: You said it appears our nation is having a national nervous breakdown.

HST: That's what I recognize it as.

Russert: Explain that.

HST: Oh, God, explain that. Well, it seems that I think in a nervous breakdown, you kind of seize up and go sideways, more or less paralyzed. I wouldn't want to get into psychotherapy, psychiatric research here, but that's how it seems. The utter torpor of the American people in voting for a person who makes them broke, takes away their education and their libraries and refunds taxes seem to be wrong. I live out in the mountains and the woods and that's the way it seems to me. And I've done this for a long time, you know, covered a lot of elections and seen a lot of politicians. I've disagreed with a lot of them. But I haven't been this appalled. Nixon—yeah, Nixon—well, he was fun compared to Bush. He was a liberal.

Russert: Nixon was a liberal.

HST: Compared to Bush.

Russert: When you look at Saddam Hussein, do you see any evil? Do you have any fear? Do you think he is a threat? Do you think he has chemical and biological weapons?

HST: Well, I wouldn't invite him out to my house, but I think we have to look at this with the fact that everything we know about Saddam, we know through the CIA. The only firsthand account I have of Iraq is through Sean Penn,* my friend, who went there to see it for himself. This is a war we're going to be bogged down in for, oh boy, a generation. And it's going to—the—the budget—budget deficit, the financial pit we're going to get into to do this, to just go over there and bomb people back to the Stone Age. That's Curtis LeMay thinking, isn't it? Remember Curtis LeMay?

Russert: He was George Wallace's running mate in 1968.

HST: Yeah.

Russert: But after September 11th, do you not think Americans looked at the world differently and are concerned that Saddam Hussein could, in fact, attempt to deliver biological or chemical weapons upon America or give them to al-Qaida or another terrorist group and the president wants to remove that threat before it strikes our own shores?

HST: Well, certainly, we look at it differently. It's hard to ignore that whole thing downtown at the World Trade Center, but I don't know that we've ever linked Osama bin Laden or Saddam to the disaster. And you couldn't take this case to court—to court—in an American courtroom and win. It's speculation. It's—I don't even know if there's circumstantial evidence is there? Or do you know?

---

* Sean Penn is an American Academy Award–winning film actor and director.

Russert: Well, Colin Powell's* case that he laid out to the United Nations, two-thirds of the American people believed that it made the case.

HST: Yeah, that's—that was the situation with the State of the Union, I think.

Russert: Mm-hmm. Very much.

HST: I think. Two out of three . . .

Russert: Yeah, very much. Do you think Al Gore, if he happened to be president, would be handling this situation differently?

HST: Oh, I think without question, differently. He is—what we have here is a very tight, very organized, very tunnel-visioned bunch of people in the White House. And what I'm curious about is who's in charge here in the White House? Now Karl Rove† or Cheney or Ag—it's hard for me to believe that this—this president is really in charge as a leader . . . I just wonder who is in charge.

Russert: Overwhelmingly, the American people give George Bush very high marks for leadership. And it—the irony they point to is that Colin Powell, who had been the one most skeptical about war with Iraq, is now the one who is making the case and is probably the most effective messenger the administration could have.

HST: Yes. And his—his conversion is—well, I—I never had that kind of faith in Powell, but he is a smart and intelligent guy and like the other generals. Hell, Norman Schwarzkopf** came out against the war. You know, it's—going, "Well, we're—we're—when we—when we get in a war, we must pull together." What is happening now looks to me like dangerously war.

Russert: Let me show you the photograph of someone back in 1972. This is George McGovern and Hunter Thompson on the campaign trail. *Fear and Loathing on the Campaign Trail*—of '72. He was dubbed the candidate of acid, amnesty and abortion.

HST: Yeah.

Russert: Is that the George McGovern you know?

---

* Colin Powell is a retired United States Army general and served as the secretary of state under President George W. Bush from 2001 to 2005.

† Karl Rove is the former deputy chief of staff to President George W. Bush from 2001 to 2007. Rove has worked as an influential Republican consultant and strategist.

** Norman Schwarzkopf is a retired United States Army general. He was the head combat commander during the first Gulf War in 1991.

HST: Oh, no. He's one of the great people and one of the most serious.

Russert: He's a decorated war pilot.

HST: Yeah, oh, yeah, and proven.

Russert: And yet—and yet at the '72 convention, he didn't give an acceptance address until 1:00 in the morning surrounded by people with bandanas and all kinds of things. And it set an image or a symbol to the country that clearly turned them off. Richard Nixon beat him in a landslide.

HST: Well, yeah, won it by 22 points.

Russert: You have a soft spot for Richard Nixon, don't you.

HST: I do definitely. Compared to this administration, and we know the Bush dynasty is disturbing, but with Nixon, it was so much fun, compared to these people.

Russert: Let me show you a photograph from your book. This is young Hunter Stockton Thompson. Look at that angelic presence.

HST: Oh, my God, yes.

Russert: At the age of nine, that little devil became involved with the federal agents because you were toppling federal mailboxes. True?

HST: True. Well, it was only one box that I was accused of.

Russert: One?

HST: Yeah.

Russert: And what did you do?

HST: We did drop it, yes, in front of a speeding bus, yeah, call it a speeding city bus, to defend the honor of the neighborhood because the bus driver was rude and impatient. He wouldn't wait for us while we ran down the hill trying to catch the school bus. We were just kids.

Russert: Was that a defining moment in your life?

HST: Well, it wasn't until the FBI came after me and wanted to put me in prison.

Russert: At age nine.

HST: Yes, my mother cried. Yes, it carried a mandatory five years in prison for defacing federal property. Yeah, that's when I learned that they just—they were fishing, and they didn't know that I did it. I'm very concerned and every part of my constant thinking has to do with the Fourth Amendment. I've talked—you know, started the Fourth Amendment Foundation to—although the Fourth Amendment is just about shredded now. There has to be some defense against handing this government in vain, seize, take over, invade our lives and our personal, well, privacy in that—every day.

Russert: But—but after that episode, when you were 19 in Danville, Kentucky, you were arrested for vandalism and shortly after, arrested for robbery. The outlaw spirit took hold.

HST: Robbery? Robbery? It's been so long. What did I rob, you know? Well, all right, I probably did it. Yes, I was a child criminal and I guess after that, when I was 18, I just had one too many nights in jail and I gave up crime as a way of life, turned to writing.

Russert: Which is white-collar crime in many ways.

HST: Well, it's an argument. It's arguable.

Russert: You have said, "I can't believe I get away with it."

HST: Well, no, I couldn't at first.

Russert: All right. After the—the robbery charge, they said to you, "All right, don't go back to school. If you join the United States Air Force, we'll put you—set you on your way." True?

HST: No.

Russert: No. Fix it, correct it, clarify it.

HST: Yes. After I came out of jail on my birthday, juveniles can't make bail in Kentucky, so I had no choice. One lesson, the wisdom I got out of it was that it was disturbing to be in jail, but I did learn to get along with people even in jail. They called me the president. But, I realized I didn't want jail to be my way of life.

I joined the Air Force because I wrecked a truck that I was driving as a parts delivery boy. It was a brand-new Chevy truck. And I was very proud of my driving. And one day, I took it down an alley—a downtown alley at about 60 miles an hour and just—I mean, one inch off, just opened up the side like a can opener. So, I joined the Air Force instead of going to jail.

Russert: You joined the Air Force, and you were a sports reporter in the Air Force?

HST: Editor.

Russert: Sports editor.

HST: Yeah.

Russert: And how long were you in the Air Force?

HST: Two years.

Russert: And honorably discharged.

HST: I got in a tangle—well, it's a long—all these stories are stories are long.

Russert: You think the draft is a good thing, don't you?

HST: Absolutely.

Russert: Why?

HST: Despite the fact that I protested against it for a—so many years, end the draft, I think [it] democratizes the Army, and it makes the Army a civilized bunch of people instead of the hired gang of mercenaries. And you know lifers in the Army that—who are just professional soldiers, they're in their own world. And to have college people, draft people, you know, mixing in and out of the Army every two years, it puts a little constraint on it.

And they don't—the Bush people don't want the draft because they don't want the—the draftees for that very reason, because, they're hard to discipline, they're likely to be smart enough to say "why?" once in a while.

Russert: I don't see any huge support amongst Democrats for reinstating the draft either.

HST: Right. Democrats are a bunch of eunuchs, and it's disgusting. I'm tired. It's shocking that there is no opposition, really, in this country.

Russert: Are there any Democrats you respect?

HST: Well, there's some that I like and . . .

Russert: Candidate for president or someone who's been president or been a candidate.

Russert: McGovern? How about Bill Clinton?

HST: Well, I kind of like him in a dark way. He's the—well, sort of a traveling salesman from Arkansas, which is what he always was.

Russert: But you wouldn't vote for him again for president, you said.

HST: No.

Russert: Would you vote for his wife, Hillary Clinton?

HST: No.

Russert: Why?

HST: Well, I went down there to—to Little Rock under the impression that he was kind of a yo-yo, but she was the brains with a sense of humor. Wow. That is a steely woman. She still hates me.

Russert: You're also friends with James Carville.

HST: Yeah. James is a good one.

Russert: How—how do g—well, how do you get on with the Ragin' Cajun?

HST: Fine. I like him. We talk. He's one of the three or four top operatives—you know, political, not wizards, but in a rhetoric way, as in evil perhaps, although there's no evil in politics. It's all irrelevant. But—Lee Atwater.

Russert: Lee Atwater . . .

HST: Yeah.

Russert: . . . who was Mary Matalin,* James Carville's wife—Atwater was her boss.†

HST: God, that's unbelievable. Yes, love conquers all, eh? Yes, I was down there. I had to talk James out of leaving town on the day of the election, going to Paris with the opposition's chief strategist. He was going to run off with her on Tuesday night of the election, and . . .

Russert: This is back in 1992.

HST: Yes. He was persuaded to stay until the next night when—the victory party and staff, and he was gone. People were very stunned. Yeah, it is queer, isn't it?

Russert: He actually went to the transition meetings at the governor's mansion—after he came back from his vacation, came out to the press and said, "Well, they wouldn't give me secretary of State, so I'm not taking anything."

HST: He didn't want to be in the government. Yeah, James, he needs to work in semidarkness and with a whip in his hand. Yeah, his image is a little hard, but he's a good one.

Russert: You must respect, in a political way, the skills of Karl Rove.

HST: Goddamn, you bet. That's what I mean by who's in charge. And, yeah, his record speaks for itself. And given the fact that I don't think much of Bush's analytical powers, Rove must be more—and more influential. I hate to think he's totally influential, that he's the main voice and—and brains. Well, those—those kind of Svengalis come and go in politics, but they don't stay around long.

Now if—if 49 percent or 48 percent of the people in this country vote, and if, say, if all the Deadheads voted, Grateful Dead, we'd have a different president today. And that's the only real power that we have, and just to throw it away like that is, well, you know, we got the government we deserve.

Russert: Gary Hart ran George McGovern's campaign.

HST: Yes.

---

* Mary Matalin is a Republican political consultant and head editor of Threshold Editions, a conservative imprint of Simon and Schuster. She is married to Democratic political strategist James Carville.

† Lee Atwater was a chairman of the Republican National Committee and a political strategist for presidents Ronald Reagan and George H. W. Bush.

Russert: He's thinking about running for president again. Would you support him?

HST: I would definitely think about it. He's a friend, but I think it's important to win this one. So I would . . .

Russert: Can he win with the way he withdrew from the last campaign?

HST: I doubt it. It's a handicap to start with that. And me and Warren Beatty* were the only two people who told him not to drop out. I thought, and wrote, "Gary, there's the 'adulterer's vote."

Russert: The primary?

HST: Well, it—enough—enough people out there who identify with you that it's a vote of your own. I don't know (screams)—oh, God, the decadent vote is what I was getting at.

Russert: So if you get the Deadhead vote and the decadent vote . . .

HST: Yeah.

Russert: . . . you think you're on your way.

HST: Of course. Of course.

Russert: The gos—the gospel according to Dr. Thompson.

HST: Oh yeah.

Russert: Let me—let me show you another picture from your book. This is you and Johnny Depp with guns—shooting guns. Yeah, there you are holding it. You are fascinated with guns, aren't you? You have how many . . .

HST: I appreciate the fine machinery.

Russert: You have—what?—you have roughly 30 shotguns?

HST: No, no, no, no.

Russert: No?

HST: Well, maybe seven or eight shotguns, Tim. They're all the best of the best. And I—I just enjoy them. Like motorcycles, I enjoy the precision, the—how they work. I don't consider them weapons or, as much as tools, or toys.

Russert: I—toys. Are—are you still a member of the NRA?

HST: I think I—I bought a lifetime membership. I think I'm a lifetime member.

Russert: Would you ever think of challenging Charlton Heston for head of the NRA?

---

* Warren Beatty is a film actor, director, and producer. In 1981, Beatty won the Academy Award for Best Director for his film *Reds*. Beatty has campaigned and advocated for Democratic presidential candidates since the 1968 campaign of Robert F. Kennedy.

HST: Yeah. That's a good—that's a good idea, yeah.

Russert: Now that's an interesting Gonzo campaign for Hunter Thompson. You can announce tonight that you're going to take on Charlton Heston for head of the NRA.

HST: Yeah, that would be interesting, but that's a lot of work, too. Yeah, that would be—What is it? Kabuki theater. I wouldn't mind that. But Michael Moore's in it. That's an idea. My home out there in Colorado, Owl Farm, is a chartered Rod and Gun Club, so that we could legally keep weapons.

Russert: Let me show you a picture of a—from your book of the O'Farrell Theater in San Francisco.

HST: Yes.

Russert: And there it is—surrounded by young ladies.

HST: Yeah.

Russert: What was your job there?

HST: I was a night manager.

Russert: And what kind of facility was it?

HST: It's the Carnegie Hall of public sex in America.

Russert: OK. Why would you take a job like that?

HST: I was writing a book. Well, I started off writing an article for *Playboy* about feminist pornography, and I got so deeply involved in that that I started writing a book called "The Night Manager." So I figured, "I'd better be the night manager."

Russert: Did you enjoy the job?

HST: Yeah. Of course. That was wonderful, and it taught me a lot. Got me deeply into San Francisco politics; got me arrested a lot, too.

Russert: A lot of discussion—things have been written about Hunter Thompson, the amount you consume in terms of alcohol, the amount of drugs you've ingested. Are you surprised that here you are, at age 66 . . .

HST: Five.

Russert: . . . 65 . . .

HST: Yeah.

Russert: . . . approaching 66, that you're still alive and kicking?

HST: Oh, it baffles me. I never expected to be anywhere near this kind of age. But it—since it's here . . .

Russert: Will you donate your organs to science?

HST: Hell, yeah, to Harvard Medical School. But I'm not sure—well, I—I haven't signed one of those—I mean, you know . . .

Russert: Organ donor . . .

HST: . . . organ donors that I—

Russert: Well, you should. What—are you afraid of death?

HST: No, no. It'd be silly to be afraid of it. And, yeah, I just don't look forward to it, you know, like, "Whoo, whoo. Let's die and have fun."

Russert: What's after death?

HST: What's after death? Well, for me, I figure I'll be back around. I'm sort of a road man for the lords of karma.

Russert: "A road man for the lords of karma."

HST: Yeah, the great hall of karma.

Russert: And you'll be reincarnated?

HST: Yeah, in some form. I don't want to get into the biology of it now, but, yeah, on this—on—you know, it's a—I take a little rest, maybe a little, as long as possible, right? It's a hard job. Then I'll come back around in some other form.

Russert: As what? What would you like to come back as?

HST: I think I've been through that once, and I think I ended up either a dolphin or a seagull.

Russert: Both majestic in the way they fly through the air.

HST: Yeah, and free. I pay a lot of attention to freedom, and I think this country is throwing it away. This—this onerous, this compulsion to trade our freedoms for security, which is an illusion of security, is horrifying to me.

Russert: You have a son, Juan Fitzgerald, born in 1965.

HST: Yes. Yeah.

Russert: How would you rate yourself as a father?

HST: Pretty good.

Russert: Why?

HST: Well, I look around me, and I think other people would, would tell you the same thing. Juan was born into the middle of an extremely active time, '64, I think, and into an extremely active, weird family. And he grew up perfectly. He's extremely proud, and I like him, and get along fine with him.

Russert: What's he do for a living?

HST: He's a computer guy. He's into some food chain, Mexican food I forget the name of it or I'd plug it. But he's into the financial computer part of it. He's totally different from me . . .

Russert: And I'm told there's a young man named Will . . .

HST: Willie.

Russert: . . . who's about—about—Willie—about four or five years old, who calls you Ace.

HST: Ace, yeah, and from the very beginning.

Russert: This is your grandson.

HST: Yeah.

Russert: Why does he call his grandpa Ace?

HST: I didn't want to get into that—in that sentimental, old, yeah . . .

Russert: Pops, Granddaddy.

HST: Yeah, right. So I figured "Ace" was about right.

Russert: You said, "Call me Ace"?

HST: Yeah. He writes me letters and faxes all the time. Yeah, it's he's never heard me called anything else. He knows I'm Hunter. Two weeks ago, whenever this book, the first copies showed up, he was talking to, I guess, my son's wife, and she was talking about me being a writer or writing books, and he said, "Well, I've never seen him write books." And then we showed him this.

Russert: What's your next book?

HST: Oh, there's *Polo Is My Life.* That if I want to drift into the perverse and the fun—yeah, I've been working on that. It's not a story of polo, but it's an attitude.

Russert: Gonzo journalism to be continued. Hunter S. Thompson, we thank you for joining us tonight. His new book, *Kingdom of Fear.* Stay healthy, keep writing. We'll see you all next weekend right here on CNBC.

Boulder Weekly—April 3–9, 2003

The Doctor Will See You Now

BY BEN CORBETT

It's always because we love that we are rebellious; it takes a great deal of love to give a damn one way or another what happens from now on. The situation for human beings is hopeless. . . . For the while that's left, though, we can remember the Great and the gods.

—KENNETH PATCHEN

Gonzo journalist Hunter S. Thompson pleaded no contest to spraying a man in the face with a fire extinguisher after the charge was reduced to a petty offense. . . . Thompson, who entered a plea to petty disorderly conduct Friday, was initially charged with misdemeanor assault in the April fire extinguisher episode at Boulder's Fox Theatre. . . . At public speaking appearances, Thompson sometimes sprays a fire extinguisher toward the audience to close shows. He was showing some people the technique in his dressing room when . . .

—LAS VEGAS REVIEW-JOURNAL

The Doctor's new book, *Kingdom of Fear,* comes as the author's autobiographical pummeling of the senses that dates back to his childhood when, at 9 years old, the FBI grilled him for destroying a mailbox and he called their bluff. "And I learned a powerful lesson," writes Thompson. "Never believe the first thing an FBI agent tells you about anything—especially if he seems to believe you are guilty of a crime. Maybe he has no evidence." Its style is fragmented, jumping from prophecy to flashback, and segues through some of the most impacting events of the 65-year-old's life as a journalist, author, and now icon. The volume ends at Thompson's first encounter with his assistant (and now fiancée) Anita, one of the inspirations for the book, who enlightens Thompson with the words, "You have the soul of a teenage girl trapped in the body of an elderly dope fiend." In high Thompson fashion, during the interview, the Good Doctor was sipping whiskey, smoking fine hashish, writing his column, and gambling all at once.

BC: What are you watching?

HST: Yeah, hold on, you caught me at a . . . Kentucky/Butler. Hold on just a second . . . Goddamn, Kentucky 25 straight wins! This is gonna go on for about three minutes or so, uh, Indiana/Pittsburgh. Yeah, I'm predicting these games. I write the column for ESPN on Sunday nights.

BC: You're writing the column right now?

HST: Yeah. Well, I also have a significant financial investment in these games. Yesterday I was No. 2 of all the ESPN people predicting it. I did well yesterday.

BC: How much did you win?

HST: Oh, Christ that was about a $5,000 investment. And I have others. But boy, it looks like Louisville and Butler fucked me up today. (To himself) Let's see, Irvine/Michigan State, oh boy, that's tough. Texas/Connecticut . . . I think Texas will win there. I don't know. Fuck. I haven't seen Connecticut play.

BC: What's the most you've ever won?

HST: I can't remember. I remember losing $4,000 to Ed Bradley one time. Somehow I don't remember the wins quite as well as I do the horrible losses. He was out here for this year's tournament too, and then he got called off to the fucking war.

BC: So what's your status with *Rolling Stone* these days?

HST: I don't really like talking about *Rolling Stone.* People ask me all the time. Well, you know, that was a great run for me. *Rolling Stone* was one of the . . . well, maybe the best magazine of the time. But things changed drastically. The attitude's changed. I didn't fit in there anymore, and I still wouldn't now. It got very corporate.

BC: They probably wouldn't be around today if you hadn't written a lot of that stuff.

HST: Yeah, you're probably right. A lot of people have said that. I think you're all right. I don't like to uh . . . Well, fuck why not? Wenner is a pig. Yeah, he actually turned into one.

BC: With your new book, why the title *Kingdom of Fear?*

HST: That's what I perceived this country to be at the time. From any direction you look at this country, everything that's happening is motivated by fear and terrorism and war. It's a national panic encouraged by these low-rent, evangelical punks in the White House. In two years, Bush and his crowd—or rather, his crowd and Bush—have turned this country from a prosperous nation of peace into a broke nation at war. In two years they've destroyed the economy, our place in the world, and the future of the children. And the next three generations are going to be paying for this war.

BC: Why the subtitle *Loathsome Secrets of a Star-Crossed Child in the Final Days of the American Century*?

HST: The American century ended in 1999. Well, let's say 2000. And that's what it was called, "The American Century." A man named Henry Luce came up with that. But this isn't the American Century for sure, and it has nothing to do with the American Dream at all. The country has gone back to the worst of its kind of evangelical right-wing freaks. And what really bothers me is that the voters keep voting for Bush, even though they're going broke more so every day. We've raised several generations of stupid people. Ignorant and stupid. And I really can't understand that. Hell, it happened so fast.

BC: How did you get into doing your "Hey Rube" column for ESPN?

HST: John Walsh, the managing editor at ESPN, in an old friend of mine. He was an editor at *Rolling Stone* when I was there. We became good friends, and one day he asked me if I thought I could write a sports column for ESPN. I was in a decent mood and said, "Yeah, of course." The column is one of my favorite things. It keeps me on deadline and it's a relief to get to the column to write. Just pure writing.

BC: Well, here's my favorite one. I want to read a segment and maybe get some comment. This is from February 11, 2002, titled "Terrorism at the Superbowl":

"The news out of Washington is getting darker and weirder by the hour. On some days it has the look of a full-bore Terrorist cell operating out of the White House basement, spewing fear and desperation on a nation of suddenly impoverished patriots. Where is Bill Clinton now that we finally need him?"

HST: Jesus Christ. Well, I hate to say it, but it seems to be all accurate and prophetic even. I mean it's not that difficult to be prophetic with this country and this administration. You can imagine your worst fears, and then figure they'll probably come true.

BC: That's pretty edgy stuff. Especially written only five months after September 11. Nobody was criticizing Washington yet. You seem to make a career of taking a sportswriter's approach to politics.

HST: Well yeah. That's an interesting mix, writing a sports column and politics. Being a sportswriter, I guess I've kind of brought that style to everything I've done since then. And I'm still a sportswriter. But I branched out—heh heh. Excuse me a second.

[To Anita] I'm looking for that pipe. Where is that goddamn . . .

BC: So we have bin Laden and Saddam, and then we have the American propaganda machine. Who exactly are the terrorists here, and why should we fear them?

HST: Well, we should fear the White House I think more than the terrorists. In the *Kingdom of Fear,* people tend to be a lot more obedient. Fear makes people behave differently.

BC: What do you think about the anthrax letters being sent to Congress?*

HST: I think that was bullshit, and they were probably planted. My feeling from the beginning was that the tragedy at the World Trade Center was also rigged. I can't say that for sure, but I've had that uneasy feeling from the very beginning. I haven't been convinced of anything otherwise. They haven't done a goddamn thing yet to convince anybody that bin Laden actually did that. I never believed that a gang of Arabs sitting around a fire in Afghanistan cooked this up and pulled it off.

[To Anita] Where's the *New York Times* story from today? Here's a story out of the *Times.* "Reporters Respond Eagerly to Pentagon Welcome Mat." (From the March 23 edition.)

"Carefully devised by the Pentagon to counter years of complaints by news organizations about restrictions on combat coverage, the new policy of 'embedding' more than 500 reporters with invading troops has produced riveting images of fighter jets on carriers and tanks plowing across the Iraqi desert, accompanied by household faces like Ted Koppel† . . . and of surrendering Iraqi soldiers with their hands held high. [To himself: Oh goddamn!] . . . Pentagon planners have also reached out to diverse outlets where public opinion is shaped

---

* In September 2001, letters containing anthrax spores were mailed to the offices of six Democratic senators and to major U.S. media outlets. Five people died from coming in immediate contact with the anthrax.

† Ted Koppel is an American television journalist and former host of ABC's *Nightline*.

by including reporters from MTV, *Rolling Stone, People Magazine* and *Men's Health,* and foreign journalists running the gamut from Al Jazeera, the Arabic language television channel, to Russia's Tartusk news agency. News organizations have expressed satisfaction with the arrangements."

BC: What do you think?

HST: Jesus Christ, that's absolute bullshit. I've covered wars. By being embedded, it's almost like being captured. You're given access to whatever they want to give you access to, and they make you really grateful for it. It's like doling out the access. That happened in the Vietnam War a lot. But the Pentagon decided journalists would never have access to another war.

BC: So what access do they have now?

HST: They don't have access. That's the point. By embedding them, they totally co-opt them. And then their copy is, let's say, "approved." Nothing gets out of there without going through the military machine. All of our news really from Iraq and Afghanistan for probably the last two years has strictly been the product of Psyops and the CIA.

BC: Was it the same when you were reporting on Vietnam?

HST: Not at all. They didn't have that censorship in place. The first time they implemented it was in [1983] Grenada, and I was shocked. It was a practice run for the next war in Panama. Grenada was the first time really that all access was cut off.

BC: But you were independent at the time. You didn't have to take orders, right?

HST: There was no control over the press, but that was their first attempt to do that. I remember the first time I'd ever seen concertina wire, and they tried to kick me out of my hotel. They took it over, and I refused to leave. That was the first time I'd ever been ordered around by the Army.

BC: How does the media coverage compare to when you were in Saigon?

HST: I was in Saigon at the end, but I went out to various places in the field. For journalists, Vietnam was a very free war. That's why the Pentagon blames the media for losing the war. We had a lot of violence down there with the reporters.

BC: During Nixon, who controlled whom? Did the press control the White House or did the White House control the press?

HST: It was about 50/50 on any given day. That was the beauty of it. That was also true in Vietnam. You could go anywhere you could get. You know a lot of people were killed and shot over there. Our photographer was killed on the last goddamned day of the war. But at least we got the truth out about that war. We haven't had the truth about any war since then.

BC: What do you think will happen with this war?

HST: This war is going to go on for 20 or 30 years. It's been going on for 12 already. We'll be there certainly the rest of my lifetime, and pretty much into infinity. Look at Korea. That's a country we invaded and went to war with 50 years ago, and look what we got out of that. Fifty years is nothing. For what amounts to one person's lifetime, we've been fighting a war with the same country.

BC: You wrote in your book that Bush is now getting us into a war with the entire Arab-speaking world.

HST: Oh yeah, this is World War III.

BC: And what will be the end result?

HST: A fascist police state for one. I mean that's necessary in wartime, right? Let's just call it Bush—(It's not Bush, but it's his administration). He's clearly the worst president in the history of the U.S. The negativity of his accomplishments is going to take a long time to recover from. The same people that control the "goofy child president," as I call him, also controlled his father.

Oh yeah! We were talking about *Rolling Stone* and Vietnam. On my way to Vietnam, actually I was on a 747 crossing the Pacific. At some point along the way I was fired by Wenner, which also cancelled my life and health insurance. Nobody should be forgiven for that. That was kind of a turning point in our relationship. Then it just got worse, and everybody with any talent who has ever worked there was fired. Wenner just stopped caring about what was going on in the country. He just got into being a celebrity publisher.

BC: That happened to a lot of people of that generation.

HST: Well, it didn't happen to Bob Dylan. I was talking to him a few weeks ago out here, and he was asking me about what happened to *Rolling Stone.* I told him it was the greed, and fuck it, one of the most evident factors in the change in *Rolling Stone* was when he [Wenner] came out of the closet. And I don't know if there's any connection at all, but when he started hanging out with Ralph Lauren and the Velvet Mafia, the power and money, he just got into that life, and he cut himself off from his friends from the past and his wife, certainly, the editor of *Sports Illustrated* now, the editor of ESPN, hell all of our Black Alumni Club. I'm proud to be a member. We all are. Some of the best talent he ever had. Oh, Jesus, if you look at that group picture of the *Rolling Stone* taken in 1971, that was the very beginning. Annie

Leibovitz took the photo. It's in one of my letters books. It's a famous photo. Goddamn, just the names.

BC: Would you say that those were the golden years of American media?

HST: Yeah. During Watergate—but not for long after it—I really believed it was the beginning of a new era for American journalism. I thought we were heroes, and we had done heroic work getting Nixon out of there. I feel like part of a ring of what Nixon called "The Conspiracy." And there was a conspiracy between certain people. I thought we were going to develop a new generation of journalism and I'm still baffled at what happened. It did not get better or smarter. The word or the message did not get passed on.

BC: What exactly did happen to the American Dream?

HST: That's a big subject. It seems to me that history goes—in this country anyway—in eras of 20 years. Look at the period between 1960 and 1980—from the introduction of the birth control pill until the arrival of AIDS. That was distinctly 20 years. And then the generation 20 years after that, that's really like comparing two worlds. Everything seems to lead back to 1980 to the real beginning of the downfall of America. Living in this country is gonna be a different experience from now on, and nobody's gonna know or much less remember at all what it was like to live in the '60s or '70s. That was a very special 20-year period, and then 1980 to 2000 was a downhill slide.

BC: Were the 1960s a failure?

HST: Oh, hell no. Not by my light. There were a lot of failures, but it was the birthplace of the journalism and the writing and thinking that brought Nixon down and should have continued, but didn't after 1980. Carter was a good man. Compared to Bush, Carter was one of the best presidents ever. But since then, they were all Republicans—I don't have to stress that too much—Reagan and the Bushes. Clinton was all right. Whether he knew or not that all these people were stealing out of the stock market I can't say for sure. I think everybody knew, except the poor bastards that invested their life savings in retirement plans.

BC: Is democracy in America dead?

HST: Well, I think it's very ill and this administration wants to get rid of it. And it doesn't seem to be working when more than half the voters don't vote. Democracy just can't function without the participation of the "governed."

BC: Why don't the people participate?

HST: I don't really know. I don't think in terms of journalists as smart people. Just the best—and I'm talking about my own tribe here. That quality didn't disappear. It's just that the corporations took it over. Shit, Viacom now owns everything that I write for. Except *Vanity Fair.*

BC: Any predictions for the 2004 presidential election?

HST: Well, I don't see any other way possible to stop this frenzied Jesus freak, this *Kingdom of Fear,* except by beating Bush in 2004. The last election was stolen. Imagine how they'll have to scramble to make sure they win this election. We're the enemy now, and we're going to have to pay attention in '04. That's one way of possibly stopping this runaway train and the fall of the empire. It's crumbling.

BC: So you think America will be finished soon?

HST: Yeah. Or at least what they're still trying to claim it represents. What? Freedom? Democracy? Excellence? I don't think we're making much progress in those areas. This is not a free country.

BC: You write a lot about civil liberties and our continual loss of them.

HST: "Giving them up" is what it is, goddamnit! This "loss" . . . I'm tired of people . . . Never mind. I'm getting kind of wild.

BC: Go ahead.

HST: Ahhhhhhhh Gooood!!!!

BC: So what's at stake?

HST: What's at stake? The difference between journalists covering the Vietnam War and covering this war. The weird thing is that this [*New York Times*] story says—and it is true—that the journalists like it. "Reporters Respond Eagerly to Pentagon Welcome Mat." Now if that's not Hitler, if that's not the Third Reich . . . Well, this is the Fourth Reich, I'll just come out and say it. It's getting wild up here. I was talking to Charlie Rose on the air last week or the week before, and when I compared Hitler to George Bush, goddamn, they cut it. That was impossible for even me to say in New York. That was over the line. So I'm just telling you in case you want to read *The Rise and Fall of the Third Reich* again.* Hitler is an apt and very good comparison to this regime, this fucking crusade. It's all the same. Same plan. Same old format.

Goddamn, I've really wandered far afield. I was concentrating on sports when you called. We really covered the, uh—heh, heh—territory there.

---

* The book *The Rise and Fall of the Third Reich* is a comprehensive history of Nazi Germany by journalist William L. Shrier. The bestselling book was first published in 1960.

High Times—September 2, 2003

The Gonzo King

BY MATT HIGGINS

Gonzo journalist Dr. Hunter S. Thompson is a survivor. During his career of 40-odd years Thompson has survived a stomping by the Hell's Angels, a running feud with Richard Nixon, and a dubious sexual assault and drug case, all while consuming superhuman quantities of drugs and alcohol. At age 65, this heavyweight of American letters is still fighting, still smoking, and still churning out humorous and propulsive prose with his latest book/memoir, *Kingdom of Fear: Loathsome Secrets of a Star-Crossed Child in the Final Days of the American Century* (Simon & Schuster). His weapons are his words, and his victims are those who would cheapen the American Dream. Thompson talked to *High Times* as bombs were being dropped on Iraq about subjects dear to him: pot, politics, war, and the law.

High Times: How are you doing?

HST: I won a big legal case today. I didn't win it. We won it, of course. You asked, "How are you doing," and I'm saying, "We won a big legal case today." I think *High Times* would be real interested in it. Well, shit, it's pretty quick. Maybe two years ago I decided to get involved with what was then a murder case in Denver. A cop was killed. A skinhead committed suicide, they say. A girl, Lisl Auman, who was only vaguely connected to the skinhead, if that, was put in prison for murder for the rest of her life, with no parole.

High Times: You write about this in *Kingdom of Fear*.

HST: Yes. Well, the Supreme Court in Colorado yesterday agreed to hear her case soon, based on one question in the appeal, which was turned down by the appeals court, so we appealed it higher, to the state Supreme Court. To my surprise really, they agreed that they would hear it. Which means that our chances of success have gone from zero—prison for life—to about fifty-fifty. Pretty good.

High Times: That's great.

HST: Yeah, we got on that case with the lawyers from the National Association for Christian . . . what is it? It's not Christian. I'm watching these goddamn Jesus freaks raving all over television. Christ, Where was I? I just smoked some hash, actually. Oh yes, the NACDL, the National Association for Criminal Defense Lawyers. I'm the poet laureate of the NACDL.

High Times: How did you get involved with them?

HST: Shit, I was on the board of NORML. On the national advisory board, and I got to know these people. Needless to say, a lot of criminal lawyers there. When I got busted about ten years ago, these guys, along with my master lawyer, Hal Haddon from Denver, came and rescued me. These guys have one way or another come out of NORML and the politics of the '70s and '80s. They helped me completely and totally destroy a nasty case against me. We got to know each other and we got to be friends. It's very much like a political campaign, with horrible stakes for the losers. If I had lost this, I would no doubt have ended up in prison doing time.

I really appreciate the guys who came over the hill, like Keith Stroup* from NORML. I came to know these guys through the Mitchell brothers [Artie and Jim], and we formed the Fourth Amendment Foundation. The purpose was to have a lawyer—a big one—available at all times in all fifty states. We did a lot of thinking about it, but our purpose was to make it a fact in law that the state had to pay the legal expenses of anybody the state accused of a crime and failed to convict.

The case we took on in Denver was a convicted cop-killer. They don't get much worse than that. But all these cases . . . the mind is running at top speed here. Stop! Get a grip on yourself! I was thinking that since we do have a choice of winning the coin toss, pick a good case, a winnable case. The NACDL filed a friend-of-the-court brief, they brought their muscle to the appeal. This was the public defender's office in Denver, a broad coalition of people, including Benicio del Toro and Warren Zevon.

High Times: Does this apply to the dictum that appears in *Kingdom of Fear:* "All that it takes for evil to prevail is for good men to do nothing"? Do the Lisl Auman case and your interest in protecting the Fourth Amendment lie in that sentiment?

HST: Well, my thinking is that's where all of our interest lies. Bobby Kennedy used it the first time I noticed it. It's a universal sentiment. How

---

* Keith Stroup is a criminal defense attorney and founder of NORML.

the shit did I get myself involved in all this? To say, "For evil to prevail" sounds like a distant possibility. It's not going to happen right away—but no! It's happening right now in this fucking savage year. Evil is triumphing. It's right in front of us and it's on us as individuals personally and collectively. It's not going to be down the line. You know, civil rights aren't just for Negroes. Oh, shit, where did that come from? Bobby Kennedy said that.

That's what *Kingdom of Fear* was based on. It all came true much faster than I thought it was going to. It started off as a benign kind of memoir, and in a very short period of time, events like politics . . . That's us. That's you and me fighting over there, paying for those bombs. I guess I'm a little embarrassed of my generation as the first one in a long time in America, maybe forever, to leave the world, the country, the nation, in worse shape than when we inherited it.

High Times: You wrote about the death of the American Dream in *Fear and Loathing in Las Vegas.* Now the country is currently at war, and the Constitution is under attack by the Justice Department. Do you feel like it was a prophecy when you wrote about these things thirty years ago?

HST: That's exactly what I'm saying. Prophecy? It kind of looks like that now. What did Edward Abbey call me, a seer?* It's one of the highest compliments ever been paid by Abbey or by anybody. A seer: one who sees things. But there's really nothing mystic about it. We could all see it coming. Some saw it and some not. I don't know if we want to get into this war with Iraq. Let's save that question for later. As you can see I'm very sped up here and acting wild.

High Times: Do you still smoke marijuana?

HST: Of course I do. Why would I quit?

High Times: As someone who's reputed to have tried every drug out there, is there one that's your favorite?

HST: I would say that acid is still walking with the King. After all these years, it's almost always pleasant. I would say acid is my favorite. I don't do it that often. You might want to be careful with it. But it is the real thing. Now I'm talking LSD-25, not what you might buy on some market today. Real LSD-25 is the king of drugs. I use it. I don't necessarily recommend it. I don't recommend anything that I do.

---

* Edward Abbey was an American writer and environmental essayist. His books include *The Monkey Wrench Gang* and *Desert Solitaire.*

High Times: Is there a drug that you would absolutely never try again?

HST: Oh shit, yes. One that particularly comes to mind is PCP. Hell, I hear about a drug I would not try every day—drugs I cannot even tell you about or repeat the names of, or something that puts you into a steroid rage. Oh, yeah. That's the newest one. It's a supreme downer. It's like a 'roid rage. Downers in general and drugs like that just get you fucked up. I always said that drugs are no excuse and neither is booze. I hold myself to that standard and other people too.

High Times: There was a referendum last year that would have legalized marijuana in Nevada. I think people were optimistic, but then it was defeated. Why do you think there's still resistance to decriminalizing marijuana?

HST: Well, what you're telling me is old news. That's in the NORML files. We fought that battle a long time ago. That's the same thing we were talking about earlier. I'm surprised, shocked really. Christ, we got marijuana decriminalized in like twenty-five states in a very short time [Actually, it was 11—Ed.]. We kicked Nixon out of the White House, ended the war in Vietnam. It was a bitch of a time—a very special twenty years. At the time my war with Nixon was a symbol of a larger war, what Nixon brought in with him. All of that now is being trashed by the Justice Department—everything that we stood for.

High Times: It seems that the Justice Department has zeroed in on the medical-marijuana movement in California.

HST: Wait a minute. California's worked and then that goddamn shithead . . . what's his name? Ashcroft. They overruled the California Supreme Court, and it was still a federal crime in California even though it wasn't a crime in state law. So they went in and busted all these medical-marijuana growers. The marijuana laws are getting tougher. It all has the look of a glaze of Nazism, and it looks very much like the Third Reich. I've been rereading *The Rise and Fall of the Third Reich*. Have you ever read it?

High Times: No.

HST: It will scare the shit out of you. Maybe it won't. This country has never been invaded or bombed. That's one of the reasons, of course. The Pentagon thinking started during World War I: If you must go to war, make sure it's not on our soil. So they decided we must go to war.

High Times: You mentioned Nixon. I know you're no fan of the current president. How do you think George W. Bush compares to Nixon?

HST: This administration makes Nixon and his people look like a gang of liberals. Almost goofy, childlike. The mentality, the atmosphere around the Watergate trial. That was fun. Yeah, I'm proud of my fight.

High Times: Well, you won.

HST: Lots of people were resigned in the '60s to the Vietnam War. It took a while to turn even the president around on that. We did run Lyndon Johnson out of office. I was quite proud of that. And then Nixon. That was two in a row. Winning got to be a habit in a lot of ways. Winning is a habit, and failing is, too, or losing. The McGovern defeat in '72 didn't seem like the end of the world. We knew we were going to get Nixon. Watergate had already happened. It was like a pause in the real war. George McGovern is still saying the same thing, saying it eloquently, and is still right. I talk to him all the time.

It started with Reagan, this deconstruction of everything we had fought for and achieved since World War II. Yeah, I'm shocked and I have to look around me. I know how much more progress we had made, and the difference between that and the mood of the nation now is one universe away. This afternoon I was talking to Gary Hart and some other people on that kind of subject. My mind is going wild now. It was just a good focused time. We weren't winning, it turns out. How that happened in twenty years is really an interesting question. It's happened so fast, like the nation has plunged into something like World War II, which changed the world forever. But this was no goddamn World War II until we started it. The world is against this war, and I agree with the world. I'm used to being out of step.

The US sank the League of Nations, and this administration is hell-bent on sinking the UN. It's a tradition, but it looks to me like the forces of darkness have prevailed for a while. The evil that's down the road is here. It has a lot to do with people refusing to vote and calling it irrelevant. This is what happens when people don't vote. You think it's cool not to vote? Take a look around you, jackass!

High Times: How do you think the Bush administration has hoodwinked America into thinking this war is the right course of action?

HST: No, I don't think many people outside the Pentagon or the White House really believe that. They have succeeded in selling that message. It always happens in times of war. But that's all the time now. Clinton came out today or yesterday saying, "It's time to forget our differences and get behind our president and pull for our troops." And Clinton was a jackass, or a treacherous bastard anyway. It's "You're either with us or against us" that I think they have sold.

Americans are cheap and chickenshit, and they're going along with the police state. I don't know why exactly, but we can go back in American history. There's been some war ever since I was born. There was a long period between World War I and II, but not very long. It's been pretty much a constant war.

Cheney was on TV last night repeating that thing that Saddam must be killed because he turned chemical weapons on his own people. They're classified as weapons of mass destruction. I remember a lot of gas being used against me. Shit, that CS gas and pepper gas would qualify as chemical weapons for sure. And this government used it during the '60s on many people, including me.

High Times: You mentioned Bill Clinton earlier. Do you feel, like a lot of people, that Clinton let America down?

HST: Come on! Bush has plunged us into a goddamn vicious stupid foreign war, and Clinton let the country down by getting a blowjob in his office? I'd like to talk to somebody on TV and have them ask that question. That's a good one: "Do you think that Clinton let the country down in the context of a political discussion and Bush and the war?"

High Times: Do you think he fulfilled the promise a lot of people had for him, or do you think he failed to fulfill that promise?

HST: He did a lot better than Bush has. In two years, this little, half-bright creep has taken the United States of America, a prosperous country, a nation at peace, to a dead-broke nation at war. How in the fuck could that happen? That gets back to our original question of generations, and how I felt a certain shame for mine because of these bastards. I respect power when it moves, as [Chicago] Mayor Daley used to say. I have to admit these bastards are good, like Hitler was good. Goddamn, you wouldn't even compare Clinton to Bush. I don't know who you would compare Bush to. This is a whole new world for American politics. The American Century did end with the year 2000.

I had a conversation with Bob Dylan last September. He was out here talking about the Bush administration, bitching about what they're doing now. Bob is one of the real heroes of our time. I said to him, "Goddamn it, we've got ourselves into a hell of a fight with these bastards. This gang is serious. They're not amateurs. They're not going to be as easy as Nixon was." He looked at me, and we could call it a wry smile, and said, "Yeah, yeah, but we don't have to join them."

Late Night with Conan O'Brien—November 6, 2003

Conan: All right everybody, my next guest wrote such classics as *Fear and Loathing in Las Vegas, Fear and Loathing on the Campaign Trail 1972,* and *Hell's Angels.* His latest book, *Kingdom of Fear,* is in bookstores now. Please welcome Hunter S. Thompson.

HST: Oh fuck . . . fucking chair . . .

Conan: Most people come around the front but you do things your way and that's cool. Sir, very nice to have you here.

HST: Yeah good to be here . . . yeah hi. (Shakes Conan's hand)

Conan: How are you? Good to have you. You and I had an experience once because you're a fan of firearms. You like to fire guns . . .

HST: I enjoy it, yeah . . .

Conan: You enjoy guns. You and I once. Remember the time we went out. You and I with a camera crew and we fired lots of guns.

HST: You bet. You bet. I'm remembering.

Conan: Clearly that had no impact on your life. That was a big moment for me. What was your impression of me? Did you think I was a good shot? Let's talk about me. How was I as a marksman? What'd you think?

HST: Me, me, me . . . yeah right.

Conan: *Late Night with who?* Not *Late Night with Hunter S. Thompson! Late Night with Conan O'Brien* man!

HST: I heard you had a drug problem, but this is horrible.

Conan: (Laughs) Those rumors are not true. Those are some good times you and I had, remember, we were firing those guns? Want to take a quick tour down memory lane. This was just a couple of years ago. I forget when this was. We've been doing this show . . .

HST: An original experience.

Conan: This is an original experience. Let's show this to the people.

(Video clip is shown where Conan and Hunter S. Thompson are drinking whiskey and shooting guns at a stuffed bear and a cardboard cut out of Bill Buckner.*)

---

* Bill Buckner is a retired Major League Baseball player.

Conan: Let's talk. It's a little controversial. Last year, it was a total accident and your assistant is fine now, but you accidentally shot your assistant. Let's talk about that.

HST: Well, it was not that way. She rushed into the path of a shotgun pellet.

Conan: So you were shooting a shotgun and your assistant happened to be in the way?

HST: I was shooting at a bear in front of her door . . .

Conan: There's a bear in front of her door?

HST: Uhuh. So I called her and said, "Don't go out your door, there's a bear there." And I was pissed off. Anita got me out of bed and said, "There's a bear outside." I just wanted to move it. It was right outside of her door. She'd step on it.

Conan: Did you think for a second of using the McConaughey* method of rushing the bear? And hugging it and caressing it? No this is your method. It's quite different.

HST: Laughs. Well. Mine works.

Conan: So you shot at the bear and what happens? She came out the door around the same time?

HST: Walked right . . . Instead of not opening the door. Like the very thing, "Do not touch: wet paint." Bang. Right out the door just as I pulled the trigger. I didn't shoot at the bear; I shot at the gravel underneath it. So the rocks bounce up and it gets him. Stings him in the ass but it . . .

Conan: Doesn't hurt the bear.

HST: No. He got up kind of annoyed and lumbered off. But just as I pulled the trigger, Deborah stepped out her door and "Bang": bounce here, bounce there. I think two pellets. It embarrassed me. And embarrassingly it ruined my safety record.

(Audience laughs.)

Conan: Yeah. What a terrible thing for you. But your assistant is fine now.

HST: Oh yeah. She was fine in a hour. It made a lot of headlines and people got excited. "I wanted to kill the bitch. I lured her out there . . . "

Conan: Now you've been portrayed in film not just once but twice. Johnny Depp played you in *Fear and Loathing in Las Vegas.* And appar-

* Film actor Matthew McConaughey.

ently he practically lived with you and shadowed your every footstep so he could learn how to be Hunter S. Thompson. Is that true?

HST: Yeah. Yeah. He came out there—God dammit . . .

Conan: What's the matter?

HST: Never mind, never mind. See my shoes there? (Waves shoes to the audience.) Yeah I went and got these things. I made these shoes.

Conan: You made those? You didn't make those! Those have the Nike swoosh on them! You didn't make those! Hold that up. If you're making those shoes, why are you putting the Nike swoosh on them?

HST: Ah, it adds a kind of panache to it, you know what I'm saying?

Conan: (Gesturing to his watch.) Yeah I made this myself. It's pretty nice. Isn't that nice? Something I like to wear.

HST: Yeah. I have my bracelet here too.

Conan: So Johnny Depp, he lived with you?

HST: Yeah. It was weird. No a serious actor will apparently. Well Johnny is serious. The bastard moved in and we had to put him in a cell in the basement.

Conan: Johnny Depp slept in your basement?

HST: Yeah. A guest room sort of. But it's a dark, dark place. There is all kinds of books in it. It also had in it, well—he discovered a keg of dynamite. Well, actually flash powder. Gunpowder—right next to his bed.

Conan: What was dynamite doing right next to his bed? Why do you have all this dynamite?

HST: Well. For bombs.

Conan: Well. If you're going to be making some bombs, it's good to have dynamite around. If you're making a cake, have some flour.

HST: Mentioning bombs or making bombs. Don't talk to me about that. What do you mean making bombs? Why do you want to make bombs?

Conan: I'm . . . I'm guilty. How did this get turned around to me? I'm not making bombs. You're the one making bombs and fake Nike sneakers in your basement. What am I doing? I'm not doing anything. You know what? This is ridiculous. We don't have any time. There is so much. We haven't even gotten to—but we're completely out of time. You have to come back. We have to talk about all these things.

HST: Let me just explain one thing to you. That this is the Kingdom of Fear as I say here. You are the perfect example of being a victim. It's clearly rattled you badly.

Conan: I'm a victim?

HST: Yeah.

Conan: How do you say I'm a victim? Look at me. I'm happy-go-lucky. I'm a happy guy.

HST: Yeah, me too. That good.

Conan: He just touched me. And I liked it. *Kingdom of Fear,* by Hunter S. Thompson, is out there right now. Go out there and get this book. Sir, thank you very much for being here, for making time for us. We'll take a break, everybody. We'll be right back. Stick around.

Freezerbox.com—March 9, 2004

The Hunter S. Thompson Interview

BY ADAM BULGER

Bulger: (To Answering Machine) I had an interview scheduled with Hunter Thompson—

(Explosion of music over the telephone)

HST: Hey hey hey hi. Sorry, this thing is just dragging on longer than I thought. I'll call you, I'd imagine, in like ten minutes.

Bulger: OK. Sure.

Bulger: (TWENTY MINUTES LATER) Hello?

HST: I got caught up in some goddamn weird old English romance of some kind.

Bulger: Was it something you were writing, or reading?

HST: I was watching a movie. (Yelling to someone in the room) *Sense and Sensibility,* I think. I couldn't believe it, I was wrapped up in this ancient goddamned thing.

Bulger: Jane Austen, right?

HST: Yes, it is.

Bulger: I've never seen it, I think I've read the book, though.

HST: Goddamn, I must be in a unique mood of some kind because I got completely into it.

Bulger: Really. I wouldn't think you'd like that.

HST: I wouldn't either. I've never been into Jane Austen, particularly. But that was well done. A nicely done movie.

Bulger: OK, then. What is the state of the American dream today?

HST: Oh, god. That's a pretty pre-thought out, written-on-a-list kind of question. Not very good. Yeah, I would say not. The American Dream ran out with the American century. I'm still figuring it out. That's a pretty strong statement. I'm still putting the pieces together right now.

Bulger: What do you think Horatio Alger would do if he was alive today?

HST: He'd probably be a terrorist.

Bulger: Do you think it's possible for a man to be free in present-day America?

HST: Well, it depends on who it is. I'm doing pretty well. I don't know about you. I have a feeling it's going to be more of a struggle than it's been for a while.

Bulger: Why's that?

HST: Look around you. The military state we're being formed into—shit, I wrote about this last night. The military structure—did you read the book I just wrote?

Bulger: Yeah. *Kingdom of Fear.* I thought it was a very apt title.

HST: Yeah, more so than I realized when I came up with it.

Bulger: What do you think of the state of political journalism?

HST: Very bad. Very lazy and almost cowardly in its obsequiousness.

Bulger: What important questions are they not asking?

HST: God damn, man. Who wrote these questions for you?

Bulger: I did.

HST: Well, they're all kind of pertinent, but let's take a break and kind of work up to some of these.

Bulger: OK. I'm going to ask you some more softball questions. What are you driving these days and what's its top speed?

HST: Oh Jesus, you really are one of these, aren't you? It's snowing out. I drive a Jeep Cherokee through the snow.

Bulger: If they offered you the post of the governor of Samoa today would you accept it?

HST: Oh. That's interesting. Well, yeah, if I thought I could really have free hand. It would be an adventure. I'd try it for a year.

Bulger: You're the last public figure to use a cigarette holder. What's the deal?

HST: For one thing, it is not a holder. It is a filter. A big difference. A filter clears a full ounce of scum and tar a day, keeps it from ruining my lungs. The first time I used it, I saw what came out of a filter and I never stopped.

Bulger: How does that compare with your double life as a character in the *Doonesbury* comic strip?

HST: Well that's a horrible piece of shit. I got used to it a long time ago. I used to be a little perturbed by it. It was a lot more personal. The bastard was, well, I don't read it or follow it. It no longer bothers me.

Bulger: What's the best drug to write on?

HST: You've got dumb questions.

Bulger: Um, sorry. Have you ever done Ecstasy?

HST: Yeah. It seemed kind of mild and talky. I didn't mind it. It's not in the nature of the kind of drug I am normally accustomed to, it was a quasi-drug, I guess.

Bulger: What kind of music are you listening to?

HST: Let's see. I just got the new Bob Dylan box set from the Rolling Thunder tour from 1975. It's kind of a big package with a book and several CDs in there. It's maybe the best rock and roll album I've ever heard.

Bulger: You don't think that was after his peak?

HST: Shit. You really are dumb. You have to listen to it and find out. If you think that, you really are ignorant. What do you want to talk about—Eminem?

Bulger: Is writing still fun for you?

HST: Yes.

Bulger: What's the best firearm for home security?

HST: Twelve-gauge short-barrel shotgun.

Bulger: And what's the best for just fucking around?

HST: Machine guns are kind of nice. You can have a lot of fun with them. It's like watering the lawn. I don't get to play with them very often.

Bulger: Ralph Steadman said that you almost killed him in a gun-related explosion while he was visiting you in Aspen. What happened?

HST: I don't know that story, but no doubt it's right. I can think of several times. Ralph is well acquainted with my lifestyle.

Bulger: He also said that you claim that you are one of the few people who should be allowed to own a handgun, and he said that you definitely shouldn't be allowed to own one.

HST: (Laughs) Ralph is one person who definitely shouldn't be allowed to drink whiskey.

Bulger: Why's that?

HST: I'll wait for his reason why I shouldn't have handguns. Whiskey is not beneficial for Ralph.

Bulger: You were a very vocal critic of the Clinton administration, but you were in correspondence with Sandy Berger, Clinton's [national security advisor]. Are you guys still friends?

HST: Oh, yeah, definitely, he's a good boy. I disagree with a lot of my friends. Just because he's my friend doesn't mean he has to agree with me.

Bulger: Are you still in touch with Patrick Buchanan?

HST: Occasionally. We're still friends. Patrick is a libertarian, or at least in that direction. I think of politics as a circle, not a spectrum of one line not just right and left. Patrick and I are often pretty close. Patrick's an honest person. He's a straight guy and very smart guy.

His magazine, the *American Conservative,* is really interesting. It's all anti-Bush, basically.

I'm pleased with that. I frequently agree with him. He's an intelligent—you might call him a politician.

Bulger: He did run for President a couple of times.

HST: Yeah, he's a politician.

Bulger: Why exactly did you try to deliver an elk's heart to Jack Nicholson's house?

HST: I thought it would be fun and it's in the spirit of our relationship. A little humor. I don't know, it just came to me tonight. I had a few bombs, you know. We do that pretty frequently, exchange bizarre presents. I couldn't have foreseen the horrible circumstances around it. He had just gotten in from LA. I didn't know it, but he had a stalker. I saw him the afternoon he got in. I said I'd see him later. I figured, shit, I have some presents for the kids. I was supposed to get there a little earlier. I feel a little queasy looking back on the night. Of course it was all in good humor. It went wrong in so many weird ways. I went out there and sort of did my thing and left, feeling rejected sort of. Bear in mind I was pretty much wanked up, in the mood I frequently get in with Jack. He's pretty fast. He's one of the natural aristocrats of our time.

Bulger: He's fast?

HST: Oh, yeah, we have a good time talking. Jack is quick. One of the smartest people I know.

Bulger: What do you think of how the Hell's Angels have gone mainstream?

HST: Don't confuse the Hell's Angels that I wrote about with what the Hell's Angels are now. I consider Sonny Barger to be a friend of mine.

Bulger: Really. Even after his boys beat you up?

HST: Shit, he didn't do it. You swim with sharks, you're going to get bit once in a while. I wasn't surprised by that. In fact, I thought it was long overdue by the time it happened. I always got along fine with Sonny. I haven't seen him in a while. He's an extreme case of a sociopath, but I like him.

Bulger: After Altamont, too.

HST: That was way over the line. I've seen stuff like that before. Not kill people in that sense, but I wasn't surprised at all at the Angels' behavior. That's what they do. The Stones and Rock Scully,* the people who decided to have the Angels as their personal security, I would blame them.

You would blame the incident on whoever chose the Angels as security.

HST: Right. I don't know who I would have chosen, but that's a guarantee of an explosion and a disaster.

Bulger: Do you ever watch Fox News?

HST: Very rarely.

Bulger: What do you think of their level of discourse?

HST: I think it's low and dumb.

Bulger: I heard that you and Allen Ginsberg had the same weed dealer in the '60s.

HST: That's an obscure and arcane story, isn't it? But yeah, yeah. I had met him before in New York during his poetry readings and things. In San Francisco, it turned out that we did have the same weed dealer. That's when you bought weed in tins, tobacco tins. Ten dollars, fifteen. I lived in an apartment right next door to the guy he was buying it from. I was working on the Hell's Angels book. I got to talk to him about it, and he was a big help. Allen was a good one.

Bulger: You liked him a lot.

HST: He was the real thing, in the way. He was involved in everything. Allen was a gentleman and an honest man. He was fun, wonderful sense of humor. He helped me with the book. He took some time.

Bulger: How was he in a crisis?

HST: He did that ohm thing (starts chanting) OOOOOOOOOOOOHH HHHM. He just tried to hum it away. I first saw that in La Honda. There were cops, he was trying to get people out of jail. I was being a journalist. I had more or less a neutral zone pass. I could go back and forth between the Angels and the cops. I could negotiate. I had gone down there. My son was two years old at the time.

Bulger: In La Honda?

HST: No, I was out in Sonoma. I went down to La Honda for a little fun. I took my kid with me. Fun, you know. Allen and I got in a police chase. I

* Rock Scully is a San Francisco Bay area concert promoter and the former manager of the Grateful Dead from 1965 to 1985.

was driving. The cops had pulled some people over. It was a madhouse over there, that whole La Honda scene. Blinking, blazing, lights going on all the time. I know that I've described that someplace else, so I won't get into it. We stopped to intercede on some other arrest the cops were making. As a journalist I could do that.

Bulger: You have claimed to be the most accurate reporter people could read. A lot of people would disagree. How would you defend that claim?

HST: With the exception of typos, I have some ungodly typos in my work. In terms of my . . . I might not get the dates right every once in a while. I try to be more accurate than other journalists, which is not that difficult. You have to distinguish between what happened and what the situation was. I'm not doing a very good job of this. And imagination.

Bulger: Do you think that's due to your willingness to put objectivity by the wayside?

HST: Well, you can't be objective when you're dealing with passionate situations, politics and so forth. I guess you can, I never have. For instance if you were objective about Richard Nixon, you would never get him or understand him. You had to be subjective to understand Nixon. You have to be subjective to understand the Hell's Angels. Would you be objective about Altamont, I guess. A million people gathered, a riot started. I was supposed to be there.

Bulger: Oh yeah?

HST: I took one look at it on the last day and figured fuck this. Like a million people. Guaranteed explosion and disaster. Imagine having gone in there early and going down by the stage and not having a helicopter to get you out? I know people who were trapped under there for eight hours! Just horrible . . . then I don't know . . . it [inaudible] of police brutality. I can't really be objective. I can claim I am. Well, I mean, free press, street press, it's the goddamned street press right now that's the only, that's doing this job with us, on us, with Bush and passing propaganda. Just, uh—disgusting!

Bulger: The mainstream press, you mean?

HST: Yeah, the mainstream press is uh, is uh, in the bag, in the pocket of Bush and the military and they seem to like it there! Not all of them, I've got a lot of good friends, good people in journalism, that feel more strongly than I do, or at least as strongly.

Bulger: Right.

HST: The uh, *New York Times,* eh, yeah, it's a different animal. There's not too many papers like that. But the press in general, the media, the TV, is doing a disgraceful job in covering this situation in this country and around the world. This is where I have to bring some subjectivity into it that I believe is right! A president that came in here, uhhh . . . about two years ago . . .

Bulger: Right, barely elected.

HST: Barely elected, yeah, and I guess it's only been two years, and he's taken this nation from a, uh, um, let me think looking at it from a, uh, just objectively, from a prosperous nation at peace to a broke nation at war.

Bulger: Right, but I mean, there were those assholes who flew the plane into the World Trade Center.

HST: Who were they indeed? Now, (cough) do you believe that, that a bunch of Arabs jumped up from some kind of a campfire and fucking mountains over there and snuck into this country and hijacked those planes and did that by themselves?

Bulger: Well what are you proposing? I mean I think they were funded years ago by the CIA and it was a blowback, but, I don't think there was any direct . . . Are you saying there might be some other American agency or some international agency that directly supported them in that?

HST: Uhh, this is tricky territory, but yeah, that's what I'm getting at.

Bulger: Really.

HST: I can't sit here and jerk up documents like Joe McCarthy,* there's no proof of that. But I'm sure there is. And the idea that we're getting the whole story, uh, through the uh, the media, or from the president, is absurd on its face because you never do, for one thing. And there's so many unanswered questions and loose ends and uh, let's see, well, lies! Yeah, about what happened. That they, in the run-up to that day, the years, I wrote a column about it right after it happened.

Bulger: Yeah, I've read it. I thought that was great, the thing about your phone conversation with Johnny Depp, right?

HST: Yeah, that was one of them. Yeah, that one and the one right before it. I was just finishing my sports film for ESPN when, I was about to go to bed, and I had been up all night, you know the usual, you know struggle, deadline . . .

Bulger: Mmhmm.

---

* Joseph McCarthy was a Republican senator from Wisconsin. He served in office from 1947 to 1957. McCarthy is infamous for his anti-communist "witch hunt" and trials of suspected Soviet sympathizers and spies at work in the United States during the Cold War.

HST: And sort of on my way to bed, I saw something on the, heard or saw, something about a plane hitting the World Trade Tower. The first reports were of the "small plane"—like one of those things that sometimes hits buildings around the world. That got my attention just enough not to go straight to bed. I turn around and have a look at the TV set, just in time to see that other one go straight in. Jesus.

Bulger: Um . . .

HST: Hang on a second there . . . there's so many things about who uh, oh boy, this is a dangerous area. But I talked to witnesses, I'm just thinking of one in particular, a guy, a driver who watched the, just happened to be taking uh, maybe the owner of the Giants, I forget who he was, but he was out at the Meadowlands. But he saw both of them hit.

Bulger: Right.

HST: Direct line of sight. The first one, he didn't get really get a line on, but it got his attention, though he hadn't seen the approach. But the second one, he said, uh, and I heard this from other people, but very few, really, calm and sane accounts the moments of insanity. I happened to see the second one go in, but just the last few seconds, as it came out of the left, stage left, and then plowed right into the front of the center of the TV picture and the center of the building, uh, perfectly. And I wrote that it was one of the most efficient, uh, most skillful and just about impossible um, acts of piloting . . . That's a very rare, uh, uh pilot . . . can take a big plane and plant it right as if a target or bull's-eye was on the side of the building. Apparently that second plane approached, and veered off, and made sort of a half-loop and then sort of came back and aimed again and then hit the building.

Bulger: Right.

HST: Have you heard this, or did you see that, or do you know about it?

Bulger: Yeah, well I've seen the tape so many times.

HST: But have you seen what would be before the tape that we see, like a minute before the hit?

Bulger: No, I haven't.

HST: Well, I haven't either, really. But there were eyewitnesses. And several people have said that, but you had to be watching. This guy happened to be at the Meadowlands. 'Cause I've kind of seen it as something that's really horrible and atrocious but not that hard to pull off. I mean it just seems like they got some box-cutters and they hijacked a plane and they flew it into a building. It doesn't seem like there was that much skill or that much preparation really. It's pretty broadly assumed that there's a lot more to that story than the uh, the simple, kind of evil guys who just wanted to learn enough about flying to take a plane off but not land it.

Bulger: Right.

HST: Remember, everything we know about that, that incident, and it was a horrible thing, I mean tragedy! Uh, and about Iraq and about Afghanistan and the people allegedly inside those countries, you know, Bin Laden . . . Everything we know in this country is spun through the CIA or NSA, but let's call it the CIA.

Bulger: No, they want to spread democracy now, that's the message.

HST: Well I've been dealing with these guys for forty years. I've been covering politics and I was in the air force and I've been around this kind of thing. I know something about the structures and behavior of the military, politics, the White House. And it gives you a certain perspective, at least to ask questions.

Bulger: Yeah, your depth of knowledge and personal experience . . .

HST: Well, plus if you go back and read some of the things I've written, I don't stand by that first column I wrote on the World Trade Tower tragedy. Like I said, I was just going to bed, and they called back and said, "you gotta write another column about the bombing in New York." Nobody really knew what it was. And I wrote a column, and it's in the book.

Bulger: What newspapers and magazines are you reading right now?

HST: Well, I mean lemme look here, *New York Times, New York Observer, The Nation,* uh, *Consumer Reports, Sports Illustrated.* Now I look up and I see the *Statistical Abstract of the United States* . . . I see *Legal Affairs,* uh, let's see, *Time, National Geographic, Foreign Affairs Quarterly,* uh, *The Progressive, The Economist.* It goes on and on. It's a, it's a load. But I find that I really stay uh, more, certainly not more knowledgeable out here than I would be if I were in Washington, but the people I know and can call and then see frequently, I stay pretty well informed out here. There's a network that has taken me forty years to cultivate and build.

Bulger: The end of your ESPN columns it says you live in a fortified compound in Aspen. How exactly is it fortified?

HST: Well it's not really fortified, it's, I put that in there I guess, it helps me keep gawkers away. And it helps to—somebody gets shot out here every once in a while.

Bulger: You get shot out there?

HST: There was a story about me shooting my secretary a while ago. It was bogus. But now I have, it keeps me a little bit, it keeps people from being too eager to rush in here and knock on the door. I had a lot of that. Huge amount of curiosity seekers.

Bulger: Ok. What do you think of um, I'm sorry, I'm getting back to my list of questions.

HST: You can tell that right away, "what do you think of? . . ."

Bulger: Yeah I know, I'm sorry man.

HST: Go ahead.

Bulger: What do you think of the state of America today versus when you were writing in the '60s and '70s?

HST: Ho, it's a whole different game. This is a corporate state, really. Pretty much on the order of uh . . .

Bulger: Like the Weimar Republic, kinda?

HST: Exactly. There we go! And it's National Socialism in a way, that would be a good conversation. Let's, wait, let's say something about that. Let me hear what do you think about that. I've been reading *The Rise and Fall of the Third Reich* again. I see parallels throughout the Third Reich to the extent where I often refer to this as the Fourth Reich.

Bulger: The post-American Century then.

HST: Well it's a convenient break you know, the new century. And it just happens to be that we started off with, well, you might call it a bang, you know? Why the voters in this country continue to vote for the same people who plunge them into economic doldrums and real trouble?

Bulger: Why do you think that is?

HST: That is what brings us I guess to the, uh, Third Reich and that comparison. It baffles me, enrages me. And I can't, it seems to me like simple stupidity.

Bulger: You think people are just dumb?

HST: Well, the education [in this] country, the patriotism, the boom boom drum, and the propaganda, and the cooperative media, yeah.

Bulger: Yes, that's why they weren't so opposed to getting the Nazis in.

HST: Exactly but, the country on paper, in a state of prosperity. And we know better about who was, you know, what stocks were really worth what. But, it was a prosperous country, seemingly, people weren't wheeling wheelbarrows of dollar bills through the streets to buy a loaf of bread. And, just to watch the quality of life in this country go down and down, and lesser expectations of happiness and freedom and discretionary income, leisure, all the things that seemingly defined this country, uh, in the past let's say 50 years. It has been . . . moving forward and upward, a lot of quarrels in there, a lot of things to argue about, but I don't think it has been, in most people's eyes, a nation where the current generation of children can, and does look forward to a standard of living lesser and lower than their parents. You know, not live as well.

Bulger: What's that?

HST: Oh, well it's the diminishing of personal expectations in this country. And the hope, the feeling of hope. I talk about this all the time to a lot of people: Are you more optimistic about the next ten years than about the last, when you started?

Bulger: Who, me?

HST: Yeah.

Bulger: No! I . . . man, not to rip you off, I'm full of fear and loathing. I am a citizen in the Kingdom of Fear. I'm scared every waking moment, man.

HST: Well, uh, Jesus, that's horrible! That's a kind of prevailing sentiment.

Bulger: Yeah.

HST: And you know, you look at fear and people, a population that's just riddled with fear and confusion and, loathing, goddamn. Never did it occur to me when I came up with those words that I would be using them to describe the state of the nation 30 years later.

Bulger: Yeah, you said that 30 years ago, and fear keeps coming through in your works. I mean it's so powerful, like your use of it. And I was just kinda wondering what you're fearing right now.

HST: Well I don't, I'm past fearing things. I'm old enough to, not really worry about some of the things that maybe I once did. I'm a successful writer, I'm . . .

Bulger: I just had one last question, and it kind of plays into what we were just talking about. Your friend Warren Zevon was diagnosed with inoperable cancer. [Warren Zevon died on September 7, 2003—Ed.]

HST: Yep.

Bulger: And I just wanted to know how you have reacted to this, if you've mellowed out at all, if this has kind of affected what you're fearing, or your concept of fear.

HST: Well, no, I'm very sad about Warren's situation, but I think it's my job to console him, or to ignore it. They're all quacks out there, and many people have come through fatal prognosis. I assigned him to write the music for this movie we're working on here, the *Rum Diary.*

Bulger: I'm curious about why you're doing the kinda sports-centric thing with ESPN. I know you started as a sports journalist, but . . .

HST: I got a soft spot in my heart for sports and what the hell, I bet on it, I'm into it all the time, I might as well make some money on it. One of the things I think I've learned over time is I have to make movie on, excuse me, money on, I have to get paid for my vices somehow, or else it's gonna be destructive. If you're paid for being crazy, then you're not crazy, is that right?

Bulger: And when the going gets weird, the weird turn pro.

HST: I think the real difference is functional and dysfunctional rather than sane or insane. And John Walsh at ESPN is an old friend. And I like it, it keeps me, the column kept me kind of sane, a regular deadline every week. I have to finish it and read it the next day. I like the regularity of it. I grew up in newspapers. And it just gives me a nice little break every week.

Bulger: Well, that was my last question.

HST: Well, that's, uh, good luck! And you're going to need it.

Bankrate.com—November 1, 2004

Hunter S. Thompson: Surprised He's Still Here

BY JAY MACDONALD

Bankrate: "Hey, Rube," your weekly sports column on ESPN.com, kind of completes a circle for you, having started out as a sportswriter, right?

HST: A lot of people start in sports writing. It's kind of a taproot. It's great because you can use fun words, all the adjectives you can put in there.

Bankrate: Were those lean times for you?

HST: Oh, yeah, man. If you've been a sportswriter under any circumstances that are normal, you would know what that lifestyle is like, living in basement apartments.

Bankrate: Some of your funniest letters have been browbeating, expletive-dense tirades directed at editors who owed you money.

HST: Normally you get paid on newspapers or you get fired, it's a pretty clear-cut choice. But being a freelancer, you never know if the things that you send out are going to bear fruit and create a river of gold for you. They never seem to come through, and it's the weird ones that you don't expect. That's been my experience.

Bankrate: You've been particularly scathing to Jann Wenner, editor and founder of *Rolling Stone*.

HST: Oh Christ, yeah. Yeah, he never paid on time. Never has, never will. Ask all my good friends: You're nobody in the publishing world if you haven't been fired by *Rolling Stone*. Two come to mind right away, the editor of *Sports Illustrated* (Terry McDonnell) and the editor of ESPN.com (John Walsh). It's a really distinguished alumni. He didn't pay them either.

Bankrate: Did you jump at the chance to do a weekly sports column?

HST: I always like to have an immediate outlet. I wasn't really looking for that, but John Walsh, who has been a friend of mine for 30 years from *Rolling Stone*, came out here with a couple other guys. I like writing columns. The lag time between when a piece is due and when it's published can be very disturbing to me. Those small, quick ideas that pass through your mind, a column gives you an opportunity to spit them out.

Bankrate: "Hey Rube" is filled with gambling stories, one of your favorite pastimes.

HST: I like gambling. I learn a lot about people when I gamble with them. If you bet on just about every play in a football game plus the outcome of the game, it will come out pretty close to even. We make bets here while the ball is in the air all the time.

Bankrate: Did you gamble during the lean years?

HST: Well, I hate to say it, but yeah. I wasn't taking the milk money, that sort of thing, but I'm kind of a believer in gambling. Sports and gambling are just my constant factor, a red thread through my life. That's sort of a background, sports.

Bankrate: Is there anything you wouldn't bet on?

HST: Well, I don't do much betting when I go to Las Vegas. I don't like the machines. You know what's going to happen when you go in there, on the numbers. If you bet every roll of the dice, if you can live through your bad times, the odds are you'll come out pretty close to even, but if you don't bet on all of them, you never can tell how you're going to come out. You bet on, well, not hunches; I've been in this business a long time, you're bound to learn something.

(At this point, Thompson takes another call, also on speaker phone, from a friend who tells him he just saw Hunter's appearance on an old episode of *To Tell the Truth*.)*

HST: Holy s—! No, that was my second appearance. I was on an earlier afternoon show, really early, like 1961, and Johnny Carson was the interviewer. I thought I was pretty cool; I saw an ad in the *New York Times*. It was a show where you paired up with a strange woman, in my case, but the point of it was, you made $50. If you have a good story and you want to tell it on TV, come on.

Bankrate: Sounds like *Who Do You Trust?*

HST: Yeah, that must be it, I guess. And when the cameras came on, my knees began to knock. I had read about that and heard about it, people's knees knocking, and goddamn they actually were. And I looked over at the host,

---

* *To Tell The Truth* was an American game show produced by Bob Stewart. Hunter appeared on the game show in 1967.

and I didn't know Carson from Jim Baker, and he saw that I was trembling and shaking and he calmed me down. But I still lost the main prize.

Bankrate: Among your many bizarre encounters, your limousine ride with Richard Nixon during the 1972 presidential campaign was surely a high point.

HST: Oh, boy. The Raiders were playing against the Packers, which was Nixon's team, and nobody else on the press bus could talk about it, they were afraid of Nixon on football. He was known to be a hard rocker and very involved. And (press secretary) Patrick Buchanan—I've always liked Patrick Buchanan—he was looking for somebody to ride with the boss and talk football, and these other guys, political wizards, nobody volunteered. I was the only one on the press bus who volunteered.

Bankrate: You've been pretty outspoken in your dislike of our current commander in chief.

HST: I was candid about Nixon, too.

Bankrate: Yet you say Nixon pales in comparison to George W. Bush.

HST: Oh, yeah, he looks almost like a liberal. You look at the Clean Air Act* and several others back then. Nixon was a crook but at least he operated off of an individual base. But this yoyo, this stupid little . . . It's cheap opera. Take a look at your pocket. Take a look around you. It's a hold-up, a looting of the national treasury, and that's what they're doing. The combined spending of the Kerry campaign is far less than $5 million for advertising. Five million dollars, that's like a goddamned Susan Anthony dollar compared to $60 billion that is just routine going out to Halliburton. We might lose if we went to war with Halliburton.

Bankrate: You are neighbors with Prince Bandar, the Saudi ambassador and longtime Bush family friend featured in Michael Moore's *Fahrenheit 9/11*.

HST: I can see him from my front porch. He's been a pretty good neighbor; that counts for a lot out here. He will shoot some skeet now and then. I don't want to say anything really ugly about him. He's an enlightened plutocrat, I guess you call it. Michael Moore is dead right on that, and it's even worse than you think. Bandar. All kinds of roads cross out here. Networks and wires.

---

* In 1970, President Richard Nixon signed the Clean Air Act into law, allowing federal and state authorities to regulate industrial and automobile emissions.

Bankrate: The Bush Administration seems to have lit your fuse. Are you angry again?

HST: Very angry. I'm very angry. That's why I guess I have to write this (campaign) piece for *Rolling Stone*. This is the darkest hour that I have seen in my long experience as an American. This is evil.

Bankrate: As a betting man, what do you think of John Kerry's chances?

HST: If there is an election on schedule—if—I would say 60–40 Kerry right now. I think if we can get the sportswriter's vote, the dope fiend's vote and the Grateful Dead vote, that would make a big difference. Hating Bush is not enough. You've got to vote now in self-defense. If we have another administration like this, it will be so bad that what's happening now will look like a small breakfast for what's coming next.

Bankrate: Are you surprised at where you find yourself in life?

HST: No. Not at all. I mean, the fact that I'm here at all, yeah. But since I'm here, I'm not surprised. If you're going to be crazy, you have to get paid for it or else you're going to be locked up.

Playboy—May 2005

Post Cards from the Proud Highway

What follows is the final collaboration between Hunter Stockton Thompson and *Playboy,* based on a series of interviews he gave to Assistant Editor Tim Mohr last December. The two spent the better part of a week at Owl Farm analyzing a variety of subjects, from firearms to physical fitness, all of which interested Thompson deeply. "To live outside the law you must be honest," Bob Dylan wrote, but you must also possess great sensitivity to your environment and a wide range of esoteric skills and wisdom. In his 67 years on earth Thompson made himself an expert in matters great and small and loved nothing more than to expound on what he had learned. This assignment was interrupted by his death on February 20, but we could think of no better tribute to a great American writer than to present this small storehouse of vital knowledge in his own words. This is for old fans as well as those who may have come to the party only recently.—The Editors

ON FREEDOM

Freedom is a challenge. You decide who you are by what you do. It's like a question, like a fork in the road. An ongoing question you have to keep answering correctly. There's a touch of the high wire to it. I've never been able to walk high wires, but I get the feeling.

ON DRIVING

The only way to drive is at top speed, with a car full of whiskey. It takes commitment, especially out here with so many deer and elk around. Car lights paralyze deer. You've got to lean on the horn, brace on the wheel and stomp on the accelerator. When you hit the brakes the front of the car dips down—that will put the beast into your windshield. Now, the significant impact will still occur if you step on the gas, but you're not helpless. It'll still destroy your grille and lights, but—unless it's a bull elk—it will kick the animal out of the way. Hitting the beast head-on will move it instead of popping it up onto the windshield.

It's the swerving that gets people killed.

You know how powder snow is great for skiing? It's great for driving, too. You just have to know the limitations of the car if you're going to drive on snowy roads. Once you've done 360s and drifts, you know what the road is like. And I always test the brakes, just to be sure I'm not going to go 400 feet when I think I have a grip. Once you get yourself into a full-bore drift, just downshifting won't get you out of it. A combination of things can, but downshifting alone can get you out of it only on asphalt. And Jesus, driving on "all-weather" tires . . . I can't imagine driving on those. I use studded snow tires. The metal studs sound like a tank and wreak havoc on the roads, but they are like bear claws. The difference between hitting your brakes in a blizzard with snow tires and the all-weather tires they put on rental cars? Goddamn.

ON COURAGE

I set the speed record on Saddle Road—in Kona, on the Big Island of Hawaii—in a heavy rainstorm. There are always going to be things like monsoons when you're trying to set a speed record. What do you do? Think better of it? Come back another day? Your life will change on decisions like that. I take a street-fighter mentality, an Ohio riverboat gambler attitude: It's out of the question to go back or turn around.

ON VIOLENCE

Never hesitate to use force. It settles issues, influences people. Most people are not accustomed to solving situations by immediate and seemingly random applications of force. And the very fact that you are willing to do it—or might be—is a very powerful reasoning tool. Most people are not prepared to do that. You can establish the right reputation in this regard—you might, right in the middle of a conversation, just swat some motherfucker across the room. Make his blood shoot out in big spurts. I'm giving away trade secrets here.

I've been beaten worse in New York City than I ever was by the Hell's Angels. I used to go out looking for punch-ups in New York. It was worth it just to see an oncoming mob of angry preppies. These weren't fights. There was nothing personal about it. I didn't hate the people. I was just a brawler. It was good American fun. It was all frivolous. There wasn't any right or wrong. Just fucking Saturday-night whoopee.

ON FATE

I'm doomed all my life to violent actions. I'm closely associated with the gods of the underworld—not crime so much but the underworld.

ON FIREARMS

My parents weren't gun people. Growing up I didn't know much of anything about guns except that my parents didn't want me to have a .22. A BB gun was okay. But I found a .22 anyway. I would shoot at lights out of the back of my house, out my bedroom window. There was an alley between the houses. There were light bulbs on the brick garages in the alley. They had metal grilles protecting them, like jail bars, so it was kind of a trick to hit the bulbs.

It was extremely dangerous. Some kid who shouldn't have had a gun, experimenting, shooting out of his bedroom, shooting down into the alley. I had no intention of doing anything other than putting out light bulbs. But I think about it now and think about what could have happened. The odds are going to catch up to you sometime if you keep shooting into the same passageway.

When I got to the military all I knew was the .22. The most accurate weapon in my house is an Olympic pellet gun—single shot, .17 caliber, pneumatic. I can hit a dime across the living room with it. It was given to me by the Mitchell brothers. I would pack it when I worked at their cinema. At the time it was the standard for Olympic shooting competitions.

For conditioning gunstocks, linseed is a good natural oil, but it has a tendency to be sticky. Tung oil is the thing.

ON HUNTING

I used to get most of my meat from game. A wild boar running out in the open is kind of rare. But it makes for a hell of a hunting day. All this fear of cooking pork rare? Shit on that. With wild boar you just cut it into steaklike slabs, more like pork chops, and cook it on a grill. It's delicious. One of the best things I've ever had. Dressing the animal is a huge part of it. First kill it by surprise so the adrenaline doesn't get released from the glands. A frightened animal tastes a lot worse than a peaceful one. You want to take it when it's grazing, not when it's running or panicked.

With a good rifle it's the shock more than the tissue damage that kills them. The shock sends out death rays all through the body. The animal can't operate. It's too much trauma on the nervous system.

ON PHOTOGRAPHY

I took all the Hell's Angels photographs. Those were all mine. But I learned after trying for years that I could not keep the same focus as a photojournalist. The myth of "take your own pictures, write your own story" didn't work for me. As a photographer I had to keep getting longer and longer lenses. I didn't like to get up close. I didn't want to get in people's faces because you couldn't talk to them much after that.

ON GAMBLING

I don't play cards much. Only once in a while for fun, to play around. I like to gamble where my own knowledge helps me—where if I'm smart about my betting I can affect my chances of winning. Unlike slot machines or dice games.

With sports betting it's always better to strike at the partisan, the home crowd, the emotional bettors. Go into a hostile town at night, visiting, and bet against the desperate, emotional bettors—they'll give you points, and that's the way to win at gambling. And the way to lose is to be one of those emotional bettors.

As a kid I played football, basketball, baseball. I was very much into it. I didn't start gambling until after I quit playing. But about halfway through high school I decided to fuck football and become a criminal. I made my choice between the sports life and the criminal life. Once you quit playing, you need that competitive factor. I don't give a fuck about a game unless I have a bet on it. You have to see it as an opportunity. Nongamblers see it as a chance to lose—and often feel they can't afford to lose. A gambler sees it as an opportunity that can't be passed up. Hell, go into debt.

Ed Bradley came out here one day and beat me for about $4,000 on a basketball game. I think it started as a hundred-dollar bet. But we kept doubling up. I paid him, of course. After all, I would have looked askance—and mentioned it in public—if he hadn't paid me. That's what makes it fun: the reality of it, having to pay up. It's good for it to hurt. Being labeled a cheater or a welch is much more painful to a gambler than getting beat up in the parking lot.

ON KARMA

It's extremely bad karma to brag about things you've gotten away with. I'm a great believer in karma in a profound sense: You will get what's coming to you.

ON READING

All the King's Men, by Robert Penn Warren, is one of my all-time favorite books. If you don't know the book you should grab it and read it as soon as possible because it will teach you a lot of things. *The Ginger Man,* by J. P. Donleavy, was one of my seminal influences. It was kind of a password in certain circles. The Ginger Man got the piss beat out of him more than a few times, as I recall. The reading experience is important: *All the King's Men,* George Orwell's *Down and Out in Paris and London,* F. Scott Fitzgerald's *The Great Gatsby. Gatsby* is 55,000 words long—amazing economy in a book like that. With *Fear and Loathing in Las Vegas* I was determined to make it shorter than that. I may have failed. I think I beat it. But it's like the speed record on Saddle Road: I'm not sure I still hold it. In fact, I'm sure I don't if I could do it just by getting my hands on a Ferrari.

I get tremendous pleasure from reading aloud and having other people read to me. I like to hear how other people hear things. I like women's voices, foreign accents. There's a music to it.

When you're reading aloud, just remember that you want to understand it yourself. You have to hear it. That's the key to other people comprehending. You've got to hear the music. You need to hit each word. Not the way journalists read but with a dramatic rendering. It takes awhile. It's easier to comprehend when you creep along, like driving in second gear. The listener should be impatient for what's coming next.

ON REJECTION

For the better part of two years, while I was working as a copy boy at *Time* magazine—after my time in the Air Force—I took courses at Columbia and the New School. I had the fiction editor of *Esquire,* Rust Hills, as a creative-writing professor at Columbia. I still have a note from him saying, "Never submit anything to *Esquire* ever again. You're a hateful, stupid bastard. *Esquire* hates you." It was kind of a shock at that age.

ON FREE WILL

In Orwell's *1984,* rigidity is imposed by the will of the state. Whereas with soma, in Aldous Huxley's *Brave New World,* it's the will of the people. I've always operated on that second theory. Nobody is stealing our freedoms. We're dealing them off. That's the dark side of the American dream. I've always seen myself as a carrier of the torch against that urge. I always took it for granted. Just like I always took it for granted that if I wanted to run for president I could. I could do it. It's a nice way to think for most of your life, to be able to sustain that. Attitude counts for a lot.

ON DEMOLITION

When you push a car off a cliff and blow it up, be sure to roll the windows down to avoid shrapnel. Also, strip the license plate so you're not billed for the cleanup.

ON JAIL

My class in high school was the first one in the history of Louisville Male High to have girls in it, though still no blacks. I fell in love with a cheerleader. I can't say it was distracting—I was just not in the habit of going to class. But I wasn't cutting school to go back and jack off in an alley and eat cotton candy. My friends and I would go drink beer and read Plato's parable of the cave. We would go to taverns and read things like *All the King's Men.* Yes sir, it was a smart gang. When a judge at juvenile court sent me off to prison, I saw there was not a lot of future in jail. That is a vital piece of knowledge. I've never been back. I've been in holding tanks and such, but they've never convicted me.

ON PUBLIC SPEAKING

When I was in the Air Force I would take classes on the base. One of the classes I took was for something that terrified me more than anything in life: public speaking. It was terrifying. I don't know how I ever became a sought-after speaker.

When the Hell's Angels book came out I was forced to go out and do publicity for it. It was still hard for me. They told me that if I could write a convincing article I could write a speech. I'd seen senior officers try to master public speaking in order to get promoted to field-grade positions—it was like survival for them. Succeed or die. Public speaking was a required skill. But when I got the sports editorship at the base newspaper—because the guy who was doing it was drunk, busted for the third time for pissing in public—I never had to master it.

One problem I have with public speaking is the sound system—I rarely get there in time to do a sound check. So the sound ends up distorted or you lose the bass.

ON NUTRITION

Grapefruit is vital to my lifestyle. I eat grapefruits, oranges, lemons, kiwis. I also need something green with every meal—some vegetables on the plate. Even if it's just some sliced tomatoes and green onions in a pinch. It's both aesthetic and healthy. If I take a look at a plate and see brown, gray, white, I can't eat it. I want to see some red and green.

Drink six to eight glasses of water a day. When you don't drink enough water you lose your taste for it. When you're chronically dehydrated the body misses it, but it has a self-fooling mechanism where you don't think about it. Then you have to reeducate your taste buds for it. At first you can't drink much pure water. I've worked up to five or six glasses a day. At first I could barely do one.

I had started the hydration process before I broke my leg in Hawaii at Christmastime in 2003. Everybody had been telling me. I was going into the Aspen Club—to the sports medicine department—to learn to walk after my spinal surgery earlier that same year. I wasn't supposed to recover from that.

I've really enjoyed my body. I've used it. One of the things I've been most impressed with in my life is the resiliency of the human body: They did both my spinal surgery and my leg surgery without putting any metal in me. No metal, Bubba.

ON MEDICINE

A lot of doctors are reluctant to take responsibility for me. Nobody wants to be the doctor who killed Hunter Thompson. I don't trust the medical establishment, but I do trust individual doctors. I'm straight with doctors. They have to learn that they can talk to me straight, too. There's no point in trying to conceal anything. I appreciate the ones who take risks on me, and I have to look out for the chickenshits.

Most physicians are quacks. In Hawaii, when I broke my leg, they wouldn't give me any painkillers because I'd been drinking. Alcohol is supposed to be dangerous with painkillers. But depending on the person, that can be unnecessarily dogmatic. Body weight makes a big difference. If I sit around here doing hit for hit of almost anything except acid with a 100-pound woman, she'll get twice as ripped as me.

Anyway, the doctors wouldn't give me painkillers. They wanted me off the island. Nobody wanted responsibility. The doctors, the university where I spoke, the organizers of the marathon I was covering, the hotel where I stayed—they all wanted me out. It was hell. When they tried to load me onto a full commercial flight, they jammed my broken leg into the fuselage of the plane. I was the last to board. Imagine the wonderment of the other 200 passengers upon hearing this incredible uproar at the front of the aircraft—my ever-increasingly violent screams. All those passengers delayed 45 minutes, unable to see what was going on and unable to get up from their seats. Finally the airline had to give up. I've learned that when you get that mean, most people try to get away from it. And if they are assigned to handle you physically, they really want to get away from it.

ON MOBILITY

I was helpless when I got back from Hawaii. I had to shit in buckets. I had to learn how to move between wheelchairs. I had to learn to walk for the second time in one year. That was survival. It's very hard controlling your environment when you're in a wheelchair. Or in pain.

There are some advantages to being in a wheelchair but only when you can get out of it. It can be a wonderful way to travel. But not as nice as in a private jet. I'd do just about anything in this world to avoid flying commercial.

ON DRUGS

Most drugs have been very good to me. I use drugs, and if I abuse them, well, show me where. What do you mean abuse them, you jackass? What's abuse? Like most anything else, it's about paying attention. It's simple. It's not some exotic school of thought I picked up somewhere; it's paying attention. Concentrating. It's something you have to do your whole life.

I watch it and make sure people can handle things. You have to be super aware of who is fucked-up, who is angry. Not at you necessarily, but who is dangerous. Who is not the same friendly guy you were talking to yesterday. See how different things affect different people. Then avoid them if you have to, or keep an eye on them. You can help people at some stage of their anger, but there's a point beyond which you can't do anything.

Steroid-based nasal spray can turn you into a monster.

The worst side of drug use is getting the drugs. Yeah, the police are my drug problem. You just can't travel with drugs anymore. That forces you to get your drugs from the local market when you go to a strange town. That affects the people you spend time with.

I've never made a nickel or dime off drugs. Never sold them. That's vital to the karma. Keeping a balance—not getting greedy. I would also feel somehow responsible for my clients. And most full-time dealers I've known have spent time in prison. It's part of the bargain. You have to put some of that profit away—probably half of it—against the day when you have to make a big bail or pay a lawyer. The one thing the Hell's Angels did religiously was pay their bail bondsman. Every month, every bill. He's the guy who would be right there when anybody got busted. Call him anytime day or night, anywhere. He'd always come get you.

I don't advocate drugs and whiskey and violence and rock and roll, but they've always been good to me. I've never advised people who can't handle drugs to take them, just as people who can't drive well should not drive 80 miles an hour on any road. That's a point.

ON ALCOHOL

I have no patience for malevolent drunks. No patience. Drugs, drink, it's no excuse. Booze is probably the most dangerous substance—it's so available, and it's easy to get really wrecked. I felt a sense of amusement when I first read a book called *Nation of Drunkards*. It's a beautiful book—in the rare-book category. It's a history of alcohol and the forming of America. The nation really was conceived in a river of booze.

There's a basic difference in consumers of whiskey or any other substance, and that is the difference between being a binger and a chipper. I have understood for many years that I'm a chipper. The binger sets time aside to get wasted, to go on a binge. The chipper, like me, just does it all the time. It takes awhile to get settled in your patterns like I am—if you live that long.

ON BEING OUTNUMBERED

Taking on groups of people was the ultimate fun. And then running off with their women. The Genghis Khan approach. It was romantic. I got the shit kicked out of me a lot. But it was fun. That's an unhealthy attitude—which is why I don't recommend it to other people.

Getting into rumbles without having any idea what you're doing is dangerous. I did it, but I learned. There are some basic rules. For one thing, any crowd or gang can murder you—no matter what kind of crowd. A crowd of schoolgirls can kill you.

Fighting gangs of people is very risky. If you ever get caught trying to defend yourself, attack one person in the crowd. Just try to kill that person. Concentrate, like a shark. Don't attack randomly. I've found that's about the only way to fight a mob. Kill one of them, or try, or seem eager or willing to. People will want to kill you for doing that, but it usually turns the momentum of a senseless brawl where you're just a soccer ball. When the soccer ball can attack you and bite your cheek off, the game changes.

I was ahead of the game when I realized that if I tried to kill one person the rest would back off.

You want to take on a large one. Take on a symbolic leader, the spokesman, the bully. A swift and violent kick to the nuts after a glass of water to the face is always good—and I mean a crotch twister, boy. There's a big difference between a sort of snap-kick to the nuts and one with a follow-through, where you go all the way through the crotch with force. Use the leg—hit with a higher part than the foot so there's a narrow point of impact.

Though it's probably better to stay out of rumbles, I miss it in a way. I hate bullies and like to take them on. There's that red line. It becomes like a two-minute drill in a playoff game. There's no reason, just survival. It's game time. I've frightened myself and other people with the extremes to which I can carry it.

Just because you give up fighting with your knuckles doesn't mean you give up fighting. That's the deadly serious underbelly of Gonzo—the fist inside the glove. I'm still every bit as willing to take on a fight. You just have to figure out where and when. You need to know by gut instinct when the numbers are against you. You need to choose your battles—and your battleground—carefully. You don't want to volunteer to be destroyed. Pick your spots.

And there's no reason to see it all as a battle anyway.

ON POTENTIAL

That old thing about "this kid has a lot of talent" will take you a long way. But eventually it has to pay off. Potential will run out—and it can run out suddenly.

ON DENTISTRY

I'm usually not sensitive to pain. I have a high tolerance for it. But I've never thought of pain as an option in any kind of dentistry question. Pain has always been a given. An assumption. Pain? Of course you'll have pain if you do a root canal. I've never had dentistry without pain—until a recent epiphany that is going to be one of the main clinical discoveries of our time.

I don't fear the dentist. It's just not someplace I'd choose to go. You don't look forward to a root canal. They put that rubber dam across your mouth. You can't talk to the dentist. You can't say, "What the fuck are you doing?" One of my problems is that I'm too conscious of what he's doing. I kind of critique him as he's going along. I make the classic mistake of dumb people: I think I know more than the dentist.

I want as little pain as possible. My dentist—a half-bright quack; not a bad dentist but a simple one—will not give anybody pain pills. He hates giving me the gas. I don't have much use for the gas anyway, though the first whiff or two can be nice.

Turns out music is really the best remedy for pain. Not just music but dominant music, top volume. I hadn't fucked around with headphones since the 1970s, but recently I introduced music on a scale that I had not thought of before. It was with a little CD Walkman. I finally figured out how to turn it up to top volume. I used this Discman properly for the first time. Boom. I had my own studio, my own speakers.

I did have a normal quotient of whiskey. But I wouldn't say the whiskey was a factor. Another ingredient was the weed I thought I'd try. When I finally told the dentist, "Goddamn it, your stuff sucks. I'm going to go out and smoke some weed in the car," he said, "Yeah, that's the way to do it." It's not like he's a goddamn Jesus freak of some kind. Now they say, "Of course you should have self-medicated. You should have done it all along."

Be sure to self-medicate. I used to think of needing painkillers after dentistry. Ho-ho.

I could barely get into the dentist's chair. I was as high as four dogs. In a good mood. But it was hard to get to the chair and socked in. I felt like I was in command of the world. I had my sunglasses on. I had the CD player in my crotch. I had a strong drink of Chivas Regal and ice in easy reach to my left.

None of the things you're normally conscious of—probes, sticking cotton in your mouth, the pain of the injections—mattered once I turned the music on. At top volume you can't ignore it. The music is louder and more intense than the pain. And then when he brought in the drill—which you can normally feel even if it's not always painful . . . nothing.

Hot damn! I was so excited about my discovery that I tried to tell the dentist about it while I was in the chair. But I had that rubber in my mouth. So I just put the fucking headphones back on.

ON EX-PRESIDENTS

When addressing a former president, Mr. President is the proper form. But I also call one Jimmy. Of course, some of them are best addressed as Swine.

ON HUMOR

Humor is important—I can't think of anything much more important. Not necessarily to make people laugh but to make them smile. I find that if I can laugh with someone or get them to laugh with me, that's an immediate bond.

It's not something I write down or memorize before I go out. It becomes a habit, a survival technique.

Making your enemies laugh once is no big trick. But making them laugh twice, three times, against their better judgment, makes them notice.

It's like when you shoot a gun in public. The first shot doesn't get people's attention. Hell, I don't notice a shot unless it's right outside my window. But the second shot gets everybody's attention.

ON FASHION

When it comes to clothes, it's easier to talk about the dark side of the American dream in a clown's garb than a clergyman's. But dressing with a sense of humor has its drawbacks. I have a shirt covered with fishing lures—they're silver rubber minnows. Sometimes when I'm wearing it I'll reach down to scratch my rib and feel this scaly shit. God, what a shock. I'm used to finding weird things wrong with me—what the fuck is that?—but not scales.

I like the way sunglasses look, but I seldom wear really dark glasses. I've found that if people can see my eyes through the lenses it's more comfortable. I try not to have my costume be a problem for me or other people.

I'll wear Chucks with a tuxedo. Is that confrontational? There are times when I'll wear a blazer for no particular reason. They have good pockets. It's easy, comfortable.

I love what people call my Coat of Many Colors, which I bought at Abercrombie & Fitch in the early 1970s. Every once in a while I wish I had bought the pants, too. It's a hunting outfit, sort of a precursor to those blaze orange outfits. It's a very well-made coat—it has a game bag that folds out of the back. The bag's waterproof, plastic lined—you can shoot a duck and pop it into the pouch. It'll carry ice for drinks. And it doesn't leak blood. Somewhere in there are loops for shotgun shells.

I've always bought, been treated to or stolen the highest-quality clothing I can. Shit, it saves a lot of money not having to go out and buy new shirts every year.

When I carry a gun it's always in a shoulder holster. That's when you want to have looser-fitting coats. There are times when it's better not to be obvious with your gun—most of the time, really. Unless you're out shooting with people or doing something where other people have guns, it's better not to advertise it.

ON SKINNY-DIPPING

Total darkness and no clothes is the only way to swim. Swimming in clothes seems almost obscene to me.

ON SURVIVAL

Choosing the right friends is a life-or-death matter. But you really see it only in retrospect. I've always considered that possibly my highest talent—recognizing and keeping good friends. And you better pay attention to it, because any failure in that regard can be fatal. You need friends who come through. You should always be looking around for good friends because they really dress up your life later on.

In the end, it's not so much how to succeed in life as it is how to survive the life you have chosen.

ON PERSPECTIVE

I'm too old to adopt conceits or airs. I have nothing left to prove. It's kind of fun to look at it—instead of a personal challenge to the enemy out there, just enjoy the evidence. I can finally look at it objectively. Not "Who is this freak over here?" but "Who am I?" I've gotten to that point where it's take it or leave it. Whatever way I've developed seems okay to me on the evidence. So what if the score is against me? I've been on the battlefield for a long time. I suppose I always will be—just my nature.

Contributors' Biographies

Lynn Andriani is an associate editor and book reviewer for *Publishers Weekly.*

Robert Sam Anson began his career as a journalist at *Time* magazine, where he was a correspondent from 1967 to 1972, working in the Chicago, Los Angeles, New York, and Saigon bureaus. He is a contributing editor for *Vanity Fair*, and his work has appeared in numerous publications, including *Life* and *Esquire*. He is the author of *McGovern: A Biography, Best Intentions: The Education and Killing of Edmund Perry, War News: A Young Reporter in Indochina,* and *The Opportunist: Dick Cheney's Path to Power.*

Marty Beckerman is the author of *Generation S.L.U.T.* and *Dumbocracy: Adventures with the Loony Left, the Rabid Right and Other American Idiots.*

Adam Bulger, currently a staff writer for Connecticut newsweekly the *Hartford Advocate,* has written for *New York Press, Inked Magazine, The Believer,* and other publications.

Douglas Brinkley is an award-winning author, distinguished professor, and American historian. He is the editor of Hunter's volumes of letters: *The Proud Highway, Fear and Loathing in America,* and the forthcoming *The Mutineer: Rants, Ravings, and Missives from the Mountaintop, 1977–2005.* He is the editor of President Ronald Reagan's personal diaries, published as the best-selling *The Reagan Diaries,* and is the author of *The Boys of Pointe du Hoc; Jimmy Carter: The Unfinished Presidency; The Great Deluge: Hurricane Katrina, New Orleans, and the Mississippi Gulf Coast;* and *Bobby.*

Lynn Carey is a features writer for the *Contra Costa Times* in the Bay Area and editor of the paper's book section.

Ben Corbett is a writer described by *National Review* as a "thirty-something countercultural journalist out of Colorado." His work has appeared in *Salon, Reason, High Times, Easyriders,* and *Tattoo,* among others. He is the author of *This is Cuba: An Outlaw Culture Survives* and the forthcoming *Forever Che.*

Bill Dunn writes about men's fashion, motorcycles, cars, travel, and culture. He has been style director of *GQ* (United Kingdom), and senior editor of *Esquire* (United Kingdom). He has been a scriptwriter and has written many books, including *Man About Town,* a history of menswear in the twentieth century.

David Felton began his journalism career at the *Los Angeles Times* and is a founding editor of *Rolling Stone* magazine. He is currently the Senior Vice President of MTV Networks.

Tad Floridis is a former freelance writer. He is current an associate publisher at Grove-Atlantic books.

John Glassie, a contributing editor for the *New York Times Magazine,* has written for the *New York Times, Salon, Wired, The Believer,* and many other publications.

Peter Gzowski, who died in January 2002, was a Canadian writer, television and radio journalist, broadcaster, and talk show host. He interviewed over 25,000 guests ranging from Margaret Thatcher to Wayne Gretzky and won an International Peabody award for broadcasting excellence.

Matthew Hahn lives in Richmond, Virginia, with his wife, Elizabeth, and daughter, Allie. He has written for newspapers and various publications. He currently spends his spare time curing his own meats.

Matt Higgins is a freelance writer based in New York City. His writing has appeared in the *Village Voice, High Times, ESPN Magazine,* and other publications.

Christopher Hitchens is a contributing editor at *Vanity Fair* and a regular columnist for Slate.com. He has written for *The Atlantic, The Nation,* and *Free Inquiry.* He is the editor of *The Portable Atheist: Essential Readings for the Non-believer* and author of *God Is Not Great: How Religion Poisons Everything; Thomas Jefferson: Author of America; Love, Poverty, and War: Journals and Essays;* and *Why Orwell Matters.*

Paul Kaihla is an award-winning investigative journalist with *Business 2.0* magazine and an author whose career was kick-started by Hunter.

Simon Key is a former contributor for *I-D Magazine,* based in London.

Phoebe Legere is a New York City–based composer, poet, performer, and multi-instrumentalist. She has been critically acclaimed as "a genius" and "the female Frank Zappa." In addition to a wide array of luminous accomplishments, Legere is the founder of the New York Underground Museum, and she has had many one-woman shows of her paintings, including a recent show at the Patterson Museum of Art.

Jay MacDonald is a gypsy journalist and contributing editor to *Bankrate.com* whose work spontaneously appears in U.S. newspapers, magazines, and websites. He has proudly followed Hunter's sage advice, "When the going gets weird, the weird turn pro."

Dee McLaughlin, a former editor and writer, is now Vice President of Marketing for the Virgin Entertainment Group.

Tim Mohr is a staff editor at *Playboy* magazine. His writing has also appeared in other publications, including the *New York Times.* He is the translator of the German novels *Guantánamo* by Dorothea Dieckmann and *Wetlands* by Charlotte Roche.

Sara Nelson is the editor-in-chief of *Publishers Weekly* and a journalist who has been published in the *New York Times, New York Observer, Wall Street Journal, Glamour,* and *SELF.* Additionally, she is the author of a memoir, *So Many Books, So Little Time: A Year of Passionate Reading.*

Peter Olszewski, Siem Reap Bureau Chief of the Phnom Penh Post, Cambodia, is a former rock magazine editor, editor of Australian *Playboy,* creator of *Nation Review's* cult hero JJ McRoach, and official Australian minder to Hunter S. Thompson. He has written for most major Australian publications and was a journalism trainer at the *Myanmar Times.* He is now a contributor to *Mediaweek,* and editor of *MediaBlab,* published by Dow Jones' Factiva. He has written four books, his latest being *Land of a Thousand Eyes* (Allen & Unwin) about life in Yangon, Myanmar (Rangoon, Burma).

Mick O'Regan is a journalist, producer, and on-air radio host for the Australia Broadcast Company (ABC). He has won the United Nations Association Media Prize for a *Background Briefing* documentary on the El Salvador peace accords. He has hosted Australian programs *Radio National* and *The Media Report.* Currently, he is producing and presenting *The Sports Factor* on Radio National.

P. J. O'Rourke is a best-selling humorist who started his writing career with *National Lampoon,* of which he was editor-in-chief. He has also written for *American Spectator, Playboy, Esquire, The Atlantic, Vanity Fair,* and *Harper's.* O'Rourke has served as the Foreign Affairs Desk Chief for *Rolling Stone* and has written many books, including *Parliament of Whores* and *Give War a Chance.*

Hugo Perez is an award-winning filmmaker and writer whose work has been presented on HBO, Showtime, PBS, and venues such as MoMA and the Smithsonian.

John Perra has written for *George, People, Time,* and *Runner's World* among many other publications. He has covered the White House, reported on the death penalty, investigated meth labs, and filed from New Orleans in the immediate aftermath of Hurricane Katrina in 2005. He lives in New York City with his wife, Aine.

Jane Perlez is the former chief diplomatic correspondent for the *New York Times.* She is currently the paper's Southeast Asia bureau chief and has been nominated for the Pulitzer Prize for her coverage of Somalia, Indonesia, and Pakistan.

Tobias Perse is a former assistant in the features department at *Rolling Stone.* He was one of Hunter's New York–assigned assistants. He is currently a documentary film director and producer.

George Plimpton was an author and founding editor of *The Paris Review.* He was heralded by Hunter as "an aristocrat of the spirit . . . a gigantic influence in my life" and "a genuine Man of Letters." He died in September 2003.

J. Rentilly is a Los Angeles–based journalist who covers film, music, and literature for a variety of national and international publications, including *US Airways, Spirit, Planet Syndications,* and *Mean.* He is currently honing his chops as a marching band pianist.

Judd Rose was a four-time Emmy award–winning investigative journalist with ABC and CNN. His extensive broadcasting career also included reporting for the Associated Press and NBC on domestic and international affairs. He died in June 2000.

Ron Rosenbaum is a journalist whose work regularly appears in the *New York Times, Esquire, The New Yorker, The Atlantic,* and *Vanity Fair.* He is the author of *Explaining*

Hitler: The Search for the Origins of Evil; Those Who Forget the Past: The Question of Anti-Semitism; and *The Shakespeare Wars: Clashing Scholars, Public Fiascoes, Palace Coups.*

Tim Russert was an influential American political journalist, the host of NBC's *Meet the Press,* and the author of *Big Russ and Me* and *Wisdom of Our Fathers.* He died in June 2008.

Corey Seymour was one of Hunter's New York–assigned assistants for *Rolling Stone.* He is a former senior editor for *Men's Journal* and is currently the senior editor for *Travel and Leisure Golf* magazine. He is the coeditor of the oral history *Gonzo: The Life of Hunter S. Thompson* along with Jann Wenner.

Mary Suma is the former station manager at KDNK in the Roaring Fork Valley, Colorado.

Craig Vetter is a freelance magazine writer and novelist. He lives in Chicago and is currently working on a memoir about his father.

Jann Wenner is the editor and publisher of *Rolling Stone* and the chairman of Wenner Media.

Jerry Williams was known as "The Dean of Talk Radio." He was a groundbreaking, nationally syndicated talk radio personality for AM and FM stations in Boston, New York, Chicago, and Philadelphia. He died in April 2003.

Cliff "Skip" Workman is a founding member of the Oakland chapter of the Hell's Angels Motorcycle Gang. He left the group on good terms in 1981 after a bike accident left him paralyzed with spinal stanosis. He currently fights for the rights of disabled U.S. veterans.

Credits

"Interview with reporter about Hell's Angels." Originally aired on ABC News, February 20, 1967.

"Interview with host Alan Davis and Hell's Angel Cliff 'Skip' Workman." Originally aired on *Sunday*, Canadian Broadcasting Corporation, 1967.

"Interview with Jerry Williams." Originally aired on WBZ Newsradio 1030, Boston Massachusetts, August 8, 1972. Transcribed with permission.

"Playboy Interview: Hunter Thompson," by Craig Vetter. Originally appeared in *Playboy* magazine, November 1974. Reprinted with permission.

"Interview by Peter Olszewski." Originally appeared in *Loose Licks* (Australia), Spring 1976. Copyright © Peter Olszewski. Reprinted with permission.

"The Hunter Thompson Interview," by Robert Sam Anson. Originally appeared in *New Times*, December 10, 1976. Copyright © Robert Sam Anson. Reprinted with permission.

"Interview with Peter Gzowski." Originally aired on *90 Minutes Live*, Canadian Broadcasting Corporation, April 12, 1977.

"Hunter S. Thompson: The Good Doctor Tells All . . . About Carter, Cocaine, Adrenaline, and the Birth of Gonzo Journalism," by Rob Rosenbaum. Originally appeared in *High Times* magazine, September 1977. Copyright © Ron Rosenbaum. Reprinted with permission.

Transcribed from lecture at the University of Colorado (Boulder), November 1, 1977.

"The Hunter Thompson Saga: A Savage Burlesque in Three Parts," by S. M. Jackson. Originally appeared in *Commonwealth Times,* student newspaper at Virginia Commonwealth University in Richmond, Virginia, November 28, 1978. Reprinted with permission.

"Interview by Jane Perlez." Originally appeared in *Washington Journalism Review*, November/December 1979. Copyright © *Washington Journalism Review*. Reprinted with permission.

"Interview by David Felton." Originally appeared in *Rolling Stone College Papers,* May 1980. Reprinted with permission.

"Thirty-Six Manic Hours in Toronto with Dr. Hunter S. Thompson, Guru of Gonzo Journalism," by Paula Kaihla. Originally appeared in *T.O.* magazine (Toronto), November 1986. Reprinted with permission.

"Fear and Loathing: On the Trail of Hunter S. Thompson and Ralph Steadman," by Simon Key. Originally appeared in *I-D* magazine, November 1987. Reprinted with permission.

"Interview by P. J. O'Rourke for the 25th anniversary of *Rolling Stone* magazine." Originally appeared in *Rolling Stone* magazine, November 25, 1987. Reprinted with permission.

"Thompson on Thompson," by Jack Thompson. Originally appeared in *Studio for Men* magazine (Australia), February 1989.

"Down and Out in Aspen," interview with Judd Rose. Transcribed from *Primetime Live* (ABC News), February 27, 1992.

"Interview by Kevin Simonson." Originally appeared in *Spin* magazine, May 1993. Copyright © Kevin Simonson. Reprinted with permission.

"Proust Questionnaire." Copyright © 1994 Conde Nast Publications. All rights reserved. Originally published in *Vanity Fair*. Reprinted with permission.

"NuCity Goes Gonzo," by Alma Garcia and Norma Jean Thompson. Originally appeared in *NuCity Press*, Albuquerque, New Mexico, March 1, 1995.

Originally aired on *Weekend Edition Sunday* (National Public Radio), November 24, 1996.

"Interview with P. J. O'Rourke." Originally appeared in *Rolling Stone* magazine, November 28, 1996. Reprinted with permission

"Interview by Sara Nelson." Originally appeared on The Book Report.com, June 1997. Reprinted with permission.

"Hunter S. Thompson," interview with Jacki Lyden and Linda Wertheimer. Originally aired on *All Things Considered* (National Public Radio), August 7, 1997.

"The Godfather of Gonzo Defends His Oeuvre and Stomps on His Enemies," by Tom McIntyre. Originally appeared in the *Village Voice*, August 19, 1997. Copyright © Tom McIntyre.

"Writing on the Wall: An Interview with Hunter S. Thompson," by Matthew Hahn, as first published in *The Atlantic Monthly*, August 26, 1997. Copyright © 1997 Matthew Hahn. Reprinted with permission.

"God of Gonzo: Hunter S. Thompson Still Railing After All These Years," by Lynn Carey. Originally appeared in *Contra Costa Times*, August 30, 1997.

"Interview with Hunter S. Thompson," by Pheobe Legere. Originally appeared in *Puritan* magazine, 1998. Copyright © Phoebe Legere. Reprinted with permission.

"Vegas Stripped: Guns, Drugs and Johnny Depp. Hunter S. Thompson Has Waited 25 Years for His Warped Vision to Hit the Screen," by Tobias Perse and Tad Floridis. Originally appeared in *Arena* magazine (UK), September 1988.

"Night of the Hunter," by Bill Dunn. Originally appeared in *Esquire* magazine (London), November 1998. Reprinted with permission.

"None More Gonzo." Originally appeared in *MOJO*, April 1999.

"Hunter S. Thompson: The Art of Journalism No. 1," by Douglas Brinkley with contributions from Terry McDonell and George Plimpton. Originally appeared in *The Paris Review*, Autumn 2000. Copyright © *The Paris Review*. Reprinted with permission.

"Q & A: Hunter S. Thompson," by John Perra. Originally appeared in *George* magazine, December/January 2001. Reprinted with permission.

"A Twisted Wired Guy: The Original Gonzo Returns to the Spotlight to Fight the Good Fight Online and Settle Some Old Scores," by Hugo Perez. Originally appeared in *Yahoo! Internet Life*, August 2001. Reprinted with permission.

"Interview with Mick O'Regan." *The Media Report*, "Patriot Games—American Journalism post 9/11," by Mick O'Regan, was first broadcast on ABC Radio National. August 29, 2002. Transcript is reproduced by permission of the Australian Broadcasting Corporation and ABC Online. Copyright © 2002 ABC. All rights reserved.

"Interview with Mary Suma." Originally aired on KDNK Community Radio (Carbondale, CO), January 2003. Printed with permission.

"Bedtime for Gonzo," by J. Rentilly. Originally appeared in *Razor* magazine, January 2003. Reprinted with permission.

"Fear and Loathing in the New Millenium." Originally appeared in *Publisher's Weekly*, January 13, 2003. Reprinted with permission.

"Oh, Loathsome Me: Hunter S. Thompson Checks in from Woody Creek and Rants Nostalgic About a Life Lived in Fear," by Corey Seymour. Originally appeared in *Time Out New York*, January 30, 2003. Reprinted with permission.

"Hunter S. Thompson: The godfather of Gonzo says 9/11 caused a 'nationwide nervous breakdown'—and let the Bush crowd loot the country and savage American democracy," by John Glassie. Originally appeared on Salon.com, February 3, 2003. Reprinted with permission.

"My Chat (and Hash-Smoking Session) with Hunter S. Thompson, Gonzo Journalism Legend," by Marty Beckerman. Originally appeared on martybeckerman.com, February 3, 2003. Copyright © Marty Beckerman. Reprinted with permission.

"Interview with Tim Russert." Originally appeared on CNBC, February 8, 2003.

"The Doctor Will See You Now," by Ben Corbett. Originally appeared in *Boulder Weekly*, April 3–9, 2003. Reprinted with permission.

"The Gonzo King," by Matt Higgins. Originally appeared in *High Times* magazine, September 2, 2003.

Originally aired on *Late Night with Conan O'Brien* (NBC), November 6, 2003. Printed with permission.

"The Hunter S. Thompson Interview," by Adam Bulger. Originally appeared on Freezerbox.com, March 9, 2004. Copyright © Adam Bulger. Reprinted with permission.

"Hunter S. Thompson: Surprised He's Still Here," by Jay MacDonald. Originally appeared on Bankrate.com, November 1, 2004. Reprinted with permission of Bankrate, Inc.

"Post Cards from the Proud Highway." Originally appeared in *Playboy* magazine, May 2005. Reprinted with permission.

Every effort has been made to contact all copyright holders. If notified, the publisher will be pleased to rectify any errors or omissions at the earliest opportunity.

Index